CW00828096

RIDING LUCIFER'S LINE

Big Iron in Hand is an original 24" x 36" oil on canvas painting by Donald M. Yena, copyright 2011 and used by permission.

RIDING LUCIFER'S LINE

Ranger Deaths along the Texas-Mexico Border

by
Bob Alexander

With Foreword by Byron A. Johnson
Executive Director
Texas Ranger Hall of Fame and Museum

Number 11 in the Frances B. Vick Series

University of North Texas Press
Denton, Texas

©2013 Bob Alexander
Foreword ©2013 University of North Texas Press
All rights reserved.
Printed in the United States of America

10 9 8 7 6 5 4 3 2 1

Permissions:
University of North Texas Press
1155 Union Circle #311336
Denton, TX 76203-5017

The paper used in this book meets the minimum requirements of the American National Standard for Permanence of Paper for Printed Library Materials, z39.48.1984. Binding materials have been chosen for durability.

Library of Congress Cataloging-in-Publication Data

Alexander, Bob (James R.)
Riding Lucifer's Line : Ranger deaths along the Texas-Mexico border / by Bob Alexander ; with foreword by Byron A. Johnson. -- 1st ed.
    p. cm. -- (Number 11 in the Frances B. Vick series)
  Includes bibliographical references and index.
  ISBN 978-1-57441-499-8 (cloth : alk. paper) -- ISBN 978-1-57441-513-1 (ebook)
  1. Texas Rangers--History--19th century. 2. Texas Rangers--History--20th century. 3. Texas Rangers--Biography. 4. Peace officers--Mortality--Mexican-American Border Region. 5. Law enforcement--Mexican-American Border Region--History--19th century. 6. Law enforcement--Mexican-American Border Region--History--20th century. 7. Texas--History--1846-1950. 8. Mexican-American Border Region--History--19th century. 9. Mexican-American Border Region--History--20th century. I. Title. II. Series: Frances B. Vick series ; no. 11.
  F391.A29 2013
  976.4'05--dc23
                          2013000151

Riding Lucifer's Line: Ranger Deaths along the Texas-Mexico Border is Number 11 in the Frances B. Vick Series

On the cover: *Big Iron in Hand* is an original 24" x 36" oil on canvas painting by Donald M. Yena, copyright 2011 and used by permission.

All photos are from the Texas Ranger Hall of Fame and Museum, Waco, Texas. Used by permission.

The electronic edition of this book was made possible by the support of the Vick Family Foundation.

Contents

Foreword

Across three centuries now the history of Texas Rangers has been interwoven with the history of the U.S.-Mexican Border. The Border is a convention, a state of mind, not an unalterable physical reality, but a line on the map that affects people's lives at many levels and in many ways. Whenever the Border has been redefined or described it has sparked controversy that has frequently led to violent confrontation. Over the centuries the boundary line has been as fluid as the Rio Grande, changing constantly with shifts in national sovereignty, politics, surveys, economics, and the course of the river itself. After Rio Grande floods, some early residents living by the river awakened to find their homes and property lay in another country—some more than once. Today, the U.S.-Mexican Border is the most active border in the world with an estimated 350 million legal crossings a year.

The story and tribulations of the Border began in 1821 with Mexican Independence from Spain. The boundary Mexico inherited extended from Louisiana to Missouri and northwest to Oregon and thence to the Pacific Ocean. It encompassed all of the modern Border States of Texas, New Mexico, Arizona, and California—and more. The almost inconceivable vastness of the territory assured that newly independent Imperial Mexico could neither adequately settle the land nor defend it. As a fallback, foreign immigrants from the United States and Europe were recruited to become Mexican citizens in exchange for land. To provide protection in the face of raids by Native Americans, the governor of Coahuila y Tejas, José Félix Trespalacios, gave administrator Stephen F. Austin authority to raise a militia. Austin recruited the first "ranging men" in 1823, regarded by most historians as the first Texas Rangers.

Political turmoil in Mexico, and fears of the foreign-born immigrants in Tejas, resulted in the revocation of provincial rights and freedoms and the curtailment of immigration. Peaceful dissent took root among the hardscrabble farms, ranches and adobe haciendas of Tejas. The outcry crossed racial lines with Anglos and Tejanos demanding constitutional freedoms. Ultimately the movement blossomed into nationalism, revolt, and the Texas Revolution of 1836.

General Antonio López de Santa Anna's inopportune loss of the Texas Revolution left a legacy of Border problems that have persisted almost 200 years. The Treaties of Velasco he signed ended the Revolution and saved his life. One treaty provision established the Mexican Border with Texas at the Rio Grande. However, the Mexican Congress refused to ratify the Treaties of Velasco. Mexico did not formally recognize the sovereignty of the breakaway province and, but for pragmatic reasons, regarded the Nueces River as the *el paso al Tejas*. This disagreement sparked an era of Border conflict and sowed the seeds of war.

Mexico was obviously not pleased or amused by Santa Anna's actions: he had lost Texas and publicly exposed Mexico's shaky hold on the rest of the Southwest to those promoting Manifest Destiny. Furthermore, the Texas Revolution incited separatist movements in the Mexican states of Coahuila, Tamaulipas, Zacatecas and Yucatan.

Texas Rangers, who had responded to Indian raids, died at the Alamo, and fought rearguard actions against overwhelming odds during the Revolution, were now in the thick of it under the Republic of Texas. After the cessation of hostilities in 1836, the Texian Army essentially dissolved and the soldiers left for home to rebuild their farms and ranches. The Texas Rangers and other hastily formed militia units were the only means of defense for the new Republic.

Mexico soon began to test the resolve of the Republic and the United States by sending troops across the Nueces River on punitive expeditions. From March to September of 1842 Mexican General Ráfael Vásquez and French mercenary General Adrián Woll led approximately 2,000 men on raids that managed to briefly retake San Antonio. A few hundred Texas Rangers and militiamen engaged and routed them.

As tensions and skirmishes escalated, roughly half of the U.S. Army was relocated to Texas during 1845 and the star-shaped Fort Texas was constructed on the north side of the river. Mexico regarded the Nueces River as the *de facto* border, and thousands of Mexican troops were sent north to scout and ultimately lay siege to Fort Texas, which they regarded as a foreign invasion of their territory. The siege ultimately led to the Battle of Palo Alto and the U.S.-Mexican War. When hostilities ceased in 1848, the Treaty of Guadalupe Hidalgo realigned the survey from Texas to California, firmly establishing the Rio Grande as Mexico's boundary with Texas. Estimates are that Mexico lost a staggering fifty-five percent of the land she had previously claimed.

For the time being, the line that stretched from Texas to the Pacific was ill-defined. Surveys conducted to shore up America's claims were inaccurate; the reference maps agreed upon in various treaties were flawed. Language in treaties describing the boundary was left intentionally vague. It did not matter too much as neither the U.S. or Mexico considered the unpopulated and inhospitable desert lands of New Mexico and Arizona of immediate value. Silver and gold strikes were decades away.

For a period of time the Texas-Mexican Border was uncharacteristically quiet. The United States was preoccupied with the California Gold Rush, political turmoil, the formation of new states and territories, slavery and the Civil War. Mexico was busy with its own civil wars of reform during 1857–1861. The turmoil split the country into political factions. The country also had to attend to the ejection of a French interventionist monarchy proclaiming the Second Mexican Empire, 1861–1867. Calm along the Border would not last.

After the U.S. Civil War, returning veterans and Southern expatriates hardened by war discovered that the area between the Nueces River and the Rio Grande—the Nueces Strip—had a valuable resource. Small bands of Spanish Longhorn cattle wandering the area had been ignored. They had been left to breed on their own. Herds estimated in the millions roamed the Strip and many were unclaimed. Postwar America and postwar Mexico were expanding and cattle driven to markets or new railheads were money on the hoof.

As result Texan and Mexican cattle barons proliferated, as did *de facto* warlords like Juan Cortina on the Mexican side and King Fisher on the Texas side. They and their bandits constantly rustled cattle, raided the other's ranches, and committed homicides and abductions. The Strip had become as much of a lawless war zone as Afghanistan. Hostilities were no longer military engagements regarding national sovereignty, but civilian outlawry fueled by the demand for cheap cattle. Crossing the Border served as refuge for the lawless.

In the face of national pressure and a U.S. government unwilling to take action, Governor Richard Coke authorized a Special Force commanded by 31-year-old Confederate hero Leander McNelly. The Special Force was funded by Texas cattlemen. During a legendary few months in 1875, McNelly and 41 recruits pursued bandits, recovered stolen cattle, clashed with border warlords, operated autonomously under ostensible martial law and caused an international incident by invading Mexico. Cattle theft and banditry was reduced, but it would remain a common occurrence until the Mexican Revolution.

In 1910 Francisco Madero attempted to depose Porfirio Díaz from the presidency, setting off the Mexican Revolution. For almost three decades the Border became a place of refuge for bandits, revolutionaries and ne'er-do-wells. Death tolls reached the hundreds on both sides of the Rio Grande and continued to climb. Tensions escalated when, in 1915, a plan created by Mexican revolutionaries hiding in San Diego, Texas, was discovered. The plan called for a revolt by a "Liberating Army of Races and Peoples" that would return to Mexico lands lost in the Treaty of Guadalupe Hidalgo. Summary execution of every white male over the age of sixteen was also a part of the plan.

The resulting furor manifested itself in a massive and unplanned increase in the ranks of the Texas Rangers and the deployment of U.S. Army personnel to the region—and into Mexico—in force for the first time since the Mexican War. The poorly devised increase in the Ranger ranks resulted in a corps riddled with undesirables who were untested and untrained; some Rangers resigned rather than serve with the new inductees. Atrocities were committed by both sides. Eventually the U.S. Army intervened to restore a level of order. Stability slowly retuned to Mexico. Complicating the matter was the "national experiment of Prohibition." In addition to revolutionaries and bandits, bootleggers smuggled alcohol into Texas by the burro-load with Rangers and a small cadre of U.S. Customs officers the only effective forces to intercept it.

Since 1836 the Texas-Mexican Border has been characterized by violence due to issues of national sovereignty, cattle, revolutionary politics, and bootlegging. The majority of citizens on both sides have been peaceful and productive. But they have spent generations dodging armies, staying out of the way of bandits, and avoiding insurrectionists. Often their lives have been punctuated by tragedy and random violence. Into the third century of Texas Ranger and borderland history it does not now appear much relief is in sight.

Beginning in the 1980s, drug trafficking exploded along Texas' 1,254 miles of Rio Grande frontage; narco kingpins taking advantage of a benignly administered Border protection program. Today up to 48 billion dollars a year in marijuana, methamphetamine, cocaine and heroin are crossed into the U.S. The contraband comes in daylight and under the cover of darkness. Illicit drugs are floated or flown across the Rio Grande, driven through international Ports of Entry, and despite hundred-degree heat carried in backpacks through the chaparral and across Texas borderland ranches.

Cartel members terrorize the Mexican and U.S. side of the Border at will, murdering Mexicans and Americans, literally skinning some alive, and in certain cases executing policemen and wiping out entire police departments, along with depopulating Mexican towns. During 2008 more than 5,700 murders occurred on the Mexican side of the Texas Border, with 1,600 in Ciudad Juárez alone. Two years later the murder count in Juárez nearly doubled. I have been shown horrific cartel crime scene photos the Texas Rangers have on file. The sickening images reveal some of the violence cartel members have committed against Mexican people. Even in this desensitized age, the brutality and torture is gruesome.

In response, Governor Perry has once again employed Texas Rangers to provide protection to citizens along the Southwestern Border. During 2009 he announced the formation of specialized Reconnaissance Teams led and staffed by Rangers and incorporating Texas Department of Public Safety criminal and special tactics personnel. The hand-picked teams are deployed to high traffic, high crime areas along the Border. They are equipped with aircraft, particularly outfitted patrol boats, armored personnel carriers, high-caliber military weapons, surveillance equipment and state-of-the-art command and control centers. But above all, these Texas Ranger Recon Teams rely on some of the best trained, experienced, and most effective law enforcement personnel in the world. Thankfully there has not been a Ranger fatality despite numerous firefights with cartel members and drug runners.

Regrettably, the Texas-Mexican Border truly remains dangerous. We owe the Texas Rangers of old a debt, as well as their modern-day colleagues in the various divisions of DPS, the multiple agencies of the Department of Homeland Security, the sheriff's offices and police departments, as well as military units deployed along the river. Their commitment is remarkable.

In this book Bob Alexander draws upon investigative skills and experiences he gained as a career Special Agent with the U.S. Treasury Department. Subsequent to retiring from active enforcement activites he taught Criminal Justice classes at an area community college. With a base of both practical and theoretical experience Alexander is exceptionally positioned to recount this absorbing compilation of interconnected stories. He paints an informative and colorful picture of Texas Rangers enforcing laws and forfeiting their lives along the near unmanageable Texas-Mexican Border. Alexander's research is meticulous. His reasoning is logical and the interpretations are impartial. Bob pays attention not only to "what happened" but also places an incident in its appropriate historical context. These Texas Rangers had a compelling story and Alexander, in his relaxed and easygoing style has told it well. It is a noteworthy contribution. The collection of Ranger histories in hand offers an accurate boots-on-the-ground type look at many episodes from the 1870s to the 1920s and justly honors the sacrifices that these fallen Texas Rangers have made.

Byron A. Johnson, Executive Director
Texas Ranger Hall of Fame & Museum
Official Repository of the Texas Rangers
Waco, Texas

Preface and Acknowledgments

The Texas-Mexico border is trouble. Like a Black Widow seductress the borderland is at the same time alluring, deceitful—and heartless. Haphazardly splashing across the meandering Rio Grande into Mexico is—or at least can be—risky business, hazardous to one's health and well-being. On the border nonchalant inattention to geographical surroundings and any childish naivety about inhumanity can get one killed. Television news reports and current newspaper headlines corroborate the rather apathetic, harsh, and less than stellar public relations message: The Texas/Mexican border is a nightmarish mess.[1] Eminent nonfiction writer Leon C. Metz, himself an El Paso County resident, in *Border: The U.S.-Mexico Line* succinctly drives home a spear of disturbing reality: "Crime has become the leading growth industry along the border."[2] Substantiation of Mr. Metz's contention is ubiquitous.

Visiting with an Assistant Director for the Texas Department of Public Safety is enlightening. Kirby W. Dendy, that veteran law enforcing official, who also serves as Chief of Texas Rangers, corroborates the sobering reality: "As their predecessors for over one-hundred-forty years before them did, today's Texas Rangers continue to battle violence and transnational criminals along the Texas-Mexico border. In spite of the dangers and hardships they face, the dedication and resolve of the Texas Rangers to enforce the law and protect the citizens of the State of Texas is stronger than ever."[3]

Another salient case in point would be that the U.S. Department of Agriculture, during the 1980s—subsequent to legal authorization by an act of Congress—mandated its horseback "tick riders" working along the Rio Grande carry sidearms for personal protection. And they still do, despite the fact their job description is to protect America from diseased and parasitically infected animals, not fill border town jailhouses and federal penitentiaries with smugglers and murderers and decapitators.[4] Early on in this century's first decade a honored Texas writer, educator, and author of *Kings of Texas*, Don

Graham, in speaking of the Lower Rio Grande country, warned that indifferently wandering around in the area is "....not such a good idea, for this is drug smuggler country and anybody poking around in this isolated place, a true borderland, vague and undefined, is asking for trouble."[5] Nowadays, 2012, borderland chambers of commerce are hoeing the tough row, desperately trying to lure once eager tourists and noticeably scarce vacation dollars to their economically distressed and arguably dangerous neighborhoods. It's a tough sale. Separate accounts appearing in March 2012 newspaper editions zero in on tormenting Texas/Mexican border reality, at both ends of the Rio Grande: The *Dallas Morning News* highlighted the mass kidnapping and disappearence of a Matamoros family, while the *El Paso Times* chronicled the calculated and ferocious murders of five Juárez policemen during just one bloody episode. Scarcely two months later, shocking headlines revealed the discovery of 49 headless corpses just south of the border. Closer in—right on the border—the bodies of nine lifeless victims were found suspended from a bridge at Nuevo Laredo, Mexico's sister city to Laredo, Texas. Through passage of time little has really changed along sovereignty's edge. Suave and smooth-talking elected officials, along with the debonair bureaucratic pencil-pushers from both countries, literally cringe at having to admit this unsettling bit of political incorrectness: Neither country has real control of the border. It truly is a hard expanse of real-estate now and was then too, a hundred and more years ago.

So hard in fact that even in the early twentieth-century women—some women—resorted to carrying guns. No male chauvinism here, not along the line, not when the times and place suggested the no-nonsense wisdom of going armed, even for play and everyday business. One of the borderland's iconic personalities, a Big Bend treasure, Hallie Stillwell, recalled that while teaching public school along the Rio Grande at Presidio, Texas, she unfailingly carried a six-shooter to class—she was nineteen years old.[6] Drs. Charles H. Harris III and Louis R. Sadler, award-winning writers and indefatigable researchers with a sterling international reputation did not shy away from legit border reality when titling their highly praised masterpiece, *The Texas Rangers and the Mexican Revolution: The Bloodiest Decade, 1910–1920*.[7] Spilt-blood washing against and drenching the support pillars of most borderland nonfiction writings is not only commonplace but necessary—if truth be told. In commenting about a specific sector of the Southwest borderlands an illustrious chronicler of exhilarating

Old West lore and literature, Dr. Charles Leland "Doc" Sonnichsen, wrote that part of the region "….is a parched desert where everything, from cactus to cowman, carries a weapon of some sort, and the only creatures who sleep with both eyes closed are dead."[8]

Doc Sonnichsen's journalistic hyperbole is rich. The unspoken caveat that alertness is a key component for survival is sound. Perhaps his sage advice can best be exemplified in the context of law enforcement narratives, and nowhere better geographically spotlighted than along the Texas/Mexican border—then and now a fertile hotbed of violence.

The Rio Grande marks the southern edge of Texas and correspondingly an international boundary line with Mexico. Depending on who's doing the measuring, how they're doing it, and what time of the year the calculation is underway, reveals that the Rio Grande—as the Texas borderline—computes as a rough 1000 miles from the vicinity of El Paso to near Brownsville where it empties into the Gulf of Mexico.[9] Though biography of the Rio Grande is historically bountiful, abundantly so, there is a quantifiable downside.[10] As stated, many pages of that history are written with the blood of good men, bad men, and men altogether innocent—except for their latitude as cultural bystanders. The purpose of this book, however, is not to explore the Rio Grande's illustriousness or its bloodiness in the round. Rather the intent is, in a narrowly focused approach, to survey the personal tragedies of one body of men, Texas Rangers, as they scouted and enforced laws throughout borderland counties adjacent to the river. Walter Prescott Webb, one of the early Texas Ranger chroniclers and, admittedly, a Ranger legend builder, was not standing clueless in left field when speaking of the Rio Grande's sinister intrigues: "Perhaps the river knows, the river that conceals its mysteries more effectually than the graves along its banks conceal the bones of men…. Lead sinks more men in the Rio Grande in a year than gold does in a decade."[11] Since this is a story, more precisely an anthology of nonfiction stories about Ranger deaths by gunfire, appropriately it would not be incredibly outlandish to postulate that many of those state-paid lawmen might very well have characterized the Rio Grande as Lucifer's Line, the most perilous strip of ground in Texas. Certainly selected actuaries did, refusing to even underwrite life insurance policies for Texas Rangers assigned to the Texas-Mexico border.[12]

The format of this book is simple: Criteria for earning a biographical chapter easy, but disheartening. For inclusion herein a Texas Ranger must have made the ultimate sacrifice, and that sacrifice must have been made in a county bordering the Rio Grande—the Texas/Mexican boundary. Broadening the scope of this narrative to include violent deaths of all Texas Rangers killed in the line of duty would have proved unwieldy. In fairness, exclusionary clauses are necessary. The timeframe will commence in 1874 with formation of the Frontier Battalion and the Special Force which is when the Texas Rangers were actually institutionalized as a law enforcing entity. This review will conclude with the last known Texas Ranger death along the border, be it in the twentieth-century or, this one, if demoralizing news breaks before a final submission of the manuscript. Similarly, since the spotlight is on law enforcing issues, mortally succumbing to an Apache's arrow, or giving up the ghost due to the Grim Reaper's parting gift of pneumonia, influenza, malaria, or an advanced syphilitic condition falls outside the framework of this tome.

At first blush an academic pundit might underplay the historical worth of peeking in on fatalities incurred by but a single outfit, along a distinctly pinpointed backdrop—Lucifer's Line. At second look, an evenhanded appraisal is enlightening on more than one front.

Much has been written, particularly after earlier publication of venerating Texas Ranger histories, about an institutionalized vestige of bald-faced misbehavior, racism, and deliberate murder carried out by Rangers under the guise of enforcing the law. Some of those tales, unfortunately and inexcusably are true. There were—as with any law enforcing outfit—the proverbial bad apples within working and managerial ranks of the fêted Texas Rangers. Well, more precisely, there were some real rotten apples. This is not breaking news. Legislative investigations and agenda driven scholars—and an occasional condescending thinker—have sometimes gloried in exposing examples of malfeasance and malevolence on the part of Rangers as if it were, until they had come along, a dark secret. Overstepping that perpetually readjusting line of legality does not go unnoticed today, nor did it in the nineteenth-century. Whether with just cause—or not—Texas Rangers were no strangers at finding themselves often trapped in the quagmire of negative publicity.[13] Narrow-mindedness regarding social and cross-cultural issues was not foreign to ethnic subgroups. Texas Rangers were but a microcosm. They were but a piece of the puzzle on behalf of humanity's bizarre contradictions. Controversy swirled around their very boot tops, and had since before their inception as a peace keeping outfit. Hullabaloo concerning what Rangers did and how they did it and who they did it to, is often fodder for a class of contemporary detractors. In certain quarters focusing the lens of sociological truths is somewhat awkward: Especially for proponents with predetermined and grossly evident agendas, those fashioning their own versions of reality. Sharpening the picture leads to a discarding of that one-dimensional sales pitch weaknesses, the patently overworked ethnic exculpations. Drs. Harris and Sadler lay hard truth across the anvil and forge unbendable reality: "All along the Rio Grande the population was predominately Hispanic, which inevitably meant that most of the criminals were Hispanic, which inevitably injected a racial component into law enforcement—predominantly Anglo peace officers versus predominantly Hispanic outlaws. What tends to get overlooked, however, is that the vast majority of law-abiding citizens in this area were also Hispanics."[14] Morality is not singularly hammered from ethnicity.

Disappointedly, degrees of machinating muckraking still creep to the forefront within the context of selected historic explorations. Smugly suggesting "....the general view of many Chicanos and Mexicans is that 'every Texas Ranger has some Mexican blood. He has it on his boots,'" might bear prejudicial weight as a belief in specific quarters, but any such blanket accusations are unsustainable, factually.[15] They won't hold water. In fact, such dogmatic overstatement exposes an undercurrent of its own bigotry. There were—and are—many Texas Rangers with no blood whatsoever on their boots. Likewise there were many "Chicanos and Mexicans"—in fact the majority—who were not then or are they now bandidos or smugglers or border-jumping ne'er-do-wells. Perhaps a rational and frank policy position would be to historically bring indictments with evidence and skip blind generalizations. There was/is plenty of borderland criminality and murder and misbehavior that should make all uncomfortable—no matter their ancestry.

Though the comparative weight may be debated, sometimes there were petitions requesting Texas Rangers be forthwith removed from a given community, as well as offsetting pleas that they be stationed in a locale plagued by crime.[16] The truth is often thorny, but even when the Texas Rangers were wrong, dead wrong, now and again public sentiment issued them but a sly wink and a nod of endorsement. For other circumstances, when the wrongdoings cried for public redress, the shamed or culpable Texas Ranger—or Rangers—were asked to resign, dishonorably discharged, and/or even criminally prosecuted.

On the other hand, taking a hard nonpartisan look at the other end of the spectrum is, too, revealing. Texas Ranger history—bona fide history—is burgeoning with examples of the state salaried peace officers standing tall, bravely, honestly, selflessly. Many are the accounts of authentic Texas owlhoots ferociously and foolishly crossing paths with a gritty six-shooter-wearing Texas Ranger—once. Not all Texas Ranger gunplay was unwarranted—far from it! The seemingly inexhaustible Robert J. Casey in *The Texas Border and Some Borderliners* more than half a century ago reiterated the genuine peril associated with living life up and down the Rio Grande, on either bank, through the voice of his uncle who entertainingly swanked, "....the only legitimate industry was coffin making."[17] Certainly it was said with tongue in cheek, but that, in and of itself does not make gist of the message untrue. Elaborating, Uncle Ben characterized some of those border country towns as being "tough to the limit of human endurance."[18] Indisputably—the old-time records and newspaper trails are there—Texas Rangers contributed their fair share at keeping borderland undertakers and pine-box builders busy.

So what do we gain by rehashing six-shooter stories of bygone days? The answer is not elusive. Unlike historians and writers and fun-loving aficionados of Wild West nonfiction looking into the past from a time and distance well removed, the borderland Texas Rangers profiled in this volume were living in real time—making hard decisions in real time—and paying the highest price for miscalculation—in real time. This particularized cadre of Rangers were robbed of hindsight and not opportunely awarded a "do over." Perhaps in accessing their stories there is a tendency to be myopic, zeroing in on particular details for a particular time at a particular place and a particular Ranger, and then rendering an intellectual judgment from afar. The societal dynamic is much broader—and was so during the milieu of riding Lucifer's Line. Repeated individually these authentic Wild West stories are, hopefully, exhilarating vignettes of breathtaking escapades: True tales putting the "Western" in a Western for those looking in vicariously from the safety of a comfy reclining armchair. From the perspective of Texas Rangers living in real time, these adventuresome newsmakers were seen in the aggregate, one after the other—pulled together with the taut sutures of apprehension and dread. What had happened to their comrade-in-arms, though miles upstream or miles downstream, and on an indeterminate horizon of time, could very well be stalking their earthly existence, too. That's why the job description demanded they carry a gun or two—or three. Their adversaries sure did. Not surprisingly then, as psychologists and sociologists ably confirm, human beings may be products in generous extent to genetic makeup, but everyday experiences and crucibles of environment are relevant dynamics in shaping personality and attitude—how we act—and how we react.

That then would be one cerebral justification for threading these stories together, one after the other. Individually they are but mini-biographical tales, profiles, sketches: Strung together they offer societal commentary. Aside from what may be learned practically, another good reason is elementary. By forfeiting their lives in the line of duty these Rangers deserve at a minimum the posthumous honor of acknowledgment, their stories should not be pigeonholed in the dustbins of history. Collectively those boys dying along the tough Texas border offer pieces of sociological insight into the ceaseless turbulence and turmoil allied with enforcing laws and apprehending *mal hombres* on the line: We are but products of place and time. There is nothing new or earth-shattering about that, but cogent thinking and rethinking might—just might—be beneficial in profiting from the experiences of those tasked yesterday and today with patrolling the treacherous and unforgiving and yet untamed Texas/ Mexican borderlands. Lest there be misinterpreted unfairness, it is duly and freely acknowledged that the professors and preachers, psychotherapists and shoe salesmen, short-order-cooks and physicians going about their routine business in a Texas border town are not necessarily at risk, but they are not working down along the river in the labyrinth of cattails and willows, cacti and chaparral. It is a reasonably safe bet, a surefire bet, they are not pleasantly picnicking with their families and wading barefoot in the Rio Grande while skipping pebbles into Mexico as nighttime shadows close in. They are not lost in the twists and tangles and terrors of Lucifer's Line. These Texas Rangers were.

On the other hand everyday life along Lucifer's Line in a Mexican border town is intrinsically chancy. Contemporary journalists present a wide array of books and articles, many supplemented with gruesome photographs, depicting horrors near unspeakable taking place on the Rio Grande's south side. Aside from innocent civilians suffering murder, kidnapping, and extortion, the pandemic violence splashed across newspaper pages and television airways detailing the death of Alejandro Dominguez Coello: He lasted in the job as Nuevo Laredo's chief of police for a grand total of six hours, before mortally attacked by assassins pumping thirty bullets into the lawman who had promised he was "beholden" to no man.[19]

Grinding an understanding of those sociological matters in play and honing an awareness of the very real everyday dangers facing lawmen—then and now—makes easier the unscrambling of mythology and preconceptions while setting straight reality, discomforting as it sometimes might be. Startlingly and scarily looking into a Winchester lever gun's or Colt's six-shooter's muzzle then, or a high-capacity Glock's or AK-47's today is a situation best avoided. Men and women on the line don't need a tutor to know that.

Quite often it's written—frequently with pompous gusto—that during the nineteenth and early twentieth centuries hard-edged and saddle-toughened Texas Rangers would shoot first, ask questions later. History bears witness, sometimes they did. That mindset, however, does not necessarily equate with a calculating murderous intent. Should the cold circumstances be right, in real time, getting in the first lick is but damn smart. Self-preservation is not an abnormal or discreditable phenomenon. The well-known, at least in certain circles, modern era shootist and late Southwestern lawman Bill Jordan, U.S. Border Patrol, smartly titled his near classic volume about six-gun survival *No Second Place Winner*. In a general context steely-eyed Bill Jordan was right as rain, right on target. Many are times red ribbons are awarded posthumously—to widows. While riding Lucifer's Line, survival mattered, sentiment didn't.[20]

The reader should not be misled. Herein there will be no effort wasted as a whitewash defense for aberrant or abhorrent misbehavior, even if committed by the hand of a Texas Ranger. Nor will the word count be capriciously extended trying to validate some inane excuse for Mexicans or Mexican-Americans behaving badly—criminally, murderously. It will be transparent while thumbing these pages this unlucky set of Texas Rangers met their Maker and a mortician as byproduct of wrongness by native speakers of Spanish and mean blue-eyed desperadoes of the deepest dye. Lucifer was not bigoted. The borderline was an impartial zone for his handiwork. And, yes, he must have thought it a special treat when one Ranger cannibalized another—with a twin-barreled shotgun or Colt's .45 six-shooter.

This venture will not spin on an axis of trying to justify or condemn aspects of interaction between cultures, with its typically abortive attempts at setting right today, social injustices of yesterday. This narrative will adhere to history, not atonement. Or, in the sagacious words of the late Elmer Kelton, former president of the West Texas Historical Association, who had a no-nonsense outlook about apologetic folks wanting to blame great-granddad for all that went wrong in the West: "I feel that it is time to blow the whistle on them and tell it like it *was*."[21]

Too, as would factoring into the equation all of the Texas Rangers killed on the job make the book unmanageably cumbersome, there will be no crack at particularizing the not insignificant number of other lawmen forfeiting their lives while riding Lucifer's Line. During one harrowing incident a Texas Ranger and a U.S. Mounted Customs Inspector went down together. In another shooting rampage a borderland deputy sheriff fell lifelessly alongside his working partner for the day, a Texas Ranger who also made the supreme sacrifice as blood ebbed from his head, painting red the barroom's hardwood floor. Suffice to say, enforcing law on the Texas/Mexican border was/is risky employment, a tough method for earning a paycheck. Some folks, though, are drawn to police work with abandon, willingly and involuntarily so—a dichotomy defying any sane commonsense explanation. Whether a peace officer was representing city, county, state, or the U.S. Government the narratives of those fatally gunned down are worthy of memorialization: As is the ultimate sacrifice of all lawmen killed in the line of duty, even those far removed from the Texas/Mexican border.

Likewise this is not a book about situations, thrilling as they may be, where a Texas Ranger was legitimately forced into a dicey gunplay—or callously acted absent self-restraint—killing one or more adversaries, either rightly or wrongly. Although it skews adherence to chronology by scrubbing out any suspense and telegraphs an ending for each chapter, in *Riding Lucifer's Line* the subtitle *Ranger Deaths Along the Texas-Mexico Border* is purposefully unambiguous.

Clear-cut too is another dynamic. Nonfiction writings are an amalgamation. Substantiated data, from a number of sources, is welded together to tell, hopefully, a good, but factual story. The process takes many helpmates. Acknowledging their enthusiastic input is not only obligatory as a matter of politeness and professionalism, in this situation it's a personal pleasure as well. There were—for the most part—three wellsprings tapped for writing *Riding Lucifer's Line*. All were indispensible. Each is more than deserving a carve-out of special and heartfelt appreciation.

Ronald G. DeLord has always stepped to the forefront when asked. Formerly serving as Executive Director for the Combined Law Enforcement Associations of Texas, the acquaintance and friendship with Ron was result of his wearing another hat, that of President of the Peace Officer's Memorial Foundation, Inc. Untiring have been his efforts at identifying Texas Peace Officers killed in the line of duty, and making sure their sacrifice is not forgotten. It is no easy task to properly identify and meet the rigid criteria of proof necessary for placing names on monuments in Austin and at Washington, D.C. Not surprisingly such unsettling events occurring nowadays are more easily reconstructed than those happening during the nineteenth-century. However, Ron, taking a most commendable approach, is thoroughly committed to honoring all of Texas' fallen peace offi-cers—regardless. When broached with the infant idea that writing *Riding Lucifer's Line* was a genuine possibility, Ron unhesitatingly offered counsel and encouragement. He pledged—and has kept his word—that he would gladly share any tidbit of information he had collected over the years dealing with a Texas Ranger death on the border. Not only is the affable working relationship never underval-ued from this writer's viewpoint, now readers thumbing these pages are beneficiaries of Ron DeLord's graciousness and dedication.

For folks addicted to Texas history—researching, writing, or just reading—Donaly E. Brice probably needs no formalized introduction. Undoubtedly his name appears more times in the Acknowledgment Sections of nonfiction works about the Lone Star State than any-one's. A working career with the Texas State Library and Archives Commission put Donaly squarely in the right place for not only researching materials for his own writings, but for answering the innumerable requests from others in want of retrieving this or that document—or a whole pile of documents. Donaly's sheer enthusi-asm for finding and forwarding copies of primary source records is unmatched—by anyone, anywhere! He wants a writer of Texas his-tory to get it right. And to that end he is unbending: Donaly's intrin-sic desire is for a researcher and/or nonfiction writer to have access to *all* pertinent material. After that they may decide what's relevant or how to fashion independent interpretations. Of course Donaly

Brice's backing on this project was immeasurable, but more importantly, his friendship is the real treasure.

Research delving into Texas Ranger history obligates the writer to fully explore library and archive materials—and photographs—at the Texas Ranger Hall of Fame and Museum, Waco, Texas. Failing to do so is folly. Not only is the institution first-class in everyway, it holds distinct honor for being the Official State Hall of Fame and Official Repository of the Texas Rangers, as designated by resolution of the Texas Legislature. State lawmakers may have made it the official repository, but the staff—the entire staff—makes TRHF&M a blue-ribbon winner. Under the brilliant overall management of Executive Director Byron A. Johnson, a good personal friend, the facility has really flourished, not only as a vacation destination for visitors, but as a topnotch research resource, especially after opening of the brand new Tobin and Anne Armstrong Texas Ranger Research Center, housed on the same grounds as the museum. Though there is an affinity for and working relationship with the whole cadre of museum employees, for particular research help with *Riding Lucifer's Line* were Deputy Director Christina "Tina" Stopka, and Research Librarians Christy Claridy and Amanda Crowley. Their help was crucial, their smiles contagious.

Although it might prove an awakening for some readers of Old West chronicles, many incidents herein cited were bloodstained episodes taking place during the early twentieth-century, a timeframe corresponding with the Mexican Revolution. Drs. Charles H. Harris III and Louis R. Sadler, acknowledged experts of that conflict and era are friends. Thankfully, and it does indeed speak well of them, they were never too busy to take a timeout, answering questions or making critical clarifications about a number of seeming inconsistencies regarding Rangers positioned along the Texas/Mexican border and their law enforcing activities—good or bad. Jointly, Charles and Ray are a formidable research and writing and award winning team; individually they are gentlemen who falter not at taking a neophyte under their wings of principled historical research, sound reasoning, and practical advice.

As with two of my Ranger works from University of North Texas Press, *Winchester Warriors,* a history of Company D, and *Rawhide Ranger,* a biography of Austin Ira Aten, the cover of *Riding Lucifer's Line* is again graced by the unrivaled artwork of Donald M. Yena. Don is a master storyteller—with a paintbrush. The cover illustration for this Texas Ranger volume is his striking *Big Iron in Hand*; a paradigm of Don's creative canvas magic. The rangy horse's suddenly inter-rupted drink—muddy pond water dribbling from its mouth—with ears perked in suspicious inquiry at the possibility of closing danger is what one would see, in real time, if squatting behind that prickly-pear cactus. It could be downright scary. Gauging the Ranger's salt-iness as he thumbs back the Colt's hammer is not fuzzy: He's one tough *hombre* making ready for tough times. Running is not in his repertoire. Are the approaching horsebackers friends or foes? The leathery sun burnt face, graying hair, and his luxuriant but drooping moustache are weathered marks of age—experience—good sense. There is a foreseeable outcome. If a gunfight is eminent, the oldtimer is primed for a first place finish—second place won't do. Nor will it do for Don Yena! Thank you, my friend.

Particularly helpful—and always willing to be so—were *bueno amigos* also afflicted with the unshakable desire to spend every wak-ing minute scrambling for time to drown themselves in Old West history. All are published authors; all are contributors to making *Riding Lucifer's Line* whole. The simplest of thanks may really be inad-equate, but it's not forgotten for Doug Dukes, Liberty Hill, TX; Dave Johnson, Zionsville, IN; Cliff Caldwell, Mountain Home, TX; Rick Miller, Harker Heights, TX; Harold J. Weiss, Jr., Leander, TX; Deen Underwood, El Paso, TX; and Chuck Parsons, Luling, TX.

For their role in helping tell this story are four friends owed a special debt—and thanks. These folks are either particualry now focused on border law enforcing issues, and/or perserving that his-tory. One is the aforementioned Chief of the Texas Rangers, Kirby Dendy, Austin, TX. The other champions are Charles L. Wright, Assistant Port Director, U.S. Customs and Border Protection, El Paso, TX; Brenda Tisdale, Museum Administrator, Border Patrol Museum & Memorial Library Foundation, El Paso, TX; and David Turk, Historian, U.S. Marshal's Service, Washington, D.C.

Though it's quite a distance—all the way across the Atlantic—a particular voice of appreciation must be sent to Jeff Burton in England, an amazingly knowledgeable specialist on the American Southwest's notable bandits and man-killers. Jeff is not only one fine historian; he willingly and courteously answers the calls for help and/or guidance. The thoroughness of his research sets a standard to be emulated; the depth of his friendship is never forsaken.

As always, Bob Pugh, Trail To Yesterday Books, Tucson, AZ, unfailingly pitched in when that obscure out-of-print book or pamphlet was a "must have." His expertise is extraordinary.

The following cast also deserve mention by name: Jim Bradshaw, Haley Memorial Library, Midland, TX; Monty Waters, Austin, TX; James Wright, Whitney, TX; Michael Toon, Texas Collection, Baylor University, Waco, TX; Gillian Wiseman, Reference Librarian, Waco-McLennan County Library, Waco, TX; Jerri Garza, Archives of the Big Bend, Sul Ross University, Alpine, TX; Lisa Cornelius, Director, Red River County Library, Clarksville, TX; Denise Burnett, Director, Portales Public Library, Portales, NM; Vivian Grimes, Reference Librarian, Clovis Carver Library, Clovis, NM: Frances Mosley, Librarian, Throckmorton Library, Throckmorton, TX; Amber Wilson, Barry County Museum, Cassville, MO; Sheron Barnes, Special Collections Librarian, Victoria Regional History Center, Victoria College/University of Houston, Victoria Library, Victoria, TX; Sarah Bellian, Curator, Scurry County Museum, Snyder, TX; And surely it would be remiss not to mention Jan Devereaux, an award-winning writer of merit, who understands the ups and downs, highs and lows, linked with researching and writing nonfiction books. She's right there, every step of the way.

Karen DeVinney, Assistant Director/Managing Editor, University of North Texas Press, is worthy the gold medal. Working with Karen, taking the work-product from manuscript to book, is an unadulterated pleasure—pure and simple. Her matchless editorial competency is surpassed only by her cordiality. Easy-going collaboration with Karen guarantees a topnotch volume and upholds UNT Press' first-rate reputation within publishing circles. And, under the most capable stewardship of Ron Chrisman, Director, in but a few short years UNT Press has earned those well-deserved accolades. Ron's commitment to preserving and promoting an understanding of Texas history within the subtext of exploring issues and personalities of its law enforcing past is remarkable. Assuredly these nonfiction volumes focused on the Old West genre are yet popular for the general reader, as well as probing scholars. Thankfully, Ron has long recognized the sociological and educational commentary that may be captured by following Texas Rangers, understanding blood feuds, and watching societal misfits self-destruct during the thundering stampede aimed at burgeoning communities' try at civility. Ron Chrisman's acquisition skills put the proof in the pudding: Many, both aspiring and reasonably well established Old West authors make their first stop Denton, TX. Certainly the day-by-day operations keep any worthwhile organization afloat. Such is indeed the case at UNT Press. So while Ron Chrisman and Karen DeVinney are immersed on their end, two other dedicated staff members are at the wheel, steering the ship. Paula Oates, Director of Marketing and Lori Belew, Administrative Assistant, admirably do their part weathering the storms and landing the cargo safely in the readers' hands.

Introduction to Part I

The Frontier Battalion Era
1874–1901

Setting the chronological and geographical stage seems but obligatory before tackling the challenge of recounting true-life Texas Ranger stories within an anthology. By and large it is acknowledged that birth of the Texas Rangers—as a legit law enforcement agency—can be traced to 1874 when the Frontier Battalion and Special Force were legislatively built and launched. To say there were no Rangers prior to that—besides being Texas blasphemy—would simply be historically erroneous. Ranging companies dating to the days of Stephen F. Austin during the early 1820s are a genuine part of the Lone Star State's abundant and unique portfolio.[1] Thrilling campaigns pitting part-time Rangers against barbaric marauding Indians raiding the Texans' farms and ranches, or, from that other perspective, peacefully disposed Indians resisting wild-eyed and merciless Anglos invading their territory, is meat on the bone for generic and often slanted treatments of Texas history. Perspective does matter. Perhaps manifesting itself no more prominently than when probing the conflicts between warring cultures speaking different languages, owning generations of fixed tradition, and exhibiting conflicted sets of what is right and what is wrong.[2] Before stepping away, advancing the century's clock for this particular narrative, hearing from a salty old-time Texas Ranger about a dollop of Indian fighting ethnocentricity is enlightening:

> We rangers, as well as Indians, fought under the black flag. We asked no quarter and gave none. Whenever we met it was simply a case of outfight or outrun 'em, whichever could be done the best. When we fell into their hands they scalped us and frightfully muti-

1

lated our bodies, frequently cutting and hacking us to pieces. We didn't do as bad as that but scalped them just the same....[3]

Competing cultures along the borderline, once again, fostered an indefensible but predictable example of intolerance; the poisonous head of perspective injecting its communal toxin into another bloody fracas. Certainly Texas Rangers during the United States' 1840s war with Mexico had earned an evocative nickname spoken—or spit—by the Mexican tongue, *Diablo Tejanos*, the Texas Devils. In the main, during this orchestrated international conflict Texas Rangers had embraced what may be euphemistically transported into the modern-era, the wartime strategy of Shock and Awe. Mexicans were awed by the brutality and callousness and vindictiveness of ruthless Texas Rangers crossing the disputed Rio Grande and assaulting them on their native soil. Though impressed with the Texas Rangers' ability to live off the land, scout behind enemy lines, gather valuable—crucial—intelligence, and do battle asking for no quarter and giving none, U.S. Army commanders were shocked by Rangers' atrocities and extraction of coldhearted vengeance. Not shocked enough, however, to relinquish the bloody Rio Grande as part of America's permanent southern boundary with Mexico. Nor were the Texas Rangers' consciences bothering them for once more settling overdue scores for Goliad and the Alamo and other real or imagined affronts. For war-weary Texians those no-nonsense Rangers were the right stuff.[4]

So while the Texas Rangers were indeed garnering a reputation, a mystique, they were an outfit generally composed of citizens volunteering on an as-needed basis. Enlistment as a provisional Texas Ranger was not a long-term career move, not a job with dependably recurring paychecks—month after month—year after year. Once the raiding Indians were chased out of the neighborhood or run to ground past the frontier's edge, part-time Texas Rangers disbanded, picking up the plow and tramping after a team of mules or saddled-up once more, hunting for the festive cow to rope, trip, and brand. America's internal struggle, the Civil War, would stymie any notion whatsoever of attaching law enforcing permanency to these Texas Rangers.

At war's end Texans faced multiple troubles. On the western frontier Indians were raiding for reward and revenge with impunity. In South Texas, along the Rio Grande, Mexican bandits were overrunning Texans' cattle ranches and attacking Texas towns. The interior counties were plagued with lawlessness, epidemically so—though not as the byproduct of any grandiose conspiratorial scheme as a few over-thinking intellectuals sometimes feebly argue. Local law enforcement authorities—often outgunned and outmanned and underfunded—were unable or unwilling to act. Adding to the heartburn, at least to Texans, was imposition of a Reconstruction government and the ostensible radical Republican administration of Governor Edmund J. Davis.

Recognizing the genuine need for a state-sanctioned law enforcing body with statewide jurisdiction the governor, as midwife, birthed the Texas State Police during 1870.[5] Governor Davis' progeny was in the eyes of most Texans but an unwelcome and unwanted bastard child. Although there were not just a few dedicated and competent fellows making up the State Police roster, there was, too, a rather healthy sampling of guys not suited for impartially insuring justice, anywhere—at anytime.[6] A few mean-eyed stone-cold killers had wormed their way into the State Police ranks. Governor Davis may have had his heart in the right place, but many of his inappropriate appointments and a policy of allowing perhaps 40 percent (a debatable estimate) of his police force to be comprised of freedmen did not set well with dyed-in-the-wool Texans of a Democratic Party persuasion. Black men carrying Colt's six-shooters and putting white men in jail was a big and bitter pill. Way too big and way too bitter for most resident Texans to swallow. And they didn't! After regaining political control of the Texas Congress, one of the first acts of Democrats was abolishment of the Texas State Police. The legislative act of April 22, 1873, generally met with statewide approval:

> The people of Texas are today delivered from an infernal engine of oppression as ever crushed any people beneath the heel of God's sunlight. The damnable police bill is ground beneath the heel of an indignant legislature.[7]

Politically the detested State Police had been destroyed. Practically the reason of their existence had not. Texas was awash with lawlessness. Too, on the western edge of the frontier raiding Indians were yet making incursions, stealing horses and cattle, sometimes killing isolated settlers, kidnapping kiddos and enslaving captured wives and mothers. Particularly incensed that the federal government was not doing, or was incapable of doing, enough to assuage their concerns over interloping Mexican bandits and Plains Indian raiders and Anglo feudists, the Fourteenth Texas Legislature jumped, enacting several pieces of legislation, which in part said: "to provide for the protection of the Frontier of the State of Texas against the invasion of hostile Indians, Mexicans, other marauding or thieving parties."[8]

Among other governmental matters, new legislative statutes created the Frontier Battalion, six seventy-five-man companies and, later, the Washington County Volunteer Militia, Company A (the only company) which was broadly dubbed the Special Force, a unit at first specifically tasked with cleaning up a mess in DeWitt County, the Sutton-Taylor Feud. Afterward the Special Force was drafted to put the wholesale kibosh on livestock thieves and murderers breeching the Rio Grande and setting aflame, sometimes literally, South Texas, that section below the Nueces River.[9] With the births of these two corps the Texas Rangers had been institutionalized. It was now a real paying job—with a real future—if a man wanted it, and if the man could cut it.

And it is at this moment in time that some pointless nitpicking and/or wrangling about semantics typically pops up. Now and again well-meaning historians and an occasional newsprint journalist pride themselves at pointing out that the Washington County Volunteers, Company A, under command of Captain Leander Harvey McNelly were not, in truth, real Texas Rangers. Interestingly, everyone—even those fussy fault-finders—have not problem number one with labeling all of the officers and men of Major John B. Jones' Frontier Battalion as Texas Rangers. In truth neither the Frontier Battalion or Special Force personnel were legislatively—or even in a formal administrative sense—officially designated as Texas Rangers.[10] Such as it is, the inconvenient formality changed nothing—then or now—not in the minds of most Lone Star folks: For everyday Texans at large, newspapermen, politicos, bandits, fugitives from justice, store clerks, cow thieves, schoolchildren, and government bureaucrats at the local, state, and federal level, the men and boys making up the two units were Texas Rangers.

Shoring up the assertion is not inappropriate. Leander McNelly's adroit biographers make their viewpoint emphatically clear: "the McNelly company in all aspects [was] a Texas Ranger company except for the name. The men were paid by the state, the captain reported to the adjutant general, and McNelly as well as the ordinary Texan of the day considered the group as much Texas Rangers as the official six companies of the Frontier Battalion."[11] Two twenty-first-century historians, both with broad-spectrum two-volume treatments of the Texas Rangers, seem to concur: One skilled writer penned, "McNelly and his men showed up in South Texas wearing what they wanted to. A militia company on paper, in appearance and function they rode as Rangers."[12] The other, a widely respected Western historian, put his cards on the table: "The men regarded themselves as Rangers, and so did the public—'McNelly's Rangers.'"[13]

Perhaps even carrying more weight than what is propounded by secondary sources, peeking in at the actual written remarks of Texas Governor Richard Coke to Captain McNelly in a contemporary letter dated July 9, 1875, is unequivocal and should—for most folks—put the matter to bed (emphasis added): "the pride of true Texans in the historic fame of the Texas *ranger* is fully gratified in the record your command is making...."[14]

Reverting back to the present era, another item is worth bearing in mind. The Official Repository for the Texas Rangers, designated by the State of Texas Legislature, is the Texas Ranger Research Center (the newly built and christened Tobin and Anne Armstrong Texas Ranger Research Center), an integral division of the Texas Ranger Hall of Fame & Museum, Waco, Texas. Although the museum's Executive Director, Byron A. Johnson, and Deputy Director/Chief Archivist Christina Stopka maintain a first-rate facility in every regard, they do not make selections for inclusion in the institution's Ranger Hall of Fame. Nominees and Inductees for the Hall of Fame are chosen from within ranks, by the Texas Rangers themselves: Captain Leander H. McNelly has been so honored. Texas Rangers credit McNelly a Ranger, a real Texas Ranger.[15]

In the same vein: For purposes of honoring officers killed in the line of duty, the Texas Peace Officers' Memorial Foundation recognizes and officially designates members of the Frontier Battalion and the Washington County Volunteer Militia, Company A, as Texas Rangers.[16] For anyone intent on splitting hairs, quite naturally the prerogative is and remains theirs, but for the common-sense purpose of *Riding Lucifer's Line*, we'll line up with the old-time Texas governor, most contemporary historians, and the twenty-first century Texas Rangers.

Subsequent to passage of enabling legislation and the selection of Major John B. Jones of Navarro County (Corsicana) as commander of the Frontier Battalion the May 1874 recruiting began.[17]

The staffing model called for putting on the payroll 450 fighting men. Enduring budget shortfalls would reduce personnel numbers appreciably throughout the Frontier Battalion's lifespan. Privates were to draw $40 per month, paid quarterly. The new Ranger was expected to report for duty with a personally owned six-shooter, "Army size," and a "horse" which meant a gelding, not a temperamental sexually cycling mare or an easily aroused and sometimes hard to manage hormonally stirred-up stallion. The neophyte Texas Ranger's mount would stand appraisal by the enrolling officer and two "disinterested" parties for good reason; if the horse were killed in the line of duty the State of Texas would reimburse the Ranger so he could purchase another. A Ranger without a horse was no Ranger. The policy of replacing dead or severely wounded horses, in and of itself should have been a not subtle warning about what might be expected of the green recruit. A novice Texas Ranger was to be furnished with a .50 caliber Sharps carbine, but it would not be free. The gun would become his personal property only after the cost had been deducted from his quarterly pay.[18]

The state would supply ammunition for the firearms, feed for the horses, and a hearty but monotonous diet of "bread, beef, coffee, and sugar & salt," for the enlistees. Naturally, the eats could be supplemented with wild game, fish, and fresh honey robbed straight from the beehive. The term of enlistment on paper was for four years, by administrative decree shortened to twelve months. Nonetheless it was outside work, twenty-four and seven. The Frontier Battalion boys would be allowed the niceness of covering tents if available, if not slumber would be beneath the stars—or thunderstorms. Their job, as it was understood, was to "scout" not whine.

Rangers were not furnished, nor expected to have uniforms. Wide-brimmed hats and high top boots were obligatory—tradition and practicality called for that much of a dress code. They had no official—state issued—badges and would not have for the next half century. For those intervening fifty-plus years if a Ranger wanted a badge he ordered one from a jeweler or out of a catalogue. Or, had someone hammer out one to his liking, of his own design—now and again from a *cinco peso*. Then and now the badge is but a symbol—not the official authority. A Texas Ranger's official power came in the form of a Warrant of Authority and/or his Descriptive List, which particularly identified him. However, both papers were carried in a leather pouch or pocket, not openly displayed. How would one know a real Texas Ranger? Well, they just should! A Ranger captain explained why everyday folks should be able to recognize a Texas Ranger, simply "because of their general appearance, they ride big shod horses and have pack mules."[19] The cavalier dearth of identifying Texas Ranger accoutrements would from time to time lend itself to heartache and heartbreak.

Company captains, appointed by Governor Coke and Adjutant General William Steele, possibly with some input from Major Jones, were awarded the discretion of staffing their respective commands, as long as they complied with explicit guidelines: "Persons under indictment or of Known bad character or habitual drunkards will be rejected."[20] There was another stipulation, too. Privates and noncommissioned officers had to be unmarried, single men, absent the responsibility of wives and children, because: "As it is expected that this force will be Kept actively employed during their term of Service only young men without families with good horses will be recruited."[21] Captains and lieutenants were exempt from the stricture banning married men from service.

This administrative diktat, wholly an arbitrary decision, would in the final analysis not bode well for the Frontier Battalion, though the prohibition was not draped over the Special Force commanded by McNelly. True professionalism demands levels of hands-on experience. That comes with time. Restricting Texas Rangers from having a wife and children may have seemed logical in the short term, but social mores of the times expected men—mature career-minded men—to marry and start a family. Until the prohibition fell by the wayside, which would happen in large part due to racing technological developments, the personnel turnover rate of the Frontier Battalion was atrocious: undoubtedly a case of unintended consequences![22]

Nevertheless there was no shortage of fellows wanting to enlist for an outdoor life of adventure. Some were but "beardless youths" but that was not a disqualifier. Most had reached the age of majority, but not by too much. They were, however, all white. There was also another common thread drawing them together. The prohibition vis-à-vis marriage had hollowed a shallow recruiting pool, paring down the average age of Texas Ranger candidates. Excluding some company captains and lieutenants, but few of them had ever even seen a real live Indian, much less suffered through a difficulty with some blue-eyed desperado or Mexican bandit—or exchanged gunfire with anyone. What they didn't know they would learn on the job. Most would be quick students; inattention to lessons in this classroom could promote disastrous results.

At the outset both the Frontier Battalion and Special Force were tasked with annihilating the enemy, not imposing the sanctions of criminal law in a courtroom. Traditional law enforcement duties there would be, but not during the start-up timeframe—apart from a limited basis in the broad overview. For Frontier Battalion fighters the enemies were Comanche and Kiowa and Apache; for the Special Force troops, who would soon find themselves deep in the Lower Rio Grande Valley, the adjutant general's orders were plain, damn plain: "destroy any and every such band of freebooters" that had crossed into Texas from Mexico with thoughts of plunder muddying their minds.[23]

Unlike the single company Special Force led by McNelly, the Frontier Battalion's Texas Rangers commanded by Major Jones were subdivided into six companies, A through F. These units were widely scattered—strategically—along a north/south line at the western frontier's edge. At the time much of the vastness of western Texas and the Panhandle was for the most part uninhabited by whites. It was the domain of Indians and buffalo, not Ned the hardscrabble farmer and his brood. The Texas Rangers of Major Jones' command were to act first as a buffer between painted warriors and palefaces. And, if raiding Indians breeched that imaginary line they were to chase them with vengeance—to the burning gates of Hell if need be. For the Lower Rio Grande Valley the message for Mexican bandits was similar: crossing the Rio Bravo would not be cost free; the toll could be paid with blood. Neither McNelly nor Jones was disposed to sit behind the desk; they were field-commanders and, as such, spent most of their time squaring off with the enemy—or trying to!

Enumerating in detail the clashes between Texas Rangers and marauding Indians is doable, but not necessary within the pages of *Riding Lucifer's Line*, a storyline thematically centered on true Texas Ranger tales with a law enforcing bent. Wide-ranging histories of the Texas Rangers, and there are several, more than adequately explore the uncompromising role Rangers played in subjugating Indians. After the 1874–1875 Red River War of which the U.S. Army really owns any credit or criticism, the threat from Indian raiders in Texas while not wholly eliminated, was appreciably diminished. What was not lessened was the need for Texas Rangers.

Although it is and can be effectively argued that Governor Richard Coke did not envision the part Frontier Battalion personnel would take with regards to civilian law enforcement in the original enabling legislation, State Senator David B. Culberson did. Section 28 of the April 10, 1874, law is explicit:[24]

> Each officer of the battalion and of the companies of minute men herein provided for, shall have all the powers of a peace officer, and it shall be his duty to execute all criminal process directed to him, and make arrests under capias properly issued, of any and all parties charged with offense against the laws of this State.[25]

For the last quarter of the nineteenth-century Texas Rangers were on the road of transition; from a ragtag assortment of young men wanting to taste adventure, to a corps of professional lawmen steeped in traditions of days past, and building—in most instances—a positive legacy for those who would afterward march in their footsteps. Unquestionably that road was fraught with danger. Progression down the timeline was at times rocky and near immobilizing but nevertheless it's fascinating nonfiction—moving them from then till now.

As the narrative moves forward there are discernible subchapters. The Texas Rangers' learning processes, the adaptation of untried law enforcing techniques, the utilization of new technology, and the hard realization that they were playing on a field with rules they didn't write, but were now Constitutionally mandated to adhere to, makes for a first-class Old West story, a humdinger. A contemplative student can watch the transition as it unfolds.

Remembering that at the outset Frontier Battalion boys signed on to hunt Indians is crucial. Not in their wildest dreams—for most of them—at that time did they think they would be called on to make arrests and put folks in the penitentiary or shoot it out with a bad man—the bad white man—from Bitter Creek. Such work was not universally tolerable. Some Texas Rangers opted out. A few flatly refused to arrest a friend. Others caught the law enforcing fever, but not unwisely sought the better pay and working conditions generally afforded a county sheriff or federal officer, or as a cattlemen association's hired gun. Many, in the final analysis, were simply using Ranger service as steppingstones to healthier and more lucrative prospects.

One of the initial law enforcing tests—real tests—laid in the Texas Ranger's lap were criminal violations, offshoots from the

Mason County War, aka the Hoo Doo War. If judgment is impartial—
which it should be—the Texas Rangers failed, and miserably so. But,
in fairness, they were beginners in the law enforcing game. Certainly
a nighttime episode wherein the Mason County jail was mobbed as
a Texas Ranger lieutenant and a civilian stood as witnesses dispels
the staleness of "One Riot—One Ranger." An ex-Company D Ranger,
William Scott Cooley, committed a coldly calculated murder, and
several of his former colleagues actually resigned from the Frontier
Battalion rather than arrest him.[26] And even Major Jones was forced
into admitting: "Within a few days however I became convinced that
it would only aggravate the troubles to leave Lt. Roberts company
here [Mason] for the reason that the sympathies of his men were
entirely with one of the parties to the feud.... and entertained a violent prejudice against Sheriff Clark and the German population."[27]

Though not necessarily looking for historical redemption, the
Texas Rangers under Major Jones' leadership chalked one up. Kimble
County (Junction) was near out of control, the rougher element having created a reign of lawlessness. Crime was running rampant and
unchecked. Too, even certain county officeholders were participants:
"Buckskin officials were in full blast."[28] Employing a technique normally reserved for Pinkerton operatives, Major Jones dispatched a
Texas Ranger to Kimble County in an undercover capacity. Shortly
thereafter the major received the lawman's secret report, uncor-
rected for the sake of its original flavoring: "I find that Kimble County
is a thiafs stronghold, the two Llanos and all tributaries are lined
with them.... the County is unsafe to travil through."[29] Jones acted.
Prepositioning Rangers from several companies, on April 19, 1877,
the major kicked off what would go down in history books as the
Kimble County Roundup. Forty-one suspected outlaws were jugged,
including the county sheriff and county judge. In retrospect it was a
watershed moment for the Texas Rangers, who, according to Major
Jones had tirelessly labored to assure success in such "arduous and
unpleasant service. The work was very fatiguing much of it having to
be done at night."[30] The Texas Rangers—good Texas Rangers—were
now taking pride in their new line of work—law enforcement. *Esprit
de corps* was conspicuous. Routine scouting for Indian sign which
might or might not materialize was suspended, officially, by direct
order. Texas Rangers were to "concentrate on the suppression of lawlessness and crime in the frontier counties and along the cattle trails

to the north."[31] The Texas Ranger job description had morphed from soldiering to policing.

Early on Frontier Battalion hierarchy had recognized one of its newfound law enforcement mandates was the chore of arresting and returning to sheriffs or locking up wanted fugitives. Perhaps one of the earliest indicators Rangers were on the march toward taking a professional approach to law enforcing work was management's implementation of the Fugitive List, popularly known to lawmen in the field as the Book of Knaves, Black Book—or even the Ranger's Bible. In today's lexis it would wash out as something akin to Information Technology. For nineteenth-century Texas Rangers it was a handy tool, a written compilation of wanted fellows, their physical descriptions, crimes they were charged with, rewards that had been posted and, when appropriate, notations about a fugitive's specific idiosyncrasies or peculiarities. Local sheriffs and city marshals supplied the data, and statewide many were the criminals that could credit their undoing to a Ranger thumbing pages and matching names and/or descriptions to the list each carried in their saddlebags.[32]

There would be a hiccup or two as far as professionalism was concerned, such as the much ballyhooed El Paso Salt War (Chapter 2), individual instances of foul behavior, and a few exhibitions of sheer stupidity, but for the most part Texas Rangers were making a good name for themselves, especially after catching John Wesley Hardin in Florida and killing desperadoes Sam Bass and Seaborn Barnes at Round Rock, Williamson County, Texas. After shedding their Indian-chasing duties, Rangers, many times over, found themselves at the epicenter of complex and thorny Texas doings. Embroilment in such flare-ups as the Fence Cutting Wars and Jaybird/Woodpecker Feud would be but two high-profile instances where Texas Rangers were dispatched to put the damper on overt criminal behavior. There were a host of other episodes.

The salient point to draw from this Part I Introduction is not particularly complicated—but relevant. Law enforcement is ever evolving. Such was the case then in the life of Texas Rangers, individually and institutionally. Such is the case today. Taking that quarter century overview of the Frontier Battalion's lifespan is thrilling to be sure, but above all else—downright enlightening. Aside from particularizing crimes and criminals and reliving gunplays, the evolution of Texas Ranger enforcement tactics and incorporation of available tools and the speed with which it was all taking place is near mindboggling.

In but reasonably short order the Texas Rangers underwent a philosophical and operational change during the nineteenth-century. For the most part the transition was handled quite proficiently. Rangers had tailored, and continued to tailor themselves for changing times and progressing technology.

Even before crossing into the twentieth-century the observant student is afforded opportunity to watch the Texas Rangers move from law enforcing "by the-seat-of-your-pants" to developing Probable Cause, signing sworn Affidavits, obtaining Search and Arrest Warrants, capably testifying before district judges and/or justices of the peace, as well as complying with demands of the law regarding having a formalized Inquest when they or another killed someone, or when the death was of a suspicious or uncertain nature—external to the medical care of a physician.

Those same observations—over time—reveal that the Texas Rangers were on the road to becoming competent criminal investigators, employing, or trying to employ, the very latest forensic advances: identifying bodies through dental examinations, matching the cut pieces of rope or barbed-wire, and comparing crime scene soil samples to the mud on a suspect's boots. Though we'll use today's familiar terminology, even during the nineteenth-century those industrious Texas Rangers were bringing into play such law enforcement techniques as mail covers, sting operations, surveillance, informant development, witness protection, undercover undertakings, crime scene reconstruction, tempting would-be perpetrators with bait ploys, and exploiting an effectual task-force model for interdiction and investigations. Too, regrettably, but progressively, Internal Affairs-type inquiries became a part of the Texas Ranger hierarchy's administrative toolkit. As an outfit the Texas Rangers did not shy from trying something new.

Texas Rangers especially were fond of new firearms, taking advantage of the very latest developments. Through their old-time correspondence, which is voluminous, and by reviewing period photographs, of which there are many, the progression from days of the single-shot Sharps .50 caliber carbine, to the most up-to-date smokeless powder Winchesters may be followed. They were, in truth, Winchester Warriors. Still, during the nineteenth-century the preferred handgun was a Colt's New Model Army Metallic Cartridge Revolving Pistol, which is more commonly known as the .45 Colt's Peacemaker or Single Action Army.

As early as 1885 the Texas Ranger command structure had been communicating via the telephone, which is somewhat surprising to most folks, but perhaps one of the most momentous measures impacting Texas Rangers was expansion of the railroads. Once railway lines were operating pervasively, criss-crossing throughout the Lone Star State (about 1888) a dramatic change in Texas Ranger deployment and its managerial style resulted. Heretofore, especially during the Indian chasing days, Texas Ranger actions were typically movements involving large numbers. Sometimes the entire company responded to a real or imagined threat. At other times the company was subdivided and a squadron of Texas Rangers answered the call, but nearly always with numbers. Easy access to railroad connections prompted a change. Texas Rangers, those from within the same company—sometimes just one or two—could now be stationed in widely separated camps or different towns, covering much more territory within their allotted sphere of jurisdiction. Should the need arise, it was but quick work via the telephone or telegraph to summon Rangers, even from multiple companies. Loading their saddle-horses and pack mules into a livestock car, the Texas Rangers, the whole company plus others if necessary, could converge in but a matter of hours in most cases—anywhere in the state.[33]

Those same railway links shaped Texas Ranger service otherwise, too. With transportation time cut to a matter of hours, not days, the granting of furloughs became relatively common. The outcome was noteworthy. Although a specific order reversing the policy of Texas Ranger privates and noncoms having to be sans a wife has yet to surface, it appears a sly wink and a nod supplanted the limitation. Just as with responding to a distant spot on the map in an "on duty" status, with the ease of train travel a lonesome Texas Ranger could now easily visit his spouse, children, and/or parents—or girlfriend—and be back at his duty-station in but short order. The dynamic lent itself well to sound personnel management practices—employee retention.

Naturally it will come as no earth-shattering surprise that the days of the Frontier Battalion were numbered, but thankfully not an end-of-the-line for Rangers. Inside *Riding Lucifer's Line* the first eleven chapters cover that time period consistent with a named Texas Ranger's service in the Frontier Battalion. Then, with new legislative and administrative statutes in place and a suitable Introduction for Part II intended to—hopefully—orient the reader, the story continues.

Perhaps though, prior to moving on to succeeding chapters a simple caveat is worth noting. Generally it is more-or-less proffered—notably by academics—that there was no longer a frontier after the close of the nineteenth-century, and some thinkers want to shut her down even before that. Skirmishing with such a premise would be a scholarly exercise—and for the purpose of this work—valueless, even if otherwise it was meaningful. Occasionally theoretical arguments are just that, theoretical: Rousing but abstract nevertheless. Maybe such is fine for the classroom or beer-table debate, but is such conjecture diluted or knocked sideways by real world truths?

It may be plausibly argued that law enforcement work, no matter the timeframe, is entitled to define its own frontiers. Not with the chronological ticking of a clock, but by on-the-ground perspective. Then or now a law enforcer finding him or herself in a deadly confrontation could very well postulate they were living and standing and fighting on a bona fide frontier, a frontier between constrained civility and unchecked chaos. That space was a perilous frontier then and is today. The Frontier Battalion Rangers enumerated in Part I would attest to that—if they could!

With that said, let's ride Lucifer's Line.

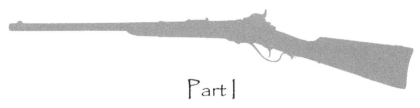

Part I

Photo Gallery

Texas Ranger Hall of Fame & Museum

Leander H. McNelly, Captain of the Special Force. His short-term results were dramatic and bloody, but his enforcement methodology was/is undyingly controversial.

Major John B. Jones, Commander of the Frontier Battalion.

George Durham, even into old-age was proud to be carrying distinction of once being on the state's payroll as a "McNelly Ranger." He also authored (with help from Clyde Wantland) one of the Texas Ranger classics, Taming the Nueces Strip.

Cicero Rufus Perry, a genuine fighting man. "Rufe" was a charter member of the Frontier Battalion and one of its first company captains, a veteran of numerous hard campaigns in early day Texas.

Life in the Frontier Battalion was an outdoor experience, as evidenced by this photograph.

Texas Rangers, horseback, strike a handsome—and recurring—pose for the traveling photographer.

Frontier Battalion Rangers of Company D under command of Captain Dan Roberts. Top row L to R, Doug Coalson, Ed Wallace, Lewis Cook, and George Hughes. Second row L to R, Nick Brown, Billy Sheffield, R. G. Kimbell, Tom Carson, Dick Russell, and L. C. Miller. Middle row L to R, Ed Sieker, L. P. Sieker, Captain Dan Roberts, Henry Ashburn, and Doc Gourley. Fourth row L to R, Tom Sparks, Bob Roberts, William "Slick" Clements, J. L. Rogers, George Bingham, and Jim Renick. Bottom row L to R, Jim Moore, Sam Henry, E. J. Pound, and Henry Thomas. Killed during the battle with the Jessie Evans gang in southern Presidio County was Private George R. "Red" Bingham, fourth row, fifth from left.

Three of Austin Cunningham Aten's five sons would become Texas Rangers, and all three would, at one time or another, experience the horrors of shoot-outs wherein the second place winners were carried to the graveyard. Standing L to R, Austin Ira Aten, a future Ranger; Clara Isabel Aten; Thomas Quinn Aten; Margaret Angelina Elizabeth Aten; and Franklin Lincoln Aten. Seated L. to R, Calvin Grant "Cal" Aten, a future Ranger; Austin C. Aten and wife, Katherine Eveline; and Edwin Dunlap Aten, a future Ranger.

Although enlisted Rangers of the Frontier Battalion were in the beginnings prohibited from having a wife, the stricture did not apply to captains or lieutenants. Captain Dan Roberts married and brought his wife Lou to the Company D camp. Tentative identification for this unique photo is L to R, Captain Roberts, Lam Sieker, unknown female visitor, and Lou Roberts inside the canvas fly of her new "home."

These gritty Rangers of Captain Joe Shely's Company F, Frontier Battalion scouted the middle Rio Grande Country between South Texas and the Big Bend area. Standing L to R, J. W. Buck, Pete Edwards, Captain Shely, George Farrow, Brack Morris, and Charlie Norris. Seated L to R, Washington "Wash" Shely, Tom Mabry, Bob Crowder, and Cecilio Charo.

Many notable Texas Rangers working the Texas-Mexico border were headquartered at this picturesque spot, Camp Leona, Uvalde County, not unduly far from Del Rio or Eagle Pass, both on the Rio Grande.

Texas Ranger Austin Ira Aten, horseback, armed and ready for war. He was involved in his first—but not last—gunfight with supposed bandits along the Texas/Mexican border.

Oscar D. Baker was one of the Texas Rangers—along with Ira Aten—involved in the border country shoot-out wherein Private Frank Sieker was killed, and was also one of the several Rangers arrested at Laredo and held in the Webb County jail for 26 days.

Ranger Charles Henry Vanvalkenburg Fusselman was killed trailing mal hombres in El Paso County's Franklin Mountains. His killer, Gerónimo Parra, aka Jóse Nuñez, was hanged at the city ten years later.

These Company F Rangers were stationed in South Texas, commanded by Captain James Abijah Brooks, standing at far left in suitcoat. The time frame is the early 1890s parallel to the so-called "Garza War" wherein Texas Ranger Robert E. Doaty (Doughty) was mortally cut down.

The seizure of more than 3000 quarts of liquor (tequila and/or mescal) smuggled from Mexico into Texas by mescalleros strapped to three dozen pack horses was a case of damn good work or damn good luck! Regardless, this was one pleased-as-punch squad of South Texas Rangers.

Headquartered at Alice but dispersed throughout the South Texas border country were these Rangers of Company E, Frontier Battalion, under command of Captain J. S. McNeel, seated in center of photograph.

Frank Jones, Captain of Company D, seated third from left. After surviving several gunplays he would be mortally gunned down on the Rio Grande's Pirate Island, below El Paso. Rangers in this photograph suffering violent deaths at the hand of others are identified by *: The Rangers are, back row from L to R, Jim King*, Baz Outlaw*, Riley Boston, Charley Fusselman*, James William "Tink" Durbin, Ernest Rogers, Charles Barton, and Walter Jones; Front row L to R, Bob Bell, Cal Aten, Captain Jones*, J. Walter Durbin, Jim Robinson, and Frank Schmid*.

Fittingly the Texas Rangers sometimes had a chaplain. Whether it was for show or preparedness for any eventuality is unknown. However, Ranger Chaplain Pierre Bernard Hill was clearly ready to pray at the bedside, eulogize at the funeral, and kill a bear—or a badman.

Although here he is depicted as one of the Texas Rangers dispatched to Temple, Texas, to dampen tensions during a labor dispute, Edwin Dunlap "Eddie" Aten, standing fourth from L, was to suffer more than one gunplay while enforcing the law along Lucifer's Line. These Texas Rangers are, back row from L to R, Captain J. A. Brooks, Captain John R. Hughes, John Nix, Eddie Aten, Edward Fulton "Big Ed" Connell, T. M. Rose, Lee Queen, A. A. Neeley, G. J. Cook, and Dan Coleman; front row from L to R, Jack Harwell, Will Schmidt, C. B. Fullerton, G. N. Norton, Ed Palmer, Joe Natus, James V. Latham, and E. E. Coleman.

Old-time Texas Rangers paying respects at relocated headstone of Captain Frank Jones. Standing L to R, Eddie Aten, his brother Austin Ira Aten, and Edward "Ed" Bryant. Kneeling, John R. Hughes. Both Eddie Aten and Ed Bryant were veterans of the furious dustup wherein Captain Jones was viciously cut down on the Rio Grande's Pirate Island by murderous fugitives.

Though pictured here while a Texas Ranger, fifth from left, Bazzell Lamar "Baz" (sometimes Bass) Outlaw was "in a close place worth two or three ordinary men," but when drinking, which was often, he was all but a "maniac" and "always wanted to shoot some one." At the backyard of an El Paso whorehouse he murdered Texas Ranger Private Joseph "Joe" McKidrict. In turn, Outlaw was fatally gunned down by man-killer John Selman, who would later kill the notorious John Wesley Hardin inside El Paso's Acme Saloon. Thereafter Selman's earthly existence would be snuffed out—second place in a gunfight— the six-shooter triumph of another notable Old West gunman, George Adolphus Scarborough, who that day took home the blue ribbon.

A near mandatory photo for inclusion in any Texas Ranger book is this emblematic image. And, in truth it does illustrate that with a much improved transportation and communications network Texas Rangers from various companies could be assembled at one place in but short order, this time at El Paso to prevent a prizefight—though it was more for show than any actual interdiction. Also illustrated in this photograph is the hard fact that Rangers now could easily doff the rough duty look of cowboys, and don suitcoats and ties. They could not—and would not—shed their Winchesters, the primary weapon for a gunfight despite any Hollywood hype about fast-draw hip-shooters. The Frontier Battalion's command structure was all there, in the front row from L to R, Adjutant General W. H. Mabry, Captains John Reynolds Hughes, James Abijah Brooks, William Jesse "Bill" McDonald, and John Harris Rogers.

Ernest St. Leon was one tough cookie, a Texas Ranger specializing in undercover work behind the scenes. Near Socorro, Texas, he and a companion were murdered during a shoot-out with suspected evil-doers. St. Leon's on-duty death was the last for Texas Rangers during the nineteenth-century.

This Texas Ranger photograph is a near classic: Standing L to R, Robert "Bob" Speaks and James "Jim" Putman, Seated L to R, Alonzo Van "Lon" Oden and John Reynolds Hughes. Oden and Hughes were involved in the gunplay near Shafter, Presidio County, wherein Ernest St. Leon eternally tapped out the running lights of ore thief Matilde Carrasco by shooting him squarely "between the eyes."

Chapter 1

Sonny Smith
1875

Sonny Smith's death earned him distinction. It was not a highly sought-for spot in the Lone Star State's overall history, but nevertheless a unique spot. The seventeen-year-old Ranger was the youngest Texas peace officer to forfeit his life in the line of duty—by gunfire.[1] And not surprisingly the tragedy took place while the teenager was riding the Devil's line.

Smith was very much a real Texas Ranger in the Special Force, a rookie private in Leander Harvey McNelly's hard-riding and sometimes high-handed company.[2] Though his initials were L. B. the young Ranger was popularly known as Sonny, and occasionally as Berry, name designations as yet to be fully and satisfactorily untangled, as is Captain McNelly referring to him as Benjamin and L. B. or Texas Ranger George Durham calling him Febe.[3] Factually, as previously stated, Sonny was the youngest lawman in McNelly's company and somewhat ironically his father D. R. "Dad" Smith was the oldest. Father and son, previously from Travis County, and later from the recently created and organized Lee County (Giddings), had enlisted on the twenty-fifth day of July 1874.[4] Their platform of action as Texas Rangers would in due course place father and son in woolly and sparsely populated country known as the Wild Horse Desert, that area between the Nueces River and the Rio Grande. An unforgiving section of real-estate that Austin's *Daily State Journal* avowed was home turf to "a vagabond population, inured to rapine and violence, and who make it the theater of incessant lawlessness."[5]

An assertion that this portion of the borderline—and above— had long been a fermenting bed of hostility, fertilized with bloodshed, cannot be honestly refuted.[6] The effort at hand, however, will not serve as the springboard for an asinine blame game. Badness can be traced to both banks of the Rio Grande. There's plenty of that untidiness to go-around. Since this vignette focuses on Sonny Smith but the briefest of generic recaps is necessary.

Corpus Christi, at one time boosted as the "Naples of the Gulf" or the "Italy of America," lay in Nueces County bordering the Texas Gulf Coast. Named for an abundance of towering pecan trees shading the Nueces River—*nueces* is Spanish for nuts—the county had been artfully carved from San Patricio County during April of 1846 and officially organized by the twelfth day of July that same year.[7] During its earliest stages, the Mexican War period, Corpus Christi like any other fledgling community flooded with unmarried or married soldiers far from home, was awash with "Houses for drinking, gambling, theatrical entertainment, and other diversions...." Undertow of the money-hungry sporting element was threatening to drown discipline of U.S. Army troops bivouacked on the beach. Characterizing early day Corpus Christi one high-ranking military man grumbled that it was "the most murderous, thieving, gambling, god-forsaken hole in the Lone Star State or out of it."[8]

Also sited in Nueces County thirteen miles northwest of Corpus Christi, the county seat, was the little settlement of Nuecestown, frequently referred to by locals as "The Motts."[9] The little village is an important geographical spot for recounting Sonny Smith's story. Likewise, due west of Corpus Christi by about twenty miles was the then near forsaken Hispanic settlement of Banquete. It was a place candidly referred to by an on-scene Texas Ranger as the "jumping-off place into the lower Nueces country.... it was pretty well known as the sheriff's deadline. Men on the dodge figured if they made Banquette [sic] they could make the Rio Grande without too much trouble from the law."[10] Writing for the *Galveston Daily News* a newspaperman cautioned that traveling between Corpus Christi and the Rio Grande was an extraordinarily hazardous undertaking.[11] In fact, if it's to be believed, area rancher William Woodson "W6" Wright would frequently, after assessing their toughness, place bets that folks headed south for the border from Banquete would never reach the state's southern tip at Brownsville—alive![12]

One bunch of Mexican bandits, at least nominally sponsored by Juan Nepomuceno Cortina, was willing to gamble that American lawmen would issue them "not too much trouble."[13] During the tail end of March 1875, the *banditos* began slipping across the Rio Grande in small sets, then furtively forging themselves into a singular and robust gang on the Texas side. Fixing social grievances from bygone days was not in the blueprint. These guys were gangsters. Their grand scheme was to cut off, attack, and loot Corpus Christi.[14] The big plan went awry due to "internal squabbling" and fouled up communications.[15] Not all of the mean men were where they were supposed to be, at the time they were supposed to be there. An alternate target was selected, Nuecestown. On Good Friday, March 26 the bandits struck, and struck hard.[16] Below Nuecestown they murdered two Anglos, stabbing them to death, then hanged two Hispanics, raided the ranch of Sam Page, and hanged another fellow. Continuing, and on the warpath, the bandits robbed anyone unfortunate enough to be traveling alone, unprotected, and took prisoners. Both women and men, old and young, were fair game.[17] After arriving at Nuecestown the desperadoes bit from a hard plug, John Thomas Noakes' general mercantile and U.S. Post Office. The landmark store was well known "as a border outpost for Anglo civilization on the edge of the Nueces Strip."[18]

An Englishman by birth, the forty-six-year-old Noakes was not a man to underestimate. If need be he would shoot you. And this was one of those times. Mr. Noakes wounded a bandit, incapacitating him. Then he calculated the odds of doing battle with overwhelming numbers arrayed against him.[19] Common sense prevailed. The store owner escaped through a trapdoor and tunnel he had designed for just such an emergency. Luckily his wife and five children, after a tense confrontation with the outlaws, escaped grave physical injury. The bandits, meeting no further resistance, looted the combination home and storehouse and post office. Subsequent to plundering the premises the place was torched, burned to the ground. After working hard all of his remarkable life John Thomas Noakes could pocket ashes, nothing else.[20] Conversely, others nearby could pocket something more: Revenge!

Initially, two civilian posses were put in the field, one led by the Nueces County Sheriff, John McClane, and another captained by Pat Whelan. A member of the latter squadron, George Swank, was mortally dumped from his saddle when they overhauled the fleeing raiders who were racing for sanctuary across the Rio Grande, more than a hundred and fifty miles away.[21] The exhaustive running gunfight produced two more indisputable results: Hooligans outran the citizen lawmen and the possemen ran out of ammunition. A fellow unable to run fast or far was Felix Godinez, the marauder gunned down by Mr. Noakes. He had been abandoned by his pals and fallen into American hands. For the next play excuses were abundant: "The jail is insecure, the time for the holding of court distant, and the prospect of another raid for his rescue great. The majority of our citizens now out by the late pursuit and patrol duty at home were [are] unable to stand guard over the jail," more especially for "one of the most cruel and determined of the raiders." After a kangaroo court hearing and sham trial with an assured verdict of *guilty*, Felix Godinez was summarily executed.[22] Perhaps understandable, but by no measure defensible, the ugly head of vigilantism had emerged.

For frontier-era journalists the newsy item about the murderous raid on Noakes's store was a corker—a humdinger. "The brutality and brazenness of the attack on Nuecestown sent shock waves across South Texas."[23] Most folks noted and, rightly so, this raid by border bandits was a northern penetration into Texas heretofore unknown.[24] It too was a tale igniting and reigniting passion and prejudice. South Texas—in fact the whole Lone Star—during this spate of time was no bed-ground for tolerance. But then again, neither was Mexico. Unauthorized militia units took to the field resulting in the deaths and property destruction of altogether innocent and inoffensive "Mexicans." The pretexts for summary judgments were many, but consistently absent even a hint of good cause—such as evidence.[25]

It was into this blistering cauldron that Ranger Sonny Smith had ridden, an inexperienced private riding a jaded horse, but proudly high-stepping mentally behind his captain, the sometimes revered and the sometimes unkindly, but justifiably criticized Leander H. McNelly.[26] The orders from the Texas adjutant general, William Steele, were explicit, no reading between the lines required:

> As you are doubtless aware, the country bordering on the Rio Grande has been subjected to frequent raids of armed robbers who, crossing from Mexico in small numbers, elude observation until gathering in the interior, they carry destruction to isolated ranches and small villages. Your object will be to get as early information as possible of such gatherings, and to destroy any and every such band of freebooters. At the same time, be careful not to disturb innocent people who speak the same language with the robbers....[27]

One of Captain McNelly's first acts was genuinely necessary, but near unanimously unpopular with the local Nueces County citizenry, the Anglo citizenry. He declared that bands of armed folks, unless at the time actually accompanied by a bona fide and commissioned lawman, were to be declared outlaws, subject to arrest—or worse![28] The local press was incredulous at such bossy arrogance. A particular editor chided: "This high-handed way of ordering citizens to disband by a Captain of Police, exceeds anything that ever happened under the Davis police; martial law had some semblance of authority, but McNelly issues his orders like an Emperor."[29] Regardless, Captain McNelly's decree won the day. He and his men would be the law of the land, a law unto themselves.[30]

Another of Captain McNelly's directives was implementation of an operational procedure for his men, but its real value would be lost should it be a secret and it wasn't. McNelly's company would operate under the hardcore policy of *la ley de fuga*.[31] Prisoners—once they'd spilled the beans—were valueless and expendable. Custodial possession of a person presented logistical nightmares, too: They had to be guarded, housed, and fed. A policy of *la ley de fuga* alleviated other little messy irritants; no prisoners meant "no lawyers wrangling in a courtroom, no bail bonds, no judge, no jury."[32] With a spirit of evenhandedness it is important to take stock of border country reality; ruthless treatment of prisoners would not be solely confined to America's side of the line. Later, Russian-born Emilio Kosterlitzky, riding at the head of *La Gendarmería Fiscal*, more commonly known as *Rurales*, since they scouted Mexico's northern and mostly rural frontier, was equally as harsh: "Hence, where Mexican criminals were concerned there would be none of the judicial shilly-shallying and legal niceties practiced in other sections of the world. Bandits were tried when caught, but the trials had none of the guarantees and practices of English common law. Instead, a few questions were asked, and if a suspect could reasonably be thought to have committed the crime in question, he was pronounced guilty and executed."[33] In practice the merciless convention of *la ley de fuga* in Mexico's northern borderland provinces was commonplace. "It has been said with sardonic humor that those who received such primitive justice—'got away, but just a little way.'"[34]

Passionately offering an excuse or apology for such coldblooded procedures practiced on either side of the border somewhat satisfies an intrinsic need for fashioning a macho persona, but is really reprehensible and unpardonable—aside from being statutorily unlawful. Even in the nineteenth-century along Lucifer's Line. Texas Ranger George Durham, thought so, coughing up the rough truth, though it bothered him:

> The military had to fight by the books as written in Washington. But those Nueces outlaws didn't fight by any books. Neither did Captain McNelly. They made their own rules, and Captain made his. They didn't mind killing. Neither did Captain McNelly. They didn't take prisoners. Neither did Captain McNelly.[35]

Private Sonny Smith and his fellow Rangers were assembled for a "pep talk" and given tactical orders for engaging the enemy: "If two or more of you flush out some bandits, whether they're running or forted and holed up, put yourselves at five-pace intervals and shoot only at the target right in front of you. Don't shoot to the left or the right. Shoot straight ahead. And don't shoot till you've got your target good in your sights. Don't walk up on a wounded man. Pay no attention to a white flag. That's a mean trick bandits use on green hands. Don't touch a dead man except to identify him. And treat the law-abiding people with respect."[36] Clearly McNelly saw himself as a warrior, not a mealy-mouthed diplomat. Whether or not Private Sonny Smith, young and tenderfoot green, was listening to his captain's admonitions is iffy.

After an overall update regarding general news of the raid on Noakes' store, Captain McNelly was apprised of a worthy of note tidbit, at least according to Private Durham. Purportedly during the raid and before the fires were lit, the gleeful bandits had appropriated eighteen brand-new Dick Heye saddles from Noakes' storehouse.[37] Writing years later Ranger Durham said these items were "the Cadillacs of the saddle world." The Dick Heye saddles were heavily festooned with oversize silver conchos in a distinctive pattern, and could be easily recognized at a distance.[38] Theft of the saddles is genesis for a smidgen of take-it-or-leave-it Texas Ranger history—or mythology.

George Durham wrote that Captain McNelly laid down a dictate that anyone, moreover a Mexican, observed sitting atop a brand-new Dick Heye saddle should be shot forthwith: "Empty those saddles on sight. No palavering with the riders. Empty them. Leave the men where you drop them, and bring the saddles to camp."[39] McNelly's

adept biographers, acknowledging there was a noted saddle maker
named Heye doing business at San Antonio, postulate the emptying
of saddles tale is just that—apocryphal.[40] Perhaps it is. There could
be a ring of truth, however. Not so much in the minuscule details,
but in the tenor of a generalized inference for public consumption—
by Nueces County citizens and Rangers alike. A "Mexican" riding a
spanking new saddle had best be prepared to show proper ownership,
proof of purchase—a receipt, a corroborating witness, something.
Or suffer the consequences! Captain McNelly's Texas Rangers were
in the area tending to business, serious business, and there best be
no mistake about it. With emphasis added another penman maybe
hits closer to the truth, declaring: "On glimpsing a Mexican riding
new leather a Texan was wont to say, 'Yonder goes a Noakes.' Unless
a *quick and satisfactory explanation* could be furnished the Mexican
was killed."[41] Even more reasonable and more likely would be interpretation by a twenty-first century scribe: "Anybody caught with
one of them in his possession was a thief and would be dealt with
accordingly....," which gives leeway for an arrest instead of extralegal
execution.[42]

Purportedly a Corpus Christi merchant, Sol Lichenstein, outfitted McNelly's company with brand new single-shot .50 caliber Sharps
carbines, which required a cartridge "as big as your thumb" and had
a bore diameter large enough "for a gopher to crawl through."[43]
According to Ranger Durham, McNelly preferred his company be
armed with the Sharps single-shot because the Rangers would be
more careful about making every round count.[44] An added benefit
of the Sharps, firing the whopping .50 caliber bullet, was that it was
a long-range weapon, whereas the Henry and Winchester repeaters
of the day were not. Arguably there was tactical advantage in holding an enemy at a distance—within range, and with enough ump to
knock down his horse, putting him afoot. In metaphoric chatter of
lawmen, the Sharps big fifty could "keep the wolf off of you." Mr. Sol
Lichenstein wasn't worried too much about reimbursement from the
State of Texas, rationally declaring he had rather lose the rifles to
a stingy government than to Mexican bandits on their next visit, a
nasty plundering raid.

No doubt proudly toting his Colt's six-shooter, a new Sharps
carbine across the pommel of his saddle, Texas Ranger Sonny Smith
soon found himself southwest of Corpus Christi at Santa Gertru-
dis on land under dominion of Richard King, a cattle empire, the

humongous King Ranch. It must have been pretty heady stuff, for a boy. He was armed to the teeth, traveling in the company of a few seasoned fighting men, reining in amongst saddle-hardened cowboys and hard-edged *vaqueros* at the most celebrated cow kingdom in South Texas, maybe even the whole Lone Star State. Surely Sonny noticed that horses beneath the Rangers' legs did not measure much when compared to those in the King Ranch's corralled remuda. The ranch's using horses were working stock, geldings all, well fed, well groomed, well muscled, animals with hearts of lions and plenty of bottom—staying power. Richard King took notice of the Rangers' gaunt horses, too. After bellies filled with sinfully tasty beef stew and cathead biscuits and bloodstreams clogged with near boiling Arbuckles coffee the all-night stopover ended at first light. Captain McNelly's Rangers departed King's hospitality atop fresh horses—good solid horses. Much like storeowner Lichenstein, the King Ranch patriarch had sensibly reasoned that it was better to furnish the Texas Rangers horses, than it was to lose them to thieves. Maintaining an interconnected and favorable relationship with the Texas Rangers would be a hallmark of the King Ranch's philosophical business model—for good or bad. The Mexican bandits, and no doubt some pesky palefaces, had been siphoning Richard King's cattle and horses with alarming recklessness and disquieting success.[45] Not long thereafter, McNelly and men would again return to the King Ranch for succor and sympathy after a highly controversial raid across the Rio Grande and mad dash back to the river—and the protection Texas and the U.S. Army afforded.[46]

Also enlisted in McNelly's company was a Ranger who would earn a well deserved reputation, a dubious reputation to be sure, but a reputation nevertheless. Jesús Sandoval was McNelly's inquisitor. Purportedly Sandoval's wife had been violated by Mexican bandits, his children abused, and his ranch house burned into but a pile of smoldering rubble.[47] Jesús now had but one purpose in life—to settle the score, not even it—he wanted a decisive lopsided settlement for investment of his time. His methods of interrogation are legendary, though not nice. Rawhide intricately plaited into a strong *reata* with one end noosed around a suspected bandit's neck and the other end pitched over a stout limb seemed a surefire technique for extracting critical intelligence.[48] Sandoval thought so. McNelly agreed.[49]

McNelly agreed to something else, too. He'd turn a blind eye to killings, courtesy Jesús.[50] So, while the historical record may be silent regarding a thorough accounting and specific names of all those alleged desperadoes who bobbed up and down at the far end of Sandoval's yoyo, an assertion Jesús was a skilled interviewer goes unchallenged. Compassionate and kindhearted, no! Ruthless and effective, yes![51]

After moving south, Sonny Smith and his fellow Rangers went into camp above the Rio Grande awaiting further developments. They were not long in coming. An effective raider himself, proven during the Civil War as a Confederate commander, Leander H. McNelly was cognizant of the role spies and undercover operatives could play in a wartime setting. Captain McNelly was at war. Exploiting the skills of covert intelligence gatherers McNelly learned the sometimes enigmatic but ever rascally borderland character Juan Cortina had a fat deal to supply Cuban markets with fat cattle.[52] The inventory to be shipped, no great surprise, would be drawn from the grazing herds of Texans and *Tejanos* ranching north of the Rio Grande. Cortina was an equal opportunity wholesaler, no matter the commodity.[53] McNelly's company was placed on special alert.

Knowing a hot confrontation was near, Sonny Smith pleaded with Captain McNelly that he be allowed to accompany the main body of Texas Rangers and not be detailed as a camp guard, as was his aging father Dad Smith, the Ranger charged with watching over the company's team of mules and supply wagon. The elder Smith made his feelings known, declaring that Sonny was his and Sarah's only child, and his wife would be inconsolable should misfortune sweep her beloved boy away. Sonny Smith tested his own brand of logic on Captain McNelly, lamenting that every man in the company had a mother who would be heartbroken should catastrophe befall them. Recognizing the insight and spirit of a warrior, even a warrior so young, there was no counter-argument. Captain McNelly acquiesced, allowing Sonny Smith the honor of riding with his comrades, several of whom were not too much older then he.

Adding to the daring and competent detective work of his intelligence operatives, Lady Luck made a fateful contribution. McNelly's Rangers captured suspected bandits Rafael Salinas and Incosnasción Garcia. Jesús Sandoval's propensity to stretch necks paid its dividend. The prisoners talked—snitched on their partners in cross-border crime. Captain McNelly listened. Outlaw leaders Camilo Lerma and José Maria Olguín, aka El Aguja—the Needle—were already on the American side, a herd of near 300 head of pilfered cattle being pushed towards the Rio Grande. The Rangers made ready.[54] Accordingly, thinking there might be hazardous confusion if the brigands were laid into during fading light, McNelly asked a Ranger to donate his sparkling white shirt to the communal good cause. The shirt was shredded into strips—arm bands—each Texas Ranger donning his distinguishing marker. Dad Smith broke out cartridge boxes from the wagon and divvied ammunition to the fidgeting and zealous, anxious and obsessing, would-be man hunters. No doubt several green Rangers' tongues began to swell as the metallic taste of fear coursed through their mouths, washing away the last trace of saliva, making it difficult to even spit. Not a man in ranks, however, was a whiner—not a sissy among the twenty-two Texas Rangers stepping into the stirrup.

Forthrightly Ranger Sonny Smith and his pals were in the saddle, working that actionable intelligence, hard-charging trying to overtake a band of sixteen Mexican bandits and their misappropriated herd of Cuban-bound cattle—before they were crossed into Mexico, herded to Bagdad on the northeastern coast of the state of Tamaulipas, then loaded abroad ships for transport to the island port. Hungry Cubans citizens would relish in obtaining prime cuts at below market prices. Cortina and Cuban importers, perhaps with the clandestine aid of an occasional American co-conspirator, would stuff their purses with black-market profits.[55] To that point it had been a splendid plan.

On the morning of June 12, 1875, in the Cameron County salt marshes of historic Palo Alto Prairie the Texas Rangers and Mexican bandits went to war—a shooting war. Captain McNelly was awed—not overawed—with the Mexicans' guts and gunfighting grit. They, too, were good warriors: But for a bad cause. McNelly reported, almost in a bizarre way eulogizing:

> And as I anticipated, the Mexicans turned to drive my men off, but they held their ground, and I got up with four or five men, when the raiders broke. After that it was a succession of single hand fights for six miles before we got the last one.... I have never seen men fight with such desperation. Many of them after being shot from their horses and severely wounded three or four times, would rise on their elbows and fire at my men as they passed.[56]

Two hours later fifteen Mexicans bandits lay lifeless on the battlefield, dead, buzzards with putrid breaths and vulturous eyes circling overhead. Or put in the words of a famous Texas folklorist, the ill-fated Mexicans had been "naturalized" by the hard-riding and straight-shooting Rangers.[57] McNelly's men emerged from the battle unscathed save one of their favorites, seventeen-year-old Sonny Smith.[58]

Ranger Sonny Smith and his working partner for the day, Spencer J. Adams, had followed a wounded and de-horsed bandit chieftain, Camilo Lerma. Desperado Lerma could not walk, but he could crawl. Camillo disappeared into the shielding wet veil of a waist-high salt grass motte, hidden but not forgotten. Ranger Spencer Adams stayed astride his horse, Sorrel Top, a bird's eye view of the bandit's lair before him. Both Rangers Spencer and Smith had—in the pell mell heat of excitement—defied previously issued instructions: "Don't walk up on a wounded man." There may be leeway for dispute as to whether or not Sonny Smith dismounted and began the manhunt afoot, but the irrevocable outcome of competing versions merge all too quickly.[59] When Captain McNelly rode up, pulling alongside, a despairing Spencer Adams finished the story:

> This morning when the fight started by the lagoon you all got ahead of me and Berry [Sonny] Smith and some of you shot the bandit off his horse and you thought he was dead. Berry and I saw him crawl into that Spanish dagger thicket you see there near the edge of this pond. We ran up to the thicket to shoot him again, but just as we got there he shot and killed Berry Smith, and shot at me and hit Sorrel Top in the neck. Later, after Berry was dead, he crawled out and got Berry's pistol, and a little while ago he crawled out to this pond of water. He is out about the middle of it—you can see the rush grass move when he crawls along. I think you broke his leg for he had not been on his feet today.[60]

Captain McNelly's barking further orders was unnecessary, not to Rangers with their blood up. They quickly positioned themselves around the motte, making sure not to station themselves wherein anyone would fall hapless victim to friendly fire. When reeds and tall grass hinted of sway they shot—again and again and again. Camilo Lerma was for the short term trapped, for the long term dead. In the end the Rangers' haphazard marksmanship had done the trick. The Palo Alto Prairie battlefield was littered with the dead bodies of Mexican bandits and one lifeless American desperado, Jack Ellis.[61]

The bodies were later piled into a wagon and hauled to Brownsville by local lawmen under direction of the Cameron County sheriff, James G. Browne; the city marshal for Brownsville, Joseph P.
O'Shaughnessy; and a detachment of U.S. Army personnel from
nearby Fort Brown.[62] One of the dead Mexican bandits was wearing
a new suit of clothes, ostensibly the duds removed from a popular
schoolmaster and former Brownsville policeman, Frank F. Mahan,
whose lifeless and naked body had been found earlier near the "Mesquite Rancho." After he had been stripped, the unlucky fellow had
been horribly butchered, his "head, arms and legs were severed from
his body."[63] Subsequently, a Texas adjutant general would offer his
take on this type of murderous bandit, and as would be expected
there was not a drip of flattery in his assessment. To him the raiders
were but "Mexican cut-throats and thieves, who ravaged this southwestern portion of Texas with the fierceness and pertinacity of hungry wolves."[64]

At the American border town, directly across the Rio Grande
from Matamoros, bodies of Mexican bandits were dumped and then
stacked onto the plaza like cordwood. A gruesome reminder—a touch
of preventive enforcement—forecasting the guaranteed fate of any
mal hombre should he breech the line with antics of cow thieving and
raiding on his mind. Needless to say, Mr. Cortina and many folks of
Mexican ancestry were incensed at the outrageous disrespect for the
dead. McNelly himself was not caught off guard, notifying Adjutant
General Steele: "I find that the killing of those parties has developed
a most alarming state of things on this frontier. The Mexicans on the
other side of the river are very much infuriated, and threaten to kill
ten Americans for each of their Bravos."[65] Not only were Hispanics
and Mexican borderland natives fuming; their temperature rocketed
skyward after observing the reverence and pomp awarded interment
of the lonesome dead Texas Ranger, Sonny Smith. If the reports be
true, Captain McNelly threw a little more fuel on the fire: He had one
of his Rangers "wear a captured sombrero to the funeral," saying such
an in-your-face gesture "would be good advertising and a fair warning to all bandits not to cross to the Texas side."[66]

Upon learning of his son's death, Dad Smith rushed to Brownsville. There he learned Sonny was resting peacefully in a fine coffin,
one that had been purchased at a princely cost of $130. Sonny Smith
was to receive full military tribute. With an honor guard of seventeen
countrymen surrounding his coffin, Sonny Smith was removed from

an undertaker's work place and taken to the "preisbyterian Church" where a "beautiful funeral sermon was preached."[67] Thereafter, in a colorful but somber funeral procession, a U.S. Army band playing and Texas luminaries John Salmon "Rip" Ford and Colonel H. C. Merriam serving as parade marshals, the remains of Sonny Smith were laid to rest in the northwest corner of the Brownsville Cemetery following a traditional U.S. Military rifle salute.[68] The Mexican and Hispanic community of the Lower Rio Grande was not favorably disposed. Captain McNelly noted: "And then on this side, the Mexican residents of Brownsville....are public and violent in their denunciation of the killings [bandits] and the attention given my dead soldier seems to have exasperated them beyond measure."[69] Their unflattering displeasure with Leander H. McNelly would soon proliferate, but that's another story: This one's about Sonny Smith.

Old-time Rangers, particularly N. A. Jennings, George Durham, and William Crump Callicott, in later life recounted the death of young Smith in autobiographies or correspondence with inquiring historians. Perhaps at this juncture, in closing the young dead lawman's narrative, it's appropriate to hear from another, a Texas Ranger that was right there, a witness to tragedy who took pen in hand on the fifteenth day of June 1875, poignantly posting Sonny Smith's mother from Brownsville, Texas.

Mrs. Sarah P. Smith. dear Mrs. Smith I have been called upon to furnish this letter. I can say (much against my wishes as the bearer of bad news to you). On the 12th of June McNelley's Compoany encountered a band of Mexican desperadoes about twelve miles north of Brownsville where a desperate fight ocured resulting in the annilation of the mexicans, but althou we were victorious we sustained a loss. Which to us is irrrepairable, in the death of one of our best and bravest boys. L. B . Smith was killed- - - - -he fell like a soldier at his post- - - -dear Madam he is gone, and while we (his companions in arms) deeply sympathize with a mother who has lost a Son we almost envy him his Glorious death. Who would not be wiling to die fighting for the liberty and the rights of mankind? He fell near youre humble coraspondent. He lived about half an hour, and suffered but little. Dear Madam youre son is no more on earth, but we, who knew his many virtues feel assured that he is far happier than we. Life is but short at most. You will Soon be reunited in that happy land where the wicked cease to trouble and the weary are at rest- - - -and if I could venture to ask a favor at youre hands, I would ask for one prair that you might also meet in that better world with Youre humble servant. [signed S. J. Adams]

P. S. I would beg leave to say that youre Son was buried with the honors of War by his companions assisted by the Government troups and the citizens of Brownsville. Mr. Smith, youre husband is well in body and is trying to become resigned. he sends his love to you. Hopeing you may be able to say with the patient of Job, that the lord giveth and the lord taketh away. Blessed be the name of the lord. [signed S.J.A.][70]

Hardly would McNelly's tactics be acceptable in today's marketplace of progressive thinking and enlightened policing. What he did is what he did. No mealy-mouthed justifications or condemnations need creep into this story, not with fidelity to simple truth-telling in mind. Captain L. H. McNelly rode into the history books carrying plenty of interpretative baggage. Ranger Private Sonny Smith—just doing his job—rode ahead, to the horrifying sound of gunfire.

Chapter 2

John E. McBride and Conrad E. Mortimer
1877

The earthly life of Texas Ranger Sonny Smith had been snuffed out near one end of Lucifer's Line. For this narrative the geographical setting moves upstream to an arena just as wild and woolly, but much farther removed from the Texas seat of government. As the story unfolds in El Paso County it will not go unnoticed that this isolation from legislative hallways and the governor's office contributed to brouhaha of epic proportion in the writings of history, even for Texas. Hard truths about the El Paso Salt War are readily retrievable and often misunderstood. Misinterpreting or manipulating or massaging facts is not a rare practice for agenda-driven scribes. Optimistically this try at recounting Ranger McBride's and Mortimer's journey along Lucifer's Line will set firmly the pilings of historical transparency.

Ambitiously El Paso County—in the first instance—had been one of four surveys lopping off land when Texas claimed a boundary stretching to headwaters of the Rio Grande in Colorado. Ultimately a compromise was reached ceding the two northernmost subdivisions and the boundary line readjusted so that El Paso County, as it does today, is bordered by the country of Mexico and the state of New Mexico. The county was formally organized during March of 1871 but positioning of the county seat was a seesawing affair of arguments and hard-fought elections. As the story at hand uncorks the county seat of El Paso County was Ysleta in 1877, the oldest town in Texas. The county had caught its name for a pass in the Franklin Mountains, a southern chain of the Rockies.[1] On the Mexican bank of the Rio Grande stood *El Paso del Norte* (present Ciudad Juárez) and her sisters on the American side were the hamlets of Franklin and Magoffinville until they were meshed into the city of El Paso, Texas. As expected with two municipalities facing each other across the Rio

Grande, both named El Paso, confusion flourished until the Mexican city underwent the name change in 1888.[2]

El Paso County was at the far end of the Texas world, not only in distance, but demographically as well. In fact, as far as a majority population was concerned El Paso County was but an appendage of Mexico. The Rio Grande was but a river to cross through when visiting family or friends, attending a fandango or funeral—or a fight. Such had been the case for generation after generation after generation. For those growing up along the river its meaningful significance as an international borderline was immaterial.[3] Tradition and custom were the sociological underpinnings of life for the 12,000 folks of Mexican ancestry living along both banks of the *Rio Bravo*. Tradition and custom, too, were the sociological underpinnings of life for the eighty souls of Anglo extraction living on America's banks of the Rio Grande.[4] Population distribution was asymmetrical—decidedly unbalanced. Therein lay the rub. As previously mentioned we are but products of place and time.

The Lower Rio Grande country where Ranger Sonny Smith forfeited his life and El Paso County were alike, yet at the same time so culturally contradictory. For both spots the native Spanish-speaking folks were in the majority. Though specific acts of legislation promulgated in the Austin statehouse may have been unpopular in both quarters, in South Texas there was not near the overt resistance as exhibited in far-flung West Texas. To say there was not racially rooted animosity emanating from both sides of the border in South Texas would be amiss, but after crossing the Rio Grande—either way—the general expectation was to play by that country's rules—or pay the penalty. Banditry and murder were banditry and murder in both places: However along the winding Rio Grande, as distance from the Gulf Coast increased, so too did lessen the necessity for some folks' complying with the letter of the law, moreover if it was a pesky bother infringing on long-held rights of heritage.

To be consequential a particular law must have bite, legal punishment for noncompliance. Rattlesnakes absent fangs may appear scary, but they're no real threat. Bluntly speaking El Paso County was "beyond the reach of state protection" where laws were "expressed in definite language but weak in execution."[5] Such impotence did not go unnoticed. Some citizens of El Paso County were fine-tuned in their antagonism to the "American method of government and any new or progressive laws which [were] in opposition to their accustomed views or feelings are opposed to the extent of great disorders."[6]

One prime example would be Texas legislators mandating that children go to school, at least part of the year. In El Paso County the sometimes scalawag priest, Father Antonio Borrajo, dogmatically strong in his anti-American beliefs, "particularly hated the compulsory school law." Sending chaste teenage daughters to school with boys was unthinkable, as was not allowing religious books in the classroom. Blasphemy! Damn busybody lawmakers could do whatever they damn well pleased at faraway Austin. Within confines of El Paso County, an adamant Father Borrajo would "forbid his parishioners to send their children to school. His will was law, and the children were not sent." Although several parents were actually arrested and/or fined for failure to comply with the compulsory school statutes, there really was not a feasible method of enforcement, not with top-heavy demographics being what they were. So, in the end, "the priest triumphed and the school law became a dead letter in El Paso County."[7] Post the Mexican War and the zealous political wrangling, a sharp diplomatic pen had penciled details of a treaty. The timeframe for this Texas Ranger tale is circa 1877; therefore it must be duly, prominently noted, that many of the Americans living on the Texas side of the Rio Grande, if middle-aged or elderly adults, had been born Mexican nationals. Their residence had not really changed, but their government drastically had. American expectations and unfathomable legalese overnight had stabbed them with sharpness of a sometimes unenthusiastic and disinclined conversion. They were now citizens in a foreign land, but had not geographically budged an inch. Not in body and certainly not spirit:

> There was one other quirk of the Mexican mind which no Missouri lawyer could ever accept, and that was a fine, frank disrespect for written codes of law. Among those humble *peones* and proud *ricos* flourished a set of democratic ideas which went beyond anything an American had been able to subscribe to since 1776. They knew that power originates in the people and they reasoned that what the people agree on must be right regardless of the law books. "They were the people, and the people were the law."[8]

El Paso was at the western tip of Texas. *El Paso del Norte* was staked on Mexico's northernmost frontier. For both governments it was the end of the line. Eighteen seventy-seven was yet to see railway connection to distant and forlorn El Paso County. It is then not inordinately unfair to proclaim the locale was, in many respects, cut off from the "outside world." In everyday and indisputable language, early day El Paso County was "an island in a sea of sand, hundreds of miles and decades in time from most ports of civilization."[9]

Perhaps it's handy in setting the stage to mention that an early-day stagecoach trip to El Paso County, if commenced at the state's capitol in Austin, obligated a not paltry expenditure of about sixteen days—start to finish—over a bumpy and unimproved roadway.[10] Understandably, but slowly, as roads improved the travel time contracted, but even then it remained a long, arduous, and precarious trip. The independent voyager riding horseback or laboriously cajoling teams pulling private conveyances was forced to husband horseflesh with watering stopovers and rest periods for both man and beast, which doubled the traveling time. Getting to El Paso County from anywhere was not easy. Communicating by telegraph was no simple matter either. The quickest method for a telegraph message or an eager railroad traveler getting to El Paso from Austin, Texas, was not by a westerly course across 600 miles of unforgiving desert openness, much of it under opportunistic eyes of fierce Apaches, but a northerly route into Kansas. At Topeka linkage could be established with the Atchison, Topeka, & Santa Fe Railroad or westerly planted telegraph poles. Thereafter the trip for man or message could be sent on its way into New Mexico Territory, then south into the Mesilla Valley and the quaint village of La Mesilla, and on into El Paso County.[11] Shortest distance to a point may be straight across, but in frontier Texas it wasn't the quickest.

Another measure in far West Texas was much shorter. A rough ninety miles or so east of San Elizario and Ysleta on the American side of the Rio Grande, which were downriver from *El Paso del Norte*, lay the heralded Guadalupe Salt Lakes, a patch of sometimes damp ground poor in measurable moisture, rich in easily accessible and extraordinary deposits of salt. Salt in abundant supply was very seldom appreciated, but when doing without, it became precious. Even when not pure and pristine white the crystalline mineral was a necessity of life. Salt not only made groceries palatable, it could be used in the preservation of foodstuffs. It was an utterly crucial commodity for other reasons, too—more than ever so in the scorching Southwest where sheer sweat sometimes poured from the dehydrating body, draining it of an ingredient indispensable for one's very survival.[12] History will bear witness: "Men fought and died over rights to salt deposits just as bitterly as they fought over gold or cattle."[13]

In fact, even before the Guadalupe Salt Lakes were discovered by U.S. Army personnel during the Civil War era, folks from West Texas and neighboring New Mexico Territory had exchanged gunfire due to a hot dispute over salt. *Salineros*—salt gatherers—from nearby Doña Ana County had piled their carts high with salt from the San Andres Salt Spring on the eastern face of the San Andres Mountains overlooking the Tularosa Basin. Needless to say the *salineros* hadn't paid a *peso* for the salt, an indisputable but rankling detail seriously troubling Mr. James Wiley Magoffin who owned—or thought he did—the salt. On the sixteenth day of December 1853, as 127 *salineros* and their 26 *carretas* burdened with salt encountered Magoffin's semi-official and highly questionable posse from El Paso County the sparks ignited, spewed, and fizzled. The long and the short of the story is uncomplicated. The posse's fully charged cannon had been wheeled into place and discharged, the *salineros* had turned loose their oxen which stampeded toward the posse, and unmitigated hell seemed to have broken loose.[14] Outnumbered, the pseudo law enforcers had run one way, at the same time *salineros* ran the other way. Since no one was actually killed, or even wounded, the confrontation could be graded as close to comic.[15] Such would not near be the case in 1877 El Paso County near a quarter-century later. Then and there blood will be spilt onto salt.

While the so-called Magoffin Salt War flickered and died, the ensuing El Paso Salt War ignited and raged into a full-fledged conflagration. For understanding that explosive eruption of human passions it is but appropriate to pinpoint a cultural dissimilarity. Anglo-Americans held strongly to certain beliefs about private property rights, Mexicans and Mexican-Americans, with conviction, clung to an alternative. Both camps were desperately trapped—by tradition. For the Anglo, ideas regarding clear titles to land and resultantly the fruits of its productivity, were sacredly implanted—staunchly entrenched and immovable. Native Spanish speakers had an ingrained outlook otherwise. Theirs was more of a communal attitude, especially when it came to distribution of Mother Nature's essential but sometimes scarce commodities, water—and in this case salt. In one society what the land produced unalterably belonged to the owner; to profit from such was but the work of an industrious capitalist generating his dream. For the other faction unhindered social harmony rested on specific natural necessities being shared uniformly—for the common good. Of course, there were pirates within both cultural groupings.

Although at first blush it may seem tasteless and somewhat insensitive today, the spoken language could be an impediment to good intercultural relations for those living along the Rio Grande then: Those folks living in real time. Movers and shakers within the Anglo community found it irksome that much of El Paso County's business affairs were rudely handicapped by elected officials such as justices of the peace and county commissioners' inability to speak English. Whatever else may be said of Sheriff Charles Kerber (real name Friedrick Sperfechter) this gripe bore a buzz of legitimacy: "In the event that many indictments were found by the grand jury, it would be impossible, under the laws of the State, to find enough qualified petit jurors to try the cases, because the law requires that petit jurors should speak the English language. After indictments were found the only way to try these cases would be by change of venue to another county."[16] Changing venues may sometimes be necessarily advisable for insuring a fair trial, but it's a motion that guarantees inconvenience and expense: Headaches for the overworked sheriff and county governments with their typically inadequate budgets.

For moving two ill-fated Texas Rangers' stories forward a brief recap is needed, overriding any want to skip straightaway to the six-shooting drama. Early on the famed Texas personality and cattleman Samuel A. Maverick had legally filed on land encompassing the Guadalupe Salt Lakes—but not in entirety.[17] As customary with a theory of capitalism, Sam Maverick charged a small fee for *salineros* gathering salt. They in turn eking out negligible but sufficient profit for their labors by barter after the product was transported and distributed to communities along both banks of the international river. Though it is sometimes expediently overlooked, excess salt was sold on the free market in Mexico which by definition elevated some *salineros* to the role of profit motivated hustlers also. There was an evident leak in Maverick's capitalistic venture. Upon learning that his plat covered not the whole of the Guadalupe Salt Lakes, *salineros* worked on the untitled portion—no fee, no hassle.[18] Without bogging down in the minutiae of land title legalities, technicalities, railroad relinquishments, and the longitudes and latitudes of precise surveys, there is ancillary news. With clarity it may be reported that George B. Zimpelman, a Texas powerhouse politician, ex-sheriff of Travis County, and well-fixed banking mogul, lawfully picked up salt lake land outside Sam Maverick's saline acquisition. Zimpelman had also picked up something else along the way: a fire-breathing firebrand and ham-fisted son-in-law, lawyer Charles H. Howard, a man pigheadedly determined to forever bulldoze frontward, never—ever—take a step backwards.

Mr. Zimpelman remained in Austin, focused on business interests and social affairs. Mr. Howard hotfooted to El Paso, where among other things—such as a judgeship—he made a big name for himself in El Paso County, saturated in the darkness of local political machinations and intrigues as well as serving as his father-in-law's salt lake agent. Howard's self-image was more than generous. His bitterest political rival in El Paso County was an Italian, Louis Cardis, a man similarly caught up in shady schemes with a central motivation of profit. Additionally, Cardis was a master player at manipulation, becoming a proactive voice for El Paso County's majority population.[19] Louis Cardis, too, had an outsized ego.

Unashamedly and maintaining the American theory that the owner of the land could—and moreover should—reap the profits it produced, be it a steer grazing on ranch land on top of the ground, or gold and silver deposits below ground, or apples and oranges falling from above ground, Charles Howard publicly declared that salt taken from Zimpelman's tract was not free. All too quickly two fellows put it to the test. In what today may be technically characterized as a wholly premature—and dubious—legal tactic, the ever pugnacious Howard caused the arrests of Macedonia Gaudara and José Maria Juarez not for gathering salt, but for intending to go to the Guadalupe Salt Lakes and take salt, without beforehand gaining permission and tendering the requisite cash payment. At a local hearing Mr. Gaudara declared his innocence, avowing he would never knowingly violate the Texas law. He was sorry for the confusion. The case against him was dismissed. On the other hand Mr. Juarez was defiant, hotly so, hissing that he cared not what the law said, he would go to the salt lakes anyhow. Not surprisingly his case was not tossed out, but docketed for adjudication. The bewildered Mr. Juarez was jailed in lieu of his posting the necessary $200 bail bond.[20] Therein may be hint of an innocent misunderstanding in the criminal case of a non-English speaking José Juarez, a possibility alluded to by Sheriff Charles Kerber: "when Juarez, apparently under the impression that Howard was laughing at him, and he did not understand English, jumped up and said, in a very threatening and insulting manner to the court,

that he had said he would go after salt, and that he would do so."[21]
¿Quien Sabe?

The fuse for impending disaster had been lit. Outraged folks—a
mob—absent even the slightest trace of legal authority, in an indefensible act of impetuousness made a prisoner of Charles Howard
and others. For three days the prisoners feared for their lives, but
were finally released on a provisional agreement: Howard would
leave El Paso County forever, within twenty-four hours, relinquishing any claims to the salt beds positioned below Guadalupe Peak, the
highest mountain in Texas. To ensure compliance Howard was to
post a bond of $12,000 and hightail it, letting the courts ultimately
make some resolution regarding the salt lakes. After his bondsmen
posted the surety, Charles Howard agreed to vamoose from El Paso
County, scooting into New Mexico Territory as a life saving measure.
But those closest to him knew he had every intention of returning to
Texas, proving, if nothing else, "that he was a man, not a mouse."[22]

Evocative storytellers and accomplished academics, many with
divergent viewpoints vis-à-vis societal blame games, have dissected
the El Paso Salt War with aplomb. In the context of accelerating the
part Texas Rangers played there is a hard bottom line. Charles Howard had returned from his temporary holding station, La Mesilla, just
across the line in New Mexico Territory. Louis Cardis, who may or
may not have been secretly plotting Charles Howard's early demise,
lay dead on the floor behind a maple desk in Solomon Schutz's store,
at least one eared-back Colt's six-shooter at his side. Out the front
door went an agitated and unrepentant Howard, emptying spent
hulls from the double-barreled scattergun, and trading it to his servant Wesley Owens for a blue-steel repeater, "a 16 shooter, a rifle, and
it was loaded."[23] The roadway back into La Mesilla was short. Charles
Howard was fast. The stink of burnt black-powder wafted throughout El Paso County, an unpleasant aroma swamping any remnant of
ever reaching a peaceable accord.

Sheriff Charles Kerber was in a tough spot, maybe partly due to
his own doings, but tight nevertheless. He had gone to La Mesilla
after the killing of Cardis. If he retuned to Texas with Howard there
was little doubt the prisoner would be mobbed and murdered. Correspondingly if Sheriff Kerber retuned to Texas soil empty-handed,
handcuffs on nobody, he would likely be mobbed and murdered.[24]
Therein fostered a damn good reason for the Texas governor, R. B.

Hubbard, to send in the Texas Rangers, well, a Texas Ranger—there was only one would-be riot.

By the aforementioned circuitous route through Kansas and New Mexico, Major John B. Jones, commander of the Frontier Battalion, arrived on the scene—not the Texas scene though. His personal courage was unquestionable. However for this assignment his judgment was not exceptionally smart. First, he had stopped over at La Mesilla, conferring with Charles Howard and Albert J. Fountain about the newsy hubbub, before proceeding to El Paso County. Major Jones' meeting first with the prospective defendant—beyond doubt the Italian's killer, maybe his murderer—gave off an odor. It was not perfume. Was he really there as a nonpartisan? Jones had come to remote West Texas by himself, that spoke well of his bravery. Such, nonetheless, did not bode as favorable foresight. Texas' chief executive had sent him on an investigative mission to find out what-in-the-hell was going on in faraway El Paso County.

Major Jones soon discovered—or simply had confirmed in his own mind—what the whole of Texas knew: The county was a powder-keg, volatile, capable of blowing like monkey-fingered nitroglycerin. To mollify fears in the majority community, where some were screaming for Howard's head on a platter—and those of his bondsmen too if they didn't cough up $12,000, Major Jones had assured them the accused would be, at the right time, returned to Texas—in chains if necessary—to stand trial. Upon conviction Howard would receive a sentence befitting the offense, punishment determined by the jury. Major Jones could promise no more than that.

Although it bears the weight of profound—though not necessarily flattering—scrutiny now, Major Jones was living in real time and was facing a real dilemma. He had cooled the heels of radical voices hollering for blood payment, at least temporarily, but by virtue of rank he had other fish to fry, pressing matters elsewhere demanding interest of the Frontier Battalion. Time and travel constraints, coupled with the battalions' already overtaxed workload in Major Jones' mind, prevented the deployment of an existing Ranger company to El Paso County. Texas Rangers were warranted; there was no doubt—not to Major Jones. He would recruit locally, drawing manpower to fashion a separate twenty-man detachment for Company C, but not inaugurate a totally new company. An on-the-spot commissioning of a second-lieutenant from local stock would command the unit. Jones' knotty predicament was understandable, but in truth, self-imposed.

Justifiably it may have been wholly impractical to send a preexisting company, and all their camp equipage and livestock to El Paso County at the gallop. It would, however, not have been unfeasible for Major Jones to have either taken one or two seasoned Ranger noncoms or junior officers with him initially, or telegraph orders that one or more report to El Paso County at once, via the same route through Topeka that he had taken. But he didn't!

Instead he selected John B. Tays, younger brother of the Reverend Joseph Wilken Tays, pastor of the St. Clement's Episcopal Church at Franklin. John Tays was a good man, but one shy of any law enforcing know-how whatsoever. History and more than a few Texas historians have not been overly kind to Lieutenant Tays. Perhaps the criticism is justified. Perhaps it is not, at least not all of it. As tragic events unfold it must be remembered despite twentieth and twenty-first century poppycock in a few idolizing Texas Ranger histories, Lieutenant John B. Tays was a real Ranger—as real as they come. Likewise, men comprising the rank and file of the Company C detachment were, too, real Rangers—as real as they come. Downgrading these Rangers, postulating "that not a one of them would have been a Ranger under normal circumstances" seems somewhat to border on preposterousness, politely discounting the writer's first-rate credentials.[25] If the state of affairs be "normal" there's not need for one Texas Ranger, much less twenty. And, adding straightforward and well-reasoned insight, as two acclaimed scholars markedly point out, those privates and noncoms haphazardly recruited at El Paso had received as much formal training as any other legit Texas Ranger—none: That's "none" with a capital N.[26] For Rangers it was a school of on-the-job training. Stepping up, the newly to be Texas Rangers took the following oath.

> We do solemnly swear that we will [in] true faith and allegiance bear to the State of Texas that we will serve her honestly and faithfully, that we will defend her against all her enemies and oppressors and that we will obey the orders of the Governor and the officers appointed over us according to an act of the Legislature for frontier defense approved April 10th 1874 so help us God.[27]

Two of those Texas Rangers signing on the eleventh day of November 1877 were John E. McBride and Conrad E. Mortimer. McBride at thirty-two years of age was the older by half a decade, but both had declared birthplaces somewhere in Canada. The fact McBride, a saddler by trade, appreciated good horseflesh is evidenced by the valuation of his mount, $125, contrasted with that of Mortimer's at $40, which may in someway correlate to his occupation as a "mechanic."[28] McBride, too, in the historical context, had early on pulled to himself something Mortimer had had not: A close, favorable, and working relationship with the pugnacious Charles H. Howard, having accompanied him on the salt lake survey marking Zimpelman's proprietary claim. Though a widower, raising a daughter, McBride was gauged as being both "tough and reliable" as well as thoroughly loyal to Howard.[29] Whether it was Major Jones or Lieutenant Tays who made the decision is hazy, but McBride was sworn in as the new detachment's 3rd Sergeant, while Mortimer was figuratively handed stripes of 4th Sergeant.[30] Fine-tuning would follow. With fairness the best that can be said of the Company C boys recruited in El Paso County is that it was a mixed-bag, a ragtag assortment of good men, some not so good men—and not just a few real bad men. Charitable chroniclers sometimes try—as later events will make clear—to distance this cadre of Texas Rangers from those Frontier Battalion boys stationed elsewhere—in the interior of Texas. Such a tricky ploy is anemic. Both sets were Texas Rangers, pure and simple and indisputable—real Texas Rangers!

Major Jones having yet unfinished business before departing for Austin prearranged a stopgap solution for that thorny legal issue—Charles Howard's murder charge. Major Jones accepted Howard's voluntary surrender, carried him before a magistrate and witnessed his release after posting the $4000 bail bond, which in theory was to assure his appearance should the El Paso County grand jury return an indictment. Charles Howard returned to La Mesilla. Major Jones scurried back to headquarters in Central Texas.[31] The non-Anglo community at this time was not up-in-arms, but they were stewing. Louis Cardis was dead, and his killer Charles Howard was kicking up his heels in La Mesilla. That didn't seem to square.

There was another state of affairs not squaring well, not for Charles Howard. While at La Mesilla he learned disconcerting news: A self-assured party of twenty *salineros* driving sixty yoke of oxen had started for the Guadalupe Salt Lakes intent on returning with sixteen wagonloads of duty-free salt—Zimpelman's salt. Fully cognizant of the personal danger, Howard left the relative safety of La Mesilla and rushed to Ysleta. Upon hearing that update, John G. "Limpin' John"

Atkinson, a former lieutenant in the Texas State Police and a man despised by many native inhabitants of the border, and not just a few others, did nothing to ingratiate himself, scolding that "if they [*salineros*] were men the salt question would be settled" adding that "the heads of those who went to the salt lakes would have to dance on the sand."[32] Lest one should suppose that regurgitated sourness was one-dimensional, it's relevant to repeat ill-omened remarks from the other side. Those of Cipriano Alderete: "We have marked everything down from the time when the rooster trod the hen until she laid her last egg. Everything is going to be paid for now, and we do not care what happens here after we have evened the score. You can take all these old houses. What are they worth? We will go across the river or somewhere else."[33] Not only did the Rio Grande's wetness slake thirst and irrigate crops, it served as a not make-believe barrier for skirting imposition of laws—Mexican or American.

On the twelfth day of December 1877, the intractable Charles Howard, using the in-place Texas civil court system it should be noted, filed suit in the name of the plaintiff, George B. Zimpelman, naming supposed *salineros* Sisto Salcido, Leon Granilio, *et al.*, as defendants. He, too, obtained an order of sequestration for 800 bushels of salt, placing the writ in hands of Sheriff Kerber for execution.[34] At this juncture, despite the noxious blathering of Limpin' John Atkinson, Howard was not yielding to raw cutting impulse, but was giving way for the law to take its natural course. It was too late. The last rooster had trod the last hen. Armed men, belligerent men, gathered along both banks of the river; the wringing of a neck was on their minds, the one owned by that cocksure Charles Howard.

Cutting to the chase is easy. At San Elizario positioning was everything. For Texas Rangers trapped inside an adobe building the responsibility, untenable as it might have seemed, was to protect life and limb of Charles H. Howard. For the mob outside—and that's what it had morphed into—the task seemed doable. The chickens had come home to roost. No longer were the Texas Rangers holding clear title to superiority, they were snared in a harrowing jam, wholly surrounded—besieged—by a bloodlust crowd fixed on doling out payback. These were not selfless insurgents aiming to rectify real or fancied social injustices by altruistically installing a new blueprint for government along the Rio Grande. An eventual accounting—a scorecard—will dispel any notion this uprising was cousin to the Boston Tea Party, not even a second cousin.[35] Outside the Rangers'

barricaded position the streets had filled with agitators and onlookers, some of whom were partaking of illicit opportunity: Raiding and
plundering while they rioted.[36] Purportedly that rascally Catholic
Priest, the aforementioned Father Antonio Borrajo, was doing his
part to whip the crowd into frenzy, offering absolution for anyone
with murder in their heart: "Shoot all the gringos and I will absolve
you."[37] Although it burnishes away multicultural inspired niceness,
theft on the wholesale scale, "looting anything not tied down" and
murder are demonstrative of a crowd run amok, not patriots seeking
lasting correction for perceived and/or real social injustices.[38] Lynch
mob mentality and revenge are understandable emotional concepts,
but not acceptable models for nullifying overt criminality.

The first to fall was merchant Charles Ellis. Arguing over whether
or not he was actually roped, dragged into unconsciousness, had his
throat cut and his body hacked into pieces or simply murdered at
once is irrelevant. Charles Ellis was thoroughly dead and it was not
the result of suicide or appendicitis.[39]

Next on the list of causalities would be a Texas Ranger. Sergeant
Conrad Mortimer was, bravely it would seem, gathering critical intelligence outside the Ranger's protective compound, moving from
one observation post to another. Perhaps on the jaunt he did find a
moment to meet with "a lady friend" before zipping up and resuming
his scouting duties. Regardless and unfortunately Ranger Mortimer
looked away from the window in Nicholas Kohlhaus's store instead
of glimpsing inside, not noticing a sniper named Zuñiga cautiously
peering over his precisely aligned rifle sights. Caught completely
unawares Sergeant Mortimer screamed in pain as the spiraling bullet tore through his back. He stumbled a few steps then fell to the
ground, immobilized and helpless, his five foot, ten inch, frame face
down on the dirt-packed street. Firing became general. Several rioters, those not engaged in looting the store once owned by the dead
Charles Ellis, zinged rifle and pistol balls at the Texas Rangers pinned
down in their makeshift fortress: From inside Texas Rangers
answered with bullets. Now and again a rioter catching a
Ranger's bullet screamed in pain, some dying, some were trailing
blood as they crawled to concealment. The hard numbers body count
racked up by Texas Rangers—there was one—is buried in an abyss of
burnt powder chaos. Discerning the precariousness of the wounded
sergeant's position, and the Texas Ranger's inability to protect himself, Lieutenant Tays jumped into action. Disregarding or overcoming

thoughts of personal safety John Tays broke from behind the adobe walls, rushing to Mortimer's side. During the hailstorm of gunfire, the good lieutenant dragged Sergeant Mortimer back inside the Rangers' defensive stronghold. Breathless but pleased not to be leaking blood, Lieutenant Tays watched as Doctor John K. Ball medically examined the badly hurt Ranger. The prognosis was not good. The bullet had wickedly torn into Sergeant Mortimer's back, punching all the way through red meat and muscle and gristle. Sergeant Mortimer could, by self-examination, look down with his steel-grey eyes and see the ragged exit wound below his right nipple. In excruciating pain Mortimer lingered in that never-never land between cognizance and coma that thirteenth day of December 1877.[40] Then he died.[41]

Casting aside bombast and bravado Charles Howard slowly submitted to reality: The Texas Rangers inside with him were whispering regrets and some of the Mexicans and Mexican-Americans outside were not bent toward extending a smidgen of goodwill. The noose was tightening. Howard turned to his servant, the aforementioned Wesley Owens, bringing him up to speed on his thought processes:

> I'm going to give up and let them kill me and be done; it won't do to rely upon these fellows [Texas Rangers]. I'm not going to stay here and have them all killed for me. These fellows are talking a good deal about me being here.[42]

During a parley, allegedly one wherein Texas Rangers had "raised a white flag," an accord was nominally reached, Charles Howard, and at the end of the day everyone else, Texas Rangers not exempted, would surrender to the teeth-gnashing mob outside.[43] And so it was. The rioters had possession of not only their hated foe, the accredited killer of Louis Cardis, Charley Howard, but a whole company of Texas Rangers as well, plus the sleepless lawmen's personal Colt's six-shooters, Winchesters, saddle horses—and pride. Lawmen yielding to enemies, in this instance, garnered more damning commentary during the twentieth-century legend building period for Texas Ranger histories, than it did in real time, though back East a few journalists hurled a stinging barb—but never up-close and personal, face to face, where it would stick. During 1877 there was a very real possibility in particular sections of the Southwest of finding oneself outnumbered and overwhelmed and outgunned by an ill-tempered gang of American desperadoes, merciless Mexican *banditos*, or slippery bronco Apaches who had jumped the reservation, looking for warfare and fun. An all-of-a-sudden death was a real likelihood for unlucky souls caught at the wrong place, at the wrong time. Away from peril in distance and/or time, the harshness of judgments grows easy from an armchair.

Though in today's marketplace of historically casting blame and atoning for someone else's bigotry, for this particular bloodbath ruckus, mislaid compassion might be cast overboard and washed away after assimilating hard, but enlightening truths. The crowd's leaders, a fact proven with evidence of the deathly aftermath, had been duplicitous from the get-go while negotiating terms of the sur-render—settlement of the stalemate. The verbal guarantee that no harm would come to any prisoners was defective, a clause wittingly disregarded and wholly unenforceable.[44] Not everyone's word was their bond, but in certain quarters excuses abound. Charitably let-ting folks off the hook for out-and-out looting will not sell, not in Texas, nor will it in Mexico. Downplaying the gravity associated with stealing is out of place. Thieves are thieves, period. Bestowing a wide-ranging free-pass blanket of okay to rob and loot and steal depreci-ates the honesty and restraint of those willingly and conscientiously choosing not to: the folks preferring to obey laws with integrity and show due respect for other persons and property. Although it's typi-cally underplayed due to a bona fide lack of pizzazz, far more Mexi-cans and Mexican-Americans did not participate in the skullduggery in any way—despite where their sympathies may or may not have lain. Correlating known population numbers with varying esti-mates of the mob's size is educational, although it does somewhat deflate much hot air from what in the end is still a significant and dramatic Texas story. The overall percentage of Mexican and Mexi-can-Americans actually taking part in the criminality is small, sur-prisingly small, registering in the lower single digit range.[45] Making note of such is meaningful. As it stands, buttressed by sound logic and watertight facts, it is more than perfectly clear the overwhelm-ing majority of borderland citizens did not physically participate in the turmoil whatsoever. Were they too scared to loot and murder and shoot at pinned down Texas Rangers? Did the majority sit out the shenanigans of the minority due to indifference? Had social differ-ences and rational grievances simply deteriorated into a blood feud? Or, did they, the overwhelming majority, levelheadedly want to set good examples for children, obey the law and live life according to traditionally instilled core principles? Hoeing weeds in the family garden plot or timely changing diapers are not newsworthy stories. It's but par business for the killers and crooks and rioters to get the press—nothing new. Accurately it may be proffered that what later became known officially as the El Paso Troubles was no universally accepted social uprising for redressing professed injustice, not after the thunderous clouds of a mean-spirited mob's mindset had darkened San Elizario. Whatever their private reasons—and it speaks well of them—most folks chose to peacefully remain on the sidelines while hotheads and murderers grabbed headlines.

Though it's not meant to be poking a stick in the eye of previously written accounts, in truth, the so-called El Paso Salt War in the much broader context "had little to do with salt." More to do with feuding, pitting "faction against faction" and "strong man against strong man" with tangible, frightening, disturbing, and a not awe-inspiring outcome: "Bad blood, personality conflicts, and intense personal rivalries characterized the affair, and mob violence, rape, robbery, and murder went unpunished with the breakdown of law enforcement."[46] Killing cops is a markedly unwise strategy—anytime, for any reason.

Ranger Conrad E. Mortimer had been hammered to the ground by the work of a back-shooting yahoo. Sergeant John McBride, Charles Howard, and Limpin' John Atkinson would face their killers, eye to eye. The executioners would be Mexicans, by design. Once their targets had been dispatched, the shooters could slip back across the Rio Bravo, and with great probability avoid extradition from Mexico, thwarting the best efforts of any annoying Texas prosecutors. There was a long history of lukewarm cooperation between politicos in Mexico and American law enforcement authorities when a request to extradite alleged criminals was broached.[47] The dye had been cast. "The mob wasted no time in exacting its revenge."[48] Howard went first. He was executed by firing squad, one rifleman being Jesús Telles, a Mexican well known for being "a horse thief who swung back and forth between Ysleta and Mexico." Impact of multiple bullets knocked Howard off his feet, pummeling him into the dirt, but he wasn't dead, yet, prostrate but just thrashing about. Jesús Telles sprinted forward with a *machete* to finish the job, but Lady Luck with a macabre sense of humor made her contribution to the madness. Telles, with the "*machete* raised to strike, aimed a blow at Howard's face. The dying man twisted away as the blow fell, and

Telles cut off two of his own toes. Others with better aim hacked and chopped at the body."[49] Afterward, Howard's lifeless form was tossed into a well.

John McBride was next, his personal relationship with Howard his downfall. Bone-tired Sergeant McBride had been napping when awakened and told his last day would end standing in front of a bullet-chipped adobe wall. He was resigned to his fate, prepared to show his captors no fear, no whining for gossipers to taunt his soon-to-be orphaned daughter with. The dour-faced firing squad did not dilly-dally. Texas Ranger Sergeant John E. McBride died instantly.[50]

Limpin' John Atkinson's demise did not come quickly. The first volley put him on the ground. Struggling, he rose to his feet, rebuking in Spanish, *"Mas arriba, cabrones!"* ("Higher up, you bastards!"). Two shots rang out and Atkinson sank—down but not dead. Unable to speak he raised his thumb and extended his index finger, the crude mock-up of a pistol, and pointed it at his head. The meaning was clear. Desidario Apodaca withdrew his revolver, placed it close against Atkinson's head and delivered death, a *coup de grâce*. That same day, December 17, the bodies of McBride and Atkinson were disgustingly mutilated and dumped into the well.[51]

For a time it was tetchy for the other Texas Rangers. Debate raged hot. Some screamed for their heads. Infectious murderous thoughts were putrefying saneness. Would a minority mob contaminate the masses? In the end wiser counsel prevailed. The Company C detachment was sent packing, sans anything to pack. Subsequent to regaining possession of their horses, Texas Rangers, absent even a hint of hesitation, at a fast pace left disarrayed San Elizario on the back trail—minus their six-shooters and rifles and dignity. They would return, though, with vengeance in their hearts and violence spitting from the business end of their guns.

The culturally prickly El Paso Salt War story, up unto this point, has been adroitly characterized as prime example of being a cause "wasteful and unnecessary, unless to prove to a pessimist that men can die bravely in a bad cause."[52] The Rangers—with some disquieting help—were determined to prove for optimist Texans that it was but sheer folly to think bad men would not suffer and die after taking hostages and condoning executions.

Chapter 3

Samuel "Sam" Frazier
1878

Twenty-four-year-old Sam Frazier, a North Carolinian from Randolph County by birth, was one of those privates in John B. Tays' detachment of Texas Rangers, having enlisted on November 21, 1877. Swearing his oath at San Elizario, Frazier tendered his horse for the required neutral appraisal. It must not have been a hot-blooded thoroughbred. The gelding was marked down as being worth $60.[1]

Sam Frazier would be the pattern for the type of Texas Ranger one would want by his side during a serious difficulty, gunplay. That Sam was reasonably handy with a six-shooter is backed up by his contemporaries who with envy boasted Frazier "was the best shot in the company with a revolver."[2] But, once the tunnel of immediate danger had been passed through, giving Sam Frazier a wide berth was smart. He was not a likeable fellow. In fact, as one Ranger who knew him well remarked, Sam was "abusive and insulting," classifying him "as a very dangerous man."[3] Sam Frazier's mount may not have been hot-blooded but he was, hot-tempered and coldhearted. It is important to recall that every man listed on the Muster Roll for John Tays' Company C detachment was a Ranger, a real Texas Ranger. Unfortunately—but provably—not all real Rangers were real nice guys, and some of the boys put on the payroll in El Paso County might measure as the worst of the worst. The quick and loose recruiting practices had paid a dividend—a detrimental dividend. Upholding an assertion that this Texas Ranger unit was staffed with a few seedy and dodgy and ruthless personalities is not challenging.

Jimmy McDaniels was one. Although he was from Tennessee, the twenty-five-year-old McDaniels, wearing his fiery crown of auburn hair and his hat's brim shading icy blue eyes, could already put in the bank a nefarious history of six-shooter madness and murder. Jimmy McDaniels was spring-loaded, always ready for a frolic—or a fight. Unfair fights were fine by him. As a cowboy, and later a foreman for the Cattle King of the Pecos, John Chisum, the at all times feisty Jimmy McDaniels was involved in several six-shooter situations, killing and nearly being killed. Few were his peer for a manhunt, though after making the capture his propensity for guaranteeing prisoners safekeeping was imperfect: They were gunned down while escaping! Jimmy McDaniels was a damn good horse thief, too. Apaches on the Mescalero Reservation in New Mexico Territory could and did attest to that. McDaniels ran with a pack of human wolves, men who would cleave unto themselves remarkably well-known reputations for outlawry and murder, such as Jessie Evans, Tom Bostick, Frank Baker, and Marion Turner. Two more of the better known gangsters were John Kinney—King of the Rustlers—and Charles "Pony Diehl" Ray, dead shots and dead game *mal hombres*. With wit and candor a frontier newspaperman thus inked of desert desperado Pony Diehl, "as black a picture of an unhung villain as we can find in a year's search." After coming out losers in a holiday fisticuff battle with soldiers from Fort Selden near Las Cruces, Jimmy McDaniels, John Kinney, Jessie Evans, and Pony Diehl regrouped and surreptitiously returned to the dancehall. They stayed outside. Their smoking Colt's six-shooters went inside—through windows. The act was cowardly, the mayhem measurable. Two unlucky soldiers and a civilian were dead. Two soldiers were wounded.[4] A year later the quick-triggered and bi-lingual Jimmy McDaniels became a Texas Ranger.[5]

Beside Sam Frazier and Jimmy McDaniels, another answering roll as one of John B. Tays' not so illustrious Texas Rangers, though nevertheless a real Ranger, was Jerry Barton. When enlisting as a Ranger on December 21, 1877, shortly after the murders of Mortimer and McBride, the hard-hitting and hard-fighting twenty-six-year-old Jerry Barton declared he was a cowboy, originally from Louisiana, and maybe it's true.[6] Barton may or may not have been on the lam at the time he became a Texas lawman, but evidence does suggest he'd killed a man in Tennessee with a six-shooter, flying the coop to Arizona Territory for awhile. There he tended bar at James Kellum's Phoenix saloon—for a little while. He had gotten into a fight with a rowdy and drunken Henry King, thumping him severely. King died in the streets, but at an Inquest, head trauma was ruled out, death from apoplexy ruled in. Jerry Barton was free. Free to travel and a hiatus in the Lone Star State as a Texas Ranger seemed like a damn good idea. Ranger Barton's speech impediment—stuttering—seemed not to bother Lieutenant Tays; he was looking for toughened fighters: He got more than he bargained for.[7]

Hopefully, the overall portrait of the fellows making up El Paso County's detachment of Company C is coming sharply into focus. It was not all midnight black as there were A-OK Rangers in the company. The picture is unarguably dark by inclusion of the aforementioned lawmen, and others may be splotched onto the canvas of Texas Ranger history. Men like thirty-six-year-old Ranger Jack Irvin and G. W. "Gus" Moore, a year younger, who were inclined toward "Stealing Cattle" after being kicked off the force. Shortly their bodies were found riddled with bullets, the work of vigilantes or disgruntled sidekicks: No one knew for sure. Or take the case of twenty-five-year-old C. H. "Red" Cartledge, and his crony S. B. "Sam" Northcutt, the rumored inside man for a loathsome crew of cow thieves. A good Ranger sergeant, Mark Ludwick, was obliged to kill both doornail dead after they had "turned bad."[8] Then there would soon be on the payroll Sherman McMaster, a real Texas Ranger for awhile, but one later suffering an arrest with Pony Diehl for stagecoach robbery.[9] In Arizona Territory, McMaster earned his postgraduate degree in crime after participation in a murder conspiracy with Wyatt and Warren Earp, John Henry "Doc" Holliday, and two additional ne'er-do-wells: The first a masterpiece gangland hit in the Tucson train-yard; the second a deluxe bushwhacking in the wild stretches of Cochise County—all shots to the back, naturally.[10] Obviously, misplaced hero worship aside, carrying designation as a real Texas Ranger did not automatically show linkage with ethical behavior and upright principles, not in frontier El Paso County, not in 1877–1878. Ranger Sam Frazier fit the profile—the shameful profile.

John B. Jones wasn't blind or unintelligent. He, perhaps better than anyone, knew that the recruitment of some El Paso Rangers had been from the shallow end of the pond—the stagnant and murky end. Somewhat wisely with an eye cast toward doing the right thing on the one hand, and covering his little fanny with the other, Major Jones had left Lieutenant John Barnard Tays some very comprehensive instructions concerning touchy personnel matters should they arise: If there was to be any leakage of stink, better on the lieutenant's boots, a common managerial escape valve then—and today. An explicit subsection of Special Order No. 110 was just that, plain spoken and easy to understand:

In the management of the men under his command he will maintain strict discipline and attention to duty, and to this end, is
hereby authorized in his discretion, to discharge them from the
service for drunkenness, riotous and disorderly conduct, willful
disobedience of orders or neglect of duty or for incapacity or unfit-
ness for the service in which he is engaged.[11]

Early on El Paso was jokingly tagged as Hell Paso due to a general
sense of free-for-all and instant resort to gunplay.[12] Others would
soon come to know the town simply as a "Six Shooter Capital" or
"Sin City."[13] For hapless souls personally drawn into the booming
fireworks, though, it was no laughing matter. Even in the carefully
recorded history of a house of worship, St. Clement's Episcopal
Church, nonfiction fidelity spoke to early day El Paso's earned reputation for bloodshed: "As in nearly all new places, there was a lawless
element and most of the citizens carried six-shooters for protection
and also as a means of righting their wrongs, real or fancied, which
meant, of course, many sudden deaths. It is said that in most cases
the records read that the 'deceased died of gun shot wounds at the
hands of parties unknown..... Our early parish records are, as one
rector expressed it, dripping with blood.'"[14]

Retellings of the wretched El Paso Salt War story are typically
and rightly compartmentalized into three acts: Act One is the geographical stage setting, with its complementary recap of political
infighting and intrigues. Act Two has the curtain jerked back exposing the siege, rioting, looting, murders, surrender, and release of cap-
tive Texas Rangers. The last act is where Texas Ranger Sam Frazier
attains stardom, as a villain.

Regardless of rights or wrongs, real or fancied injustices, cultural sensitivities or degrees of abject racial intolerance, nineteenth-
century Texas was not the place or time wherein forgive and forget
were coins of the realm. The widely circulated *Galveston Daily News*
heralded a forecast for pending doom:

> The blood shed by the Mexican butchers at San Elizario will hardly
> be suffered to go unavenged for the flimsy technical reason that it
> was a purely local squabble over a salt pond.[15]

Shortly after that editorial prediction the *Galveston Daily News* printed
a letter from Sheriff Kerber, who had been granted permission by the

governor to enlist aid of some-not-so-nice fellows in nearby by New Mexico Territory. El Paso County's top lawman taunted:

> I expect 50 citizens from Silver City, and then I will drive the scoundrels ahead of me like sheep.... I have no courts, no justices; nearly all were in the row, and I have to take it all in my hands. I know Texas will uphold me if no other State does. You will find I will not allow the greasers to pass unpunished.[16]

Without tumbling into temptation of biographically profiling each and every one of the fellows answering Sheriff Kerber's plea, a generic summation has before now been made: "They were hard faced and battle scarred.... they nearly all had reputations."[17] Another academic added an indiscriminate portrayal about the hard-riding, hard-shooting, and hard-hearted New Mexican posse: "Sheriff Kerber had been promised the aid of 50 men from Silver City. On December 21, 30 men from Silver City arrived; judging by their performance it is well that 50 did not come.... Many of them were men of evil reputation, and hard character...."[18] The recognized leader of the Silver City boys was none other than the altogether fearless deputy sheriff from Grant County, Dan Tucker, a certifiable man killer with at least eight deep-cut scores on his notchstick.[19] The other dominant personality in command was John Kinney, soon to be an authentic godfather of Old West organized crime. On paper, as one historian adroitly postulated, John Kinney was a "high private," but his leadership role should not be diminished or underplayed.[20]

At this chronological juncture in the El Paso Troubles enough time had elapsed since the murders of storekeeper Ellis, Texas Rangers Mortimer and McBride, Charley Howard, and Limpin' John Atkinson for the marshaling of a restoring order corps—the U.S. Army—and two retaliatory forces operating under the facade of peace keepers: Texas Rangers under command of Lieutenant John B. Tays, and the so-called Silver City Rangers captained by El Paso County Sheriff Charles Kerber with underlings Dan Tucker and John Kinney as helpmate hellions. Although some—a few—of the 9th Cavalry's "Buffalo Soldiers" riding behind Colonel Edward Hatch slipped off the half-cocked notch, their misdeeds and misbehavior pales in comparison to outright hooliganism and homicides of the two civilian elements.[21] Texas Ranger Frazier, at least for awhile, would live up to his well earned status as being disagreeable and dangerous.

Major John B. Jones' written instructions to John B. Tays—Special Order 110—is frequently cited with purpose of lessening criticism of the Ranger lieutenant's leadership role during Act Three—aftermath of the precursor acts of mayhem and murder. Part of the written order does seem to allow Lieutenant Tays a way out, afterwards, casting exclusive blame at Sheriff Keber's mismanagement:

> He [Tays] will assist the Sheriff in making arrests and escorting prisoners when called on by him to do so. Will make arrest of offenders against the law upon proper process of the courts directed to him....[22]

True, the Company C detachment's formalized orders were to cooperate with and assist El Paso County's legally installed authorities, the sheriff and officers of the court, but that same written edict placed an onus squarely on Lieutenant Tays' back:

> and will also do all in his [Tays] power to give protection to the lives and property of citizens against unlawful attacks or depredations from any source whatsoever.[23]

With ice-water running though his veins, Texas Ranger Sam Frazier would lock tight notions that Lieutenant Tays was powerless in the managerial arena of maintaining discipline and executing his not blurred charge: defending area citizens from vicious assaults and/or protecting their earthly possessions. The Texas Rangers arrested two supposed rioters and looters, Crescencio Yrigoyen and Santiago Durán. After an overnight stopover, the prisoners, hands firmly bound behind them, were brusquely placed atop empty coffins in a wagon driven by J. W. and Isaac Campbell, and the march to recover the bodies of Ellis, Mortimer, McBride, Atkinson, and Howard resumed for awhile—a little while. When the Campbell brothers looked backwards into their wagon there were no prisoners. Seventy-five yards away, dodging about in some brush, the boys did see Texas Rangers Sam Frazier and Jerry Barton and quickly reached a conclusion: "They are shooting the prisoners."[24] In but a jiffy Rangers Frazier and Barton returned to the wagon, reporting Yrigoyen and Durán had foolishly initiated an escape attempt and were mortally gunned down while hotfooting through the brambles and brush. Had they really made a mad dash? For Sheriff Kerber such a persnickety detail was immaterial. Lieutenant Tays bought into Rangers Frazier's and Barton's self-serving statements, Colonel Edward Hatch didn't! His after-the-fact investigation revealed that marksmanship of the Rangers was topnotch, one of the deceased suffered "five or six bullet-holes in his head, shot through the hat-band; the other was shot in the forehead and in the side. So near was the shot in the side it was evident the gun had been near his clothing. I was then assured in my own mind that these prisoners were killed without necessity."[25] Colonel Hatch implored the civil authorities, Lieutenant Tays and Sheriff Kerber, to make arrests. Both demurred.

Shortly thereafter, downriver, Ranger Frazier again jumped into the middle of controversy. In response to gunfire coming from a house, the Texas Rangers and Silver City Rangers unleashed hellfire. When they rode away, a very dead Pablo Nuñez and his wounded wife, Mariana, lay in their wake.[26] During this batch of meanness Sam Frazier caught a bullet to the leg, well, a spent ball inflicting not a lick of damage was retrieved from his boot—so he claimed. Unmistakably Sheriff Kerber's posse and Tays' detachment of Texas Rangers had blasted away, killing a man and nearly killing his wife, but was it a good shooting—justified? Hardly! Dutiful crime-scene investigation, again at the auspices of Colonel Hatch was informative—and incriminating. Forensic evidence, rudimentary as it was, fell short of championing any assertions that avenging peace keepers were fired on from within the house, through a closed door.[27]

Soon the state-sanctioned gunmen ran to ground Jesús Telles, the *machete* wielding mad-mutineer missing two toes. Sheriff Kerber reported the fellow "charged" the posse and was stopped with a bullet, just in the nick of time.[28] Somewhat later another witness offered his story, an alternative account: "Telles saw them coming and began to run. The whole crowd followed him. He fell as he climbed a fence and the mob shot him through the head again and again as he lay in one corner."[29]

The pattern is clear. For this cycle of revenge Lieutenant Tays failed to corral the bad behavior of his Texas Rangers. Whether it was due to overt complicity or useless ineptitude made not a whit of difference for those souls nursing bullet wounds and sorely thumped heads. Sheriff Kerber, based on his previous cries of outrage and promises, may not have shown sorry incompetence as a leader, but his collusion and condoning of criminal wrongdoings was evident—more than evident. The list grew. Pedro Cauelario and his son were accosted and abused, and stolen from. Cruz Cháves was shot two times, but, thankfully, survived this brand of law enforcement. Antonio Cadena took inventory at his home once the Texas Rangers and Silver City Rangers had moved on after hard pressing a gun's barrel into his perspiring temple: He was missing a revolver, cartridge belt, saddle, bridle, spurs—and two horses. Noverto Pais testified that the Rangers "hit me twice with their pistols, and I have the marks yet." Then Texas Ranger Jimmy McDaniels forcefully appropriated Noverto's most prized possession, a rifle—one that had belonged to his father. Salome Telles would swear under oath that her dog had been killed and her chickens had been shot. After dark when one *lawman* couldn't see the front sight of his six-shooter, he simply pushed the muzzle between Salome's breasts, "forcing her to give up her person to him."[30]

Though Lieutenant Tays' orders had explicitly instructed him with fidelity to protect persons and property from "attacks or depredations from any source whatsoever," he clumsily and amateurishly chose to do otherwise. John Tays' Company C detachment of Texas Rangers did not arrest Silver City Rangers. Sheriff Charles Kerber, nominally at the head of the Silver City Rangers, did not arrest Texas Rangers. Well, almost!

After receiving an unwelcome update via a circuitous route to Washington, D.C. and then to Austin, Governor Hubbard, with an effort aimed to throw off-target any political embarrassment, instituted proceedings wherein Texas Rangers Sam Frazier and Jerry Barton were placed in irons. The nasty allegation they had cold-bloodedly murdered prisoners Yrigoyen and Durán rather than having thwarted an escape attempt was a hot-potato issue.[31]

For moving Ranger Sam Frazier's story forward it is not necessary to delve too deeply into the face-saving blame games that the hullabaloo in El Paso County kicked up. Not at all surprisingly, the finger-pointing was widespread. The Silver City Rangers, perhaps the worst of the lot, retuned to New Mexico Territory unscathed within a context of local public relations, warmly welcomed as conquering heroes:

> A considerable number of the Silver City contingent to the El Paso army of occupation retuned to town last Saturday. They expressed themselves as well satisfied with their lark. No expense, plenty of

fun and a measure of experience which may be turned to advantage in future campaigns.[32]

This was not the Texas Ranger's finest hour. Major Jones was in a
real pickle regarding negative—and growing—commentary regarding some rather inexcusable actions of the Texas Rangers, particularly after the siege and subsequent surrender at San Elizario. John
B. Jones found himself at odds with part of the military's findings
during a post incident investigation conducted by the War Department. So much so, he felt compelled to submit a somewhat lengthy
written "Minority Report." Historically looking backwards some of
his thematic points are well taken, especially with regards to credit-
ably referring criminal cases to an El Paso County grand jury. However, that same dispassionate analysis reveals a deceptive sleight of
hand in shifting liability away from his appointment of Lieutenant
John Tays, as well as other touches of obfuscation—lame excuses
for a lawman: "I must be permitted to say that from the evidence it
appears that on the 23rd December the sheriff considered it his duty
to make the arrest of several parties, leaders of and active participants in the mob, who were known to be in Socorro [Texas], and to
search certain houses for arms. In doing this several men were killed
and one woman wounded; and transpiring in the wake of a wild,
fanatical, and brutal mob, in a period of excitement, closing up a
reign of terror by the mob which is said by the majority to have been
'brutal and atrocious,' though not justifiable, were probably unavoid-
ably incident to the duties which the officer in charge conceived that
he was called on to perform.... On the 23rd of December the sheriff,
in charge of Lieutenant Tays's company of State troops and the men
who had come from Silver City, started for San Elizario...."[33] The specifically worded clause of Special Order 110 instructing Lieutenant
Tays to "do all in his power to give protection to the lives and property of citizens against unlawful attacks or depredations from any
source whatsoever," is mislaid or forgotten or swept under the rug
of deniability? Sheriff Charles Kerber could take the blame, if blame
need be found.

Kerber didn't have to suffer even a smidgen of blame for making a
Texas Ranger out of Sam Frazier. That dubious distinction would rest
squarely on the shoulders of the man who hired him that twenty-
first day of November 1877, Lieutenant John B. Tays. By whom and
for whatever reason is unknown, but the key to leg-irons rotated and

Sam Frazier and Jerry Barton were turned out, but not out of the Rangers. Although sometimes considering the source foreshadows discounting a story's accuracy, nevertheless, a snippet in Silver City's *Grant County Herald* mentioned that Rangers Sam Frazier and Jimmy McDaniels were so despised by the before-mentioned padre, Father Borrajo, that he was publicly offering $1000 for their heads delivered across the Rio Grande in a burlap bag.[34]

Attributing bitterness to Texas Ranger Frazier for being chained to a chinaberry tree, even for a little while, won't hold water: Sam was born bitter and bad. And now he was mad! Disgruntled because of a tiff over a promotion he coveted. The principal target of his piercing anger and aggression was not Lieutenant Tays, who actually owned the say-so regarding personnel matters, but more specifically with Texas Ranger John C. Ford, a twenty-eight-year-old Louisianan. When actively recruited into ranks of the Texas Rangers with other hard cases Ford proclaimed he was a cowboy by trade, but failed to make mention of something else; certain folks rated him "one of the most dangerous men in the Southwest."[35] The actual part Texas Ranger Ford had played in the retributive madness is indistinct. If he had been behaving badly like fellow Rangers Sam Frazier, Jimmy McDaniels, and Jerry Barton it has skipped particularized notice. For the next episode in the six-shooting saga of Texas Ranger John C. Ford's life there would be plenty of particularized notice—and witnesses.

Without question the swarthy complexioned Ford, and his shock of wavy dark black hair, coupled with his no-nonsense demeanor in tight spots had yielded a lasting and favorable impression on Lieutenant Tays. He promoted Ranger Ford to the rank of 1st Sergeant. Frazier thought he should have caught the upgrade. Had he not proved himself by killing escaping prisoners, preventing their getaway? Had he not stepped to the mark when those nastily inclined Nuñez folks had decided—by themselves—to take on two posses, shooting at them from behind a closed door? What was that goddamned lieutenant thinking? Ranger Frazier was livid! He made no secret about it either, declaring to fellow Ranger Corporal H. O. "Rocky" Matthews "that there were two men in the company he couldn't live with, and they were Ford and Dr. Ball. He then threatened to kill Ford and fix Dr. Ball." Sometime after revealing his scheme to do away with Ford, Frazier grabbed his gun and began hunting for his next victim, a Texas Ranger sergeant. The man-eating tiger was hungry, cannibalis-

tically ready to feed on his own kind. Accosted by Matthews and told
to calm down, Frazier in an act of immaturity threw a temper tan-
trum by firing his six-shooter into the brush. Lieutenant Tays ineptly
interceded, admonishing Frazier: "You must behave yourself."[36] The
warning was ignored, the quarrelsome Texas Ranger piping out his
own cautionary advisory that the company "was not big enough to
hold both of us," meaning him and the new 1st Sergeant.[37]

To his supposed confidants Sam Frazier had made threats, and
those that knew him did not grade them as idle. Sam Frazier was a
real Ranger and Sam Frazier was the real deal. Sam Frazier was real
mad, too! He bragged just when he would actually settle the hash of
the brand new 1st Sergeant: "God damn him, when I get back from
Franklin."[38] Texas Ranger John Ford also had friends, good friends,
and whether or not it was worthless gossip or legit forewarning is
inconsequential; he was posted. On the last day of January 1878 Sergeant Ford put a sixth bean in the wheel—a cartridge under the hammer—holstering his Colt's six-shooter. Then, smartly, he swapped
birdshot for buckshot.

Ranger Sam Frazier had accompanied lawyer John W. Hughes
and another fellow upriver to Franklin. Upon their return to Ysleta,
where the Texas Rangers were headquartered, Sam Frazier rode into
the compound about ten paces ahead of his traveling companions for
the day. Jumping down from his horse all seemed well to Sam Frazier. That is—until—in an ordinary tone of voice but a single word
was uttered: "Sam!" Ranger Frazier did an immediate about-face and
quickly discerned the bleak picture: Four orbs staring straight at him.
Two were the steel-blue eyes of 1st Sergeant Ford, and the other two
were blue steel holes in the Ranger's twin-barreled shotgun. Ranger
Frazier screamed. Ranger Ford shot, twice. The first charge of buckshot tore into Frazier's right side, knocking him to the ground. The
second blast missed altogether, which is indicative of an authentic
close-range drama, the pellets not having had time or distance to dis-
sipate amply into a widespread pattern. Pulling himself up, into an
awkward sitting position, Texas Ranger Frazier begged for his life.
Perhaps the booming reports of the scattergun had temporarily deaf-
ened Sergeant John C. Ford, blotting out wasted pleas for compassion
or mercy, or maybe he just didn't care? Like a writhing rattlesnake,
Frazier seemed not to die. Clawing dirt and crying, Sam's luck had
played out. Throwing his shotgun aside Sergeant Ford withdrew his
fully loaded Colt's six-shooter and walked up to Sam Frazier, empty-

ing the revolver: Five fast shots in the head did the trick. One went wild. Sam Frazier was a real Ranger no more.[39]

There would be no doubt as to what result a Coroner's Inquest would render. The self-defense verdict was a foregone finale. Sergeant Ford went back to work.[40] A latter day historian of renown would write that Frazier's death was a "desirable homicide."[41] Perhaps he's right, but that should come as no shocker. Tough creatures paced Lucifer's Line. Panthers had sharp teeth and claws. Texas Rangers had guns.

Chapter 4

George R. "Red" Bingham
1880

Bad news would break from the border country. Reverberations scorched across Texas in a heartbeat, well, in the pulsations of a telegrapher's fast-tapping finger. Outlaws were on the loose in far West Texas. And, they were a nasty set indeed.

Less than thirty days had elapsed in the new year of 1880 and already a Trans-Pecos county sheriff was hollering for help.[1] Heavily armed bands of highjackers and cow thieves were rampantly gaining the upper hand, outshooting, outdistancing, and outfoxing local lawmen. These bad boys "were some pretty desperate characters ... that did not value their lives anymore than you would a pin."[2] By one report fourteen or fifteen "robberies and assaults" had been committed in but one town, inside of one month.[3] Not only were West Texas peace officers crying for relief, county administrators and private citizens were petitioning the chief executive at Austin.[4]

On the nineteenth day of May, late in the afternoon, a sensational robbery—a yet daylight robbery—occurred at Fort Davis, Texas, a prettily situated mountain village then in Presidio County, later Fort Davis County. Joseph Sender and Charles Siebenborn were German proprietors of a landmark store, within but walking distance of the U.S. Army's installation of Fort Davis, the town's namesake. Five unsmiling riders had suddenly appeared in town. Three dangerous ne'er-do-wells went inside the Sender & Siebenborn Store. The other two bandits, with fully cocked Colt's six-shooters in hand, held any would-be onlookers at bay, impolitely shoving them inside O. M. Keesey's saloon. That is, after the arctic-eyed duo had boldly relieved any terrified hostages of their personal watches and wallets and other valuable whatnots.[5] Gathering up plunder, the trio of inside desperadoes reunited with their outside comrades, then in a show of daring but reckless bravado punctuated their misdeeds with gunshots while putting iron to their horses as they raced out of town. This was no whodunit!

Real identity of the desperadoes had been established, easily.[6] Perhaps the best known today was the aforementioned Jessie Evans, murderer and veteran of New Mexico's Lincoln County War, the wasteful episode wherein two factions were vying for possession of economic strangleholds. Jessie Evans had been accompanied that day by three brothers, Charles, Dolly, and Albert "Bud" Graham, along with August Gross. All wore aliases from time to time. For this story a key handle was the false name worn by Bud Graham, aka Ace Carr.[7] West Texas citizens—the electorate—were, again, outraged at the outrageous assaults on persons and property.

John B. Jones, former major of the Frontier Battalion, but now holding down office as the state's adjutant general, heard and heeded the calls for aid. His answer to the pleas for six-shooter support was simple: Send the Rangers. This time though, he'd not rely solely on fresh recruits. Turning to a proven lawman and experienced combat leader, Captain Daniel Webster Roberts, AG Jones' instructions were explicit.[8] Outfit a detachment of good Rangers from Company D, and set them on the march toward a setting sun. That's what he wanted. More to the point, it was what Governor O. M. Roberts wanted.

Too, as a backup measure for the long haul, Lieutenant Charles L. Nevill, Company E, was to select an experienced Texas Ranger to do some on-the-ground criminal assessment work at untamed Fort Davis. Sergeant Lavoizre Blair Caruthers gained a stirrup and began his fact-gathering assignment, with laconic supplemental orders to gauge the merit—or lack thereof—of securing local talent for vacant spots on the Texas Ranger's muster roll. Or, in this regard, was Fort Davis like El Paso, a shallow pool swimming with alligators, madly biting each other and chewing their own tails?

Meanwhile, one of Company D's noncoms, Sergeant Edward Armon "Ed" Sieker, Jr., twenty-seven years old, after carefully overseeing loading of the war-wagon with essential camp equipment, a month's rations for men and mounts, plus plenty of Winchester ammunition, faced west and leisurely struck out for West Texas on the thirtieth day of May 1880.[9] Following in relaxed yet watchful formation were Texas Rangers Nick K. Brown, Henry Thomas, J. W. Miller, E. J. Pound, Richard Robertson "Dick" Russell, D. Tom Carson, Samuel A. "Sam" Henry, and George R. "Red" Bingham.[10]

As the summer sun set on the sixth day of June 1880, Sergeant Ed Sieker and his detachment unlimbered gear, establishing camp at Fort Stockton, Pecos County. Picking up on the latest criminal intelligence the Texas Rangers got an earful. Just six days earlier, thanks to the competent police work of Pecos County Sheriff Harry Ryan at the head of a determined citizen posse, the thieves had been run to ground—briefly. More precisely Will Silverstein's saloon had been target of a stakeout. An arrest attempt netted gunfire. The ensuing shoot-out cleared loafing pedestrians from Fort Stockton's streets, but sprinting desperadoes did not tarry. They had been put "afoot." Every shot—good guys and bad—went wide of the mark, nary a dribble of blood. The end result was a mixed bag—a tie, of sorts. Jittery possemen had gained custody of the outlaws' horses, but not the hotfooting outlaws, excepting one: Mr. Ace Carr was now cooling his heels in a dank Pecos County dungeon.[11] The unintended consequence was more than a little perplexing. Grabbing a tiger by the tail is risky—letting go can be ruinous.

Jurisdictionally there was a hitch. Ace Carr was locked up in Pecos County. The venue for the scene of the crime, Sender's & Siebenborn's store, was in Presidio County. There was considerable worry, and justifiably so, that Ace Carr's *amigos* would storm the jail, liberating the prisoner at the expense of a high body count. Such would surely be the case if Ace Carr was moved to Fort Davis where security issues were even more troubling due to a severe shortage of trustworthy manpower.[12] Sergeant Ed Sieker was also worried about another dimension: freeing Ace Carr with cash not bullets. He advised AG Jones that already "several attempts have made to rescue him by bribery."[13] In the interim Sergeant Sieker's Texas Rangers stood guard. A shaken county judge took pen in hand, updating Governor Roberts:

> The robbers are still in this Section waiting for departure of rangers to rescue one of their number now in jail here. If you will have Sergeant Sieker's orders extended until he shall have had time to operate we have not doubt that he will get the whole gang, he seems to understand the matter thoroughly and is doing every thing in his power. If the rangers are removed now the murderers and robbers, will flock back and some of our best citizens will doubtless fall victim to their resentment....[14]

Sergeant Sieker had been dispatched to far West Texas for the purpose of capturing fugitives, murderers, robbers, and cow thieves, putting the wholesale kibosh on criminality. Overlaying an effective security blanket requires there be no gaping holes in the coverage.

As such it is a twenty-four-and-seven set up. Instead of ranging the countryside—which was enormous—looking for mean desperadoes, the sergeant and his nine-man detachment of Texas Rangers were most of the time behind locked jailhouse doors or patrolling the close perimeter, dividing the day's hours between downtime and working assigned shifts. They, then, were really prisoners of the prisoner.[15]

Soon thereafter it was learned through the grapevine that the scandalous fugitive and man-killer John Selman, wanted in Shackelford County, was at Fort Davis having craftily reinvented himself as Captain Tyson, a butcher by trade. That he was suspected of being in cahoots with the robbers and cow thieves is a no-brainer. Selman had a secret, and the Rangers kept secret the fact they knew it.

Somewhere and sometime the proverbial light bulb switched on. How long could all of this go on? Guard duty was boring. If the outlaws could not liberate their pal Ace Carr from Fort Stockton, why not lend them a helping hand? Draw them out. Move Ace Carr to the Presidio County lockup at Fort Davis. A plan was hatched—cooked up—devised. Lure the thugs into town, graciously greeting them with a no compromise surprise—buckshot and bullets. To ensure that nasty John Selman was not free to run hither and yon spreading the word, simply make him a deputy sheriff—a jailer; figuratively tied down but not forgotten. Sergeant Caruthers feared—knew—had he actually arrested and jailed John Selman on the charges from Shackelford County, that he would have been hard pressed to "hold him."[16] In the short go, deception trumped detention. With Selman physically standing a headcount, and the plan in place for prepositioning heavily armed Texas Rangers behind storefront concealment, Jessie Evans and his crew when they rode in to free Ace Carr would be bought and paid for—dead meat—and it would be a legally sanctioned enforcement ploy.

In theory it was a good plan. In practice it was iffy. To work, mum would have to be the word. Secret keeping is always problematic when factoring in one overriding component—people. In this case it was not the hoodwinked deputy sheriff that spilled the beans, but they were floating fast on a whiskey river thanks to Presidio County Sheriff Theodore A. Wilson. The fifty-eight-year-old lawman was a genuine tough cookie, a Big Bend vicinity pioneer and Indian fighter, but when he drank—which was often—he talked. In this instance, he talked too much, and to too many folks—everyone.[17] The plan was scrapped. Deputy John Selman was arrested, and locked in the jail he thought he was guarding. Paradoxically news broke quickly. Jessie Evans and the other outlaws were seen, so it was reported, along the Rio Grande south of Fort Davis, way south—a hundred miles or so.

Purportedly the crucial bit of news had come off the forked tongue of a black fellow going by the name Louis, who not out of character for a snitch was working both sides of the street—or in this case river. If true, as has been written, Jessie Evans had advised Louis to keep him posted about Texas Rangers snooping around in the neighborhood, unless they numbered but three or four, then he need not bother troubling himself with any warning: Evans and his hard-shooting boys could handle that size impromptu. Louis bent the ear of Sergeant Sieker—or someone—that the gang they were hunting for was camping in the craggy and ominous looking Chinati Mountains on the Texas side of the borderline.[18] From that lair, when the bad boys were in want of knocking off the edge with indulgent pleasures, a southeasterly ride would spot them directly opposite Ojinaga, Chihuahua. After splashing across the river Mexican bar-keeps didn't ask questions and perfumed princesses were ready, willing, to trade time for tips. Jessie Evans and crowd were hiding, but sometimes in plain sight.

Sergeant Ed Sieker fashioned a platoon, had a pack-mule outfitted, and headed for the village of Presidio del Norte at the very bottom of that big bend in the Rio Grande—at the crossing into Ojinaga. Joining him on this scout were Sergeant Caruthers and Ranger privates Tom Carson, Sam Henry, Dick Russell, and Red Bingham. Also along, acting as local guide, was Presidio County Deputy Clato Herridio.[19] Advantaging themselves of cooler nighttime temperatures and somewhat masking their movements, the Texas Rangers husbanded horseflesh under the cover of darkness for the first day or two. When and if they overhauled the outlaws, a jaded horse was valueless. Sergeant Caruthers' horse was already graded as but "a little pony" and Sam Henry wasn't even atop a horse—he was riding a mule, sure-footed but slow.

As would be expected the Rangers chitchatted and parried with one another as they ambled toward the border, Lucifer's Line. Though it falls within the boundaries of speculation, it's not over-reach to think while he was riding along Red Bingham's thoughts drifted to an earlier time, when he was cowboying in Menard County, or even before that, tending livestock on the farm at Denison, Grayson County, in the Red River country of North Texas. Perhaps he wondered, too, what his older sister Laura was doing, or his brother Charles, four years his junior? What did his mother Ann think of his forsaking chasing wild cattle and turning into a man-hunter? Ranger Bingham needed not query why he was nicknamed "Red." George's florid complexion and a mop of flaming red hair had assured the moniker. Whether prompted by a cut at lighthearted humor or a foreboding premonition, Red Bingham straightened his five foot, nine inch frame in the saddle, gently spurring—nudging—his horse into a trot as the morning sun began peeking.[20] Pulling alongside Sergeant Ed Sieker and then checking his horse into a plodding walk Red Bingham stoically predicted: "Sergeant, I'll be in Mexico or in hell before night."[21]

Nearing the area of anticipated action on that third day of July, the Ranger's scouting tactic shifted to a daytime operation, cutting for meaningful sign on the ground and eyeing the surrounding countryside for the slightest hint of suspicious motion: curls of smoke, dust clouds, an out-of-place shadow dancing on a distant mountain's bench. Doubly hot it was, that afternoon at one o'clock. A rough eighteen miles or so north of Presidio the Ranger detachment took a break, watering their horses in Cibola Creek, not too far removed from the remote adobe mining hovels of Shafter. At a distance the Rangers detected four mounted *hombres*, one leading a pack horse. For Texas Rangers the undertaking would be clear cut: Find out who they were, what they were doing? An explanation was in order, a damn good explanation! For the four horsemen there was no inclination to stop and pass the time of day. Motives for being in the out-of-the-way neighborhood were not good, and names they owned matched perfectly with those on lists of hard wanted characters in several Texas counties. Frayed nerves bent to panic. Jessie Evans and cronies executed a sweeping 180-degree arc, emptying rifle scabbards as they spun and ran. Turning in saddles, the desperadoes were desperate, firing at the pursuing Texas Rangers, but missing. The Rangers retuned fire, ineffectively. The horse race waxed hot for a mile and a half, though Caruthers and Henry were gradually slipping further and further and further behind. The Company E sergeant's little pony and Sam's mule were struggling, but they exhibited no speed and had no bottom. Deputy Herridio had been paid to guide, not fight—a cue he understood well. Although it may have seemed an eternity with bullets zinging by, in but short order the Texas Rangers' superior numbers had melted away to equality—four against four. The ground took a gradual upturn and horses slowed on the incline then abruptly the race was over—but not the fight. First-hand, Sergeant Sieker offers color commentary:

> ....they were up on a large Mountain, we following. As soon as we were on the top of the Mtn. we soon discovered they were concealed behind a ledge of rocks, as a solid volley was fired at our little band. As there was three of us at that time, before we dismounted, a shot cut Carson's hat brim, and another passed under his leg, cutting his stirrup leather & wounding his horse in the side. They shot volley after volley at us at forty yards range in open view & they behind the rocks. Carson shot one of the party in the side but he was determined to "sell out" & Kept firing around our heads very closely, when I saw him stick his head out to shoot, I shot him between the eyes, coming out the back of his head.[22]

According to Sergeant Sieker, who made the after-action-report, during the hottest part of the fight there were but three Texas Rangers doing battle: himself, Tom Carson, and Dick Russell. Sergeant Caruthers and Private Sam Henry were yet pulling up the rear due to a shortage of horsepower not guts, and Deputy Herridio was somewhere between fireworks and foothills. What about Red Bingham, that Missouri-born boy with probing gray eyes? Well, they were closed. Sergeant Ed Sieker continues, picking up the story at the juncture his bullet exited the owlhoot's skull:

> Bingham was to my left and about 35 yards in the rear when he was shot, through the heart. We charged the party & took their stronghold & then they surrendered. Had I known Bingham was Killed at that time, I should have Killed them all. But we had disarmed them before we Knew it. Then they prayed for mercy.... Bingham must have been Killed in the first volley, after we reached the top of the Mtn.[23]

Sergeant Seeker's feigned pronouncement "I should have Killed them all," is illuminating on more than one front and favorably, at that! Unsaid it speaks well of his character, personally. Had he really wanted to, Sergeant Sieker "could have Killed them all." In a much broader context the restraint—not seeking extralegal remedy in *la ley de fuga*—places the Texas Rangers, at least these Texas Rangers, on the path leading toward professionalism. The assertion that Sergeant Sieker was moving down the right road is buttressed by his sending Deputy Herridio down the nearest road, the one leading to Presidio and a justice of the peace, the court tasked with making rulings in matters of unnatural deaths. An Inquest was obligatory by law and Sergeant Sieker was a lawman, a good lawman. While Herridio was away on his mission, other police work was on tap: a crime-scene investigation and inventory and interrogation. The gunfire had erupted with a thunderous clap. Now, in the aftermath there was time for sorting. Just who were these fellows so anxious to kill Texas Rangers rather than stand still for questioning?

The outlaw lying dead was Jesse Graham; that's what would go in the Monthly Return. One of the others, the one credited with killing young Red Bingham, was the ever incorrigible Jessie Evans, that hardheaded and hardhearted veteran of numerous six-shooter scrapes and high crimes. August Gross, aka John Gross, another of the Sender & Siebenborn highjackers, was sitting on that rocky mountain top, eternally thankful—prayerful—that these Texas Rangers were enforcers, not executioners. The fourth fellow ultimately coughed up his right name, Charley Graham.[24]

On-the-ground inventory revealed that the mean gangsters had each been armed with six-shooters, while two carried Winchester carbines, and two others sported U.S. Government Springfield trapdoor single-shot rifles, .45-70s. Unfortunately, as was noted, Red Bingham's Winchester was recovered, a fresh cartridge stuffed but halfway into the carbine's loading gate: "Bingham died bravely, being in the act of loading his gun, when he received the fatal shot...."[25]

Sitting on top of that exposed mountain shelf quickly turned miserable, more than miserable. Two dead bodies were covered with woolen blankets—and a burning July sun. Three scared prisoners with hands tied tightly, hoping for no lynch-rope outcome, were unwillingly sharing space with five saddened and weary Rangers. Tom Carson's wounded horse was sucking air. Rigor mortis was setting in—fast—on two of the outlaws' dead horses. The incomparable smell of death permeated the battle site. All of a sudden, detonation! The impulsive thunderstorm was fully-loaded. Bolts of lighting shot spears of fear. Rumbling thunder announced its presence before cracking into earsplitting booms of rockslide dread. Then it rained— and rained—hard bombarding rain fell on the out-in-the-open posse and prisoners, drenching them wet with despair. Dismally the night passed.[26]

Morning light brought better news. Daytime would be clear. Hot, but clear, once humidity dropped somewhat, diluting death's steaming stench. And at a distance the Rangers could detect movement, two approaching riders: Deputy Herridio and part-time Justice of the Peace and storeowner Richard Daly, who would officiate at the formal Inquest. The ruling came as no surprise: "G. R. Bingham came to his death in the discharge of his duty—and Jesse Graham came to his death by resisting arrest."[27]

Subsequent to the official ruling Texas Rangers were in a quandary. Wholly dissimilar to Ranger Sonny Smith, who had been laid to rest with pomp and ceremony and a military band playing the dirge at Brownsville, Red Bingham rested on a mountain top far from town; for that matter, it was far from anywhere. The Rangers knew they must move their prisoners from the battleground to Fort Davis, a substantial distance north of the borderline. The baking July temperature was punishing. The hard truth disheartening, but real: "Bingham's body wouldn't admit of moving far...." Prior to launching the long march down the mountain and to Fort Davis, a shallow grave was chiseled. Reverently Red Bingham's body was interred. Then the "little squad showed him all the respect we [they] could. We formed and fired three volleys over the grave and with saddened hearts we wound through mountain passes, to [Fort] Davis, arriving safely with our prisoners."[28]

Reassured and thankful townsmen in Presidio and Pecos Counties were delighted, and understandably so. According to Sergeant Sieker there was a movement underfoot in Fort Davis and Fort Stockton to give the Texas Rangers "12 or $1400." Perhaps they pocketed greenback gratitude, maybe not.[29] Aside from whooping it up, there were legal necessities needing attention. The capture was but one step, the first step, in pushing defendants in front of that slow grinding wheel of justice: "The robbers Evans, Gunter & Graham have had preliminary examination before Judge Duke on charge of murder of private Bingham & committed without bail, it is necessary that we guard Jail until these men are tried in October...."[30]

In the short go, then, once again the Texas Rangers were prisoners of the prisoners. Pulling those assigned shifts guarding criminals, boring as it might be, is but par business for crime fighters. Routine business for defense lawyers is getting people off the hook or out of jail where they have opportunity to earn status as "bail jumpers." The other defendants, when given the chance, skipped. Jessie Evans, not as fortunate, entered the Texas Penitentiary as Inmate 9078—where he stayed eighteen months before he, too, went over the fence, blending into the masses of humanity but thus far lost to history.

Sergeant Sieker had made a pledge, one he honored. When weather turned cold during February the following year, he and other Rangers disinterred the body of Red Bingham, and reverently removed it to the Pioneer Cemetery in Fort Davis.[31]

Ranger Captain Neal Coldwell had telegrammed AG Jones that arrests of Evans and gang would put the "quietus on trouble heretofore existing here, except horse stealing by Mexicans...."[32] Coldwell's use of "heretofore" may have been spot on right. Alas, for the Texas Rangers' dance card, waltzing and warring to the tunes of six-shooters and Winchesters on the Devil's stage was far from *finis!*

Chapter 5

Frank Sieker
1885

For genealogical lineage few families come near matching the contributions to Texas Ranger history as do the Siekers. Four of Dr. Edward Armon Sieker's sons would—at one time or another—enlist in the Frontier Battalion's memorable Company D, a frontline unit with more than its fair share of ultimate sacrifices. The oldest of the four Ranger brothers was Lamartine Pemberton Sieker, best known to history as Lamar, but family, friends, and fellow Rangers simply called him Lam. Lam Sieker, a charter member of Company D, would rise through the ranks to a captaincy, and then assistant adjutant general of the state. Edward Armon Sieker, Jr., likewise was a Company D charter member, attaining the rank of sergeant, a position he held while leading the Presidio County chase after Jessie Evans' gang and the subsequent gunplay wherein Ranger Red Bingham gave up the ghost. While age-wise Tom Sieker fit between brothers Lamar and Ed, his entry date as a Company D Ranger was early on, too, November 13, 1876. The youngest of the four brothers and the last to sign on as a Texas Ranger is the subject of this sequence of events, Frank Edward Sieker.[1]

Though born in Baltimore, Maryland, Frank Sieker had corresponded with this or that brother and made the 1878 decision to go west. There, in the beginning, he would seek adventure eking out a few dollars chasing an ever-dwindling herd of buffalo wandering the open and unfenced grasslands of West Texas. Basing operations out of San Angelo, then still known as Across the River, the band of hunters closed the year with pegged hides and sober insight; the profitability of stalking and skinning buffalo was on the wane,the high-water mark for any guaranteed financial killing a year or two past. Yet a single man, but a fellow needing a job not only for filling empty pockets, but for the sake of pride as well, Frank Sieker thought he'd follow the footsteps of older brothers. [2]

Nepotism is not new. Therefore it should be no great revelation that seemingly not an eyebrow was raised on September 23, 1884, when Frank Sieker enlisted in Company D, the working unit Lam Sieker captained, and his brother Ed Sieker oversaw as a line-sergeant further down the chain-of-command.[3] Company D's history is rich with several distinctions, one of which is the frequency boys from the same family show up on the Muster Roll.

At the time of Frank Sieker's enlistment, Company D headquarters, christened Camp Leona, was pleasantly situated and shaded at the southern edge of the picturesque Texas Hill Country near Uvalde, Uvalde County. Although not positioned directly on the Texas/Mexican borderline, Rangers working from Camp Leona with regularity made scouts due west to the Rio Grande in what would soon become Val Verde County (Del Rio) and due south to the Rio Grande in Maverick County (Eagle Pass), as well as points between—and beyond.[4]

The transition from rookie to journeyman takes time. Private Frank Sieker may have acquired outdoors and marksmanship skills as a buffalo hunter, but he was a tenderfoot in the game of policing. To straighten out that subtly defined learning curve, Frank Sieker, as would all neophyte Rangers, underwent an apprenticeship under guidance of veterans. The crucial curriculum would not be learned in a stuffy classroom under tutelage of some naive would-be or wanna-be lawman who had never, ever faced a real bad man, but in the field, on-the-job-training by real Texas Rangers, fellows who had already survived and gainfully graduated a school of hard knocks. Differentiating with precision Private Sieker's enforcement activities while engaged in learning the ropes of the Texas Ranger business is problematic. Many are the summations in Ranger reports identifying only an officer or noncom leading the scout, such as "Captain Sieker and six men." The first report actually identifying Private Frank Sieker by name is the Monthly Return of December 1884, a tad over three months after swearing his oath. On December 31, 1884, Privates James V. Latham and Frank Sieker left Camp Leona to conduct a murder investigation near the headwaters of the West Nueces River.[5] Unfortunately the two Texas Rangers, after traveling 100 horseback miles, returned to Camp Leona on January 3, 1885, empty-handed, no evil murderer in tow.[6] Though he most certainly participated in intervening scouts, Frank Sieker is next particularly identified with Private Oscar D. Baker in their effort to locate "a shooter" in the Rio Frio canyon above the headquarters camp.[7] After scouting the canyon country of the Frio and Sabinal, Rangers Baker and Sieker returned to Camp Leona where they were posted with hot news.

Redeployment had been ordered by the adjutant general; trouble was brewing on the border. Company D's Lieutenant Frank Jones, after scouting to the Rio Grande below Carrizo Springs, determined that "everything [was] in a violent state of excitement with the citizens of Dimmitt [*sic*] Co. in arms expecting an invasion from Mexico."[8] Bigwigs at Austin reacted, ordering Texas Rangers to tidy up what they interpreted as a mess.

According to Sheriff Tom Oglesby of Maverick County, unapologetic cow stealers and coldhearted killers were jumping back and forth across the Rio Grande with daring—and impunity. In nearby Dimmit County, Sheriff Joe Tumlinson and his civilian posse had chased Mexican horse thieves across the Rio Grande into Mexico, but soon had to reverse course at high-speed, racing back into Texas barely escaping wholesale annihilation on foreign soil. On the Texas side outlaw brothers, sons of Rafael Reyes, were killed during an exchange of gunfire. Captain Sieker admitted there was "uneasiness among the Ranchmen who fear the Mexicans will Kill some Americans to avenge the Reyes boys deaths."[9] Even a Company D Texas Ranger was, well, not forced to, but did spit out a stream of Lucifer's Line exactness: "The Carrizo Springs people had got into some trouble with the Mexicans across the Rio Grande. Mexicans were coming across, stealing cattle and horses, and there was a lot of feeling up. It got so bad that white men were killing every Mexican they caught over the line, and Mexicans were killing some of the white men."[10] The bodies of three "Mexicans" punctured with bullets were found beside a road leading from the Rio Grande. There was no investigation, official or otherwise.[11]

Eventually a parlay of sorts took place on a neutral island commonly referred to as *Las Isles*, but tactically the meeting netted but temporary calm. Private Frank Sieker, if there at all, was but a spectator stationed on the Texas side, though his brother Captain Lam Sieker was a key player and negotiator.[12] Any sustained peace along the border was tenuous, at best. Complicating already touchy matters was the fact two differing societies were speaking two separate languages, a niggling exasperation colorfully drawn by the personal experience of an old-time cowman, Adolph Petree: "We went to Juan Reyes's house, and Mr. Tumlinson and I saw a Mexican leave there. We went and overtaken him and he reached down to get his gun.

And that damn boss man, old Bill Thornton, like to have shot him in to. I said, 'Don't pull your trigger. He hasn't drawed his gun yet!' The damn Mexican didn't want to give his gun up but finally dropped it. Showing he didn't want any fight. We told him to take the goddamn gun and go on. He couldn't talk a word of English and we couldn't talk a word of Mexican. That is hell, you know, when you get in that shape."[13]

In double quick time the Company D camp had been strategically located along San Ambrosia Creek, Maverick County, four miles from the troublesome Rio Grande and one mile from the corner where Dimmit (Carrizo Springs) and Webb (Laredo) Counties butted together.[14] Again working in tandem with Private Latham, Frank Sieker worked a seven-day detail, guarding a sheep shearing camp on the Negley Ranch. Absent anything worthwhile to report, Privates Frank Sieker and Jim Latham returned to the newly named Camp San Ambrosia on the fourth day of March, 1885.[15] For Private Sieker and a squadron of other Company D Rangers, it was the lull before the storm.

Whether or not two fellows—convicts—escaped a work detail or scaled an ivy-covered wall at the state penitentiary in Huntsville is somewhat hazy. The fact that hunting escapees was a Texas Ranger sphere of interest is not. Just prior to Thanksgiving of 1884—before camp was moved south—Corporal Wood Saunders and an unnamed Ranger had arrested Bill Dunman and John Grace, "two escaped convicts."[16] Perhaps these two escaped again, maybe not. There were, however, escapees on the dodge and the state's governor was not happy. He had been informed—correctly or not—that a pair of native Spanish-speaking accomplices had "turned the convicts loose."[17] Thinking the fugitives and/or the co-conspirators were in the area heading for the Rio Grande, Sergeant Benjamin Dennis Lindsey, a fire-breathing no nonsense Texas Ranger who couldn't and wouldn't abide sissies, fashioned a squadron of raring-to-go man-hunters to track them down: catch them or kill them. Taking with him Privates Austin Ira Aten, Ben C. Riley, Oscar Grant, C. D. Grant, C. W. Griffin, and Frank Sieker, as well as an outfitted pack-mule, Sergeant Lindsey departed Camp San Ambrosia on the last day of May 1885.

For the day Ira Aten and Ben Riley had been tasked with herding the pack-mule. Because they had been daydreaming or debating, the duo was dawdling along lazily and inattentively, separated from the other Rangers, who were riding a somewhat oblique trail to theirs. After traveling about twelve miles southeast of camp, Aten and Riley were awakened from complacency. In the distance they observed two mounted fellows, one leading an unsaddled horse. Sergeant Lindsey's little group could see the riders too, but due to recent rains having swollen the San Ambrosia and its ancillary arroyos and gullies their clear path was choked with mud, a hindrance that would retard—not stop—response. So, Aten and Riley, while not the closest Rangers to the unidentified riders, were by happenstance prepositioned to initiate the compulsory inquiry. It was but a foregone conclusion, those guys, whoever they were, owed Rangers an explanation—according to Ranger etiquette and in line with the Ranger mindset. On the other hand, the two "Mexicans" had a wildly different picture before them. Apolonio Gonzales and his thirteen-year-old son, Pedro, could clearly see two groups of heavily armed Anglos riding big stout horses. None wore uniforms. There were no badges pinned to their vests, glittering in the sunlight. There then loomed the perfect storm for tragedy. If father and son tarried they might be overrun, robbed and killed by madmen haunting this remote section of borderland looking for plunder. If Rangers hesitated the two suspected *mal hombres*—apparently horse thieves—very likely could get in the opening lick, making the first shot count for covering their getaway. Propriety of the place and time would not prohibit Texas Rangers from shooting first, asking questions later. Private Ira Aten was not hesitant in telling of such the first time around (emphasis added). Later the story would suffer a wee bit of corrective therapy:

> I was on pack drive that day and behind the others. B. C. Riley was with me. There were six of us in all. These two men were cutting across the country, and Sergeant Lindsey, who was a considerable distance ahead of us, started across a slough with his men and their horses bogged. Riley and I saw this and avoided the slough and took right in behind the two men. When about a hundred yards from them, *we opened fire* and they returned it, all of us shooting with Winchesters....[18]

With at least two Rangers and two "Mexicans" feverishly working levers of Winchester carbines and in a day well ahead of trustworthy ballistics technology, a complete shot by shot analysis and awarding a hit to this or that participant is not doable. There are bottom lines, however. Ranger Ben Riley caught a bullet in the thigh, another in the left shoulder, knocking him out of the saddle. Then according to Ira, almost in a tone of abject incredulity: "And they commenced shooting at me."[19] Continuing with his play by play coverage Aten remembered: "I was about one hundred yards when I commenced shooting. One was a young man and one was an old man. I kept on coming, not crowding them too fast, and shooting at them."[20] Plainly it was a hot fight, a running fight—not particularly a necessary fight—but once that initial bullet spiraled down the barrel everyone had skin in the game, the fat was in the fire.

Not unexpectedly while Private Aten was exchanging rifle fire, Sergeant Lindsey and the other Rangers racing to do battle had, indeed, become "bogged." Near up to their hocks in muck the Rangers' horses were madly struggling to free themselves. Had not the situation been so serious the gyrations might have appeared comical, the bucking and lunging and humped backs, with wildly flailing Rangers grabbing for the apple—saddle horn—trying to hang on for dear life. Unluckily one Ranger, Private Griffin, couldn't maintain his seat in the saddle. Griffin had been pitched high and come down hard, knocked out of breath and out of commission with a broken collarbone.

Somehow, someway, Private Frank Sieker topped out. His horse had broken free. The young Ranger did not dilly-dally. He could see Ira Aten was alone, but not motionless. Winchesters were barking. Frank Sieker raced to back up Aten despite the gunfire.

Ranger Sieker spurring madly to close ground between warring parties tightly clutched the reins in one hand, his Colt's six-shooter in the other. From the corner of his eye, during the fog of war, Sieker's fast-approaching charge had caught Ira Aten's notice, fleetingly. With a Ranger riding to his rescue from behind and two "Mexicans" in front of him Aten wasn't befuddled with hesitancy; he kept shooting. While the gelding galloped beneath him, Ranger Frank Sieker began shooting, too. Almost at the same instant Frank began pulling in beside him, Ira Aten heard a heart rending scream: "Oh, my God!" Refocusing his attention Ira saw Sieker "falling back from his horse." Such a dramatic dismount was bizarre, according to Ira Aten: "They don't usually fall back from the horse, but forward, but the horse was going very fast, and he fell backward—still holding the six-shooter, you know." Private Frank Sieker had caught a bullet to the heart, a dead man falling. Ira Aten could ill-afford to remain idle: "I turned back and kept shooting, and saw one of the men drop his gun and fall low on his horse. I knew that I had hit him.... I saw the second fellow fall low on his horse just as he got to the top of a hill."[21]

Seemingly, in the short term, Sergeant Ben Lindsey's little squadron of gritty Texas Rangers had undergone a humiliating thrashing. Private Griffin was painfully moaning with a fractured collarbone; Private Riley was wholly incapacitated, one bullet in the thigh, another having punched through his left shoulder; and a younger brother of the company's commander, Frank E. Sieker, lay dead, lifeless atop Webb County's dirt.[22] It was Webb County, wasn't it? Well, that persnickety little annoyance would soon become a legal dispute of significant weight.

Sergeant Lindsey had been poured from the mold idealistically cast for the mythical Ranger, the one riot Ranger, the fearless Ranger, the on-no-account derailed Ranger. In Ben Lindsey's case it was for real! There was something else very real about Sergeant Ben Lindsey: He was a pragmatist, not a fool, not a reckless fellow inclined to emotionally slip off of the half-cock notch. After reuniting with Aten, Sergeant Lindsey quickly determined that Apolonio and Pedro Gonzales had sought refuge at the Loyas' Ranch on the Rio Grande. From the crest of a nearby hill the Rangers, those still in one piece, could see the commotion of armed *vaqueros*. Sergeant Lindsey's deportment was unruffled, his orders crystal clear but short—just four words: "We will go down."[23] And they did!

What next transpired can—absent a hint of derisiveness—be best portrayed as a "Mexican standoff." The two suspects, both slightly wounded, were in custody of Pendincia Herrera, a provisional deputy of the Webb County sheriff, and "about fifteen Mexicans, all armed." The bone of contention was big. Pendincia Herrera intractably wanted to take his prisoners to the county seat at Laredo, eighty miles away. Ben Lindsey demanded custody, making known his intention to remove father and son to Carrizo Springs, county seat of Dimmit County, where they could stand legal formalities. Lindsey bent to practicality:

> Our force was too small to take them to Carrizo Springs so I then told him [Herrera] we would go to Laredo with them. It was agreed that three Mexicans & three rangers should carry them.[24]

In making this part of a long story short, for diehard Texas Ranger aficionados there is an unsettling outcome. Without incident the prisoners were taken to Laredo, tuned over to the county sheriff and ensconced in the local lockup—for about thirty minutes. Sheriff

Dario Gonzales was kin to Apolonio and Pedro Gonzales and the story's twist should not come as a shocker. Father and son filed a formal Complaint that they had been unwarrantedly assaulted by a pack of scruffy looking and heavily armed strangers. Of course they didn't know, and in fact had no way of knowing they were Texas Rangers— and they had acted solely in self-defense. They had not been up to any mischief whatsoever, but had been in search of a stray horse, which they located and were heading back for the river when attacked by Anglo madmen. The aggressors hollered words in English, but Apolonio and Pedro were not bilingual and could not comprehend anything lacking an interpreter. Sheriff Gonzales bought into the story. With legally drawn warrants in hand, backed up by deputies— even if deputized for just one day—the sheriff turned Rangers into jailbirds, allowing Pedro and Apolonio to fly the coop—across the river and into Mexico.

One might think such was chicanery and met with universal condemnation. Such thinking would prove wrongheaded. The widely read *El Paso Times*, picking up the drumbeat of public opinion, reminded readership that Apolonio Gonzales "had been noted as the best guide and Indian trailer in this country and owns a large ranch."[25] The faraway *Dallas Daily Herald* punched in with a hard-hitting fact check: "Gonzales bears a high character here and his statements are received with implicit credence, he has always been honest, and he and his boy acted in self-preservation."[26] The *Corpus Christi Caller* was kind in declaring that "no more gallant ranger ever drew a breath" than Ranger Frank Sieker, then pointedly hurled its barb: "carelessness and overconfidence will down the best of them."[27] Certainly it was more than apparent that Apolonio and Pedro were not escaped convicts, nor were they the ne'er-do-wells who had "turned them loose." Ira Aten knew all too well, in a subdued tone, admitting: "As to whether they were criminals, I guess they were all criminals in there [Loyas Ranch]."[28] Webb County citizens sitting on the grand jury didn't think so: "Some days ago they retuned bills of indictment against all the rangers who took part in the recent battle on the Rio Grande, between the rangers and a supposed (?) lot of thieves; but failed to find evidence to indict the Mexicans who were in the same fight."[29] Adding institutional insult to perceived injury, a full dozen grand jurymen formally petitioned Governor John Ireland to have Captain Sieker's Company D Rangers removed from their section of the border: "Harm may occur at any moment, if the company remains. The citizens are excited and much opposed to the company remaining among them."[30] Lest there not be any untoward misunderstanding, of the twelve petitioners—only two were of Mexican decent, Juan Ortiz and C. Benavides.[31]

Is there any wonder why Captain Sieker was feverishly working to geographically place the gunplay in Dimmit County? Rangers might receive a fairer—at least more sympathetic—hearing at Carrizo Springs, at least according to his way of thinking. Legal shenanigans and loopholes were okay. Orchestrating a jailbreak was out of the question, even for Texas Rangers.

Meanwhile, downcast Rangers languished in the Webb County Jail. The period of inactivity was productive; the Rangers could make sure their independent versions of what happened were not too independent. Thus the story for public consumption and official Ranger reports became:

> They on seeing the Rangers advancing on them at once ran and were pursued. Aten and Riley came up with them first and demanded their surrender to which they agreed and when Riley reached out to take a gun from one of them he suddenly and without warning shot and the men who were Mexicans began firing on Aten.[32]

Sergeant Lindsey, in writing, notified Captain Sieker that everyone was on the same page: "I find by talking with Riley & Aten that they tell substantially as above."[33]

Needless to say in the state's bureaucratic and legislative circles such a freely publicized legal to-do was a first-class embarrassment. Too, it supplied figurative ammo for those folks who harkened great pleasure in publicly and privately sniping at Texas Rangers. In the end, after twenty-six days in jail, the pale and sickly looking Rangers had their bail posted and were released from the calaboose. Private Ira Aten was cognizant of reality, disturbing reality, but reality nevertheless: "our feeling was too great after that against the Mexicans for them to leave us there, as they knew we would be killing Mexicans whenever we got a chance."[34] With a grand jury howling for removal of Rangers from their immediate neighborhood, and the front office well aware that individual Rangers, embittered Rangers, might extract a blood payment for the Rangers' inconvenient and forced vacation, a decision was made. A not ambiguous order followed, forthwith: "I would say that you are hereby instructed to move your company to some point in the vicinity of Uvalde, Tex."[35] The adjutant general had spoken. Captain Lam Sieker moved camp. Aten chimed in: "The Governor ordered us moved from San Ambrosia after we got into our trouble. Our cases were dismissed, you know."[36]

Admirably Frank Sieker had charged into the jaws of death won over to a notion that Aten and Riley were battling escaped convicts, or if not them, two scurrilous Mexican thieves leading a stolen horse. The picture before him had been black and white. Apolonio and Pedro had either jumpily opened or fearfully returned fire "believing they were being pursued by a band of robbers." Father and son saw no gray. There was a hard bottom line, epitomized in a headline; the whole affair had been "**A Deplorable Mistake**."[37] Sometimes perspective was all that mattered along Lucifer's Line. The bullet was indifferent.

Chapter 6
Charles H. V. Fusselman
1890

John Wayne and Jeff Bridges playing the part of Deputy U.S. Marshal Rooster Cogburn undeniably owned a plateful of true grit—on the Silver Screen. For a catchy stage moniker the subject of this six-shooter vignette may have very well been outnamed, but not outgunned. Charles Henry Vanvalkenburg "Charley" Fusselman was the real deal, a Texas Ranger with documentable true grit. And, lots of it!

Charley Fusselman was not a native Texan. The son of a carpenter and farmer, Charley was born on the sixteenth day of July 1866 in Greenbush, Sheboygan County, which lay on the eastern edge of Wisconsin touching Lake Michigan. By the time he was a teenager the family had relocated to Texas, first settling near Corpus Christi, but then moving to nearby Live Oak County (George West), close to Lagarto in the southern section of the county.[1] With salty Gulf breezes blowing west across brushy plains carrying necessary moisture, Live Oak County, at the time, was cow country—good cow country. Stagecoaches running back and forth between Corpus Christi and San Antonio stopped at Oakville, then the county seat, six times a week. The little burg could proudly lay claim, until later bypassed by the railroad, of having several stores, two hotels, one livery stable, a primary school, and a couple of churches.[2] Oakville was the hub, and early day ranching spokes jutted from there. Charley's uncle, Sam Fusselman, maintained his stock raising interests in Live Oak County, too, and by the best guess it's presumed that his nephew would pick up the catch-rope, following the life of an 1880s cowboy.[3] It was not to be. Charley Fusselman picked up a Winchester.

Having ridden into the southern reaches of Duval County, twenty-one-year-old Charley Fusselman made inquiry at the hamlet of Realitos. He was in search of Camp Collins, the headquarters campsite for the Frontier Battalion's Company D, at the time commanded by

Captain Frank Jones. Charley Fusselman must have made a favorable impression on Captain Jones, at least favorable enough to land a line on the Muster & Payroll. On May 25, 1888, Charley Fusselman became a Texas Ranger.[4]

Private Fusselman's name does not appear on disciplinary reports, nor does it shine during his tenure as a rookie Texas Ranger. There is a commonsense lesson in that. Seemingly, Charley Fusselman had his head down, nose to the grindstone, and was performing at a satisfactory level, steadily earning the dollar a day the state was paying: $90 per quarter.

Although Charley Fusselman was a horseback Ranger, ever-expanding railroad connections would have a dramatic influence on his and all other Texas Rangers' working lives. Heretofore Texas Ranger deployments had normally involved squadron or near company-level responses. Now, with spider-web railroad tracks criss-crossing the state, the stationing of one or two Rangers at a specific site was feasible. Should a situation arise calling for a number of Rangers, horses could be loaded into a stock-car and in but a few short hours the entire company could converge at any given point to run down robbers, quell a riot, guard a jailhouse, or keep peace during a labor union strike. In answer to justifiable pleas for help from West Texas, a Company D detachment was sent to Alpine, formerly known to history as Murphyville, county seat of the recently created (1887) Brewster County.[5]

Hardly had Private Fusselman arrived at Alpine before speeding events overtook the gangling but gutsy Ranger. After but a stay of less than a week, three of Private Fusselman's traveling companions resigned; Corporal J. Walter Durbin, along with Bazzell Lamar "Baz" (sometimes Bass) Outlaw, and John R. Hughes had traded their silver *cinco pesos* for the promise of gold. The trio had taken employment with mining man William O. Grady at the Fronteriza Mine across the Rio Grande in Mexico. Mr. Grady needed hard men to guard the payrolls and profits, and the three ex-Texas Rangers needed hard money. There was a vacuum. Private Charley Fusselman was promoted to corporal, although Captain Frank Jones was less than enthusiastic: "Fusselman is a good man but is somewhat lacking in experience, he having been in the service only a year."[6]

Within days he was to earn those figurative corporal stripes—in spades. The first sheriff of Brewster County was ex-Texas Ranger Captain James T. Gillespie.[7] Receiving an urgent telegraph message,

Sheriff Gillespie was in a quandary. The folks at the Haymond Station east of Marathon were in desperate straits. Whether he was drunk or crazy was of little import; on June 3, 1889, Donaciano Beslanga had run amok. He was frantically shooting at frightened passersby having managed to wound at least one unlucky chap. Pressing business—legitimate pressing business—prohibited Sheriff Jim Gillespie from responding personally. Corporal Fusselman, doing what was expected of a good Ranger, stepped up, volunteering to accompany a Brewster County deputy sheriff and quickly put the quietus on Beslanga's idiocy before an innocent onlooker or passenger was murdered.

What follows is a chilling version from an actual participant, not a fretful spectator's interpretation. Too critical or an over-editing of Corporal Fusselman's official report for grammatical purposes might tend to make it palatable for those demanding absolute correctness, but such processes mask the real taste: A dish absent the peppery fire of realism. It's best served piping hot and spicy with but a dash of touchup. Charley Fusselman's recapping recipe went straight to Adjutant General King at Austin:

> yesterday morning while in discharge of my duty as Ranger I killed one mexican name Donaciano Beslanga. I will explain.
>
> Sunday eve as I road in to Alpine I met Capt Gillespie who had a telegram from Haymond station, stating that the now deceased had the town terorized. he had shot one man a bad flesh wound & was riding through town shooting & all was endanger of their lives. Capt Gillespie ask me to go with his Deputy & make the arrest. well we took the 8.52 train & when we arrived at Haymond the now deceased had gone to Maxon Springs. we got a hand car & went down but did not find him & was informed over the wire that he was at Haymond. we returned on 3.20 train & the Deputy gave up & retuned to Alpine. I stayed to try & find some other trace of him & found that he was at Maxon Springs & we had missed him by the inadequate description so I borrowed a mule & went again to Maxon Springs. found he had left at sun rise. I lay & watched his wife until 10 at night when a heavy storm blew up which drove now deceased in to camp his home for shelter. I run on him but he sliped me as it was so dark.

I followed his course to watter tank & as I was looking under the
tank for him. lightning flashed & he shot at me at about 100 yards.
I did not see where he was until he fired second shot, then I run
toward him & returned the shot. lightning flashed & he was down
on track & fired several shots & run & I lost him as it was so dark
& raining so hard. next morning I got a rifle & took his trail at daylight when about ¾ mile from Station I heard him cough. I went
toward him & the instant I saw him he saw me & sprang up to his
knees. I could see there was no chance of his giving up as he had a
bad expression on his face so I fired as he did both at same time.
witnesses said that the two shots were so near together that they
could just be distinguished, then about 15 shots were exchanged
all his happened in about 20 seconds. I emptied my gun run in on
him grabbed his gun & shot him once with pistol before he would
give up. he was hit 8 times 5 shots were fatal. he would of fought
10 minutes longer if I had no grabbed his gun & took it away from
him. I then wired Gillespie who came right with Justice & held
inquest & we returned to Alpine. The officers all say I am justify-
able in the killing as it was in self defence in the Discharge of my
Duty. Please excuse this long explanation.[8]

Indeed, Corporal Fusselman was excused of his long explanation by
Texas Ranger hierarchy, but more importantly excused by Justice of
the Peace J. R. Dawson, who at Inquest ruled the killing had been
justified, as Fusselman was acting "in the discharge of his duties as
an officer...."[9]

The following month Charley Fusselman assumed an undercover
persona, something he didn't have to do.[10] Working in the southern
reaches of Presidio County, not very far north of the Rio Grande,
before he became a face all too familiar, the young Ranger corporal
had covertly adopted the name Clem H. Fox for the task of ferreting
out parties responsible for a stagecoach robbery.[11] Stagecoach robbers may have given him the slip, but Corporal Fusselman did not
miss notice.

On the nineteenth day of June 1889, but a few days after the
killing of Beslanga, Paul Fricke, United States Marshal for the Western District of Texas, had cross-deputized Ranger Fusselman as one
of his field agents. The dual commissioning, not at all an uncommon practice in wild expanses of the frontier west, now empowered
the Ranger with investigative and arrest authority for federal law,

as well as enforcing statutes of Texas' Penal Code. Particularly U.S. Marshal Fricke noted that Ranger Fusselman could now actively— and legally—pursue violators such as "Smugglers and 'mescalleros' [liquor smugglers]." In fact, according to Marshal Fricke, the police work of the Rangers and the Deputy U.S. Marshals did for practical purposes "Dovetail" and in most instances, "very nicely."[12] Whether it was an unbending strict adherence to bureaucratic policy or a case of plain jealousy will most likely remain vague. Captain Frank Jones, who was not dually commissioned as a federal officer, was person- ally irked that Fusselman was, having "instructed [him] to resign his commission as Deputy Marshal because from information I had rece'd, I derived it hurtful to the interest of the State and am firmly of that opinion yet."[13] Infighting? Captain Jones lost the argument. Marshal Fricke didn't.

The August 16, 1889, feud and riot and killings in the city of Rich- mond led to the appointment of Company D's 1st Sergeant Ira Aten as the new sheriff for Fort Bend County.[14] Owing to his seemingly unconquerable tenacity and commendable work ethic Corporal Fus- selman was promoted, replacing Aten as the company's top noncom.[15] He remained stationed in the Big Bend country directing enforce- ment actions of Rangers assigned to the West Texas detachment.

Even a cursory review of Company D Monthly Returns reveals that Sergeant Fusselman was a whirlwind of activity, leading scouts and arresting *mal hombres* along the Rio Grande alleged to have sto- len horses, cattle, and goats, with a few highjackers and murderers thrown in for good measure.[16] Even U.S. Marshal Fricke was crediting Sergeant Fusselman with reducing crime along the border: "Fussel- man is an active and valuable peace officer and I am informed that since he has been a Deputy Marshal, there is decided less Smuggling and mescal, reducing horse stealing from Mexico, etc. than there was some months ago."[17] Good police work involves arrests, and corre- spondingly sometimes those folks demand their day in court.

Whether he responded to issuance of a subpoena or was just requested to make an appearance is moot. The morning of April 17, 1890, found Sergeant Fusselman in El Paso, a witness for the prose- cution most likely. It will later be clear as to what hat he had removed when answering the courtroom crier's call: That of a Ranger or that of a U.S. Deputy Marshal?[18] Attendant with minutiae dragging legal procedures and protocols in both federal and state court is an inces- sant expenditure of downtime for the peace officer. Posturing in the standby mode is but routine duty for a good lawman, a lawman doing a good job. Sergeant Charley Fusselman had time to kill.

Sergeant Fusselman wandered into the office of El Paso County Sheriff James H. White. Not surprisingly the sheriff was absent, sessions of court demanding his presence. Holding down the office was Deputy Frank B. Simmons who was engaged in conversation with George Herold, city policeman and the man generally credited with tapping out the lights of Sam Bass during the Round Rock shoot-out. The congenial chatter came to an abrupt end when the door suddenly swung open. In stepped, breathless and keyed up, John H. Barnes, an El Paso County stockman with a ranch at Munday Springs, eight miles north of town in the Franklin Mountains. Barnes had a story to tell and blurted it out. Sometime during the night thieves had butchered one of his calves and stolen several of his horses. Barnes told the all-ears officers that upon discovering remains of the skinned carcass he tracked the thieves. That is, until he suddenly came face to face with "a villainous looking Mexican whose appearance indicated that he meant to shoot if Barnes insisted on advancing."[19] Choosing common sense over foolhardiness Barnes did an aboutface, then raced for El Paso to report the crime and enlist aid. Once the ever-so-slow grinding wheel of justice begins grinding, judges generally don't tolerate interruption. Pending the gavel hammering an adjournment all those expected to be there, best be there. Therein lay the crux of a problem. Sheriff White and Deputy U.S. Marshal Bob Ross were busily jumping to the court's whim. Deputy Simmons, in the sheriff's absence was, if not caged, then certainly confined by obligatory duties at the sheriff's office. The bilingual George Herold was a genuine tough cookie, gunfighter if need be, and a holy terror when it came to trailing horse or cattle thieves.[20] Sergeant Fusselman had already proved his mettle, and was by now widely known throughout far West Texas as being a "very active, alert and determined man, and in the pursuit of thieves and desperadoes never lets up till he gets them, and is not at all particular what condition their bodies may be in when he does get them—so he gets them...."[21] A newspaperman's hyperbole aside, Sergeant Fusselman in this instance knew professionalism called for response and he was not known as a Texas Ranger who would step backwards. He, too, knew that stealing horses and illicitly butchering another's calf were not federal violations. He would act, but in the role of a Ranger, not a Deputy U.S. Marshal. Volunteering to lend a helping hand was Herold, always ready for a skirmish, even though he was now fifty years old. Sergeant Fusselman having come to El Paso by train had left his rifle in the hotel room, borrowed Sheriff White's horse, and scavenged a Winchester from Bob Ross. Then he, Herold, and John Barnes hit the high road for the Franklin Mountains hoping to overtake a band of horse thieves before they crossed into New Mexico Territory and then turned south into Mexico.[22]

Without inordinate difficulty the three-man posse quickly cut the trail, and while the sun was yet high overhead had captured straggling rearguard Ysidoro Pasos.[23] Somewhat emboldened by the arrest the posse charged on. By sheer luck of the draw Charley Fusselman was riding the fastest horse and took the lead, followed by Herold, with Barnes bringing up the rear guarding Pasos. Out of the blue Charley Fusselman cleared a ridge line and inadvertently rode squarely into the outlaws' *siesta* spot, a lair littered with cooking utensils, blankets, butchered beef, a sack of flour, clothing, other campsite trappings, and a whole "bucket full of tortillas." The thieves had heard Fusselman coming and quickly found cover. The ambush set. Dumbfounded that the camp seemed abandoned Sergeant Fusselman scanned the surrounding rock formations—it was too late. The booming repot of a rifle caught his attention; the zinging whistle of a bullet turned his head. An outlaw's first shot had flown wide of the mark. Not taking time to withdraw the borrowed Winchester from the borrowed saddle scabbard strapped to the borrowed horse, Sergeant Fusselman jerked out his Colt's .45 six-shooter and returned fire, simultaneously screaming warning and orders to his startled comrades: "Boys, we are in for it, and let's stay with it."[24] The words had barely been spoken when Charley Fusselman's head wrenched sideways, a bullet entering through his right temple and carrying "away nearly the whole of the right lobe of the brain." He hadn't heard the next shot. It had entered under his chin, exited through his left ear.[25]

Sheriff White's saddle was empty. Sergeant Fusselman lay dead on the canyon's floor.[26] Herold and Barnes smartly made a hasty retreat; the number of assailants unknown, the hellfire of bullets thick. Ysidoro Pasos during the chaos advantaged himself of opportunity, and "sprang into the saddle and made his escape."[27] The news broke hard at El Paso. A hurriedly fashioned posse consisting of Deputy U.S. Marshal Bob Ross, El Paso County Deputy Sheriff Dick Blacker, El Paso County Constable Charley Patterson and eight others took to the field. It was more-or-less understood: "If the thieves are captured and it proves true that they have killed Fusselman it will go hard with his murderers."[28]

Meanwhile telegrams blistered forth. Sheriff White's chief deputy, B. G. Duval, notified U.S. Marshal Fricke, at San Antonio:

> C. H. Fusselman is reported to have been killed in attempting to arrest some horse thieves about ten miles from here to-day. Have sent out posse with ambulance and surgeon.[29]

Quite naturally Ranger officialdom was notified and the flurry of telegrams and letters of notification are retrievable, but it is not necessary to repeat them in whole, verbatim.[30] Perhaps the simplest and most poignant was the one sent to John R. Hughes who had quit the guard business in Mexico and returned to the Rangers: "Have fusselman [sic] nicely buried and write his father."[31]

Unfortunately the posse failed to locate the gang of killers and thieves, but their identities were not any well-guarded secret: Gerónimo Parra aka José Nuñez, Marcus Rico, Ysidoro Acosta, and of course the aforementioned Ysidoro Pasos were the gangsters.[32] With regret, but thankfully, the posse did locate the dead body of Ranger Fusselman, still in one piece before being torn to shreds by ravaging coyotes or cougars. Reverently Doctor G. H. Sowers examined the body and assisted with putting it in the wagon driven by Frank Gaskey. On the day following the murder, at one o'clock in the afternoon, Fusselman's lifeless form was returned to mourning El Paso: "As it passed down San Antonio Street, passersby became silent, respectfully doffing their wide-brimmed hats. The sorrowful cortege turned into the Star Stable."[33] A few minutes later, Tivolor Riverall and Juan C. Franco followed herding eighteen horses, along with two cows and a calf, animals belonging to John Barnes, and discarded by the thieves in their hasty flight two jumps ahead of the posse.[34] Sheriff White's horse was not among them.

An unnamed deputy U.S. Marshal, probably Bob Ross, had also messaged the U.S. Marshal clarifying the jurisdictional status Sergeant Fusselman was carrying at the time of his death, a delicate matter soon to be administratively significant.

> Sheriff White has taken charge of Fusselmer's [sic] body just brought in, and will attend to funeral unless otherwise advised by family. He was acting as State officer at the time of the killing.[35]

Why did it matter whether Fusselman was acting in the capacity of a Ranger or Deputy U.S. Marshal? Well, there is a practical reason, a simple reason. The murdering thieves had sneakily made off with Sheriff White's saddle horse and Deputy U.S. Marshal Ross' gun—a Winchester. Sergeant Fusselman wasn't on any federal business in the Franklin Mountains when he was killed: It was an easy call. Lawmen White and Ross sought reimbursement from the State of Texas: $40 for a horse, $15 for a gun. Doctor Sowers also submitted his bill for $10 to the state, not the federal government, "for going out to where Fusselman was Killed."[36] These financial settlements—if there were any—have thus far dodged historical notice. An undertaker's bill to the State of Texas was approved, and that letter is retrievable.[37]

Though the funeral was not on a grandiose scale with the Fusselman family far away, the twenty-three-year-old Ranger was peacefully laid to rest in El Paso's prominent Concordia Cemetery—temporarily. The whole El Paso community was outraged, mad, damn mad. U.S. Marshal Fricke pledged $100 out of his pocket. Local deputy sheriffs coughed up a matching $100. Citizens and businessmen and bankers kicked in an additional $517. The state of Texas added $250. The reward was to be paid upon capture and conviction of the murderers. Lawmen were on the lookout, guarding Rio Grande crossings into Mexico. And, too, a number of private houses were raided. Several days later wording of the bounty notice was changed to read: "For the capture dead or alive of the parties implicated in the killing of Fusselman."[38]

In an act of solidarity—brothers of the badge—Charley Fusselman's "fine Winchester" had been recovered from his hotel room, and instead of holding it for family the rifle was raffled—with a purpose. Police Officer Jim Martin won the lottery, but there was a tacit understanding among area lawmen, best clarified by an unobtrusive blip in the *El Paso Times*: "Deputy Dick Blacker who is with the posse is armed with Fusselman's gun, which Officer Martin loaned him with the hope that it would avenge Fusselman's death in case the murders resist arrest."[39] Really there was little doubt there would be resistance if the yahoos were hemmed in. This was yet the bloody border, yet the day of *la ley de fuga*.

Shortly, Fusselman's brother John arrived in El Paso. He had the gravesite exhumed and escorted Charley's body home to Live Oak County. There it was peacefully laid to rest in the Lagarto Cemetery on April 29, 1890.[40] Charley Fusselman was lost but not forgotten. Though it took ten years, and is a riveting story within itself, Gerónimo Parra was hanged in El Paso for his part in the Ranger's death.[41]

So, while that fictionalized hard-drinking one-eyed Deputy U.S. Marshal based out of Fort Smith owns the memorable first name of Rooster, it's fair to postulate that Charley Fusselman was the real gamecock, a Texas Ranger with true grit.

Chapter 7

John F. Gravis
1890

Downstream from its flow through gigantic Presidio County the Rio Grande makes its most prominent dip—the big bend—in the extreme southern section of Brewster County. Both counties mutually share geographical designation: The Big Bend Country. The seat of government for Presidio County is Marfa, sixty miles due north from the river.[1] Situated on Cibola Creek, southeast of the rocky Chinati Mountains' foothills, between the blustery border town of Presidio and the county seat is Shafter, only eighteen miles above the Rio Grande. In its heyday Shafter was booming—literally.

At the time this ill-fated story unfolds bitter legal rows over land titles had already been resolved by the Texas Supreme Court. The Presidio & Cibola Mining Company was now, 1890, in full swing, employing near 300 men, mostly of Mexican ancestry. Silver ore was the product, profit was the game.[2] A workforce of lonesome men is manageable providing there is an escape valve for venting off the steam. An eighteen-mile horseback ride to Presidio or crossing the river into Ojinaga for purposes of lustful indulgence was not an everyday undertaking, not for men working twelve-hour shifts. The forty-two mile excursion to lively Marfa for satisfying such personal wants or needs was out of the question. Solution for such misery was ubiquitously easy throughout the American frontier West, Presidio County included: Take sin to the boys if they couldn't manage the trip on their own.

After a hard day's work, lifting glasses and/or raising skirts in Shafter was uncomplicated pastime, a welcome and titillating diversion.[3] Though a hellcat could go berserk and commit murder, sometimes not even an eyebrow was raised: "A Mexican woman prostitute killed an American at Shafter last night. He was no loss to the Country, but more killing may follow."[4] At out-of-the-way Shafter there was an extra persnickety phenomenon: Some folks wouldn't work.

Mexican *banditos* and Texas outlaws and a parasitical sporting crowd found Shafter to their liking. Shafter had lots of iniquitous dives and little law. Cutthroats gravitate to decadence.

The honest hardworking citizens were appalled. They began clamoring for a Texas Ranger presence: "Ranchmen on River are very impatient for rangers to go to Shafter or River."[5] Writing from Marfa, Ranger Private Calvin Grant "Cal" Aten noted that the arena of far West Texas was overly populated with "a lot of cowardly thieves and murderers in which this country abounds."[6] In the course of just one partial year intelligence-gathering mission the following information was assimilated: A Mexican was murdered on the tenth day of February 1889; a horse was stolen and crossed into Mexico; a horse and bridle was stolen at Shafter; Marcos Siog "cut one mexican very badly"; twenty-six horses were stolen in Mexico and crossed into Texas; three mules were stolen at Shafter; four horses were smuggled across the Rio Grande; a Mr. Goodman was robbed of $500 on the Texas side; A. C. Daily reported that "Mexicans were killing his cattle all the time, and he has lost 12 head in the month of July"; and Presidio County Deputy Sheriff George McCarty had arrested a "mexican for horse stealing and the prisoner was taken away from him by six armed men." The writer summarized: "I have Rangered from Brownsville to this place [and] this frontier is more in kneed [sic] of Rangers than any section I ever was in."[7] And on the opposite bank of the Rio Grande "six or eight" wanted fugitives were avoiding Lone Star lawmen despite best efforts to lure them into Texas.[8] That same year it was noted that "there is considerable stealing going on in & about Shafter & a greater amount of Smuggling which we might break up stationed for a time there...." A few months later in another missive to Ranger headquarters at Austin the top-brass was updated: "Since Aug. 17, 1889 there has been 7 murders committed in & near Presidio Co. & the murderers taken refuge in mexico & some of them american citizens & no steps can be taken to get them, the mexicans in Mexico seems to uphold them."[9] Southern Presidio County was both a figurative and literal powder keg.

Temporarily turning the compass southeast and journeying downriver is necessary for eventually moving the story back to the Big Bend Country. On February 24, 1890, a twenty-two-year-old cowboy living in or near Laredo, Webb County, made the most fateful trip of his life. Sitting tall in the saddle, the fair complected John F. Gravis had ridden due north forty miles and met with the

Adjutant General of Texas at Encinal, La Salle County. The role local Texas politics played in such a meeting between the top dog and a pup is more than murky, but the outcome is, or least it should not be, any shocker. AG William King signed Gravis up as a Private in Company F, Frontier Battalion, headquartered at Rio Grande City, but shortly moved to Edinburg, Hidalgo County.[10]

At the time Company D was maintaining satellite detachments in far West Texas, but due to certain citizens demanding their removal from Uvalde County, company headquarters was in the process of being shifted to the wild and real woolly town of Cotulla, La Salle County, with Company F on the drawing board to be redeployed somewhere in South Texas—again.[11] Provisionally Private Gravis was to stand by with Company D at Cotulla awaiting further orders.[12] Most young men entering law enforcement want a taste of adventure, and Cotulla and surrounding La Salle County were action-packed. It would have been fair to sit rookie Gravis down in front of area physician Doctor J. W. Hargus for a preview of what might lie ahead for neophyte Texas Rangers. The good sawbones knew plenty, but then again, not too much: "more than once I was led blindfolded into a thicket to doctor a wounded outlaw. I have treated gunshot wounds of 259 men and have seen 108 men with bullet holes in them that did not need treating."[13] Cotulla was one of those exceptional tough spots in the Old West where a man's—even a lawman's—reputation for being bad was worth less than a bucket of warm spit. Rocking chair talk was cheap. The moment at hand was what mattered at Cotulla; if a man wanted to survive he'd best be able to "prove that he covered the ground he stood on."[14]

On the eighth day of April 1890 Private John F. Gravis officially transferred into Company D, yet working out of Cotulla.[15] It may be suggested—though not proven—that Private John Gravis' head began to spin watching government bureaucracy at work. What he thought about moving to the Big Bend country goes unrecorded, but he was going. On next to the last day of May under orders of Captain Frank Jones, Company D Rangers "broke camp in La Salle County and started to Presidio County."[16] Three days later the Company D boys were industriously unloading boxcars and stock-cars at Marfa, their supposed new headquarters.[17] Two days later they executed a quick scout to Shafter.[18] A touch of favorable public relations was smart. Some honestly tough law enforcement was necessary.

Already a petition with over fifty signatures, including those of pioneer ranchman Milton Favor and Bill Noyes, Presidio & Cibola mining mogul, had been hand-delivered to Governor L. S. Ross at Austin. One and all they wanted a company—or portion of a company—of Texas Rangers stationed at Shafter.[19] Although the exacting conversations cannot be recreated, there's little doubt Private Gravis and his companions thrashed about that headline news earlier emanating from Shafter. It seems that Ruff Baker, an alleged cow thief and fellow of dubious distinction, had gunned down William Noel during some brouhaha in a Shafter drinking joint, fatally. Some folks were plain fed up with the felonious mischief and lawlessness. The night following the killing a few unnamed Shafter fellows "put a dynamite cartridge under the saloon & blew it to pieces."[20] Covering such maliciousness with an excuse, the bombers, co-conspirators, and sympathizers, tried their best to lay the explosion off as an act of God, a lightning strike. Their ploy was laughable, but concerned citizens and Presidio County lawmen were glad they had had the foresight to blow the place up when unoccupied—even so it "went up."[21]

Another incident would have a direct impact on the rangering life of Private John Gravis, though not at the moment it happened. At Shafter an unnamed "Mexican" got on a tear, threatening to kill a couple of Texas peace officers before he dashed back across the Rio Grande with their figurative scalps. Wholly losing touch with reality due to an overindulgence of *mescal* the yahoo exhausted his frustrations by pitilessly fracturing the skull of an "old Mexican woman" who had had the gall to scold him for misbehaving and near scaring folks to death. Forthwith he was arrested, and absent Shafter having a jail, was manacled to a tree pending removal to the Presidio County jail at Marfa. After dark, the "good" citizens, no doubt after a few drinks for themselves, on the sly unchained the stupefied prisoner. On the outskirts of town he was summarily and unceremoniously gunned down. Though it took an incubation period, sentiment of the Hispanic population gradually underwent conversion: "Word got around that the Americans had lynched him, not because he was a potential murderer, but because he was a Mexican."[22] Trouble was brewing. Yes, Shafter warranted a Ranger or two.

Certainly the adjutant general thought so. Though today's courtesies dictate watered-down verbiage, AG Wilburn King's remarks about Shafter were recorded unbridled: "The detachment in Presidio had an immense territory to control, the country very broken, sterile and dry in many parts, and much of the population an ignorant and dangerous class of Mexicans, with a mixture of desperate whites."[23]

Gratuitous guesswork in the historical context is unfitting, so at this point in the story only two hard facts are known—for sure. Somewhere along the way John F. Gravis had picked up or earned a nickname. The origin is mysterious, but fellow Rangers knew him by the handle of "Smoker" John Gravis.[24] The next sure thing is that while a precise date cannot be pinpointed, Smoker Gravis was stationed at Shafter. His partner was Private Walter W. Jones, an experienced Ranger with service dating back to May 1887. On October 31, 1889, Ranger Jones had taken a two-month vacation from Texas Ranger duties, but had reenlisted on New Year's Day 1890.[25] Also assigned to Shafter were Presidio County Deputy Sheriff Ike Lee, and a county constable, Ben Bowers.[26]

Private Gravis had signed on to do some real Ranger work and now he was walking the streets of one of the toughest bailiwicks in West Texas. There can be little doubt the near six-foot-tall Ranger with fair complexion and light toned brown hair would stand out, especially with the predominant population having darker hued physical features, and they were not openly wearing Colt's six-shooters when they went about their day-to-day business.[27] Gravis's identity as a Texas Ranger was not cloak-and-dagger stuff.

Too, it was no deep dark secret that concerned citizens of the business and working class were yet eager to make southern Presidio County a safe and viable place, rather than a locale wholly "at the mercy of the red-handed villains from Chihuahua," who in their estimation were steadily turning West Texas into the "slaughter house of the United States."[28]

For Smoker Gravis the night of August 4, 1890, would be smokin' hot. Disentangling the threads of speculation from actuality is a knotty snag in the retelling of Ranger Private Gravis's last summer night. There are two competing and divergent versions. Scenario number one:

Someone in Shafter hosted a wingding in a private residence. The party was well-attended, primarily by Mexicans and Mexican-Americans, but as would be anticipated Anglo partygoers were there also. Two of the attendees were Ranger Private John Gravis and Deputy Sheriff Ike Lee, who also carried dual commission as a Deputy U.S. Marshal. The indisputable fact that two Texas peace officers were together—side by side—bolsters the reasonableness of an assertion that they were on duty, patrolling the streets, and had stopped by the party in that capacity. Others would—and did—allege the ranger and deputy were revelers too, not acting in the role of gendarmes or under the color of law.[29]

Regardless whether or not the two boys were at a party, there is an undeniable truth in that the indiscriminate mixing of youthful impetuousness, gunpowder, and whiskey, stirred by hotheaded swizzle-sticks nets a most volatile cocktail. Celebrants drank freely; the mood soured quickly. Reconstructing the reason or reasons that someone jerked out a revolver is not now doable, if this account rings true. In the *machismos* world where there is no duty to retreat—Texas was/is such a place—the modus operandi often used for problem resolution was simple: gunplay. At the Shafter shindig, when the six-shooters came out the two lawmen stepped in. When the shooting stopped, Ranger Gravis lay dead on the floor, Deputy Lee was incapacitated with a nasty gunshot wound.[30] Hell had popped at the party. That is surefire true—if the merrymaking presumption is taken at face value.

Scenario number two is dramatically different. If a headline in the *Galveston Daily News* is accurate it would seem that Gravis and Lee attempted to make an arrest of "outlaws" and miserably failed in the attempt.[31] On the other hand, it's often written and is unquestionably clear, that Texas officials and Texas Ranger reports unflatteringly classified the mêlée as but a riot, plain and simple. The *El Paso Times* account deals in the race card: "News was brought in by the foreman of the mines at Shafter of the ambushing by Mexicans of a party of miners, rangers and deputy sheriffs yesterday. Graves [*sic:* Gravis] of the state rangers was instantly killed, and a deputy marshal seriously wounded. The fire was returned and it is believed one Mexican was killed and several wounded. The miners and rangers have about one hundred Mexicans surrounded and are guarding them until further assistance can get to them, when they will pick out those connected with the shooting and bring them to Marfa for safe keeping. The trouble came from the lynching of a Mexican some months ago."[32] Though a bit repetitious the report appearing in the *Brooklyn Daily Eagle* was much more specific. It, too, warrants repeating:

News was brought in yesterday morning by J. E. Ontbes, foreman of the mines at Shafter, of a killing which took place at 2 o'clock that morning. It seems a crowd of Mexicans had got on a spree and were firing off their weapons when several of the white miners, rangers and deputy sheriffs went down to see what was the matter. Suddenly they were fired upon from ambush and State Ranger J. F. Graves [*sic:* Gravis] was instantly killed and J. Lee, deputy sheriff and deputy United States marshal, was seriously wounded in the arm. The fire was returned and it is believed one Mexican was killed and several wounded. A physician, Captain Jones, several rangers and deputy sheriffs have left for the scene. Trouble has been brewing with the Mexicans at Shafter for some time, and it is believed that the intention was to rob and burn the mine. Graves, the dead ranger, belonged to company D. and was very highly thought of by his fellow rangers.[33]

According to one source, though it is anecdotal which is not necessarily a total disqualifier, adds this: "The man who had killed Gravis was chased and killed by the constable's party but not before several of these volunteers had been wounded...."[34]

Reconciling the two versions is as problematic now as it was then. The matter had been complicated by U.S Army Lieutenant T. R. Rivers submitting a report based on hearsay, after he had been dispatched to Shafter with a small detachment of soldiers. The Texas adjutant general wasn't buying into the vague allegations of misconduct on the part of lawmen, simply because an army man said so: "Lieutenant Rivers was evidently misled by partial reports of this transaction, and being misled he did an unintentional injustice to the character and conduct of the Ranger who was killed, and indirectly to the others."[35] A writer for the *Luling Signal* in Central Texas apparently had his mind made up, and was unapologetically plain spoken: "A row occurred at Shafter mines near Marfa, last Monday between a lot of drunken Mexicans on one side & State Rangers and miners on the other, in which a number of Shots were fired...."[36]

Certainly the *Brooklyn Daily Eagle* was right on target with one of its contentions. Captain Jones had received word by ten o'clock a.m. of the sad and violent state of affairs at Shafter. Near Marfa at the time he received the news, Jones jumped into action rounding up six Company D Rangers and raced toward the arena of action—crime scene. They paced their horses accordingly, expeditiously but not overtaxing. Because they were "splendidly mounted and there is hardly an animal that could not cover a hundred miles in one day" the Rangers arrived in Shafter at four o'clock in the afternoon.[37]

Frank Jones and his Rangers wasted no time, fanning out to make arrests. With two Rangers he arrested "seven Mexicans" charging them with Murder. Meanwhile, at the same time in and around Shafter, Rangers Charley Barton, Walter Jones, William Kipling, and John Mayfield, assisted by agitated citizens, arrested "12 Mexicans charged with riot, murder, and assault to murder."[38] For the particular dozen arrestees, custody was relinquished to a Presidio County deputy sheriff. The other seven prisoners were hauled to the county jail at Marfa. [39]

Two Rangers were detailed to secure adequate transportation and return Private Gravis' body to Marfa, so it could be properly prepared for the journey home to South Texas and ultimate delivery to his grieving parents, Charles and Elizabeth, who by the best evidence were then living near kinfolks in Duval County.

Due to but a patchy compilation of nineteenth-century Presidio County courthouse records many intriguing questions remain unanswered. A tantalizing clue appeared in pages of the *Dallas Morning News*: "The Mexican charged with the murder of Ranger Gravis at Shafter, about Aug. 8, will be put on trial at Marfa to-morrow."[40] As of this writing, disposition of the case lingers in suspension. Private John F. Gravis, a Ranger only five months, was in some sense a metaphorical sacrificial lamb. On the Texas/Mexican border rookies were but raw meat for the Devil.

Chapter 8

Robert E. Doaty
1892

Coincidence is astonishing on the one hand, perplexing on the other. At this late date with names already hand-carved into marble markers memorializing fallen peace officers, this rundown will accept written tradition and use the name Doaty as it appears in certain Texas Ranger records, though his real birth name was Robert E. Doughty.[1] The Texas Ranger killed in the previous chapter, John F. Gravis, and the protagonist in this one were relatives—of a sort—cousins by marriage. Whether she was a widow or divorcee is immaterial, but the mother of our new subject, Elizabeth Doughty, had married Frances C. "Frank" Gravis, brother of Charles K. Gravis, father of the Ranger gunned down at Shafter. At the time of the 1870 federal census both families were residents of South Texas. Thirty-three-year-old Frank was living near Concepcion, Duval County, and twenty-six-year-old Charley in nearby Nuecestown, Nueces County picking up mail at Corpus Christi. There is irony, heartrending irony, in the fact that one Gravis brother lost a natural son to gunfire while serving as a Texas Ranger, the other a stepson.

As would be expected, family and friends opted for the short version, and Elizabeth's oldest son was called Bob, rather than Robert.[2] Exactly when Frank Gravis relocated his family is indistinct, but by 1880 they were enumerated as being at San Diego, still in Duval County. Yet living at home as a twenty-year-old single man, Bob pitched in to help his stepfather with the farming and ranching chores. In fact, along the way he acquired his own flock of sheep.[3] It would seem that as a South Texas stockman, Bob had morphed into a top-hand. Although the clear-cut reasons are not indelibly marked, livestock interests or simple wanderlust resulted in adding two dimensions to Bob's life: he was thoroughly acquainted with the country between the Nueces River and the Rio Grande, and he had become fluent in the Spanish language, speaking it as good as, if not better, than English.[4] Bob's knowledge of land and language would shortly prove to be valued and in demand assets.

For carrying this story forward it is also imperative to note that another fellow in South Texas and the Rio Grande Valley had been competently and craftily honing certain skills too. Catarino Erasmo Garza Rodriguez, depending on perspective, was either a patriot or firebrand—maybe wearing both hats. Articulate and highly educated with earned college credentials, his devotion to native Mexico was not only demonstrated by time in the National Guard, but as well by a short stint as Mexican consul in St. Louis, Missouri, or by other accounts, a futile try at landing the diplomatic position. Garza had, at long last, a very real and raging purpose in life. Catarino Garza "had enjoined a small but tempestuous revolutionary cell that stood— twenty years ahead of their time—in open opposition to the dictatorial Porfirio Diaz regime in Mexico."[5]

With residence on America's side of the borderline, Catarino Garza's voice could be heard loudly, not only in inspirational and stirring oratory, but through pages of two of his newspapers: *El Libre Pensador* and *El Comercio Mexicano*.[6] Early on, while Bob Doaty was sharpening his usefulness as a borderland outdoorsman, vociferous Catarino Garza would suffer cutting pain, gunshot wounds.

Chronologically stepping backwards is a must. As result of a Texas Ranger scout during 1887, Viviano Díaz and Cicilio Ybarro had been arrested, suspects in a kidnapping. While yet in the field Rangers released the prisoners into the custody of W. W. "Wash" Shely, the Starr County sheriff. Bafflingly as it turned out, the two terrified detainees never made it to their day in court at the county seat, Rio Grande City. They had been taken from Shely's custody and lynched "by a party of men." Captain Frank Jones' comments to Ranger headquarters were not made public, and thankfully so. The words would have only fueled Garza's anger: "They were very bad characters and the good citizens here, American and Mexican, are greatly rejoiced at their taking off. There is no clue as to who did the hanging."[7] Nor would there be!

The following year during an investigation, a Company D Ranger, Private Jim Dillard, killed Abraham Recéndez to "prevent his escape."[8] The U.S. Customs Inspector at Rio Grande City, Victor Sebree, himself a former Texas Ranger, is sometimes credited with killing Recéndez due to subsequent events. Clarity of the Company D Monthly Return and a letter from Captain Frank Jones to the adjutant general prove

that Private Dillard's shot killed Recéndez.[9] Catarino Garza fired
some shots too according to comments in newspaper editorials. The
cannonade of criticism disparaging area lawmen was hot and widespread. Especially verbally wounded was Inspector Sebree, who was
so incensed he grabbed his six-shooter shooting at Mr. Garza, as
well as one of his companions, Federico Lopez.[10] Inspector Sebree
very quickly—and very smartly—hid behind the iron skirts of U.S.
Army personnel at nearby Fort Ringgold, which had been formally
upgraded from its former status as but a military camp.[11] For the
finale of this part of the overall episode a Gatling gun was called into
play, and the threat of its use kept "Mexicans" at bay, those wanting
Sebree's head severed, arterial blood pooling on the chopping block.
After his release on bond, Sebree pulled his rabbit from the hat and
had criminal libel charges filed against Garza. Dutifully a couple of
Texas Rangers arrested him: Predictably Garza posted bail and was
released. With pen in hand he continued his rant, maybe with some
justification, denouncing perceived inequalities dished out by South
Texas lawmen. Needless to say, the pot of acrimony stewed. It boiled
over, again. Hot under the collar, Victor Sebree wounded Catarino
Garza while he unwarily sat for a shave in a barber's chair.[12] Subsequently Rangers made appearances after all the disturbances—riots
in retellings—making numerous arrests, perhaps some even with
legally sufficient Probable Cause. The worsening state of affairs was
explosive, so much so that Ranger Corporal Walter Durbin—who
could say it with meaning and be believed—pledged that "the Rangers
will attend to all the killing to be done in this county for a while."[13]

Garza was intent on doing some killing, too. Amassing an army
of insurgents to overthrow Díaz's despotic regime, Catarino hatched
his plots, nurtured his intrigues, and publicly boasted of a copi-
ously ambitious 1000-man army, a figure shamelessly overinflated.
Catarino Garza's boys were not all gentlemen patriots whining for
democracy and selflessly disposed; there were bad apples in the lot,
too. After staging his followers along the border Garza launched his
assault during September 1891. Surprise attack? The would-be statesman invaded Mexico a handful of times. None of the incursions bore
delicious fruit. But the rottenness of his plan did leave a bad taste in
Porfirio Díaz's mouth. He spit out complaints to the United States
Department of State, demanding that America's neutrality laws be
enforced. As result of ineptness and military clumsiness and lack of
sustained financial wherewithal, Catarino Garza's army, deprived of

refuge in Mexico, splintered into scattered bands across South Texas and the Lower Rio Grande Valley. There they became known as *Garzistas*. With an insufficient command structure in place to maintain discipline and hold the course, fueled by weakening supply lines, and somewhat later, eroding public support, many *Garzistas* forfeited the high road of principle, assuming the role of *Bravos*, and "preyed on rancheros and behaved like stereotypical Mexican bandits."[14]

Naturally such news grabbed attention of newspapermen and magazine writers. After issuance of arrest warrants, Catarino Garza donned the mantle of a fugitive—a highly sought fugitive. That breaking news had spurred journalists. Their hyperventilated prattle amplified a damn good story: Where else would one find soldiers, deputy U.S. marshals, sheriffs, and Texas Rangers hunting for the same outlawed man and his downsized army of cutthroats and desperados—at the same time? Asserting that a huge portion of southern Texas was tight under siege would be too rich, but there was big trouble causing heartburn for both U.S. Army folks, and hardbitten Texas Rangers. Unraveling events make clear, the so-called Garza War involved real bullets, not just words. There was work to be done, enough to go around.

Bob Doaty, yet a single man, had moved to Brownsville and it seems was dividing his time between there and his old stomping grounds in Duval County, just ten miles west of Alice (now Jim Wells County). Enumerating the wholeness of his business and livestock interests is not necessary, even if the challenge could be met. The salient fact is this: Bob was well-attuned to what was going on, and was exceptionally knowledgeable about the geographical setting he had been roaming since childhood. Soldiers and Rangers brought in from afar to run down Garza and his followers were disadvantaged from the get-go. A news correspondent posed this naive question to an on-scene combatant, "What is the nature of the frontier country?" The high-ranking official bombastically replied: "Nature? Great scott; it's all nature, one terrible growth of chaparral. The brush and cactus is so thick that neither man nor beast can travel through it. There is a stretch of country about 100 miles by 100 miles that is totally covered by this brush. The Garza men, Mexican outlaws, or whatever you may call them, seem to follow secret trails and can evade any number of soldiers or rangers."[15] During an unconnected interview, for another newspaper, an added truth was hammered home, the *Garzistas* "know the country thoroughly, and without uniform can change themselves into ranchers and goat herders in five minutes."[16] Knowing well the people and places of South Texas would all too soon put Bob Doaty in the thick of the *brasada*, the brush country. A gloomy catalyst pushed him into action.

With efforts designed to cover certain legal bases, the thinkers and hard chargers of Texas adopted what today might be referred to as a task force strategy. By interlacing local, state, and federal officers together in the campaign, tactically advising U.S. Army commanders about the criminal law's finer points and holding dear their jurisdictional titles to make arrests, was but smart. There was a downside, however: No little political and personal infighting between parties and personalities—and partisans sympathetic to Catarino's dominate, but pragmatically beyond reachable objectives. Nevertheless, with so many jurisdictional representatives in the chase, coupled with the military's might to smack down *Garzistas* on the battlefield, if they could be caught, would guarantee Catarino Garza's undoing—sooner or later. One of those chances came sooner.

Father Time's opening months of 1892 revealed South Texas was awash with huntsmen thoroughly committed to nailing *Garzistas'* hides to the wall. Although contemporary newspapers are jampacked with manpower deployment particulars, the location and movements of two units would directly impact the life of Bob Doaty. Company E, Texas Rangers, commanded by Captain J. S. McNeel, was strategically situated at Alice, while Captain Chase, 3rd U.S. Cavalry, and corps were at Sweden Station.[17]

Texas Adjutant General W. H. Mabry was particularly concerned that the line between federal and state troops not be blurred, issuing orders that Rangers were not enforcers of America's neutrality laws, nor were they permitted to serve as "scouts" under command of the U.S. Army. There was no double speak, the Texas Rangers were to cooperate fully, making arrests and enforcing state law, but told to fiercely maintain an operational autonomy.[18] Rangers answered to the adjutant general and were not part of the U.S. military's fastidious chain-of-command.

Although various degrees of rancor between forces existed, Captain Chase solved some of his scouting deficiencies by relying on the services of federal officers, in the case at hand, U.S. deputy marshals, whose appointments and cross-designations were seemingly ubiquitous throughout the Lower Rio Grande Valley. Operating ahead of Captain Chase as his eyes and ears in this instance were Lino

Cuellar, Juan Moreno, and Rufus B. Glover, a former district and county clerk for Duval County, but now, like his two scouting companions, a deputy marshal. Chase received word on January 31, 1892, that his scouts had captured two *Garzistas*, formerly officers in Catarino Garza's defunct army. Anxiously awaiting arrival of the two prisoners at his headquarters, Captain Chase was distraught when they did not come in. He soon learned the reason why. At Soledad Wells, near Benavides in Duval County, the scouts had been ambushed. Deputies Cuellar and Moreno managed an escape; Glover did not. A pile of spent cartridges was evidence that he had fought valiantly, but at some point received a rifle ball to the head.[19] Though the event is thus far only somewhat explicable, there is bona fide foundation for illuminating the interconnectedness of certain South Texas bloodlines. The twenty-seven-year-old U.S. deputy marshal, originally from Clay County, Mississippi, had married into the Gravis family two years earlier.[20] Therefore it's but logical to suggest that that is why Glover's body had been taken to the Duval County home of Frank C. Gravis, Bob Doaty's stepfather, for the customary viewing and pre-burial wake.[21]

Within but a short spate of time—one month—the everyday work life of Bob Doaty underwent a drastic conversion. On the first day of March 1892 he enlisted with the Rangers in Captain McNeel's Company E, still headquartered at Alice.[22] The historical record is silent as to whether he was pressured—friendly persuasion—by Captain McNeel because of his familiarity with the terrain and a personal acquaintance with those folks roaming the *brasada*. Bob Doaty knew who were okay cowboys, *vaqueros*, sheep or goat herders—and likewise knew which fellows weren't. Or was there another reason? The killing of the popular deputy U.S. marshal had ignited a firestorm of disgust, and newspapers were not reticent with offhand predictions that Texans, not soldiers, were determined to avenge the death of Rufus Glover, who had not survived his thirty-sixth year.[23] So far, the best hint suggesting Bob's impetus for becoming a Ranger is a line lifted from a contemporary newspaper, he "going out as scout after Glover was killed."[24]

Overnight—so it seems—the tall thirty-three-year-old Bob Doaty had shown his worth, becoming, as reported by one who knew him, "McNeel's right hand man .... handsome and courageous as a lion...."[25] Ranger Bob may have had the heart of a lion, but he also owned the predatory skills of a tiger, a maneater silently moving amid the jungle of chaparral and mesquite, stickers and thorns. It was arduous and hazardous duty, scouting. Private Doaty's tenure as a Ranger had purposefully been intended to be of passing duration. Fred Feigl recalled: "I recollect about four weeks ago Bob and I were riding through the brush in the vicinity of El Gato and naturally riding side by side we got confidential....[and he] said to me: 'I am getting tired of this life; it's a big risk and no money in it. When I get through with this Garza business I'm going to quit the service and settle down....'"[26]

Often it is late March—in Texas—when dens of rattlesnakes began their annual progression of awakening, untangling, and slithering away for their holidays of solitude. In this regard the Diamondbacks and the *Garzistas* had something in common. By March 1892 *Garzistas* were dispersed into a ragtag assortment of freebooters, evidenced by Rangers finding or stumbling into their widespread abandoned campgrounds. They had divided and subdivided, fugitives in Texas and unwelcome in Mexico. March was also the time Captain McNeel's Company E Rangers uncoiled and drew blood: "On March 20, 1892, members of Ranger Company E arrested a man for aiding a Mexican bandit referred to as 'Garza.' The following day, they caught others and shot one man who refused to surrender."[27]

Two days later Bob Doaty was scouting with other Rangers "about twenty miles below Pena, on the line of this and Starr County."[28] Also scouting about, probably for venison or turkey, were three "Mexicans." During morning hours, about ten o'clock, the two parties collided in the *brasada*. For a short while it was fast and furious, the trading of shots. How did the running gunfight turn out? Tactlessly it might be said, a reporter headlined his copy: "**Fighting On The Frontier: One Of The Rangers Scouts Bites The Dust**."[29] Ranger Bob Doaty didn't eat any dirt that morning. He was already dead when he toppled from the saddle, a *Garzista's* well-aimed or haphazardly fired bullet in his skull.[30] The other Rangers pulled up, their three adversaries had somehow managed a getaway, ostensibly to sound the alarm for nearby comrades. And some mean folks were close at hand.

The brother of Starr County Sheriff Shely, who was himself a Special Ranger at the time, offered confirmation to another rightly inquisitive journalist. The Special Ranger had been out hunting horse thieves when he had found an abandoned camp near where Bob Doaty was killed. The reporter inked succinctly, repeating the Lower

Rio Grande Valley lawman's factual observations and proffered theory: "he discovered seven different camps, and at one of these camps there had been seven fires built, showing that the number of bandits was quite large." He also thought that the Rangers riding with Bob Doaty were very fortunate "that they ran upon the three Mexicans when they did, as otherwise they would have gone blindly right into the Mexican camp, and the entire posse would have been killed."[31]

A wagon was secured and reverently as possible under the circumstances Private Doaty's body was removed to his mother's and stepfather's home near San Diego. The local priest, Father J. P. Bard, officiated at the funeral, a somber Catholic service attended by many.[32]

For the story at hand it is only important to note that fugitive Catarino Garza slithered out of Texas, waltzed past Mexico and, perhaps, eventually died in tropical Panama—perhaps not.[33] Meanwhile his *Garzistas* fast depreciated, becoming a lessening headache for local lawmen and U.S deputy marshals, but no longer warranting a flexing of the U.S. military's arm. Numerous were the *Garzistas* rounded up, formally charged with state or federal criminal violations, and then ultimately fined or imprisoned—or both. Seldom do impotent insurrections end well.

Bob Doaty had been a Texas Ranger less than one month, but he was entitled to wages for those twenty-two days. The state did not wish to renege. So, "as mother and sole heir" Elizabeth Gravis was awarded her son's back pay: $22.[34] Even if a Texas Ranger survived, he couldn't get rich riding Lucifer's Line.

Chapter 9

Frank Jones
1893

The maelstrom of calls to establish a Texas Ranger presence in El Paso County was mounting as the third year of the 1890s opened. Sitting members of the El Paso County grand jury had submitted their petition to the governor on the last day of January requesting protection from "the depredations of criminal characters who flit across the frontier."[1] The next day, the county sheriff, Frank B. Simmons, made his thoughts and assessments known to the adjutant general.[2] Two weeks later George W. Baylor, a former Ranger commander and influential Texas politico, piped in with his alarming message. He was particularly incensed about the murder of two fellows just the day before, and was claiming that the "theft of horses and cattle is nearly an everyday matter." Furthermore, Baylor, if it were left up to him, would not let any blasted international limits squelch a damn good fight, pointedly reminding: "The men who Killed Fussleman [sic] were never caught, and the posse only followed them across the El Paso Mts. & down to the Rio Grande & then returned to the city. A squad of Rangers with their pack mule & 20 days rations would have Kept on the trail without regard to State or national boundaries & captured or Killed the murderers and this that element Knows and the presence of the Rangers would soon give us peace & security."[3] Collectively their reasons and logic was seamless: the county sheriff, try as he might, was a near helpless loser in the fight against rampant crime with scarce resources, a woeful shortage of tax money and manpower. The outlaw gangs were flush.

Ranger Captain Frank Jones, a widower, had shortly before remarried. The blushing bride was, too, giving marriage a second try. Helen Baylor Gillett in the suit for divorce had alleged that her now ex-husband, James B. "Jim" Gillett, a somewhat well-known former Texas Ranger, had all too often been lying around the house—a whorehouse.[4] The marriage to Jim Gillett had been "as dubious as loading a pistol with buckshot," but that was a bygone story—shallow as the grave might be—buried in the past. Captain Frank Jones was a good catch. The October 3, 1892, nuptials had taken place in the Ysleta home of the bride's father, the aforementioned George Baylor.[5]

Captain Jones' next move should come as no bombshell. High crimes and misdemeanors were spiking in El Paso County and George Baylor had invited the newlyweds to move in with him at his commodious Ysleta home. Captain Jones recommended the Company D headquarters be moved to Ysleta: "I have just retuned from El Paso County where I went to further investigate reported lawlessness and am more convinced that a Company of Rangers is more needed there than at any point in Tex."[6] Quite naturally as company commander he, too, would relocate to Ysleta or nearby. Sticking firm to his theory regarding manpower strength levels Frank Jones laid his reasoning squarely in the lap of the Texas adjutant general: "If I am sent to El Paso County I hope you can allow me to take more than 4 men. Old 'residenters' below El Paso say that 4 men will simply be murdered and will do no good."[7] Captain Jones' arguments and proposals were persuasive; company headquarters would be shifted to Ysleta. Sergeant John Hughes was to remain in Alpine with a small detachment of Rangers to cover the borderline country of Presidio and Brewster Counties. Adjutant General Mabry issued his stamp of approval.[8]

Lacking the political horsepower to land the job he really wanted, U.S. Marshal for the Western District of Texas, Captain Frank Jones busied himself making critical assessment of his new Ranger station close on the Rio Grande.[9] A native of the beautiful and sometimes green Texas Hill Country, Frank Jones was pleasantly fascinated with certain components of historically rich El Paso County; particularly the adobe architecture of the "old churches which were built in the 16th Century." Like the overwhelming majority of Anglo Texans at the time, Captain Jones had not shed sociological prejudices due to an overnight awakening and/or a change of scenery. Of the general—majority—population Captain Jones did not mince words: "I am under the impression that they have not advanced a single step in civilization. They are as ignorant and superstitious and as much under the rule of their priests as when this country was first settled."[10] On the other hand Captain Jones's appraisal of a subgroup residing along the river was not off the mark, not an example of narrow-mindedness. There were mean folks along the river, real mean folks. According to his best estimate there were at least fifty major bandits jumping back and forth across the river just below and above El Paso proper. Consequently any fairy-tale exaggerations about single-handed Rangers taking on all comers could be stood on their head. From the very start Captain Jones knew the wise course was for Rangers to work in beefed up squads, or "they would simply be murdered."[11] Not only would Rangers suffer the horrible consequences of insufficient numbers, so too would the *mal hombres* they were after. In this instance Captain Frank Jones' no-nonsense logic was spot on: "A few men so often are compelled to make a fight to effect the capture of criminals when a good number will overawe and the arrests made without the necessity of a shot being fired. Of late years the Rangers have been compelled to do Killing simply because there were so few in numbers it emboldened fugitives."[12]

The coldblooded viciousness of bandits and *banditos* along the river was not an issue that would stop Frank Jones from doing his job—that dynamic came with the territory. As an intrepid Texas Ranger he had already skated through conflict resolution with Colt's six-shooters and Winchesters, at least three times.[13] No, a desperado's reputation for badness did not earn him a free pass. That would not be an obstacle; the landscape was.

This section of the Rio Grande was tricky. Raging flood waters, periods of drought, underground currents, thoughtless carving of irrigation ditches, and plain erosion were the culprits, but an elusively meandering channel ill-defining the international borderline was the outcome. Thick and at times impenetrable stands of trees, bushes, shrubs, reeds, cacti, and cattails only served to enhance the helpless feeling of vulnerability and impregnate the psychological maze of disorientation. Distinctly relevant to Captain Jones' storyline is the geographical positioning of real-estate, a sliver of land: Pirate Island as it came to be known. The ever fickle Rio Grande had cut a new collateral channel. The resulting land mass between the ancient Rio Grande channel and the new one, before it merged back to the mother river miles downstream, was hotly disputed territory. The island was several miles long but narrow, skirted by the Rio Grande's growth of intertwined twists and tangles. On the Mexican side of Pirate Island was the impoverished little hamlet of *Tres Jacales*. An imaginary line down the island's center was supposed to have theoretically marked the two countries' sovereignty:

In regard to the dividing line between the Untied States and Mexico, there is an old river bed where the water has not run since
1854 except when river is very high that is recognized by citizens
of both nations as the line between the Untied States and Mexico.
This old channel is very indistinct and there are two or three others very near like it on the island....the Mexican side of this old
channel that is recognized as the line but there are no marks of any
international survey to show where the line is.[14]

So, what looked good to arguing diplomats had no real meaning, not
to bandits hell-bent on staking out a spot of neutrality for asylum
between highjackings and homicides. This piece of Mexico's ground
was seldom if ever patrolled by Mexican legal or military authorities.
Realistically speaking it was genuinely a "no man's land." Mexican
policía or federal troops didn't go there. Texas lawmen didn't either;
their jurisdictional reach normally ended at river's edge—as a practical matter.[15] It was not an uninhabited island. Bandits and murderers
and cow thieves called it home.

Particularly of interest to Rangers, and all other Texas lawmen
in the area, was criminal handiwork of the disreputable Olguin family, not lovingly known throughout El Paso County as the "Bosque
Gang."[16] At the age of ninety-plus years Clato Olguin, the patriarchal
godfather, had bequeathed operation of the illicit enterprises to his
sons Jesús María, Antonio, and Pedro, who captained the outfit's several tentacles. Jesús María's sons, Severio, Sebastian, and Pecilliano,
were gangland lieutenants. According to George Wythe Baylor, they
were—one and all—a "hard set." More specifically they had been
characterized as a bunch of "thieves, murderers, and smugglers" with
their sanctuary not mysteriously pinpointed: "for years they have
infested an island that has been a sort of neutral ground."[17] To be
precise, though it's really a finite line, the outlaws all technically lived
on "Texas soil." That is except for Antonio who squatted on the Mexican side. The Olguin clan were native Texans "born and raised at San
Elizario and were voters at that place until they became fugitives from
Texas." Antonio, when he crossed into the Lone Star State, treaded
lightly; he had already been convicted of rape, sent to the Texas penitentiary, and had escaped. Jesús María and Severio had just been
indicted for multiple felonies during the El Paso County grand jury's
January 1893 term, as well as having Complaints sworn to and filed
on other charges, resulting in outstanding arrest warrants.[18]

Though he had his faults, as all folks do, Captain Frank Jones owned plenty of pluck and was not a man to dither indecisively. Jones had scarcely arrived at his new duty station before swinging into the saddle and into action. Since Jones' Company D Rangers couldn't catch the Olguins on undisputed Texas ground and due to citizens along the river fearing to help as spies, snitches, or witnesses, he'd simply make a scout to Pirate Island and round them up.

Riding with Captain Jones on the twenty-ninth day of June 1893 were Corporal Carl Kirchner, Privates T. F. Tucker, John W. "Wood" Saunders, Robert Edward "Ed" Bryant, a Ranger who had reenlisted but four days earlier, and Edward Dunlap "Eddie" Aten, the youngest brother of famed Texas lawman Ira Aten.[19] Also on the scout was a young man only identified as Lujan, a fellow trying to locate and recover some missing—or stolen—horses. As darkness closed in the Company D Rangers pitched camp fives miles south of San Elizario on the Rio Grande's bank.

Up before dawn Rangers were in the saddle by four o'clock straightaway making tracks for the Olguins' rancho on Pirate Island, but barely inside that ill-defined and imaginary Texas line. Arriving at Clato Olguin's abode the Rangers found that the old man "was very surly." Seemingly the intended targets of their scout, Jesús María and Severio Olguin, had been forewarned. The Rangers thought so anyway. The most likely place for them to be found was at the home of Antonio just across the nearby Mexican borderline. Taking a break the Rangers mulled over their next move: "After getting breakfast the Capt. Started up the River on the main road which crosses backward & forward from one side to Mexico. Several times, the River being very crooked and being overgrown with this chaparral it is [was] difficult to determine when one is [in] Texas or Mexico."[20]

After tightening cinches and remounting, the Rangers had proceeded along Pirate Island's main road, if that's what it could be called. Hardly had the march began when they espied two "Mexicans" riding toward them. Upon seeing the Rangers, they "wheeled and ran back & the Rangers immediately gave chase & Kept up the road: after a run of three or [four] hundred yds—Corporal Kirchner, Pvts. Saunders and Aten passed Capt. Jones & Pvt. Tucker and ran on the Mexicans, one of them, Jesus Maria Olguin, fell from his horse and turned square off to the left of the road he being near Antonio Olguin's house & doubled back again across the road & ran into the house, the other turned off to the right of the road & threw up his hands—There were 4 houses in this settlement which is on the main road & some 200 yards from the Texas line as can best be shown by a map herewith—there being on the right of the road some 50 yds apart, and one on the left, the second house on the right was occupied by 5 or 6 Mexicans and as Corporal Kirchner passed he being ahead, a volley was fired from the door at him. One bullet Struck the magazine of his Winchester bending it so he could only fire one shot & then reload. Saunders come next & a Second volley was fired at him—Aten come close behind & a third volley was fired at him, which he retuned by a shot from his six shooter, this being first shot by the Rangers"[21] Turning in their saddles as they raced by, the Rangers could detect movement of their comrades trying to catch up.

Captain Frank Jones and Private Tucker had galloped to the sound of gunfire. Unfortunately in the heat of battle—atop keyed-up horses—they came to sliding stops but 30 feet in front of the concealed snipers outpost—a little house and outbuildings. Not wasting a precious split-second Jones' and Tucker's boots hit the ground, and they began retuning fire, Captain Jones with his Winchester. Supporting a theory that the desperadoes had been tipped off, a withering fire was coming not only from the small house, but from the cover of adobe walls jutting from each side of it like extended wings of a vulture. To the Rangers it became perfectly clear: they'd been lured into a trap—ambushed![22]

Checking their horses, Kirchner, Saunders, Bryant, and Aten "whirled and came back," dismounting and seeking cover; Ranger Bryant nesting in a spot "within 15 or 20 feet of Capt. Jones & Tucker...." The desperadoes' next volley was disastrous. A bullet slammed into Captain Jones' thigh, breaking his leg. Suffering horribly Jones drew from deep within, and somehow managed to straighten out his injured limb in front of him, firing two or three shots at his tormentors with his Colt's .45 while bearing excruciating pain. Suddenly a sombrero and rifle barrel popped up over the nearby adobe wall. Captain Jones leaned forward the best he could, trying to align the six-shooter's front sight between an outlaw's squinting eyes. The "Mexican" was quicker on the trigger, his rifle ball sledge-hammered into Captain Jones' chest, the bullet ranging downward tearing its channel. Private Tucker abruptly turned his head, inquiring: "Captain, are you hurt?" Gasping for air Frank Jones answered, "Yes, shot all to pieces." Then, "Boys I am Killed." And he was.[23]

Corporal Kirchner picks up the story:

> We continued to fire on them until they retreated & hid in the
> building[.] Just then a friendly Mexican [Lujan] who was with us
> in search of stolen horses told me we were in Mexico in the out-
> skirts of Tres Jacales a small mexican town & that the people
> had sent for the mexican soldiers who would be there in 15 min-
> utes. My first decision was to stay with our dead Captain & Kill
> or capture the mexicans but after waiting about 45 minutes I saw
> from the appearance of everything we would be over-powered &
> murdered....[24]

Private Bryant, born and raised in El Paso County, knew the Rangers
were in a jam. He quickly corroborated to Tucker, who didn't know it
at the time, that the shoot-out had actually taken place on the Mexican side of the line. Ed Bryant also counseled: "we had better get
across the line, we are in Mexico and within a mile or so of the Plaza
of Tres Jacales and there will soon be a force of Mexicans here." Lujan
the boy looking for missing horses added that "a courier had gone
to the town of Guadalupe for Soldiers & men." Fortunately Bryant,
who could speak Spanish fluently, extracted a pledge from a "Mexican to take care of the Capt's body, which he promised to do...."[25]
Although the Rangers were tough-as-nails, this was not the time to
dilly dally. Corporal Carl Kirchner, now the ranking Ranger in command, ordered the retreat. They returned to Texas, surefire identifiable Texas.

Pitiably, but in context not surprisingly, upon arriving at old San
Elizario the flabbergasted corporal found it "impossible to get a single white man to assist me." Moving over to new San Elizario on the
railroad Kirchner made use of the telegraph, broadcasting his plight:

> Have had fight with Mexican outlaws near line of Mexico. Capt.
> Jones killed. We were overpowered and have just come in for rein-
> forcements. Only had six men.[26]

Jumping into action upon learning the news El Paso County Sheriff
Frank Simmons quickly fashioned a sixteen-man posse and boarded
a special train to San Elizario. Sheriff Simmons was a bona fide go-
getter, a man not known to suffer fools, with nerves of steel—backbone—and razor sharpness in the traditions of area diplomacy. After

uniting with Kirchner's men the forces—now strong as dynamite—"went to the State line & demanded the body of Capt Jones which had been taken charge of by Mexican officials but they refused to give it up."[27]

Not ready to invade Mexico and go to war, the riled posse was forced to concede a temporary setback. Well versed in ways of the border, Sheriff Simmons was attuned to the fact that some back channel consultation would—or just might—solve the problem. Contact was made with Mexican officials upriver at Ciudad Juárez. Though the back-and-forth between Simmons and the Mexican negotiator are unrecorded for posterity—perhaps purposely—by the next day an accord was reached. Mentioning at this point a little borderland truism may be unsettling, but obligatory. Not only was the Rio Grande country sometimes overrun with viciousness and criminality, but it was also land of *la mordida*—the bite—the bribe. The reader must judge, but it's more than interesting to note that Sheriff Simmons, one week after the killing of Captain Jones, made a special request to the governor, James S. Hogg: "I have been to quite an expense in getting the body of Capt. Frank Jones, Company D State Rangers from Mexico. Will the state help me pay these expenses...."[28] Every now and again a modern era chronicler, understandably naïve about gritty law-enforcing realities, misinterprets Corporal Kirchner's next telegram to officialdom, more than twenty-four hours after the first one:

> The fight took place in Mexico but I have Recovered the Body of Capt. Jones and secured the arrests of the murderers in Mexico—letter will follow.[29]

Though he no doubt did commendable work, and at a point took possession of Frank Jones' body, even Corporal Kirchner wanted to lay credit at the rightful doorstep: "We [editorial 'we'] then made a demand on the chief officer at Juarez, Mex. Who acted very nicely (I am told by Sheriff Simmons who made the demands) & ordered the body delivered to us at the State line."[30] True, Texas Rangers had at last recovered the body—with a boat load of help from Sheriff Simmons. Too, though it took some skillful haggling, ultimately Texas Rangers—then family—gained custody of Captain Jones' personally designed Frontier Battalion badge, an inscribed pocket watch which had been a gift from Company D Rangers, and his Winchester, but not his Colt's six-shooter and handcuffs.[31] Kirchner's update that arrests had been made in the case was also correct. Three of the Olguins, Jesús María, Severio, and Antonio, had been arrested by Mexican *federales* and placed in a Mexican military jail for awhile—a little while.

Captain Frank Jones, after thirty-seven years atop Mother Earth was laid to rest on the George Baylor property, but not eternally. At a later time (1936) "his remains were taken to Ysleta, Texas and reinterred beside Zaragosa Avenue, about one mile west of the Tigua Indian reservation and Ysleta Mission."[32]

When the body had been delivered across the border Corporal Kirchner was madder than a hornet, because "it having lain in that adobe house without even having the blood washed off.... We thought of course at the time we were fired on from the house we were on Texas soil the line being only an imaginary one."[33] Also mad—or feigning anger—was M. Romero, Minister of Mexico, who had filed a formal protest with the American Secretary of State that their country had been "invaded." The hot potato, working its way downhill through U.S. bureaucratic hallways was finally shuffled off to Governor Hogg in Texas. The Lone Star State's chief executive kicked it into the office of Adjutant General Mabry for answers and "information for use of the U.S. Government in its settlement of the trouble with the Mexican Republic."[34] Over time the diplomatic complaint faded into the abyss of nothingness, as did the legal wrangling to have the Olguins extradited to Texas. There is a back-story, another type of settlement.

On July 8, 1893, Sergeant John R. Hughes was promoted to fill the vacancy created by the unfortunate loss of Frank Jones barely a week earlier.[35] Captain John R. Hughes early on was given sage advice: "The citizens here are all of the opinion that there ought to be a detective put in among the bosque people to find evidence against them, also to learn when those fugitives make their rades [*sic*] into Texas...."[36] Captain Hughes had a man in mind for such a special mission, and that fellow had a burning desire to do some detective business—and a little bit more to boot. Special Ranger Ernest St. Leon was begging the adjutant general:

> Referring to the murder of our Brave and beloved Captain by outlaws—I would respectfully ask and request to be sent out: provided his murderers are not apprehended within the next week....

but for God's sake General if those men succeed in escaping from officers now in pursuit I beg of you to send me out and there I will stay until I either bring them to Justice or go the same way as poor Frank.[37]

Ernest St. Leon, aka Diamond Dick, was well-accustomed to working in the shadows, on either side of the border. His investigative repertoire was unique. Donning a disguise Ernest could easily pass himself off as a borderland native. He could speak the language, and having a Mexican wife augmented his practical awareness of cultural traditions and folklore. Purportedly and there's not much reason to doubt it, after fixing up and fine-tuning his shrewd undercover appearance, Ernest delighted in testing his trickiness by approaching a Ranger he knew, and "ask if he had seen St. Leon any where around. When the Ranger would say no, the disguise was considered a success."[38] He, too, was savage in a fight, showing no remorse. He and Captain Hughes had already come through one six-shooter fracas together. A friend once said of him: "I have known him for some time and a more persistent traveler after criminals I have never met in all my life."[39] On the job Ernest St. Leon relished in the dark side—cloak and dagger work.

What happened next? Texas Ranger legends are plentiful and the aftermath of Captain Jones' demise is fully loaded. Legion are the accounts of blameworthy "Mexicans" doing a suicide dance suspended from Texas Rangers' ropes, or being mercilessly gunned down by a shadowy figure creeping back and forth across the Rio Grande beneath Mexico's moonlight. Early on, before Walter Prescott Webb's near classic venerating history, *The Texas Rangers: A Century of Frontier Defense*, another prolific writer had set the number of such extralegal executions at seventeen.[40] Four years later, at age eighty-three, retired Captain John Reynolds Hughes recalibrated the figure for an *El Paso Herald-Post* correspondent, loquaciously admitting and numbering the deaths at nineteen.[41] A veneer of oddness does seem to fix for such an anecdotal insinuation, a career lawman of long-standing casually acknowledging—confessing to the public—that Texas Rangers chose lynch ropes over legality. Had the onset of senility began? Or, was it the damn straight truth?

Although it is explicable, that intrinsic tendency to holler hooray when brigands bite the dust, such childlike notions of hero worship within a historical framework are unflattering and unfitting as applied to officers working outside the law, men obligated by oath to obey the law. Granting journalistic immunity from afar, a hundred or so years removed, is understandable—but unwarrantable in a non-fiction context. Gunplay is not child's play.

True to form academicians now and again dismiss such stories, absent a documentable paper trail. Despite what a smattering of well-intentioned scholars might wish to think, simply because there is no written record, doesn't mean it didn't happen. In certain instances along Lucifer's Line history is but recorded on what men opted to tell—or write down. Some real doings went understated, unwritten, and unsaid. Many old-time border lawmen coolly shrugged off queries that waxed too specific, though one did somewhat fess up: "If a smuggler was killed at night and fell in the river, we forgot about the body unless it showed up downstream on the American side."[42] Particular for the story at hand, one prominent nonfiction writer rendered his judgment: "Most of this yarn is false or improbable and all undocumented but it may rest on something Hughes recounted."[43] Well, not quite!

Before two months had elapsed since the murder of Frank Jones, Captain Hughes had notified AG Mabry that he would enlist Ernest St. Leon in Company D the first day of September.[44] Peculiarly, while extant pay records reveal St. Leon was drawing $30 per month beginning in September, and his five year old bay gelding had been officially appraised by neutral parties on September 6, 1893, as required by Ranger protocol, his name is nowhere to be found in the conventional Texas Ranger activity reports and the company's Monthly Returns for the next six months. On paper, Ranger Private St. Leon had vanished.[45]

Where was he? There is a tantalizing hint. Captain Hughes had received actionable intelligence from noted New Mexico Territory lawman Ben Williams that the outlawed Olguins, who had been released from the Mexican military prison, were keeping a low profile in the general vicinity of La Mesilla across the state line in the Land of Enchantment and/or at Canutillo just upriver from El Paso, still in Texas.[46] An old-time El Paso County deputy sheriff humbly recalled a face to face tête-à-tête with Ernest St. Leon: "Diamond Dick was a good officer....He took altogether too many chances, I think in some cases. When he was first sent to Canutillo I told him to keep a sharp lookout or some of the Mexicans would kill him. Dick replied that they would have to shoot him in the back and I told him they would do just that."[47]

Had Ranger Ernest St. Leon, working undercover, kept his promise to AG Mabry? He had pledged, it might be remembered: "I beg you to send me out and there I will stay until I either bring them to Justice of go the same way as poor Frank." For the courtroom circumstantial evidence—good circumstantial evidence—is admissible and damning. Did St. Leon settle or even the score for Frank Jones' murder? Readers may take their seat in the jury box.

Chapter 10

Joseph McKidrict
1894

New Year's Day of 1894 opened with an ear-splitting bang for some Company D Rangers stationed in West Texas. Handling firearms, an everyday task for career lawmen, is best carried out with due caution. Private Alonzo "Lon" Van Oden carelessly mishandled his Colt's six-shooter that first day of January. He "accidently shot him self in the foot."[1] Even his captain, John Reynolds Hughes, at a later date, would similarly suffer the physical hurt and emotional humiliation of a self-inflicted accidental gunshot wound: one to the "right foot from the inside."[2] All too soon other shots would be heard: No rehabilitation period with crutches for Texas Rangers would be necessary.

Hardcore details of Joseph W. "Joe" McKidrict's childhood are scant. There are, however, a couple of particulars worthy of mention. Joe's father had been killed by Indians, and his mother, Samantha Howell McKidrict, had tied the matrimonial knot a second time. She had married Alby O. Cooley, "a prominent attorney and member of the Texas legislature."[3] In those early days in and around Austin, Joe was known by his stepfather's surname, but according to the best evidence now at hand a formal adoption process had never been initiated. At sometime during the maturation process Joe began having thoughts of moving west. As a young man Joe McKidrict migrated to the Big Bend country perhaps with a plan for his future in mind, perhaps not. For the West Texas sojourn Joe had reverted to using the name given him at birth. After working a stint pulling guard duty at the mines Joe put his name into the hopper for a Texas Ranger job on July 8, 1893, along with applicant Joseph R. Sitter.[4] Captain John Hughes put McKidrict on the payroll July 15, 1893 only two weeks after Frank Jones had been coldly murdered on Pirate Island.[5] Joe Sitter, already a veteran lawman in Val Verde County (Del Rio) as a deputy sheriff, was picked up as a Company D Ranger at Comstock,

Texas, on August 1, 1893.[6] Joe McKidrict was twenty-two-years-old at the time, primed for the adventurous life of a frontier lawman.

As is the case with tracking rookie Texas Rangers, specifically identifying which scouts and arrests one participated in is difficult. Often are remarks in the company's Monthly Return listing the name of but one Ranger, followed by such generic statements as "with three men," or "in company with seven men." There is no ambiguity with one hard fact. Within six weeks of enlisting, the world of law enforcing reality was hammered home for Joe McKidrict. On August 24, 1893, another Company D Ranger was forced into a gunplay. Private J. W. Fulgham caught up to Charles Carroll. When ordered to throw up his hands Carroll "resisted and drew his pistol to shoot" at Fulgham and his partner for the day, Reeves County Deputy Sheriff George Leakey. Good luck or preparedness resulted in Private Fulgham getting in the first lick; two of his .45 bullets knocked Carroll out of the saddle, killing him instantly.[7] Another law-enforcing lesson was laid in McKidrict's lap. When firearms were brought into play and someone was shot or killed, legal wheels of a criminal justice system began turning, affecting Rangers as well as ruffians. In this instance a quickly impaneled trial jury exonerated Private Fulgham, but only after his suffering due process and considerable expense.[8]

By name the subject of this narrative first shows up in the Monthly Return for October 1893: "Joe McKidrict & F. M. McMahan made Scout to Rio Grand [*sic*] Station in Search of Smuggled cattle. Out 3 days, marched 90 miles. Cattle not found."[9] The following month McKidrict is mentioned again by name, scouting with Private Wood Saunders and a deputy sheriff, hunting for cattle thieves.[10] Before month's end that all too familiar message greeted Joe McKidrict who was yet trying to earn his spurs as a topnotch lawman. Company D Rangers were involved in another shooting. Privates Eddie Aten and Frank McMahan, while at Ysleta, rushed to the aid of two ladies in the process of being viciously assaulted by Jose Apodaca, who was hard thumping them with "a large size gun." When challenged by the two Texas Rangers, Apodaca leveled the rifle barrel threatening Privates Aten and McMahan. It was an act of idiocy. Both Rangers fired and Apodaca went down, seriously wounded. Even in this instance Aten and McMahan were forced to monetarily post bond and await formal action of an El Paso County Grand Jury. In the end they were "no billed."[11] Yes, Private Joseph W. McKidrict was being brought up to speed. This Ranger business could go haywire in a heartbeat.

During the first month of 1894, records reflect Private McKidrict was gradually being tasked with more independent assignments. On just one scout, he and Private Ed Bryant made a two-man sweep though the area around Fort Hancock, Texas, arresting a man wanted for assault to murder, a fellow accused of horse theft, and a third wanted for some other type of theft. The prisoners were jugged in the jail at El Paso.[12]

For the mid-1890s El Paso, often referred to as the Monte Carlo of the United States, was overrun with men who over time would be marked down in the bloody annals of gunfighters' history. A harsh admonishment suggesting tenderfeet and sissies would best be served in bypassing El Paso may ring of overstatement, but the city's cast of hard characters was incredible, maybe unrivaled anywhere in the Wild West. Herein there will be no time-consuming effort to match arrival dates to individual footprints. A sampling would reveal the following fellows were either residing in town or making it one of their frequent stopovers for business and/or pleasure. None were strangers at El Paso: Mannie Clements, Patrick Floyd Garrett, John Wesley "Little Arkansas" Hardin, George A. "Bud" Frazer, Jefferson Davis "Jeff" Milton, George A. Scarborough, Les Dow, Oliver Lee, James B. "Killin' Jim" Miller, Bat Masterson, Barney Riggs, George Gladden, Charley Perry, Martin Mroz, and Tom Tucker would but scratch the surface. Former Texas Ranger and Mitchell County Sheriff Dick Ware was the U.S. Marshal and John Harris Behan of Tombstone notoriety was an Inspector with the U.S. Customs Service.[13] And there were a couple of others in the lineup, two genuine tough cookies with earned six-shooter credentials.

Somehow the noted hard character John Henry Selman had beat the rap in Shackelford County, and after the nefarious escapade and association with the Jessie Evans gang around Fort Davis, he had resurfaced using his right name at El Paso. Regardless of sins of the past, or six-shooter notoriety of the near future, now, 1894, John Selman held rightful title as a legitimately elected county constable, with full powers of arrest and a free pass to go about his business armed. Constable Selman's dexterity with a Colt's revolver did not go unnoticed: "He has a reputation for courage as well as promptness and effectiveness in the use of a pistol."[14] Another fellow supplemented the contemporary assessment of Selman: "He was rather a large man, big-boned, rough-hewn and shaggy. He moved slowly, did not talk much, and drank plenty of whisky. Fearless, he was deadly with a pistol."[15]

After an involuntary separation from the Texas Rangers for unruly behavior and frequently losing bouts with the bottle, Baz Outlaw had somehow managed to worm his way back onto the Company D roster as a Special Ranger without pay. But, more notably, because he had so many friends in Brewster County, particularly in and about Alpine, Baz Outlaw had landed a deputyship from U.S. Marshal Dick Ware.[16] Most folks were not blinded by Outlaw's weakness to booze, but one and all admired his pluck. Earlier, Captain Frank Jones had recognized his grit: "He is a man of unusual courage and coolness and in a close place is worth two or three ordinary men."[17] J. Walter Durbin, a fellow Ranger, simply classified Baz Outlaw "as the worst and toughest man I'd seen."[18] Another Ranger, Lon Oden, who considered Baz a close personal friend, was forced in to admitting reality, that when drinking Baz Outlaw "was a maniac; none of us could handle him, none of us could reason with him, we just stayed with him until he sobered up."[19] Even an admiring lady chimed in with a two-pronged characterization, a ringing endorsement and a cautionary warning: "he was a true Southern gentleman, soft spoken, well educated and courteous. We loved to talk to him and to have him in our home but several drinks made a beast of him. When word got out that Bass was drinking, doors were locked, children brought in off the street and all of us kept silence and hoped for the best."[20] A newspaperman writing for the *El Paso Daily Times* confirmed the young lady's straightforward assertion:

> Outlaw has been in western Texas several years, much of the time an officer of the law, and all the time a terror to good citizens.... He was said to be a good natured man when sober, but he always wanted to shoot some one when he was drunk. And these periods of drunkenness were not infrequent.[21]

For the late afternoon of April 5, 1894, one of old El Pa so's best-known sporting queens, Mathilde Weiler, aka Tillie Howard, was hoping for the best.[22] But, just in case, though out of sight between the cleavage of ample breasts, was tucked a police whistle. It was to be used for summoning aid should a hormonally charged client overstep acceptable whorehouse protocols, becoming abusive to the nymphs or abrasive to the cash-paying customers. Tillie could suffer fools for awhile, but not loud-mouthed and disruptive belligerents, not even for a minute.

Ranger Private Joe McKidrict, like a number of West Texas area lawmen, was in El Paso dutifully responding to demands of the U.S. Grand Jury then in session. McKidrict found himself in the standby mode, his physical presence not particularly needed at the time, but unable to leave town and return to Presidio County should he be recalled to present additional testimony in the federal smuggling case.[23] Also in town was U.S. Deputy Marshal Baz Outlaw. For young Joe McKidrict the layover fostered opportunity to take in the sights, visit with fellow officers, and if he opted to sample some indulgent pleasures, he would quietly make it his own business, not public business—not talk of the town. On the other hand, for Deputy U.S. Marshal Baz Outlaw, downtime equated to drunk time. He filled himself full of tarantula juice and went on a spree, his hateful vitriolic ranting and menacing threats rising up, in equal proportion to the whiskey going down. It did not escape notice that Baz was even cursing and demeaning his boss, U.S. Marshal Ware, the man that had overlooked his shortcomings and given him employment, allowing him fees for making arrests, transporting prisoners, and serving papers.[24] During the day Outlaw had not displayed any appreciativeness for Dick Ware's kindness, but as the sun began its springtime descent Deputy Baz Outlaw was feeling amorous.

Joe McKidrict may have thought he was off-duty, but technically speaking Rangers never truly were. Shortly after five o'clock Joe heard the sharp crack of a six-shooter. Shooting guns within the El Paso city limits was not okay. The shrill screeching of a police whistle accentuated the fact that trouble was not brewing in the backyard at 307 South Utah Street, Tillie's bordello; it had already boiled over. Ranger McKidrict rushed to investigate.[25] Constable John Selman was already there. He said:

> I met Bass at the Bank Saloon and he asked me to go down the street with him. We walked away without my really knowing where we were going, but he and myself and an English man [Frank Collinson] that I have known for many years walked down to Tillie Howard's where Bass has a girl—Ruby I think her name is—and went in. Bass was drunk, but I did not think he particularly wanted to fight. He started out of the parlor with his girl, and my friend and I sat down to talk over old times. In less than a minute I heard

a pistol shot in the back yard or on the back porch. I went out as quick as I could go and found Outlaw and Joe McKidrict, a ranger, in the back yard. Joe had beat me out there without knowing what the matter was. Joe was saying that there must be no more shooting as that would call the police down there. I spoke up and said that Bass shot his pistol off by accident and that there would be no more. Joe repeated that it would not do, when Outlaw threw his gun almost against Joe's temple and fired, saying, "You want that, don't you?" He fired another shot into the boy's body and let fly at me without my ever thinking that he would do such a thing. The first shot was so close to my face that my eyes were powder burnt till I was blind, but I pulled on him at random, and I think I got him. I know that if I could have seen his bulk I would have got him, for I can't miss a man with that gun of mine.[26]

John Selman's shot didn't miss. The bullet plowed through Outlaw's chest, "just over the heart." Baz may have been seriously wounded, crimson liquid painting his blouse, but he had not been knocked down, nor put out of commission. While blood poured out of his body, adrenaline pumped Outlaw's gut reaction. He let the hammer on his Colt's six-shooter slip—twice. Each bullet found its mark, both striking Selman's right leg. Then, fully charged with excitement, he tuned and ran, stepping over Joe McKidrict's lifeless body with the bullet wound "just over the left ear" and another in his back.[27] Although stupendously drunk, Baz Outlaw's marksmanship had proven accurate, disastrously so. His flight from the crime scene was also a disaster: He ran squarely into the path of Ranger Private Frank McMahan who ordered Outlaw to immediately surrender his weapon. Perhaps sobering quickly Baz realized he was in a pickle, he handed his six-shooter over to McMahan, at the same time begging—literally begging—to be protected from any evil intent of a revenge-seeking mob. McMahan, struggling to support the fast-sinking Outlaw, hustled his detainee into the closest place of refuge, the Barnaum Show Saloon. With the patient/prisoner stretched out on a table, Doctor S. T. Turner was summoned. After a thorough examination the doctor rendered his informed opinion; the prognosis for Baz was not good.[28] Physically damaged and mentally delirious—in a state of mortal terror—Outlaw lingered four hours, incessantly muttering, "Where are my friends?" None attended his bedside. Around nine o'clock Baz Outlaw died.[29] Somewhat expressively, later Baz's brother

E. B. Outlaw, Captain, Arkansas State National Guard, lamented to the Texas adjutant general: "I had not seen my Brother for nearly (20) years, and although he came to a sad end through a weakness, yet his memory is very dear to me, as you must Know if you have a Bro."[30] U.S Deputy Marshal Baz Outlaw was buried in El Paso's well-known and well-used Old Evergreen Cemetery.[31]

Post crime scene analysis revealed that Private McKidrict's Colt's revolver was fully charged, he had not fired a shot during the barking six-shooter mêlée. Though seriously wounded, Constable John Selman, after treatment by Dr. Alward White, would satisfactorily recover, at least well enough to limp along with the aid of a hand-carved cane. Assuredly an affliction to a lower extremity didn't hinder Selman's trigger finger: He killed John Wesley Hardin the following year inside the Acme Saloon.[32] The next year, 1896, John Selman found himself in that most unenvied position, second place in a gunfight. U.S. Deputy Marshal George Scarborough killed him doornail dead in an alleyway beside the Wigwam Saloon.[33]

Private Joseph McKidrict's body had been respectfully preserved, presumably embalmed, at El Paso's Powell Undertaking establishment, and then transported by rail to his grief-stricken mother at Austin.[34] At the capitol city twenty-three-year-old Joe McKidrict, a Texas Ranger measuring service in months not years, was peacefully interred in the Oakwood Cemetery.[35]

Chapter 11

Ernest St. Leon
1898

Looks can be deceiving. In police work it is smart not to be fooled by appearance; the wolf may be wearing a sheep's clothing. Harmlessness or dangerousness cannot be accurately registered with a glance. Baby-faced Ernest St. Leon is paradigm. He would carry the childlike look of innocence into adulthood, but rest assured, throughout the Texas/Mexican borderlands St. Leon wore the stripes of a prowling tiger. He owned an overabundance of stamina and courage, enough to underwrite near any challenge a mortal human could throw down. Ernest thrived on—lived for—taking risks others couldn't or wouldn't endure.

Born at San Antonio circa the late 1860s, Ernest's mother was an English immigrant and, purportedly, his father was a politically active Frenchman of blueblood linage who had sought refuge in America.[1] An assertion that Ernest had "received a good education and was naturally bright" and that he was "intellectually above the average man" can be legitimately sustained by cursory inspection of primary source documents penned in his own hand. At some point in his maturation process Ernest studied law under the tutelage of the prominent Texas attorney Trevanion Theodore "T. T." Teel.[2]

Whether Ernest St. Leon could have legally practiced law is doubtful and in the context of his life's story it's insignificant. The young man craved much more than the spirited theatrics played out in a smoke-filled courtrooms cluttered with brass spittoons.

If the report is true, and there's not reason to doubt it, a contemporary who knew him reported that Ernest had spent time in the U.S. Army, rising to the rank of drill sergeant for cavalry troops stationed in Wyoming. Whether it was before military service or after is immaterial; at some point in time his adoring mother had given a present to her son, a fancy stickpin, one with the "largest and prettiest diamond seen on the border." Ernest St. Leon cherished the gift and wore it with pride, the stickpin becoming a part of his persona. So much so, that to friends and enemies, workmates and newspapermen, Ernest St. Leon was simply called "Diamond Dick": a nickname that stuck.[3]

Although it speaks against his seemingly aristocratic upbringing, Ernest St. Leon possessed two traits that would serve him well—and not so well. He was drawn to associate with folks of the lower economic strata and sporting classes, and he had a strong taste for good whiskey—and not-so-good whiskey.

On the first day of September 1890 the strapping twenty-two-year-old, a lad standing five foot, ten inches, had journeyed to Marfa, Brewster County, in search of a particular job. Ernest St. Leon enlisted as a private in Captain Frank Jones' Company D, Frontier Battalion.[4] Pinpointing Private St. Leon's specific participation with Ranger arrests and scouts at this stage in his new-found career is not doable. Likewise laying an exact chronology of three interrelated truths is tricky, but, one and all, relevant facts they will prove to be.

First, for reasons not yet fully understood, Ernest St. Leon cleaved unto himself a special delight in undercover work. The audacious young Ranger was not only adept at building a believable cover story, but skilled at masquerading in the appropriate garb, sometimes "getting into the loudest and gaudiest Mexican costumes, staining his face, and passing as a caballero of the deepest dye."[5] When not draped in an elaborate outfit and his true identity was not under wraps, Ernest St. Leon still cut a swath as one daring and dashing figure: "He was one of the most picturesque horseman to be seen in this locality and was a dead shot."[6]

Secondly, St. Leon took a wife, a Mexican-born wife. A precise anniversary date is elusive, but at the age of fifteen or sixteen years, Maria de Jesus Ornellas either said, "I do" and moved in with Ranger Private Ernest St. Leon—or just moved in. That she was untaught in the ways of reading and writing should not be unexpected.[7] Nor should Captain Frank Jones' displeasure with the arrangement be undervalued, although it cannot be—as of yet—specifically addressed. Captain Jones' ingrained prejudices, however, were not any deep dark secret, and can be highlighted by citing just one piece from his official Ranger correspondence: "I would not, under any circumstances, enlist any Mexican to remain in Camp among my men."[8] Private Ernest St. Leon was on shaky ground with the Company D captain.

Lastly, the unstable footing gave way on January 18, 1891. Although the scuffle was but verbal, Privates Ernest St. Leon and E. S. Fisk tangled: Ernest accusing Fisk of cowardice, Fisk alleging St. Leon a common thief. After Ranger service of but five months duration, Ernest St. Leon was "dishonorably discharged.... for committing petty thefts from the commissary."[9] Was this the sprouting of an intricate cover story? *¿Quien Sabe?* There is a related hard truth, one that did not bode well for Private Fisk; he would be discharged for "drunkenness and disorderly conduct."[10]

Although the newspaper accounts cannot be—or have not been—corroborated at this juncture, purportedly civilian Ernest St. Leon removed himself from Texas, crossed the Rio Grande, and accepted employment in Mexico guarding rich shipments of ore for the Mexican Central Railroad. By all reports Ernest St. Leon was known as "a man of good nerve," so suggestions he killed two or three Mexican train robbers does not seem too farfetched, even if lacking documentable substantiation.[11]

After the "six-shooter vacation" in Mexico, Ernest St. Leon returned to Texas, undertaking employment with the mining company, living with his housekeeping wife at Shafter. Local mining moguls were perplexed; significant quantities of valuable ore were being purloined. Texas Ranger Corporal John R. Hughes, who would later earn his Ranger captaincy, was tasked with making an investigation and putting a stop to the costly thefts. Favorably disposed toward Ernest St. Leon, Corporal Hughes cut the ex-Ranger in on his challenging assignment. St. Leon agreed to lend a helping hand, working as an informant and/or developing informants, becoming an undercover operative. Employing his best daring and intuitive and ingratiating skills in but short order Ernest St. Leon learned who was doing the pilfering and when their next heist would take place.

The critical intelligence was passed to Corporal Hughes on the quiet. After dark on January 12, 1892, after picketing their horses at a safe distance, Corporal Hughes and Private Lon Oden, armed with double-barreled shotguns, protectively secreted themselves and patiently waited. Indisputably, if the plan didn't go awry it would be an ambush, not a bushwhacking. Shooting guns and hitting the target at nighttime is difficult. By any standard it was going to be a dicey and dangerous interdiction. These *mal hombres*, when and if they came into view, would have but a split-second to decide: Surrender or die!

During the dead of night the two hidden Rangers could hear the clatter of approaching pack animals, struggling and stumbling under the weight of heavy loads. Doing their part in cajoling the mules were Matilde Carrasco, Jose Villeto, and Quinlino Chaves—and the wily Ernest St. Leon, now a part of the gang, lagging behind deceptively playing the role of a rear guard. When within range of buckshot the challenge was hollered and the shooting started—or the shooting started as the challenge issued. The Rangers' scatterguns wrecked havoc for desperadoes Villeto and Chaves, killing them—near instantly. Though wounded, Matilde Carrasco continued to fight, for a little while. Ernest St. Leon's handiwork with a Winchester was spot on. When Carrasco momentarily exposed his position, "St. Leon rose up and shot him between the eyes."[12] Captain Frank Jones' report to the adjutant general was succinct, purposely worded: "he [Hughes] and his party were fired on by the Mexicans and they returned the fire, Killing three."[13] Case closed!

Occasionally a well-meaning historian makes note that Ernest St. Leon was not mentioned in either of the after-action reports to Ranger headquarters, naively postulating if he wasn't named, he wasn't there. In this instance the application of street-sense takes precedence over academic strictures. It is not wise police work now, nor was it then, to name confidential informants or ongoing undercover operatives, more especially if there is a likely need for their covert services in future circumstances—in the same locale. For this specific situation, after Mr. and Mrs. Ernest St. Leon were safely ensconced the cat was let out of the bag. Within the same year of that shoot-out, 1892, a newspaperman informed his readers and the world: "Matildo [sic] Carrasco was killed six months ago by 'Diamond Dick'..."[14]

Afterward, Ernest St. Leon applied to be commissioned as a Special Texas Ranger. Knowing Captain Jones's opinion of Ernest was not particularly favorable, Corporal John Hughes, taking a chance, jumped the chain-of-command by making his thoughts known to the adjutant general: "He has assisted me in detecting a lot of Mexican ore thieves and is in danger of being killed at any time in this country and wishes to carry his pistol for self-defense."[15] When Captain Jones got wind of the request, he also made his feelings known to the AG, grudgingly admitting St. Leon's past undercover services had "been very useful," but yet maintained that Ernest was a man of "low character." How much weight he put on Ernest having a Mexican wife is,

regrettably, unclear. In the end, Captain Jones provisionally acquiesced: He would agree to the Special Ranger commission, but only
while St. Leon was working at the Shafter mine.[16]

Five months after gunning down Matilde Carrasco, that "thief,
murderer, and an abysmal brute," Ernest St. Leon relocated from
rough and tumble Shafter to his mother's place of residence, San
Antonio, making a home at 421 Pecan Street.[17] Still carrying commission as a Special Ranger, St. Leon penned a letter to Adjutant
General Mabry requesting that if possible any paying detective work
be referred to him, and if so, it would be "heartily appreciated."[18] For
the next few months St. Leon led a hand to mouth existence making
at-large criminal investigations, earning the meager funds financially
strapped sheriffs and parsimonious lawyers could afford to pay. Then
the world seemed to turn upside down.

News reached him that Captain Frank Jones had been murdered
on Pirate Island. It may be remembered that St. Leon had made a special request to AG Mabry that he be allowed to track down the murderers "or go the same way as poor Frank."[19] Also previously noted in
Chapter 9 was the fact that after his promotion to Captain—replacing
Frank Jones—John Hughes turned to Ernest St. Leon, enlisting him
in Company D as a full-fledged Texas Ranger on September 1, 1893.
He was in need of putting a detective in among the bosque gangsters
to either capture the fugitives, or by other accounts, extract much
more than a pound of flesh. Around El Paso, and perhaps across the
border, Private Ernest St. Leon for the next six months drew Ranger
pay, but worked—more or less—off the books.[20] More than one Mexican went missing.

Though credentialed as a Ranger, it took near six months before
Private St. Leon, atop his $65 bay gelding, began drawing public
notice from fellow lawmen and a bevy of crooks and desperadoes
he was arresting and incarcerating. Records abound identifying him
scouting with Ranger allies, U.S Deputy Marshals, federal Customs
Inspectors and an array of sheriffs and their deputies.[21]

Someone else that was favorably impressed with Private Ernest
St. Leon's overt criminal work and probably to some extent familiar
with his covert abilities was a local executive for the Southern Pacific
Railroad. He could and would beat the $30 per month St. Leon was
drawing as a Texas Ranger. And so, with the hearty endorsement of
Captain Hughes, Ernest slipped off the Company D books as a regular
Ranger, but maintained state peace officer status as an unpaid Spe-

cial Ranger.[22] In the overall context Ernest St. Leon's tenure as a Special Ranger did not last long. Ranger Wood Saunders was dismissed for becoming "drunk and disorderly," and Special Ranger St. Leon caught the same punishment for the same misbehavior.[23] Whether or not they were together overly imbibing in some celebratory mood remains a minor—and inconsequential mystery.

If he is to be believed, St. Leon swore off alcohol. He again made application as a Special Ranger. On the first day of May 1896 Ernest responded to this question: "Are you sober and temperate in your habits?" St. Leon's answer was unequivocal and hopefully true: "Yes. For the last 2 Years strictly so." He further pledged under oath that in the interim he had not been convicted of any crimes, and stated that his occupation was that of a "Frontier Detective."[24] From the best evidence at hand it would seem the twenty-eight-year-old Ranger honored his pledge. The Company D Monthly Returns reflect numerous arrests by Special Ranger St. Leon for a myriad of felony and misdemeanor infractions.[25] In the eyes of Captain Hughes, Ernest St. Leon had redeemed himself. On October 1, 1897, Ernest was dropped from the Company D roster as a Special Ranger and sworn in as a regular—state paid—Texas Ranger.[26]

That Ernest St. Leon quickly became an integral part of the Texas Ranger team in El Paso County is exhibited by two relevant dynamics. First, the following month—and for months thereafter—he was tasked with hand writing the Company D Monthly Returns. Second, for the month of December, Private Ernest St. Leon either single-handedly or with another Ranger participated in every Company D arrest.[27] There is no exaggeration in declaring Private Ernest St. Leon an absolute whirlwind of activity. During February 1898 he made eleven arrests and may have been involved in a gunplay. The Monthly Return—in keeping with the customary brevity of Texas Ranger reports—was simply inked: "Clemente Sierra, Shot and Killed prior to arrest."[28]

Another fellow, Gene Turner, aka Six-Shooter Bill, wasn't near as bad, or if he was it didn't deter Private Ernest St. Leon. The Ranger tracked him down, recovered the stolen horse and buggy, and then placed the very much surprised Six-Shooter Bill in the El Paso County hoosegow.[29] Others, a slick trio of ne'er-do-wells, were not operating behind the veneer of any six-shooter nametags; they carried real guns and were real bad.

During the waning afternoon hours of August 29, 1898, Ranger St. Leon stopped in for a visit with the local justice of the peace at Socorro, just downriver from El Paso between Ysleta and San Elizario. At the judge's request Ernest was handed warrants for the arrests of Bob Finley and John Collier, two fellows who had "taken some horses out of the city pound by force of arms." Without difficulty Ranger St. Leon executed the warrants, hauling Collier and Finley into justice court. After posting mandatory bail bonds the two yahoos rode out of town. St. Leon bid the JP adieu, departing for his company head-quarters at Ysleta. Shortly thereafter St. Leon heard a series of gun-shots and returned to the justice court inquiring about the hubbub? "The Justice told him it was the Finley party and advised St. Leon not to go after them as they were bad men and they might kill him." Never showing the white feather, Private St. Leon took off after the disorderly pair, even though by now they owned a good headstart and, unbeknownst to the Texas Ranger, had been joined by comrade-in-arms John Ray. As twilight was giving away to darkness, Private St. Leon found himself at the Lemaire Ranch. There, with a stroke of good luck, Dr. Oscar J. Breaux, visiting from New Orleans, offered to help arrest the miscreants.[30]

Somehow among the maze of intersecting trails and under night's cover, St. Leon and Breaux got ahead of the manhunt's intended tar-gets. Pausing to rest and perfect a workable strategy the Ranger and his deputy were shocked into reality when they were near overrun by the trio. Private St. Leon hollered "Stop, throw up your hands," or something quite similar. The three challenged men answered: Unleashing Colt's six-shooters they triggered responses, repeatedly. The gunfight waxed hot. During the exchange Doctor Breaux caught a bullet to the head just above an ear, killing him instantly. The night sky was illuminated with intermittent muzzle flashes, as the owl-hoots and the Ranger figuratively stood toe to toe, wildly popping caps, each hoping for reprieve but none opting to tuck tail and run. One of St. Leon's whistling .45 bullets echoed a horrendous thump; an enemy's horse staggered and fell to the ground, dead. Another of the young Ranger's bullets whipped into John Ray's right thigh knocking him out of the fight, but not out of life. Then the tables turned. A lead ball tore into Ernest St. Leon's left arm, through his shoulder, and into a lung. Losing his footing St. Leon collapsed, blood leaking from his arm, a mixture of pink/white froth trickling across his lips. Approaching a wounded tiger at nighttime is not smart. Finley, Collier, and the injured Ray opted to forego any forward movement, fleeing into the night.[31]

Naturally the fireworks had attracted no little attention. Private St. Leon was removed to the nearby Lemaire Ranch, a doctor was summoned, and Captain John Hughes, at 1:30 a.m. on August 30, 1898, was awakened by the courier carrying news of the shooting.[32] Taking Ranger Private R. C. Crawford and Deputy Sheriff Ed Bryant, who had resumed employment at the El Paso County sheriff's department, Captain Hughes jumped into action, ultimately taking custody of Finley, Collier, and Ray absent any heroics or another gunfight.[33]

Shortly Private St. Leon was admitted at the Hotel Dieu, El Paso's Catholic hospital, and the prisoners were lodged into another hotel, Sheriff Frank Simmons' El Paso County lockup.[34] While in the hospital Ernest St. Leon was interviewed by and made an oral statement to the district attorney, "but it was not made public."[35] During the evening of August 31, 1898, at about seven o'clock, Ranger Ernest St. Leon passed to the other side, "his death from the effects of a wound made by a shot from a pistol in the hands of men who were resisting arrest."[36]

Exercising constitutional rights the defendants did not waive a Preliminary Hearing. Understandably, with no surviving witnesses to contradict any testimony and the prosecution's only admissible proof a Dying Declaration of questionable evidentiary worth, the stage was set for a touch of courtroom drama. After establishing an alibi story for Bob Finley, defense attorneys went to work, mapping out their blueprint for what had actually happened that night:

> ....Ray and Collier admitted on the stand that they did the shooting which resulted in the death of St. Leon and Breaux, but alleged that they were waylaid and fired upon by the ranger. They endeavored to establish the fact that Diamond Dick was intoxicated when the fight took place and that they acted in self-defense and believed at the time their assailants were Mexicans....[37]

Adhering to prescribed and customary legalities, and with the standard of proof being but Probable Cause during a Preliminary Hearing, not belief Beyond a Reasonable Doubt, coupled with the defendants' admissions, the magistrate was justified in binding the men over for trial, even though he—and everyone in the community—could recognize the weakness of the criminal case if submitted to a jury for a

District Court adjudication. After posting $1000 each to assure their later appearance the three defendants were set free.[38] Virtually from onset the outcome was a foregone conclusion: "The state had nothing to offer in the way of evidence except the ante mortem statement of the ranger taken while he was almost at the point of death and its vagueness proved nothing." None of the three defendants suffered conviction or punishment for killing Dr. Breaux and Ranger St. Leon.[39]

At El Paso an undertaker agreed to take $52 up front, allowing Mrs. St. Leon a few days to accumulate funds for the outstanding $19.[40] According to passed down family lore St. Leon's widow divested herself of Diamond Dick's stickpin to settle the account.[41] Perhaps it's true. She was, at least temporarily, not penniless though. Captain Hughes certified the deceased Ranger had pay due in the amount of $90. Mrs. St. Leon made her X mark, accepting payment, the Spanish-speaking lawman Ed Bryant acting as a comforting friend and an official witness.[42] Ernest St. Leon was peacefully interred in El Paso's Concordia Cemetery.[43]

Diamond Dick St. Leon was one of the most colorful characters working and riding Lucifer's Line: A dead-shot fellow adept at staining his face and decking out in the loudest and gaudiest Mexican costumes while passing himself off as a" caballero of the deepest dye." He, too, held title to another, though not enviable distinction—a quantifiable distinction—Ernest St. Leon was the last Texas Ranger killed in the line of duty during the nineteenth century.[44]

Introduction to Part II

The Ranger Force Era
1901–1935

From time to time citing random facts can prove thought-provoking. Markedly, such is the case within the framework of *Riding Lucifer's Line*. As noted in closing the preceding chapter, Ernest "Diamond Dick" St. Leon was the last nineteenth-century Texas Ranger killed in action. His passing did not, however, register as the last Texas Ranger to give up the ghost while serving with the Frontier Battalion. That history will belong to another Ranger. For this narrative it's not unfitting to note that since the 1874 birthday of the Frontier Battalion, Company D, St. Leon's unit, would mortally forfeit more Texas Rangers than any of the other companies. And it's not out of place to mention that twice as many Rangers were killed along the border as within the state's interior counties during that same turn of time. Notwithstanding that the 1800s were but now days left for historians to dissect, Texas Rangers were yet living in real time and still facing real tests. Armchair thinkers looking backwards have opportunity to capriciously draw imaginary timelines. For everyday Rangers posted in the borderlands crossing a line from one century to the other was, as a practical matter, meaningless. *Riding Lucifer's Line* is but at the halfway point. The new century's opening year would hasten bitter news for a Texas Ranger's family and for the Frontier Battalion. A deathbed would receive both.

In the first instance Texas Ranger T. L. Fuller was fatally bushwhacked while washing his face at a barber shop in Orange, Texas, on October 15, 1900. Fuller had been assassinated by Thomas Poole, the brother of Oscar Poole, a fellow the Texas Ranger had killed four days before Christmas the preceding year while the ruffian was trying to liberate a prisoner from his custody. The Poole brothers were sons of the Orange County judge, George F. Poole, who from previous dealings already held dear a disdain for Texas Rangers. In fact, Captain Bill McDonald, Company B, Frontier Battalion, thought Judge Poole was unethically furnishing legal counsel to partisans during an ongoing feud. Although delving into the feud story makes for a fascinating read, for the purpose of moving this Introduction forward such will not be obligatory. Suffice to say there was no love lost between Judge Poole—along with his cronies—and the Texas Rangers. Thomas Poole was not unexpectedly put on trial for murdering Ranger Fuller at Orange and, also not surprisingly, the trial jury hastily rendered a verdict of not guilty. Feelings between Texas Rangers and the Poole faction in Orange chronically soured. And those acidic feelings had been fated not to sweeten: In the legal mind of Judge Poole most Texas Rangers did not have lawful authority to even make an arrest.[1]

Such an assertion was not brand-new. Near twenty years earlier the niggling little question had been broached, all because of a Texas Ranger gunplay. At about midnight on May 16, 1881, at Colorado City, Mitchell County, Rangers Jeff Milton, Jim Sedberry—"a regular bear in a fight"—and rookie private J. B. Wells responded to a disturbance at the Nip and Tuck Saloon. There they confronted W. P. Patterson, full-time cowman and part owner in a local newspaper, the Colorado City *Courant*. By most accounts Patterson was a real decent fellow—when sober. But alas, he was a gritty, hard-bitten West Texan "who got drunk often, and stayed drunk long."[2] During the ensuing arrest attempt Patterson yanked out his Colt's six-shooter, firing a shot at the Rangers who answered in kind. Patterson's shot had missed; the Rangers' had not. In fact, Private Wells put a hot round into Patterson while he was at least critically wounded—maybe already dead—but in any case sprawled horizontal in the dirt street. Patterson died but the uproar about his demise didn't. Mitchell County folks were outraged![3] The trio of Rangers had to face the legal music, dancing into and out of courtrooms for quite an extended time. One legal question then, was the same one Judge Poole was bringing two decades later. Eventually the three Texas Rangers came free of being legally imprisoned or executed or lynched. However, rather than remedy any disputes arising about Texas Rangers' legal authority—as is so typical for a bureaucracy—the tin of nuisance was just kicked down the road of complacency, where it laid undisturbed gathering rust, until that cantankerous Orange County judge reopened the argument—a real can of worms.

Judge Poole's reading of the law likewise sparked similar suppositions from other judicial benches: namely County Judge W. M. Pardue at Memphis, Hall County, in the Texas Panhandle. The long and short of their hypothesis was plain, elementary if one but turned to a literal interpretation of legislation creating the Frontier Battalion. You see, not that it really made any difference, but Judge Pardue was no friend of the Texas Rangers either.[4]

The two jurists were hanging their legal hat on a single word: *officer*. A quick recap from part of the law—even though it appears elsewhere in this narrative—is imperative for understanding what the brouhaha was all about. The 1874 law creating the Frontier Battalion said, in part:

> Each officer of the battalion and of the companies of minute men herein provided for, shall have all the powers of a peace officer, and it shall be his duty to execute all criminal process directed to him, and make arrests under capias properly issued, of any and all parties charged with offense against the laws of the State.[5]

The bone of contention was this. By strict reading of the law only the Frontier Battalion officers, captains and lieutenants, were vested with the authority of Texas peace officers. The privates and noncoms were not and, in point of fact and law, all of the arrests they had made for the past quarter century had been taboo—or by that tougher benchmark, criminal: False Imprisonment. Common sense, of course, would intimate that such had not been the intent of Texas legislators writing the law, but in the pitched battles of legalese rationality counts for little—sometimes. This was one of those times. Regardless how nonsensical it may now appear, at the time, it was a major concern with the potential for enormous legal ramifications.

Texas Governor Joseph D. Sayers was dumbfounded by the twist, booting the prickly matter down to Adjutant General Tom Scurry, who in turn made inquiry with Texas Attorney General Thomas S. Smith—the state's top lawyer. Could it be true? It was! Smith had concluded—the way the law was worded—that only the Frontier Battalion's commissioned officers actually had legal arrest authority—privates and noncommissioned officers did not.[6] Therein, then, was a predicament. Texas had a Frontier Battalion—a tiger absent most of its teeth—and the state legislature necessary for amending the wording and fixing the problem was not sitting in Austin, and would not be until its 1901 session. A cat needed skinning. There was more than one way.

Working within parameters of legal assurances from Attorney General Smith that it was within Governor Sayers' power to reorganize the Frontier Battalion, he and Adjutant General Scurry set to work. If those goddamned fussy judges demanded only commissioned officers making arrests, that could be arranged—right fast! The Frontier Battalion was restructured. Without delay the battalion was beefed up. Multiple lieutenants per company were named and two new companies were created.[7] The new lieutenants had been promoted on paper, but voluntarily had forgone the commensurate pay increase. It was a stopgap measure to be sure, but entirely legal nevertheless. As typical with bureaucracy there was an underbelly story. The newly promoted lieutenants were required to submit one dollar apiece—out of their pockets—to the Texas Secretary of State for covering the cost of issuing new commissions.[8] The few remaining privates in the Frontier Battalion could not lawfully make a custodial arrest, but nothing prevented them from working with and "assisting" when the lieutenant deemed taking a prisoner was in order.[9]

Texas desperadoes could not have cared less about any finer points of the law. They stayed busy. Reviewing records from but one Frontier Battalion company for the so-called period when the Rangers were in limbo is enlightening—the boys hadn't missed a lick despite all that legal mumbo-jumbo. For that period the Texas Rangers of Company D made fifty-six physical arrests for numerous felony and misdemeanor violations, including five suspected murderers, four fellows charged with trying to murder someone, a rapist, a kidnapper—and one dumbbell charged with Burglary of a Boxcar.[10]

When the 1901 legislative session was gaveled to order, fixing the Frontier Battalion mess was reasonably high on the lawmakers' agenda. By the end of March state senators and representatives had blueprinted a new outfit: the Ranger Force. It should be no shocker that Texas Rangers thus employed—regardless of rank—were to be awarded all the powers granted to Texas peace officers, not a smidgen of doubt about any nonsensical uproar over semantics. The new law would take effect ninety days after the legislature adjourned.

Over the signature of Adjutant General Scurry dated July 3, 1901, General Order No. 62 was the administrative foundation for structuring the new Ranger Force: four companies, each commanded by a captain, and not more than twenty privates per company under the first-level supervision of a sergeant. As with the Frontier Battalion, the men would still furnish their own horses and the cost of state-issued firearms would be deducted from their quarterly paychecks of $150 for sergeants and $120 for privates. The state, however, would continue furnishing the Rangers' bacon and bullets. In Austin, at Ranger Force headquarters, a quartermaster with the rank and salary of a captain, $100 per month, would attend to matters of payroll and logistics.

Five days later the Frontier Battalion was officially disbanded. Although the legal wrangling over language had created a stir, in the overall scheme Texas Rangers had hardly missed a beat, much to the chagrin of their detractors—and there were not just a few. And here it is but fair to mention—since there is no longer a Frontier Battalion—that the death of Texas Ranger T. L. Fuller in that Orange, Texas, barbershop had been that outfit's last casualty. The Ranger Force would now start carrying the burden.

Though there actually might be room for some finagling upon what would now be a much more expansive platform, it's generally accepted and reported that there were four great Texas Ranger captains of the twentieth century. The quartet had all been products of the Frontier Battalion era; now each captained a company in the new Ranger Force. The initial deployment model was thus: Captain James Abijah Brooks, Company A, Alice, Texas; Captain William Jesse McDonald, Company B, Amarillo, Texas; Captain John Harris Rogers, Company C, Laredo, Texas; and John Reynolds Hughes, Company D, in El Paso County at Fort Hancock. At headquarters, Quartermaster Lamartine Pemberton "Lam" Sieker, a charter member of the Frontier Battalion, oversaw day-to-day operations of the Ranger Force.[11]

Recalling that *Riding Lucifer's Line* is not a sweeping history of Texas Rangers in general, but a limited treatment with straightforward guidelines for inclusion, it is yet appropriate to move this Introduction for Part II ahead. Explicitly commenting that it would be Ranger Force personnel who would march—and stumble—through such epochal chapters touching Texas and American history as the Mexican Revolution, World War I, Prohibition, oil-well boomtowns, and into the gateway days of a so-called Gangster Era. Prior to kicking off Chapter 12, speaking to several background topics of substance is pertinent and, perhaps, beneficial for the reader.

Though seldom if ever mentioned in a historical context, there are and always have been two divergent types of criminal law in the eyes of societies throughout the world—including Texas. Some crimes are just communally graded as inherently evil. Murder, rape, robbery, burglary, theft, and burning someone's house to the ground are not acceptable—anywhere. These crimes are *malum in se*, bad in anybody's book! On the other hand, there are offenses that are registered as *malum prohibitum*, criminal conduct that may not be necessarily evil, but conduct that is prohibited in certain places and/or at certain times, such as violations of liquor and gaming laws, Sunday and curfew laws, or written statutes banning prostitution and/or pornography—and in some places—even carrying concealed six-shooters. In plain talk, what is completely legal in one state or town may be outlawed in an adjoining state or town. The local voting populace chooses just how much personal freedom of choice they will endorse or how much perceived sin they will stamp out—or at a minimum, making it seem they're stamping out. With *malum in se* crimes—normally felonies—the whole community is in widespread agreement. To the contrary, with *malum prohibitum* crimes—typically lower-level misdemeanors—rarely is there unanimity. In fact, often the public is about evenly divided. For the Ranger Force these distinctions would be—and continue to be—relevant.[12]

Much of the criticism leveled at Rangers during the first decade of the twentieth-century can be traced to involvement—an untenable involvement—with being tasked to squelch, or at least tamp down, infractions stemming from rowdisim and overindulgence in some pretty wild and woolly towns—burgs booming as result of money-ginning energy gone mad. For the most part locking up slobbering drunks and pickpockets and dog-tired fist-fighters should have been work for the sheriff, his deputies, and/or the city policemen. But often was the case local lawmen, for one reason or the other, furtively looked the other way making one bloc happy but infuriating another. The losers squawked. Politicians listened. When pleas hit the governor's or adjutant general's desks, not long thereafter Texas Rangers were walking the boardwalks keeping order in some unfamiliar town—typically scooping up miscreants and payloads of censure from one angered faction or another. Chasing after murderers or bank robbers or child molesters earned little scorn; state peace officers with *malum prohibitum* wrongdoers ground under their boot heels did. Predictably then, the Ranger Force was not universally popular everywhere in Texas. Many folks thought Texas Rangers were but an anachronism, a relic of bygone days. Lawmakers were constantly tinkering with the Ranger Force's funding, which snow-balled into staffing level shortages. At the same time political hacks were disproportionately casting their dark shadow over any sound management practices and unassailable recruiting policies. Crony-ism was no stranger to the Ranger Force. From time to time an indi-vidual Texas Ranger would figuratively (or literally) shoot himself in the foot injuring the outfit's reputation, clouding any appearance of professionalism. Taken as a whole though, the Ranger Force had some good courageous men and did good work—unless temporarily hamstrung by the ill-timed actions of that overbearing or inebriated or tactless Texas Ranger.

Riding Lucifer's Line hubs on borderlands doings, and although there are a couple of chapters rightly earning mention during that first decade of the twentieth-century, Part II is weighted—by chance, not design—for the years 1910–1921. At first blush there most likely would be an assumption that the subsequent storyline is tied hard and fast to the Mexican Revolution. Such a whim is understandable but unwarranted. Mexico's political upheaval certainly plays its part in several of the unfolding events, but at times only secondarily, and sometimes none whatsoever. The entire Texas/Mexican border was then—as it is today—a damn tough piece of real-estate. Nonparti-sanship peels back the abrasive hide of truth: There were mean Mex-icans, mean Hispanics, mean Anglos and, as a subset, a few mean Texas Rangers haunting the Rio Grande from above El Paso to below Brownsville. No group owned exclusivity.

Not infrequently it's written—especially within an agenda-driven context—that during this timeframe of turbulence there were between 300 and 5,000 border Mexicans/Hispanics killed by Texas Rangers and their cooperative, but mean-spirited cohorts. There is a lot of room between 300 and 5000. A dispassionate social scientist or conscientious historian or capable nonfiction chronicler might find a difference of 4,700 quite a stretch—absent quantifiable evidence—to manufacture such an indictment. *Riding Lucifer's Line* centers on Texas Rangers killed along the Texas-Mexico border, not who they justifiably killed in the line-of-duty or who they outright murdered cloaked behind the color of law. Subsequent chapters herein expose both instances. Murder is *malum in se*! Anemic would be the defense of any Texas Ranger guilty of murder or wanton brutality. Likewise, lame from the get-go are any undocumented and/or unproven and/or uncorroborated accusations of killing and arrant cruelty hurled at any institution or individual, from any quarter—anecdotally—or from underneath the guise of scholarship. Admissible evidence—not hearsay, not gossip—is what counts in the courtroom: Specifics sustained are what matter for the history book.

And one chapter in those history books—and now, thankfully, a whole book (Drs. Harris and Sadler, *Plan de San Diego: Tejano Rebellion, Mexican Intrigue*)—deals with *Plan de San Diego*. The plot was nefarious. Stated simply, certain Mexican adherents and their sympathizers on the north side of the Rio Grande were geared to retake Texas and the Southwest from the United States, keeping parts and magnanimously returning portions to Indians and Blacks as their own separate state homelands. Too, there was another component to *Plan de San Diego*: Murder all male Anglos over the age of sixteen.[13] A sobering gut check by conspirators should have waved them off because of over ambitious goals, but a fantasy it was not!

In today's climate of revisionism it is not uncommon to read that after the *Plan de San Diego* was exposed certain Mexican Revolutionary insurgents and their border country allies were not bandits, but seditionists—*Sediciosos*. Too, it is readily acknowledged by near everyone that *Sediciosos* raided and looted and murdered. But in some quarters it's written the *Sediciosos'* major thrust of Texas maliciousness was aimed at attacking visible models of American capitalism and expansionism, such as an infrastructure symbolized by bridges, railroads, power plants, irrigation pumping stations, and waterway head-gates, etc. Such assertions may be—at least in part— true. There is another hard truism. Violently attacking non-military targets to further political and/or ideological goals is known worldwide by a single appellation: Terrorism! The whole of the Lower Rio Grande Valley population—no matter political persuasion or party affiliation—or cultural and ethnic heritage—were living in real time, and by extrapolation so, too, were men of the Ranger Force.

Looking backwards—with no skin in the game—it's easy to historically grade pitched battles and tally body counts with blanket terminology, such as gauging that losses were really not too severe. That is, not too severe, unless one were actually there lying beside wounded buddies and a dead woman—her brains blown out—looking across an embankment through rifle sights at the enemy *Sediciosos* hustling to collect their piled up dead *amigos*. Or, identifying innocent murder victims of *Sediciosos* sprawled between their seats in the coach of a derailed passenger train. Perspective does matter, in real time.

Although some of the following vignettes in Part II will bring to the forefront fascinating details about the Mexican Revolution, the reader wishing an in-depth breakdown should consult more general treatments of the Rangers or works by design aimed at the upheaval. That said, the Mexican Revolutionary period and the so-called Bandit War in the Lone Star State's Lower Rio Grande Valley were by most accounts the Ranger Force's blackest days. There will be no white-washing in *Riding Lucifer's Line*.

José T. Canales, Representative for the 77th State Congressional District at Brownsville, wanted to give the Ranger Force a little scrub-bing. Legislator Canales is normally credited as the catalyst that insti-gated Texas Ranger supporters "quite eager for an inquiry in order to clear the organization's name" to set in very public motion a joint Senate-House committee exploring *alleged*—and not so *alleged*—misconduct and murders dumped at the Ranger Force's doorstep. The formalized hearings became known as the Canales' Investiga-tion of 1919. From the outset there may be room for argument as to whether José Canales' motives were to "gut" or "fix" the Ranger Force. Relying too heavily on hearsay and innuendo during official testimony before the committee undercut the viability of convert-ing those musings into admissible evidence for the courtroom. On the other hand, the very open and widely known nature of the hear-ings was no real plus for the Rangers. Episodes of bald-faced illegality and gross inappropriateness were exposed.[14] The net result of all the subpoenas and testimony and a few threats of bodily harm, despite wishes of zealous critics, was a fine-tuning of the Ranger Force com-mand structure and staffing level, with a solemn pledge to fill the roster with the right kind of men in the future.

There are many venerating histories championing Texas Rang-ers. Similarly there are not just a few published works excoriating the Texas Rangers, principally for their enforcement tactics along the Texas/Mexican border during the twentieth-century's first quarter. There really is a hard bottom-line. Despite what their committed and myopic detractors then or now have alleged or penned—and con-tinue to postulate—to their perceptible vexation the Ranger Force survived. And, as with studying progression of the Frontier Battal-ion, watching transformations within the Ranger Force are also iden-tifiable, informative, and interesting.

For it was during Ranger Force days that speeding technological development forevermore changed the face of law enforcement. Texas Rangers were still obligated to own a horse, but they now responded from company headquarters or sub-camps behind the wheel of a Ford, Old Dobbins pawing at the horse-trailer's plank floor, yearning it seemed, not to be tied by the reins and left out of the manhunt or "scout" along the river. Yes, in parts of the state there was yet plenty of enforcement work to be done horseback—especially far West Texas, the Panhandle, and along the Rio Grande.

Radio communications were on the near horizon. Those new gismo typewriters were in vogue for making reports. Dusting for fingerprints and making plaster casts of tire-tracks and footprints were forensic techniques Ranger Force personnel were being forced—by captains and changing times—to learn. Rather quickly they understood the value of sketching a crime scene and taking photographs, preserving those images for the courtroom. Sitting in the witness-box and answering attorneys' questions was much easier, and the testimony much more accurate, after reviewing those handwritten notes and black and white pictures. Lofty judges allowed 'em. Haranguing prosecutors loved 'em. Red-mouthed defense lawyers didn't. Approving trial juries generally noted the professional approach now employed in building airtight criminal cases. Twentieth-century advancements were overhauling—and upgrading—the Ranger Force.

One thing would never change, however. Bad men were still bad. Depriving bad men of their liberty is bona fide dangerous work: gun-carrying work. By and large lawmen are fascinated with firearms—tools of their trade. Desperadoes are too. And just as with watching near spontaneous adjustments Frontier Battalion era Rangers had made with regards to getting their hands on improved weaponry, the same dynamic was evident with lawmen of the Ranger Force. Examination of vintage Ranger Force photographs and perusing their archived correspondence files is illuminating. Transition from Winchester lever-action carbines to the latest improved semi-automatic rifles is conspicuous—and striking. The classic Thompson sub-machinegun was no stranger to many a Ranger Force fellow. The transition away from the .45 Colt's Peacemaker was slower—every nostalgic Texas Ranger needed that handgun—but gradually their sidearm of choice drifted toward Smith and Wesson double-action revolvers, and then to another belt pistol—their near trademark Colt

.45 auto, the famed 1911 model. Carried in fancy hand-tooled holsters and personalized by elaborate engraving and normally sporting handles of ivory or pearl or sterling silver inlaid with gold, the pair of twin Colt .45 autos became almost as an iconic symbol for the more modern Rangers as was their distinctive *cinco peso* badge.

As previously noted, law enforcing ever evolves; techniques and tactics and technological tools are repeatedly subject to examination beneath the administrative and public microscope. Organizational configuration is not exempt. Structurally the Ranger Force's lifespan would outlast the Frontier Battalion's by about a decade, but it too would eventually surrender to changing times. With inauguration of the state's latest chief executive during January 1935, days of the Ranger Force were short numbered. Governor James V. "Jimmie" Allred had campaigned on a guarantee of revamping Texas' methodology for statewide policing. He kept his promise.[15]

Governor Allred appointed a three-man commission to oversee the newly christened Texas Department of Public Safety. Placed within the progressive framework of the brand-new outfit were the Texas Highway Patrol, a fledgling State Crime Lab, and remnants of the now-on-paper evaporated Ranger Force. Although it's perhaps a little challenging to grasp in light of all the previously penned hoopla about Steven F. Austin's ranging companies, the Frontier Battalion, and the Ranger Force, there are sidebars worth mentioning. At long last, Rangers were furnished state-issued badges, no longer having to purchase their own. Now, too, placed under the umbrella of DPS, Rangers were designated by name as Texas Rangers, formally—for the very first time. This is where the modern-day Texas Rangers remain, an investigative and crime fighting and peace keeping arm of the Texas Department of Public Safety.[16] Since that 1935 Texas Ranger birthday there has been no shortage of richness for rapt historians, or nonfiction writers, or armchair law enforcement buffs. The body of work is there.

This narrative, however, must now revert back to picking up the Ranger Force story with Chapter 12. Days of the Texas Department of Public Safety are on the far horizon. In real time, down along the river, Rangers riding Lucifer's Line were yet in store for more thrilling hot times and, sadly, too many heartbreaking farewells.

Part II

Photo Gallery

Texas Ranger Hall of Fame & Museum

Emmett Robuck, a Texas Ranger from Caldwell County, made the supreme sacrifice when fatally bushwhacked by lurking assassins in the South Texas border country near Brownsville, Cameron County.

Texas Ranger Tom Goff, mild mannered but a deadly shot. He was so good with a gun that for awhile Tom was an exhibition shooter with Buffalo Bill's Wild West Show. There was, however, a bullet with Goff's name on it, one of his own. Tom was killed by an escaping prisoner near Terlingua, overlooking the Rio Grande.

These six Texas Rangers had smartly outfitted themselves with the latest improved smokeless powder Winchesters, but yet clung to one of the Rangers' favorite handguns, the Colt's .45 caliber six-shooter, popularly called the Peacemaker. Standing L to R, Herff Alexander Carnes, Sam McKenzie, and Arthur Beech. Seated L to R, Tom Ross, Albert Mace, and John R. Hughes.

Five Company G Rangers near Alice, Texas, align their sights for a shutterbug. The lackadaisical stance of the Texas Ranger on the right exposes this lineup was for show, not legit target practice—at least not at the instant a cameraman snapped this picture.

James W. "Jim" Fulgham, Texas Ranger. A second-place finish was a last place finish for desperado Charles Carroll who chose to test Fulgham's no-nonsense resolve—and skill with a Colt's six-shooter.

Though a former Texas Ranger, Joseph Russell Sitter was a Mounted U.S. Customs Inspector when he and rookie Ranger Private Eugene B. Hulen were ambushed and murdered and horrifically mutilated in the lonesome Big Bend Country of far West Texas by Chico Cano's band of cutthroats.

Second from left, horseback, Texas Ranger Robert Lee Burdett, murdered during gunplay with a "Mexican gang" in the border town of Fabens, El Paso County, Texas. The mounted Texas Rangers L to R are R. L. Morris, Burdett, Sue M. "Mac" Jester, Jim Mercer, R. G. Askew and M. C. Cathey. Captain James Monroe Fox is standing in foreground.

Herff A. Carnes and Pat Craighead. Craighead would undergo amputation of his left leg as result of a border country shoot-out gone horribly haywire—friendly fire: Herff's brother, Texas Ranger Quirl Bailey Carnes, would die of gunfire spit out by a conspiratorial crowd of not so friendly Texas/Mexican border country murderers.

Scouting the tough West Texas Rio Grande Country, riding their favorite mounts; Rangers Charles Brown (left) on "Buckskin" and James C. "Doc" White atop his trusty steed, "Old Sorrel."

For this photograph Rangers Charles Brown (left) and Doc White may not have been scouting the Big Bend Country on their preferred "rides" but scouting they were, nevertheless. Note the fact Ranger White is carrying a Colt's six-shooter at each hip.

Texas Ranger Lee Trimble demonstrates the handling ability and fine-tuning of a flashy reining horse. Note his sidearm is not the standard single-action Colt, but a modern era double-action revolver.

These four representative Rangers were scouting the late nineteenth-century Texas-Mexico border country, riding into the twentieth-century and into the history books.

Heavy hitters in any impartial Texas Ranger assessment. Standing L to R James Abijah "J. A." Brooks, John Harris Rogers, and Thurlow A. Weed. Seated L to R, Lamartine Pemberton "Lam" Sieker, John Barkley Armstrong, and William Jesse "Bill" McDonald.

Samuel H. "Sam" Newberry was a legit border country Texas Ranger, but nattily dressed he was an iconic symbol of Rangers in transition—on the bumpy road to professionalism. Note his ivory-handled Colt's .45 six-shooter along with his Mexican-loop holster and cartridge belt nearby, also iconic essentials for any self-respecting Texas Ranger of the era.

These South Texas Company A Rangers were primed and ready for war, deadly serious—and deadly. They are L to R, unknown, unknown, William "Bill" McCauley, Captain Frank Johnson, Crosby Marsden, Oscar Rountree, and Gus T. "Buster" Jones. Interestingly, somewhat later Buster Jones as a well-respected agent for the U.S. Government's Bureau of Investigation will be tasked with checking up on a band of ex-Texas Rangers, prime suspects in the lucrative—and criminal—hijacking of a Mexican military paymaster below Marfa, Presidio County.

This photograph suggests—though it's not conclusive—that Texas Ranger Lee Trimble [L], an unidentified U.S. Army soldier, and Ranger Charles Brown had official business or monkey-business on the south side of the Rio Grande.

Long known was the favorable association between South Texas' legendary King Ranch and the Rangers' hierarchy—and everyday working Rangers. This quintet of mounted Texas Rangers poses in front of the Norias Division's main house. The Rangers are from L to R, Howard C. Craig, Ira J. Heard, Sam P. Chessher, Joe B. Brooks, and Lloyd A. David.

Although another photograph taken at the same time has these Texas Rangers of Company E bristling with Winchesters in hand, make no mistake, this group of borderland lawmen scouting the Rio Grande just west of Del Rio were not sissies but shootists. Front row L to R, Nat B. Jones, James Malone, Sidney Roberts, Captain W. L. Barler (slightly to front, center), James A. Wallen and C. F. "Dee" Perkins. Back row L to R, John F. Herzing, Sie Bell, Charles A. Carta, Charles McBee, Troy R. Owens, John Carta, W. B. Davis, Richard "Red" Hawkins, Monty Kirkland, and Henry Glasscock.

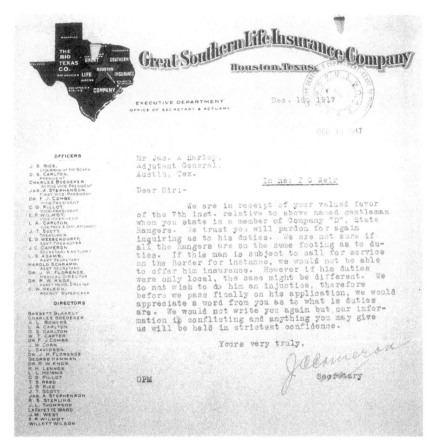

That riding Lucifer's Line was tough business may be drawn by the following extract from an insurance company executive's letter regarding issuance of a policy to a Texas Ranger: "If this man is subject to call for service on the Border for instance, we would not be able to offer him insurance."

Francis Augustus "Frank" Hamer. Frank was present and involved with other lawmen in the shoot-out when fellow Texas Ranger Delbert Timberlake was mortally gunned down along the Rio Grande by the headman for a "gang of dangerous Mexican smugglers," Enacarnación Delgado.

CAPTURE OF A BUNCH OF ARMY DESERTERS DURING WORLD WAR I, BY TEXAS RANGERS, IN SOUTHEAST TEXAS, AFTER ONE RANGER

Although this photo was taken after a roundup in East Texas, it clearly marks reality. Texas Rangers were often faced with arresting sometimes dangerous deserters and slackers, those men already AWOL or others evading the World War I draft. American draft dodgers were a multicultural lot; many skipped across the Rio Grande, not just those of Mexican ancestry, which added to the "depopulation" of the Lower Rio Grande Valley. Others thought service in the Ranger Force would provide an exemption—it proved to be a wrongheaded idea.

Standing: (1)   (2) Jules Baker, ranger; (3)
(4) Levi Davis, ranger; (5) Lee Anders, ranger; Seated: (6) Capt. Henry
Ransom, ranger; (7) Jim Dunaway, ranger; (8) M. G.(Blaze) Delling, former
ranger, U. S. Immigration Inspector; (9) A. Y. Baker, former ranger; and
sheriff;(10) R. M.(Duke) Hudson,former ranger, -Sheriff Anderson county.

Most serious historians seem to concur, man-killing Captain Henry Lee Ransom, seated on left, was an integral cog in the wheel giving Rangers a bad name— sometimes well deserved, sometimes not—during the Mexican Revolutionary period of the twentieth-century. Self-defense is by definition defensible, extralegal executions are not—not by Rangers or borderland Sediciosos, no matter lame pretexts.

Captain Will Davis' Ranger Force, Company L, stationed by the Rio Grande below El Paso at Ysleta. From L to R. Sergeant James C. Perkins, Arthur Jay "Art" Robertson, Edmond B. "Edd" Hollebeke, James Dixie McClellan, Sullivan Ross "Sully" Ikard, Frank Black, Robert Ernest Hunt, Warren Richardson Holland, Santos Duran, Benjamin L. "Ben" Pennington, T. E. Paul "Elzey" Perkins, and Captain Davis. Texas Ranger Elzey Perkins would die of bullet wounds and mutilation. Rangers Pennington and Hunt would mortally succumb to infectious Spanish Influenza while enforcing quarantine laws.

Pictured here is Captain W. L. Wright's Company D. Kneeling L to R, Light Townsend, Captain Wright, Tom Brady, and Webb County Deputy Sheriff W. B. Wright. Standing L to R are John E. Hensely, Dan Coleman, W. S. Peterson, unknown, unknown, and John W. Sadler. Truly a fascinating Texas Ranger photo on its face, but a few bits and pieces warrant mention: Note that Captain Wright's and Private Brady's 1895 model Winchesters have had the barrels sawed off to a point just ahead of the forestock, real handy for up close and personal work in the brasada. Ranger John Sadler's brother George, also a Texas Ranger, had been one of the prime suspects in the "disappearance" of Florencio García. Although Sadler was not indicted by any of the three grand juries looking into the mysterious dilemma, Florencio's "evaporation" was a festering sore spot for many folks in the Lower Rio Grande Valley. Another brother, also a Texas Ranger, Lennard Tillman "Lenn" was killed as a result of six-shooter fireworks near the Devils River by a fellow Ranger—at least according to one account.

Here Rangers Arch Miller, behind the wheel, and Lee Trimble advantage themselves with progress: utilizing roads if feasible, but having personal saddles handy for those instances when it was necessary to borrow horses from area ranchmen. Horse trailers, at the time, had not gained widespread use.

These Rangers were on duty at Brite's Ranch following the homicidal raid by Mexican bandits. Note the wide array of firearms ready for instant use, and also that even at this time the Rangers and Sam H. Neill (far right), a former Ranger, yet clung to the Colt's six-shooter as their sidearm of choice, though their cartridge belts are stuffed plumb full of high-power smokeless powder rifle ammunition.

Though they were definitely on the march to professionalism, sometimes stupidity and recklessness rained on the Texas Rangers' parade. Alligators have sharp teeth, and are dangerous—even to each other. So, too, are besotted Texas Rangers wearing real guns loaded with real bullets. Company D's Bert Clinton Veale, pictured here, may or may not have been the drunker of the two, but in the whacky competition to see just who could kill who—first—Ranger Bert finished second. Ranger Captain Kinlock Faulkner Cunningham got there first, though the aftermath cost him his Texas Ranger commission.

These fellows, too, were legitimate and plucky Texas Rangers. L to R, Hubert Patrick "Red" Brady, James C. "Doc" White, unidentified, Herff Alexander Carnes, and Milam Harper Wright. Subsequently, as a U.S. Mounted Customs Inspector Herff Carnes would be murdered by nighttime smugglers shamelessly crossing the Rio Grande into Texas.

Somewhat of a rare Texas Ranger photograph, this image depicts the Ranger horse-camp near McKinney Springs in the far southern reaches of Brewster County, that part now inside the Big Bend National Park. Standing L to R, Ranger Sergeant J. R. Hunnicutt, unknown native of the area, U.S. 5th Cavalry soldier, Ranger Robert William "Bob" Sumrall, and Ranger John Robert Hollis.

Another photo from the McKinney Springs Ranger Camp set is informative. Clearly it illustrates a level of cooperation between local, state, and federal forces. Ranger Sumrall is standing by the horse as is a U.S. Army soldier. Former Ranger but then Brewster County Sheriff E. E. Townsend—the Father of the Big Bend National Park—is standing by the auto, talking with Ranger Captain Joseph Lee "Joe" Anders sitting in passenger seat. Standing at front of the car is an unidentified Ranger. Ranger John Hollis is atop the horse, while Ranger Sergeant Hunnicutt—apparently wearing an Army campaign hat—and a U.S. soldier sit by the building, at least so says a handwritten inscription in the scrapbook.

With advancement of the motorcar came improved methods for livestock transportation. This Ranger photograph is enlightening. These Rangers have come together on official business or a boondoggle, but in either event at least three horse trailers are visible, as well as the horses outfitted with later styled and more comfortable Western stock saddles. Note a newfangled radio on the camp table. And as always, the Rangers' tools of the trade—Winchesters—are omnipresent.

"Killer Moustaches" and long sideburns are expressions of the past for this clean-shaven and dapperly turned out company of professional lawmen, Texas Rangers dispatched to Galveston when a labor dispute threatened to and did shut down the port. Several of these dandified Texas Rangers had seen hard service along the Texas/Mexican border. Seated from L to R, William M. Molesworth, Edward "Ed" McCarthy, Jr., Captain Joseph B. "Joe" Brooks, John Monroe Rooney, and Benjamin T. Tumlinson, Jr. Standing L to R, James W. "Jim" Milam, Dee W. Cox, T. T. "Tell" Hawkins, John Lewis Bargsley, Thomas J. "Tom" Cole, Claude Darlington, and James Taylor Martin.

In this near-classic Texas Ranger photograph, Frank Hamer, in the dark suit at left end of roulette table, along with representatives from other agencies, have executed a high-profile raid on an iniquitous business house at Mexia, Limestone County, Texas. These types of enforcement actions—augmented with publicity on a wholesale scale—were directed at crimes classified as malum prohibitum, not the inherently evil offenses which are tagged in legalese as malum in se.

Though these stalwart South Texas Rangers are also clean-shaven and wearing ties, as they move into the Gangster Era they are modernizing themselves with the latest advances in firepower, a Thompson sub-machinegun in this instance. The Ranger carrying the full-auto has also upgraded to a more modern double-action revolver, whereas the other four Rangers—not surprisingly—still cling to that old reliable standby, the Peacemaker, Colt's .45 six-shooters. The Ranger at right is even decked out wearing two.

During 1935 the Texas Department of Public Safety was created, comprised by inclusion of the Texas Highway Patrol and Texas Rangers, as well as a fledgling Crime Lab, as encapsulated in this interesting period photo. Modern day Rangers work under the Department of Public Safety organizational umbrella.

These two old-time and salty Texas Rangers, John R. Hughes (left) and Austin Ira Aten, spent their fair share of time scouting Lucifer's Line, luckily. Now in twilight years the bueno amigos contentedly relax at Aten's spacious and well-appointed Southern California ranch home, no doubt now and again reliving the terrors of gunplay and the thrills of bygone days—from the safety and comfort of an armchair.

Chapter 12

W. Emmett Robuck
1902

Emmett Robuck's family tree was fashioned from sturdy oak. Service in the Confederacy had claimed the life of his paternal grandfather. Emmett's father Elias A. "Berry" Robuck was a first-rate stockman, having early on gathered and trailed cattle into the faraway Rocky Mountain country while but a lad of sixteen years. Of this particular trip, one of many up the well-worn cattle trails, Berry recalled:

> I made my first trip up the trail to Utah Territory with old man Coleman Jones, who was boss for a herd belonging to Colonel Jack Meyers. This herd was put up at the Smith & Wimberly ranch in Gillespie County. I gained wonderful experience on this trip in the stampede, high water, hailstorms, thunder and lightning which played on the horns of the cattle and on my horse's ears. We suffered from cold and hunger and often slept on wet blankets and wore wet clothing for several days and nights at a time, but it was all in the game, and we were compensated for the unpleasant things by the sport of roping buffalo and seeing sights we had never seen before.[1]

Emmett's uncle, Terrell "Tully" Robuck, likewise was a cattleman from Caldwell County (Lockhart) southeast of Austin.[2] Aside from its population of pioneering folks, many with a Mississippi heritage, the Robucks included, Caldwell County was/is perhaps best known to Lone Star history as home turf for the Battle of Plum Creek. There on August 12, 1840, Texans intercepted a band of 600 Comanches returning from their incursion to the Gulf Coast after raiding and plundering Victoria and the seashore storehouses at Linnville. The resulting victory for Texans did not end fights with foraying Comanches, but it did dampen their enthusiasm for raiding into the more settled portions of the state. Thereafter isolated ranches and lonesome homesteaders were warriors' targets of opportunity.[3]

Berry Robuck finally settled near Lockhart and married Ella Lucas Brite.[4] On the twenty-seventh day of January 1877, Ella gave birth to William Emmett, the principal character of this narrative. Caldwell County, with open and level grasslands, accented with plentiful stands of timber and creeks draining to the sparkling San Marcos River, was near a perfect place for a boy to make the journey to manhood. Numerically tallying the number of whitetail deer Emmett killed, or truthfully weighing the strings of catfish he pulled from named creeks is, from this vantage point, impossible. On the other hand, there are several items that may be registered with clarity. In addition to developing handiness with firearms and making a tophand cowboy—though he preferred to call himself a stockman— Emmett stood just under six feet tall, looking out at the world with steel-blue eyes from beneath a sweat-stained Stetson shading his light complexion. Sandwiched between whetting his outdoor skills at home or in the classroom Emmett had gained enough education to read and write. He also learned to "speak some spanish."[5]

Emmett's level of bilingual ability is not known, but even rudimentary knowledge of Spanish would be of service in his newfound job. At twenty-three years of age Emmett Robuck became a rookie 2nd lieutenant with the Texas Rangers—a South Texas Ranger.[6] Working under the command of Captain James Abijah Brooks, destined to be named one of the Four Great Captains, young Emmett Robuck was in the Company A detachment posted at the extreme southern tip of Texas in Brownsville, Cameron County. Headquarters for the company was 100-plus miles north at Alice, then Nueces County, now Jim Wells County.[7]

That an entry-level Ranger was commissioned a lieutenant rather than a private was but a stopgap measure, buried in bureaucracy's bungling and lawyers' persnickety tinkering with legislative intention by means of technicality, that temporary handicap about Ranger's arrest authority as alluded to in the Part II Introduction. Numerous were the temporary appointments of new commissioned officers, but only on paper: No commensurate pay increases, just compliance with a definition. During the next legislative session the old Frontier Battalion was disbanded, officially replaced by the Ranger Force, wherein all sworn personnel were officially designated as Texas peace officers, sidestepping the best laid plans of Texas Ranger critics and enemies, at least for the short term. Emmett Robuck was a 2nd Lieutenant no more. He was a Ranger private in the newly created state policing outfit.[8]

Trifling with name designations about what to call the state salaried lawmen did not hamper the extraordinary linkage between South Texas' King Ranch and the Texas Rangers. The understanding, though not contractually reduced to writing, was reciprocal. The Ranger management team and allied elected officials could count on King Ranch hierarchy to come through in times of political or pecuniary crisis. Likewise, when needed, or perceived to be needed at the King Ranch, hard-edged and tough-minded Texas Rangers would answer the call, riding to the rescue, saving the day with Colt's six-shooters at the hip, Winchesters in saddle scabbards, and warrants of authority in hand. The arrangement was not necessarily inappropriate. Cow stealing was cow stealing, no matter who owned the cow. During the springtime of 1902, most especially in the gargantuan El Sauz (sometimes El Saenz) pasture stretching to near the Cameron County line, sharp-eyed King Ranch bookkeepers and well-seasoned *vaqueros* noticed the herd was lessening—rather than growing. Cow thieves were about. Rangers were needed.

Captain Brooks was in receipt of a telegram from the governor: Send three Rangers to the King Ranch and investigate the outbreak of cow stealing.[9] Riding from camp near Brownsville on May 15, 1902, Sergeant Anderson Yancey "A. Y." Baker, along with Privates Harry J. Wallis and Emmett Robuck, sallied forth to make an investigation and, hopefully, catch some cow thieves. At the El Sauz pasture they were joined by King Ranch cowboy Jesse Miller. Scouting through the 17,000-plus acres of El Sauz the Rangers encountered Reyes Silguero who claimed to be a fence rider for this section of the King Ranch. There is a degree of vagueness in regards to whether Jesse Miller did or did not personally know Silguero. However there was no murkiness about a suspicious fact. Fence riders were tasked with riding the fence line. In this instance Silguero was at a loss to explain what he was doing over three miles away from any fence whatsoever. The Rangers were skeptical. Private Wallis makes that perfectly clear: "We thought that he was either there as a spy for thieves or he was there looking out for some big unbranded calves." Fearing Silguero would warn any *amigos* carrying running irons and working the *brasada* looking for unmarked cattle, the Rangers were not hesitant with employment of an unsophisticated preventative tactic—a tough, though undeniably helpful tactic. They handcuffed one of Silguero's hands to "a small live-oak tree and went off about a mile looking for thieves." Perhaps it was but a face-saving measure, or perhaps it's true, but as an afterthought Ranger Wallis remarked: "Before going we gave him all we had to eat, going without anything to eat ourselves."[10] Silguero spent a lonesome and uncomfortable night shackled to the tree. Rangers passed the night elsewhere.

Next morning shortly after daybreak the lawmen's suspicions were again aroused. During their scout they found several calves just like Reyes Silguero, all tethered to trees. The sign was easy to read. Cow thieves were roping and tying while they could, intent on returning and burning brands when their supply of catch-ropes was depleted. Then they would take up the chase and toss and tripping again. The El Sauz pasture was big and screened in spots by dense undergrowth. The Rangers separated.

Near nine o'clock hell popped. Sergeant Baker, alone, emerged from thick brush nearly riding atop Ramón de la Cerda, a man in his twenties, who was afoot with a hogtied calf on the ground before him.[11] Both men were taken off-guard. Ramón jerked both of his six-shooters, one a .41 the other a .45. Sergeant Baker threw up his Winchester. Two shots were fired—at the same instant.

Complying with proper and legal protocols Sergeant A. Y. Baker got word to the foreman of the King Ranch Division that included El Sauz, Edward B. Raymond, who was asked to notify Estevan Garcia Ozuña, the local Justice of the Peace, that an Inquest was in order. Mr. Raymond carries the story forward:

> Ozuña and I arrived at the scene about 9 A.M. on the morning after the killing of Ramon Cerda by Baker. There were several witnesses present. The Justice of the Peace examined Cerda and found he had been hit over the right eye by a 30 cal. soft nose bullet. The hole over his eye was small and the wound in the back of his head was large where the bullet came out. There was but one wound which was fatal. The body was thoroughly examined by the Justice and my self and there was no other wound from a firing arm or any other character of weapon. A calf was tied down on the ground and the body of Cerda lay within four feet of him. The horse of Sergeant Baker was lying on the ground about 20 feet from the body of Cerda—The horse was shot over the left eye by a 41 cal. ball. Cerda had a 41 cal. Colts Revolver which had been fired but once.

He also had a 45 cal. Colts Revolver which had not been recently fired. About 150 yards away there were two calves unmarked and unbranded tied to one tree and about 50 yards further on there was another "Maverick" calf tied to [a] tree. About 30 feet away from the body of Cerda there was a two year old heifer with Mrs. King's mark and brand on it....[12]

An old-time ex-Ranger stabbed at summing up the gunplay with dry wit: "Cerda killed Baker's horse by shooting him in the left eye. A. Y. killed Ramon by shooting him in the right eye."[13]

Thoughtfully, during the after-incident excitement and legal hubbub someone had the good sense to turn a key and unhitch Reyes Silguero from what apparently had proven to be an unbreakable and deep rooted live-oak tree. The temporary prisoner was set free, there being no solid or incontrovertible evidence against him, though suspicion of his conspiratorial culpability ran high with on-the-ground Texas Rangers.[14]

At the time Cameron County politics were hot. Texas Rangers killing a "Mexican" was but another bucketful of incendiary fuel to throw into the cross-cultural fire, fanning the flames of racial discontent. Red Club members, forever determined to chastise the Rangers on any front, were adamant. Six days after Ramón de la Cerda's body was buried the first time, it was secretly exhumed. The Red Club had clout. At least they did with a local Brownsville magistrate, Hernacion Garcia. The second Inquest was to prove that Cerda's body would show marks of brutality on the part of Rangers. There was no evidence to sustain the allegation of unwarranted meanness. No official report was filed—or if so—it has not survived or surfaced as of yet.

Standard operating procedure for district attorneys is to prosecute—or give such an appearance, letting actions of a grand jury siphon away any negative criticism for overzealousness—or, on the other hand, any lackluster interest in docketing a criminal case for trial. Rangers Baker, Wallis, and Robuck, along with Jesse Miller, were required to post bond, awaiting action of the grand jury.[15] Not unexpectedly the Rangers could and did find support from Robert J. Kleberg, General Manager, King Ranch: ".... I want to testify to the good Capt. Brooks—Sergeant Baker & the other members of that Co. have done—and the fearless, impartial and efficient manner in which they have discharged their duty in this Country."[16] Too, ex-Ranger and South Texas rancher John B. Armstrong would chime in with his thoughts about Captain Brooks' men, pointedly expressing himself by highlighting a paradox: "The state does not help to defend a ranger when he gets into trouble, on the contrary, she becomes the prosecutor. So far as I know & believe Capt. Brooks & his men are brave, efficient rangers, capable of discharging the duties of their positions with honor to themselves, fairness to the people & credit to the state."[17]

A not insignificant number of native South Texans, when Texas Rangers were mentioned, raised an eyebrow, cocked their head, and spit. To them Rangers were *rinches*, mounted and armed Texans hunting for Mexicans to kill, and in the Lower Rio Grande Valley many viewed real Rangers as *rinches de la Kineña*—Rangers of the King Ranch. To those border folks the *rinches* "were the personal strong-arm men of Richard King [and his successors] and other 'cattle barons.'"[18]

Subsequently Rangers Baker, Wallis, and Robuck, along with King Ranch cowhand Miller were "no billed" by the grand jury, an action that more than miffed much of the Spanish-speaking population.[19]

Ramón's younger brother, Alfredo de la Cerda, fifteen or sixteen years old, was by most accounts behaving foolishly: He was openly threatening to kill Ranger Sergeant Baker on sight. Brownsville, Texas, during the summer of 1902 was not a place or time allowing a free pass for bluffs and/or death threats. The heartfelt grief was comprehensible. The threat was not smart!

What Alfredo wasn't saying, an editor for the Spanish language newspaper, *El Cometa*, was. From an outward show the words waxed hot, but then began to simmer as summer sweltered toward fall. Subsurface hostility regarding Rangers, particularly A. Y. Baker, was sizzling. The abject hatred had not cooled, not in certain hearts and minds and vengeful souls. At Brownsville whether one supported or condemned Rangers was, for the most part, "sharply divided.... along ethnic lines."[20]

On September 1, 1902, Captain Brooks left Company A headquarters at Alice, arriving in Brownsville the next day. District Court was in session and he, along with Sergeant Baker and Privates Emmett Robuck, Harry Wallis, and J. B. Puckett, kept themselves busy in between answering demands of the court. Hot tempers, courtroom theatrics, and the prospects of a few criminal defendants losing their freedom on a long-term basis always afforded a platform for disorderliness and drama. Company A Rangers patrolled Browns-

ville's streets, doing their part in keeping the peace.[21] Acrimony and
threats were not factors of too much concern to Company A's Captain
Brooks. He was tougher than the proverbial boot, and in his eyes, so
were his Texas Rangers: "My men are crack shots and I am not afraid
of them getting the worst of anything."[22] The swank was premature.

Though the timing is imprecise, others, too, left their headquarters—Old Mexico. Secretly five fellows piled into a skiff and a handsomely paid boatman piloted the shotgun-wielding men across the
Rio Bravo, depositing them on Texas soil.[23] Under the cover of darkness they surreptitiously worked their way into position, about a
mile from Brownsville.

At about ten o'clock on the night of September 9, 1902, Sergeant
Baker and Private Robuck, accompanied by King Ranch cowboy Jesse
Miller, who had been in Brownsville with them attending court,
tightened cinches, stepped into the stirrups, and started for their
campground sited in a pasture owned by Judge James B. Wells, about
a mile from town on the Santa Rosatia Road.[24] For an undisclosed
reason, which has been described both as a "boyish caper" and as a
"saloon wager," Private Robuck was riding A. Y. Baker's showy white
gelding and the sergeant was sitting in the saddle astride Emmett's
grade horse.[25]

Salty sea breezes gently wafted from the nearby Gulf of Mexico.
Routine night sounds blended with conversational tones as the three
horsemen plodded along, bantering back and forth, recapping the
day's happenings and conjecturing about tomorrow's courtroom
agenda. Underneath moonlight Private Robuck, atop the sergeant's
white horse stood out, a beacon guiding Ranger Baker and cowhand
Miller along the dimly defined roadway to camp. The white gelding
jumped sideways in response to the noisy blasts—in harmony three
shotguns had spoken. Miller's horse stumbled, crumpled, hit the
ground dead, throwing Jesse but perhaps saving his life. Sergeant
Baker lurched in the saddle, doubled over, wounded in the back.
Emmett Robuck, seemingly unscathed, sat upright on the horse,
traveling 150 yards before he lifelessly toppled from the saddle. With
six-shooters A. Y. Baker and Jesse Miller returned fire the best they
could. Target acquisition was problematic and they did no damage,
other than scattering assassins into flight. Racing to camp to retrieve
their Winchesters, Baker and Miller returned to the scene of the
shooting, only to find Emmett Robuck dead.[26]

Quickly word reached Captain Brooks. After summoning Doctor L. F. Layton, Brooks, accompanied by Ranger Privates J. B. Puckett and Harry Wallis, along with the Brownsville city marshal, rushed to investigate.[27] While rallying forces and preparing for the manhunt Captain Brooks ordered Private Robuck's body removed to the Miller Hotel at Brownsville. There, Doctor Layton performed his examination, a near full-blown autopsy. The good doctor determined "that the ball had entered just below the left collar bone, passing beneath the wind-pipe and grazing the bone of the neck, from thence it entered the cavity of the chest striking the first rib, then ranging upward and lodging in the muscle near the right shoulder, causing almost immediate death by severing the large blood vessels of the body. The ball was extracted in the post mortem examination.... and was found to be a large-sized buck shot."[28] Captain Brooks without delay notified the adjutant general by telegram:

> Baker and Robuck waylaid on road to camp last night. Baker wounded. Robuck killed.[29]

Burials, especially in tropical climates during the early twentieth-century were best carried out promptly. On Wednesday, the day after the shooting, funeral services were conducted by Reverend Beean at Brownsville's Episcopal Church, under the auspices of the Knights of Honor, of which W. Emmett Robuck was affiliated, maintaining membership with the chapter at Alice. The eulogy was touching, and "many wept outright, while there were few, if any in all the throng to whose eyes the tears did not spring." Then Ranger Private Robuck was peacefully laid to rest in the Brownsville Cemetery—temporarily.[30] Emmett's father Berry Robuck at Lockhart would have it no other way; he wanted the body of his son returned to Caldwell County. So, after but one day at the Brownsville Cemetery, Emmett Robuck's "body was taken up.... transferred to a metal casket, which was afterwards hermetically sealed, and taken to the railroad station, for shipment by the steamer [via Galveston]."[31] Too, Berry Robuck wanted something else: Justice! He personally offered a reward of $500 for the capture of Emmett's killers, and the governor of Texas coughed up an additional $300 for the arrest and conviction of the murderers.[32]

Captain Brooks recognized reality: "Some of these people are sullen and mad. Think we are too severe on some of their people. We have to do something or Wells and other good citizens will be picked off at anytime."[33] Two days later he followed up: "Some of the people who have been the cause of Robuck having been killed are now asking for protection, claim that they will be killed by the rangers."[34] The captain telegraphed Company A headquarters ordering reinforcements, full well knowing: "We have a tough lot to contend with but we will come out in the end. The feeling against rangers both in the city and country is very bitter."[35] Augmenting his small contingent Captain Brooks named Jesse Miller a Texas Ranger, filling the slot left open by the untimely death of Robuck.[36]

Soon two Rangers normally posted at Alice made their appearance at Brownsville, W. F. Bates and A. W. Livingston, the latter one of Brook's favorites: "I ask for no better man to be with me when serious trouble comes up."[37] And serious trouble there would be.

For the bushwhacking murder of Private Emmett Robuck the Rangers arrested Encarnicion Garza, Nicolas Hernandez, Jesus Villeral, Timetao Villeral, A. Sauceda, and the deceased Ramón de la Cerda's little brother, Alfredo, booking them into the Cameron County Jail.[38] Captain Brooks's personal assessment of the prisoners was promising: "Two of the men in jail are weakening and we hope to get a confession from one of them tonight [12 September 1902]."[39]

Something else was not weakening, however: boiling anger over the death of Robuck. Rumblings of taking the prisoners by force and ending their misery with lynch rope finality was drowning prudence and common sense for part of Brownsville's "wrought up" citizenry. Stepping up to the very best Texas Ranger tradition, Captain Brooks assured any would-be lynch masters that he and his men "felt it our duty to give them [prisoners] protection and would of give our lives in their defense although we were fully satisfied that we had the right parties who were responsible for the assassination of our Comrade....[40] None chanced storming the jail.

At long last the body of W. Emmett Robuck was delivered home to Caldwell County. There in the manicured Bunton Cemetery at Dale, just a short trip northeast of Lockhart, the young Texas Ranger, but twenty-five years old, was peacefully, and lastingly, interred.

Ranger Robuck had hardly been laid to rest before things once again popped at Brownsville. Sergeant A. Y. Baker had recovered from his gunshot wound, able to resume duties patrolling the city streets and scouting throughout Cameron County. Alfredo de la Cerda, who had been released after posting bond, continued with his ranting about getting the scalp of a Texas Ranger. Though it may be politically incorrect to speak to reality, nevertheless there is a real hard truism. In a world where men—good men or bad men—customarily attend to their everyday business carrying guns it is sheer folly to think threats to kill will be lightly brushed aside as idle boasting. Altogether ignoring the man who says he will kill you, guilelessly thinking he won't, is madness. In the vernacular of policing lingo such a hostile and menacing guy is "bought and paid for." Which translates to: Chaps spitting out death threats had best follow through—or not dare make a false move.

On October 3, 1902, on Elizabeth Street in downtown Brownsville, Alfredo de la Cerda wiggled the wrong way—or not? Sergeant A.Y. Baker killed him, declaring he had made a suspicious move, as if grabbing for a six-shooter.[41] Other reports indicate the dead fellow had been trying on a new set of gloves. Alfredo was, as it turns out, unarmed. Not unexpectedly the Spanish population was astir.[42] The reviled *rinche* had murdered another "Mexican."

Attuned to duty, Captain Brooks had Sergeant Baker arrested and taken before a magistrate. The killing of Alfredo de la Cerda was a matter for the courts to sort through, not the Rangers. On the other hand, coldhearted killers had unfinished business. Brooks updated AG Scurry:

> That Herculana Berbier told Geo. Patignat and George Moore that Alfredo Cerda tried to get him to assist in the plot to kill Sergeant Baker, that he refused, and went to Patignat's the night that Private Roebuck [sic] was killed so that he could prove that he had nothing to do with the killing. Soon after Alfredo Cerda was killed by Baker, Herculana Berbier was assassinated by unknown parties, he was one of the most important witnesses for the State in the killing of Roebuck and also one of the most important witnesses for Baker in the killing of Cerda. Cerda having offered him money to kill Baker. He has been employed by us to get proof as to who killed Roebuck and shot Baker, and had given important information.[43]

From their safe quarters at Austin it seemed to Texas politicos that the wheels had come off in far South Texas, particularly at Brownsville. A suspected cow thief had been gunned down by a Texas Ranger; a Ranger had been foully murdered—right beside his partner who, too, had been bushwhacked, but only wounded; a mouthy but dangerous teenager had met his Maker and the Mortician thanks to the shooting handiwork of a no-nonsense Texas Ranger; and a state-paid confidential informant's life had been snuffed out before he could testify to a damn thing: Neither incriminating or absolving anybody. Governor Sayers ordered a full-scale investigation.

In the end not too much happened. Sergeant A. Y. Baker came clear for killing the two Cerda brothers. Company A was repositioned and replaced by Company D.[44] And the adjutant general could not find much fault with the manner Texas Rangers handled themselves along that stretch of Lucifer's Line, though he admitted the boys had "cuffed" some of their antagonists "without gloves." For the most part those actions were understandable and had been justified by difficult circumstances, he said.[45] A set from the majority population bloc held to a differing belief.

Chapter 13

Thomas Jefferson Goff
1905

Although he would become a genuine Lone Star State cowboy, Thomas Jefferson "Tom" Goff could not lay claim to Texas as his birthplace. Tom Goff came into the world at Keetsville, Barry County, Missouri. Keetsville no longer registers on the roadmap. The quiet little Ozark Mountain town in the southwestern quadrant of the state, just north of the Missouri/Arkansas line, now renamed Washburn, has somewhat confused the scant retellings of Tom Goff's thrilling life's story.[1] At about age eighteen months, after his March 11, 1871, birthday, toddler Tom accompanied his parents James M. and Nellie Goff back to Texas, where they had previously lived, having been married in Cherokee County (Rusk) on October 8, 1866. With an evident touch of wanderlust in his veins James settled his burgeoning family in surveyed but yet to be organized Jones County, almost in the shadows of abandoned Fort Phantom Hill's ghostlike towering and yet-standing stone chimneys. The county was hardly inhabited, except for Indians and buffalo. Illustratively, the legendary hide-hunter J. Wright Mooar remarked that during the entire 1876 season at their camp in what is now Scurry County (Snyder) they were only visited by one white man, James Goff.[2] The Jones County adventure was short lived. A year later the Goffs moved onto a 3,500-acre ranch in Throckmorton County, above the Clear Fork of the Brazos River.[3] The Goff homeplace was pleasantly situated along Tecumseh Creek about ten horseback miles north of Fort Griffin (Shackelford County) and its ribald civilian community known simply as The Flat.[4]

Although it had been originally lopped off from parts of Fannin and Bosque Counties during 1858, untamed Throckmorton County had not been formally organized until March 18, 1879.[5] Historically speaking Throckmorton County was rich, not only because of its industrious pioneering folks, but its geographical juxtaposition as well. At an earlier day, not far from the Goff residence, were the crumbling ruins of old Camp Cooper, a pre-Civil War U.S. Army out-post. Also close by had been the reservation domain once inhabited by Comanches until removed on an "overly optimistic promise of an extensive land refuge of their own" into Indian Territory.[6]

Life was on the upswing for Tom Goff and his brothers, Frank and Will. His sisters, Georgia and Betty, because of their striking good looks, when they reached the appropriate age would have no trouble reeling in a ranch-raised husband, starting their self-reliant lives as frontier-era housekeepers. Then tragedy struck! On February 12, 1876, mamma Goff gave birth to her fourth son, James Robert, "Jim Bob." All seemed well, until two days later, when to the aston-ishment of midwives and doctors she gave birth to a girl, a delayed twin, Nellie. Not surprisingly medical complications accompanied the birth. Ten days later Mrs. Goff surrendered her last breath.[7] Life and death came quickly along the Clear Fork of the Brazos.

Glenn Reynolds, who would play a significant role in the early life of Tom Goff, was Throckmorton County's first sheriff.[8] And Throckmorton County could stand in need of a good sheriff. Though headquartered in adjoining Baylor County the Millett Ranch cowboys freely roamed, gathering cattle, and camping throughout open range country of Throckmorton County, notably at the Old Stone Ranch. A hard lot they were: "When a man got so tough that he couldn't affiliate with civilization he would go to this ranch and get a job."[9] In speak-ing of personnel practices at the Millett Ranch a modern era nonfic-tion writer summarized: "The brothers became notorious for hiring outlaws and gunfighters as ranch hands and encouraging them to augment the Millett stock holdings by cutting out steers from north bound herds."[10] In speaking of the Millett Ranch cowhands even Bay-lor County historians admitted: "And they hired some men with all the bad traits ever attributed to the worst side of the Old West.... the largest cattle ranch in North Texas and one of the toughest spots this side of Hell."[11]

Though he was but a child at the time, there is no doubt Tom Goff heard about the six-shooting fireworks at the Flat involving Millett Ranch foreman Billy Bland, a sure enough desperate character, and his pal Charley Reed. When the smoke cleared Charley Reed ran out the back door of the celebrated Beehive Saloon while Billy Bland lay on the floor, mortally gut shot. An ex-U.S. Army officer writhed in .45 caliber pain and died. Newlywed Dan Barrow stretched out on his backside staring up at Heaven, a bullet hole between his eyes.

Not dead but wounded were Shackelford County Attorney Jeffress and Sheriff Cruger, and an array of coal-oil lamps.[12] Yes, so it seems, many of the cowhands and fugitives haunting this section of North Texas feasted on the gruel of gunpowder and gin. In fact, the Baylor County Judge, J. E. Morris, from the county seat at Seymour, penned a note to the adjutant general registering his temporary relief: "The whiskey ran out and for the last ten days we have literally 'had a rest' while the grocery keeper has gone for more."[13] Tom Goff was marching through childhood on tough ground. Clearly his daddy James was one tough cookie, too! During the timeframe Tom was challenging adolescence his father was elected to the position of sheriff for Throckmorton County.[14]

Over time, according to one report, Tom had polished marksmanship skills into "legendary" proportion with both Winchesters and Colt's six-shooters.[15] Seemingly this characterization was not hyperbole, for later, a well-regarded Ranger captain would comment on Tom Goff's extraordinary capabilities with weapons: "He was the quickest man with arms and the best shot I have ever known in the service."[16] In addition to expertise in handling revolvers and rifles, Tom could top-off a cold-backed bronc, and toss catch-ropes with deftness. On the ground he was handy with piggin' strings and branding irons, and smartly adept with the castrating and ear notching blades of a Barlow. In other words, he was a first-rate cowboy—by any man's measure. At but age sixteen years Tom had landed a job with the Reynolds Cattle Company.[17]

After gathering and shaping a herd in South Texas, the cowboys were going to trail the cattle to the Reynolds Cattle Company holdings in North Dakota. Tom Goff made the trip, living up to the hardships encountered along the trail. For the next five years Tom cowboyed for the Reynolds brothers, driving cattle to the cold country, one time even surviving the bone-chilling "freak snowstorm" on the naked plains south of Fort Morgan, Colorado, during June of 1892.[18] The following year, still employed by the Reynolds Cattle Company, Tom Goff was again gathering and holding cattle in South Texas, for the moment camped with the chuckwagon between Alice and Kingsville.[19] Tom Goff's career path was to undergo change—a big change.

Riding into the cow camp was Captain John Harris Rogers, the new commander of Company E, Frontier Battalion. Purportedly he was on the trail of robbers who had highjacked a Nueces County shipping company, making off with several thousand dollars' worth of greenbacks. Captain Rogers had fallen behind the outlaws, his horse having played out. Rogers' unassuming request to the wagon-boss was straightforward. He wanted the loan of a fresh horse, and the help of a gritty cowboy, someone not afraid to lock horns with desperate fellows. Tom Goff got the nod.[20]

Well mounted, Rogers and Goff started in quick pursuit, the four robbers' tracks indicating they were making a rush for the Rio Grande, and the safety crossing into Mexico would afford. Riding the more rested horses, it wasn't too long before the two men overhauled the outlaws. Exhibiting the coolness he was made of, Tom Goff, coming in from a different angle and ahead of Captain Rogers, put his common sense and good marksmanship skills to effective use. His Winchester targets were the *mal hombre's* horses, not the men themselves. Dismounted they would be easy to capture. Working the lever of his .30-40 feverishly Tom brought down two horses, their riders piling up into a disorganized heap—both breath and fight knocked out them. Just as Captain Rogers bounced into range a yet mounted brigand attempted to get off a shot; Goff's third bullet thumped him out of the saddle, a nasty wound to the right shoulder. The fourth robber hollered King's X. Captain Rogers duly noted that both of the downed horses had been shot in the neck, and he queried Tom Goff: "Tom had learned that shooting a deer or antelope just behind the head did not ruin much meat. And an animal shot in the neck would die instantly and not jump up and run off as they sometimes did when shot through the heart."[21] The bond of friendship between Captain Rogers and Tom Goff on that day was welded solid.

Purportedly after returning to the Clear Fork Country with a herd of Reynolds brothers' cattle and during a stopover at his father's and stepmother's (James had remarried) Throckmorton County home, Tom Goff was handed a letter from Captain Rogers, one urging him to enlist with the Rangers.[22] Tom Goff bent to the plea, becoming a Company E private during December 1893, headquartered in South Texas at Alice.[23] Private Goff's first identifiable work by name was when he and another Ranger tracked down and arrested Ismail Hinejosa in possession of a stolen horse. The prisoner was turned over to the Nueces County sheriff on Christmas Eve Day 1893. And though he's not actually mentioned by name, it's reasonably safe he participated in a hurried surveillance, one mentioned by Captain Rogers in his Monthly Return's Report of Scouts and Arrests:

From the 29th to the 31st I guarded the town of Alice with nine men secretly day and night having been informed from officers on the Rio Grande that a number of bandits has plans to rob the town of Alice on or about the 1st of January 1894.[24]

Unlike the bandit raid on Nuecestown during 1875, the wholesale raid on the city of Alice failed to materialize. Perhaps the Rangers' presence was not a secret after all. Maybe it had been bogus information from the get-go.

After undergoing the necessary orientation period, Ranger Private Tom Goff was posted at Casa Blanca, a tough railroad town near Floresville, Wilson County.[25] Surveyors and track layers were busy at work laying the twin ribbons of steel that would connect Corpus Christi and San Antonio. Along with construction gangs, came the whiskey peddlers and whores and cheating cardsharps. It was the same old story, oft repeated in the nineteenth-century Wild West.

Tracing Tom Goff's movements as a Texas Ranger is doable, though difficult, complicated by the fact that Tom bounced back and forth from being a state salaried Ranger to voluntarily holding commissions as a Special Ranger while pursuing his personal commercial interests. At Karnes City in Karnes County, southeast of San Antonio, he worked as both a regular Ranger and, later, a Special Ranger when venturing into the livery stable business for awhile.[26] Tom forfeited his Special Ranger commission; out-of-state travel was in his playbook.

After an affable *adios* to the Frontier Battalion, Tom Goff took leave from humdrum business activities from time to time—because he was a superb marksman—appearing with the legendary showman William F. Cody. A snippet in the *Austin Daily Statesman* is clear:

> He [Goff] was a crack shot, having traveled several seasons with Buffalo Bill, giving exhibitions of his skill. He accompanied Colonel Cody on several of his southern tours. He was a natural born scout.[27]

The biographical clock of six-gun episodes as a Texas Ranger or demonstrations as an exhibition shooter had come to a screeching halt. During 1899 at Waco, McLennan County, Texas, Tom had taken a fair maiden by the hand, making her his wife. Ruby would be the mother of Tom's two children, a daughter, Nell, and son Thomas

Jefferson Goff, Jr.[28] After a stint as a bookkeeper—Tom was good with numbers—in a Waco produce firm, the Goff family relocated. They moved to Tom's old stomping grounds, Throckmorton. Tom didn't stomp though, he fidgeted. His brother-in-law, Luke McCabe, had landed Tom a bank job. Ruby was pleased, Tom had a good job—a safe job. Tom was not pleased. He had a safe job all right—a boring job.[29] There was a prescription for remedying that affliction of day-in and day-out tedium. John Harris Rogers, the "Praying Captain" as he was popularly known because he was a man more comfortable "without his six-shooter than without his Bible" was yet a good friend.[30]

Dissecting all of Tom Goff's thought processes is not workable. For whatever reasons he decided once more to enlist as a private with the Ranger Force. On the first day of May 1905, at Colorado City (Mitchell County), Tom Goff swore his oath, receiving his Warrant of Authority and Descriptive List, the paper documents identifying him as a full-fledged Company C Ranger, under the command of Captain John H. Rogers.[31] After dissolution of the old Frontier Battalion and creation of the new Ranger Force, company designations had undergone alteration; thus Rogers no longer captained Company E, but was in command of Company C. The headquarters of Company C in late May shifted from Colorado City to Alpine.[32] Private Tom Goff was to be posted in far West Texas in the rugged Big Bend Country.

Brewster County, the largest county in Texas, was carved from Presidio County during February of 1887 with Alpine (formerly Murphyville) named as county seat.[33] By improved roadway, near a hundred miles to the south, and not too far above the Rio Grande, is the rock-strewn village of Terlingua. As early as the 1880s, quicksilver mines were ginning quite a local economy for this otherwise forlorn and cutoff spot. However, production took off at an unprecedented pace after the turn of the century. Mining mogul and real estate investor Howard E. Perry incorporated the Chisos Mining Company in 1903, his Terlingua enterprises becoming "the largest quicksilver producer in the entire United States.... For a number of years it boasted having over a thousand inhabitants, most of them Mexican."[34]

Captain Rogers disbursed his Ranger manpower throughout West Texas. Private Tom Goff was assigned to keep the peace and apprehend violators in the general vicinity of rough and tumble Terlingua, a lonesome and dangerous undertaking. A clichéd old adage, "One Riot, One Ranger," would have been applicable in the case of

Private Goff at Terlingua, at least for awhile—until help made a show from Alpine.

One of the places Tom Goff was responsible for covering was Big Bend, a mining community five miles east of Terlingua. The spot was aptly named after the Big Bend Cinnabar Company developed and organized by Will Study, to whom present-day Study Butte owes its name. Though the little burg wouldn't survive, at the time Tom Goff was scouting for the Rangers, tiny Big Bend could boast of several business houses and a U.S. Post Office.[35]

On September 13, 1905, at Big Bend, Augustine Garcia, a Mexican between thirty-five and forty years old, began creating a disturbance in a makeshift saloon. His state of drunkenness is unknown, but the fact he had a throat impediment causing him to speak in low tones with a squeaky or squally voice, adding to his alcohol-induced slurred speech, was not helpful. The five-foot, eleven-inch man with a "yellow Mexican complexion," was a sometimes peddler and sometimes common laborer, usually making a "pretty good hand." On the downside Augustine Garcia was "very fond of liquor and frequently gets big drunk."[36] This was one of those times.

Ranger Private Tom Goff, "who was liked by everybody in the camp" was summoned to the scene.[37] Ranger Goff was all-too-familiar with Garcia; he had just arrested him for felony theft two months before.[38] There, at Big Bend, he arrested Garcia again, this time for drunkenness, which wasn't a big deal for the time and place, but Augustine had been trying to fight, making it unsafe not to physically take custody of the fellow, at least until he ascended the stairway to sobriety. There was no jailhouse at Big Bend. Alone, Private Goff would have to march the cantankerous guy to Terlingua where there was a lockup—crude, but a jail nevertheless. The distance was short, the pathway winding.[39]

Straddling his saddle Tom Goff ordered Garcia to make slow foot tracks for Terlingua. If ever an arrest was routine—there really are none—from outward appearances this one seemed to fit the nomenclature. Stumbling along, probably mouthing as most drunks would, Augustine Garcia preceded Tom Goff. The arrest and belligerence of Garcia had attracted no little attention: Witnesses there were aplenty. On the outskirts of Big Bend settlement the trail to Terlingua forked. A shortcut was okay for a man afoot, the other trail more suitable for someone horseback. Private Goff ordered Garcia to walk in front of his horse. Garcia demurred, taking the footpath. Garcia's pathway was on the steep side of a hill. Jockeying for position, to cut off the prisoner, Goff sought to get ahead of Garcia. On the loose rocks the Ranger's horse lost its footing and fell.[40] At least temporarily Tom Goff was pinned underneath the somewhat stunned horse, his Winchester rifle loaded with but three rounds in the leather scabbard on the saddle's topside. Augustine Garcia jumped at opportunity. He jerked the rifle free, hurriedly working the lever thinking he would chamber a cartridge. Instead he ejected a .30-40 round already under the hammer, and was forced to lever another bullet into the barrel. Then he fired—and missed. In a panic Garcia fumbled to recharge the Winchester. Private Goff, dazed, began trying to get back to uprightness, pulling his Colt's six-shooter as he regained equilibrium. It was too late! The third bullet tore through his hip and into his spinal column knocking him to the ground, before he "rolled down the mountain thirty or forty feet."[41] Onlookers had no knowledge about just how many loads were in Private Goff's rifle. So, when Augustine Garcia pointed it at them while retreating, they moved aside, none attempting to make a citizen's arrest.[42] Based on proximity to the Rio Grande, the general presumption was that Garcia had crossed into Mexico, leaving Ranger Tom Goff immobile and at death's threshold.

Hurriedly, medical assistance was sought, and by two o'clock in the morning Goff was receiving treatment from a doctor from Mariposa and a Dr. Stilphen, as well as a number of concerned area citizens. They "did everything they could for poor Goff." R. W. Simmons, one of the mine managers, was brought up to speed on the prognosis: "The wound was a very bad one...." Only the "hardy nature" of Tom Goff was sustaining his lingering fight for life.[43]

Captain Rogers was notified at his Alpine headquarters, and forthrightly sent a telegram to Adjutant General John A. Hulen:

> Private goff [sic] shot at Big-Bend by Mexican prisoner perhaps fatally yesterday. Will leave for the scene at once, no further particulars party not yet captured.[44]

Quite expectedly newspapers throughout the state, such as the *Austin Daily Statesman*, *Houston Chronicle*, and the *Dallas Morning News*, published somewhat garbled accounts, of the story—printing unconfirmed details as they came in. Texas Ranger Captain John Reynolds Hughes prematurely added to the confusion, suggesting "that Goff attempted to arrest a Mexican and was shot from behind by other Mexicans. It is believed that several Mexicans took part in the murderous deed."[45] Slowly as details unwound, the truth emerged. Augustine Garcia had acted alone.

During such a horrifying ordeal the gritty Ranger never lost consciousness. Throughout that night the thirty-four-year-old Goff suffered—hanging on—dead set against giving up the ghost. By one o'clock the next afternoon, however, the Grim Reaper had whipped him into submission. Thomas Jefferson Goff was dead.[46]

Captain Rogers, accompanied by Alpine's Doctor Berkley, rushing south from the county seat met the hack carrying Goff's body north at the halfway mark.[47] From that point they reverently transferred the remains to Alpine, first thinking that the appropriate place for interment would be there. A memorial service was held at the home of Captain Rogers. Shortly it was decided to ship the fallen Ranger to his old home in Throckmorton County, and so it was, Captain John Rogers respectfully accompanying the body as an honor guard—and warm personal friend.[48] At Throckmorton, Texas, young Goff was laid to rest in the city cemetery.[49]

The death of Thomas Jefferson Goff had sent shockwaves throughout the law-enforcing community. For not only had he left a grieving wife and two young children alone in the world, Goff's death was a painful reminder of just how fragile life was for those choosing a low-paying career chasing *mal hombres* up and down the border. Though it may whack mythology sideways there was not a headlong rush of eager folks knocking down the door to become Texas Rangers. The recruiting dilemma was real! This fact was specifically highlighted in Adjutant General John A. Hulen's biannual report for the period ending December 31, 1906:

A great many changes in the personnel of the men of the force has been made, due to resignations. It has been found quite difficult to keep a man in the service for any great length of time if he is of the right material; he is continually coming in contact with people who are in search of such men for various places in civil life, and who are willing to pay good prices for such service.[50]

Tom Goff, cowboy, Wild West Show trick-shooter, and Texas Ranger was "the right material!"

Chapter 14

Quirl Bailey Carnes
1910

Texas history of the family Carnes can be written in blood. Their epic story of Lone Star adventures is punctuated with bullets. The oldest of three law-enforcing brothers, Alfred Burton Carnes, held twenty-year tenure as the elected sheriff in Wilson County, southeastern neighbor of the Alamo City in Bexar County.[1] Herff Alexander Carnes, two years younger, would see service as a Company D Texas Ranger and U.S. Mounted Customs Inspector in West Texas, surviving the Culberson County gunfight which claimed the life of Pascual Orozco, Jr. and four suspected desperadoes, only to be killed later by Mexican smugglers crossing the Rio Grande.[2] The focus of this chapter is on the youngest brother, Quirl Bailey Carnes.

Hardly a whole year had elapsed since the June 1, 1884, birthday of Quirl, when the shiretown honors for Wilson County were wrested away from Lodi and formally awarded to Floresville. West of the county seat by twelve miles was the tiny community of Fairview, the generally professed birthplace of Quirl.[3] Though it's but a ghost of its former self, Fairview, at one time, could lay claim to having "three general stores, two drug stores, three doctors, a Masonic Hall, a school, and three churches, two cotton gins, a blacksmith shop, a barbershop, a grist mill, a Post Office and a wagon yard...."[4] Fairview was the home of farmer Joseph Milton and Mary Catherine "Mollie" Carnes, Quirl's parents.[5]

Quirl B. Carnes forfeited his status as a farmer, not following in his father's footsteps: He wanted to be a lawman. By September 1908 at age twenty-four he was in service of the State of Texas, a private in Company B, Ranger Force, under command of Captain Tom M. Ross.[6] The handicapped Ranger captain walked with aid of a "cork leg." Tom Ross had recklessly and accidently discharged his six-shooter and the doctor had performed an amputation.[7] For the short go Private

Carnes was headquartered at Alice.[8] A change in duty station and captains was on the crime fighting horizon.

Captain Ross, because one of his subordinates had attempted "to make a livery stable and a morgue out of the Alamo Saloon" by riding his horse into the establishment and discharging his six-shooter, was fired. Ross was, after all, ultimately responsible for the actions of his men. Adjutant General J. O. Newton had not been happy, nor had the big boss, Governor Tom Campbell.[9] Captain Tom Ross was replaced by Marvin Eugene Bailey a native Texan from Karnes County (Karnes City) and formerly 1st Sergeant of Company C.[10]

Quirl Carnes, as so many Rangers before, had made the jump from one company to another. With the dawning of 1910 he could be found in Company A under the direct command of Captain Francis Noel "Frank" Johnson, former sheriff of Mitchell County.[11] Captain Johnson maintained company headquarters at Harlingen (Cameron County) in South Texas. He was charged with scouting along Lucifer's Line from Rio Grande City (Starr County) to below Brownsville where the river emptied into the Gulf of Mexico, and 100 miles north back to Alice. Law enforcement in Johnson's assigned bailiwick was particularly challenging, not only because of the mistrust and misbehavior between cultural subgroups, but because of another problem, one recognized by award-winning twenty-first century educators and writers: "A good part of Johnson's problem was that a lot of men carried guns. Citizens tended to give up their weaponry only when they were confident that the law could protect them. This had never been the case along the lower Rio Grande border, with its tradition of political corruption and endemic violence. The attitude seemed to be that one should go around armed because you never knew when you'd run across somebody who needed killing."[12]

Although Company A headquarters was at Harlingen, Quirl Carnes was stationed with another Texas Ranger private at Rio Grande City, some fifty-odd miles upriver. Quirl's law-enforcing partner was James Patterson Nelson "Pat" Craighead, thirty-five, a dark-headed and dark-eyed Ranger from Southerland Springs, Wilson County.[13]

Owing to what seemed to be an unprecedented crime-wave taking place at San Benito, twenty-four miles north of Brownsville, Cameron County Sheriff Celedonio Garza sought cooperative aid from Rangers. Privates Carnes and Craighead were relocated to that city. Aside from routine instances of petty thefts, cow stealing, train wrecking, highway robberies, and other felonies, a newsmaking murder case was dominating headlines. The bloody aftermath would touch the two newly deployed Texas Rangers.

According to most reports, on the twenty-sixth day of May 1910, Jacinto Treviño made suggestive and indecent remarks to the young wife of James Darwin, an engineer for the San Benito Land & Water Company. With gusto, the twenty-six-year-old Darwin issued Mr. Treviño a severe head thumping, apparently thinking he had evened the score and taught the upstart a merited lesson. He hadn't, not in the now-vengeful mind of Jacinto Treviño.[14]

The following day, as James Darwin was going about his business, leisurely walking to work at the company's canal head gates, a gunshot shattered the Lower Rio Grande Valley's stillness. The bullet zipped into and out of Jim Darwin's head, leaving him sledgehammer dead. The crime did not even come close to registering as a whodunit. There were two eyewitnesses, and one, Treviño's cousin Hilario, allegedly offered up a confession of sorts fingering Jacinto as the gutless and cowardly perpetrator.[15] There was, however, a sobering truth. Texas authorities could not expect—and were not counting on—judicious extradition from Mexico where their prime suspect was lying low. Jacinto was the son of a retired and well-respected Mexican Army officer from Monterey, Captain Natividad Treviño.[16]

James Darwin's first-level boss, Sam Robertson, chief engineer, had made his thoughts known, adamantly demanding Jacinto Treviño be brought to bay one way or the other, preferably by execution of a legally authorized arrest warrant. Mr. Heywood, the company's president, pitched his corporate ante into the pot: $500 cash for the capture of Jacinto Treviño delivered to lawmen on the Texas side of the river. In accord with his outspokenness, Sam Robertson now, too, owned the unconditional enmity of Jacinto Treviño.

The wheels of a murder conspiracy began spinning. A tantalizing aroma of greenbacks caught the notice of one Pablo Treviño, another of Jacinto's cousins, who by chance also happened to have worked at the San Benito Land & Water Co. At Brownsville, Pablo had staked out his niche as an "honest working man" assiduously earning the "confidence" of his employers.[17] Although absoluteness is elusive, it does not take much reading between the lines to suggest who the recipient of Pablo's latest tidbit of hot news was. The *Brownsville Daily Herald* staff writers didn't seem overly concerned with maintaining any cloak and dagger suspense:

> Last Tuesday, Pablo Trevino, after an absence of some time, came to San Benito and told a well known man from whom he had formerly worked and who had trusted him, that he had just returned from Monterey and, on alighting from the train at Ramirez, a station on the Mexican National line, had met Jacinto Trevino. The latter, Pablo said, told him that Sam Robertson was the ___ ___ ___ [son of a bitch] he wanted and if he could get Robertson, he would be satisfied, and that he was coming over soon to make the attempt.[18]

Sam Robertson was probably not too shocked to learn that he was a marked man, but he may have been bowled over realizing the ambush was already on the drawing-board, slated to take effect during wee morning hours of July 31, 1910, while he was traveling to work for the routine and recurring audit of the paymaster's distributions. The would-be killers would covertly cross the Rio Grande at a particular point, open the ball with a booming broadside, and then slip back though wetness to supposed asylum.[19] Behind two or three shots of tequila and the backslapping camaraderie inside a Matamoros *cantina* the plot seemed foolproof. There was, unbeknownst to Jacinto Treviño and the coconspirators, a hitch, a kink—a snitch playing in the game.

Murderous intentions could be tolerably counterbalanced by employment of deadly but lawfully sanctioned force. Jacinto Treviño stealing back onto Texas ground would give the Lower Rio Grande Valley lawmen their best chance to nab or neutralize a highly wanted man.

On Friday, July 29, Pablo Treviño crossed the Rio Grande into Texas. And, during this visit, updated "the same man" that the murderous plan was good to go: Jacinto Treviño and others would cross the river about midnight Saturday, secret themselves, and "lie in wait for Sam Robertson on Sunday morning...."[20]

On the night of July 30, 1910, a posse of commissioned lawmen and civilians positioned themselves along the river waiting to execute their turnabout-is-fair-play blueprint. Dividing into subsets, the ten-man squadron had taken up concealed spots, in their minds, covering all likely crossings the assassins might use to access the San Benito road that Robertson would travel on his way to work. Ranger Carnes, a Cameron County deputy sheriff, thirty-seven-year-old Henry Benjamin "Benny" Lawrence, and levee rider John Zoll, working for the San Benito Land & Water Company, made up one platoon. Hunkering down in the shadows, the trio waited. Upstream their comrades deployed. As night began to give a nod for the onset of wee hours, Carnes, Lawrence, and Zoll detected movement from the river, coming toward their lair, unawares of the trap. Nervousness was spring-loaded. At a distance of about twenty or thirty feet, either Carnes or Lawrence in Spanish challenged the advancing party to stop and throw up their hands. The terse verbal command was answered immediately—with a volley of buckshot and bullets. The lawmen returned fire, momentarily. Benny Lawrence went down, seven pellets of 00 in the right side of his head, killed instantly.[21] Ranger Quirl Carnes caught one whizzing rifle slug behind the right ear and another in the arm, falling to the ground, yet alive—but dying. John Zoll milked his Colt's six-shooter dry and then he ran for dear life, intent on pinpointing the shooting site for the other officers and civilians whom he knew would be—or should be—rushing to the sound of gunfire. And so they were, at least two were. Ranger Private Pat Craighead and Cameron County Constable Larkin Earl West, age thirty-two, burst from the brush in search of their teammates. Encountering Zoll the two paid lawmen were breathlessly brought up to speed as to what and where it all had happened. The levee rider was instructed to summon more help while Pat Craighead and Earl West charged through the dark toward their fallen comrades.

Stumbling ahead, the two lawmen at last discovered their downed colleagues. Obviously Deputy Benny Lawrence was dead, but Ranger Quirl Carnes was unintelligibly groaning, still clinging to life—barely. Earl West kneeled to give him comfort when to his astonishment he heard the dreaded clicks—a weapon's hammer cycling to the full-cock notch. Crouched over Carnes, his Winchester out of reach, West began rising to his feet and drawing his six-shooter in one fluid motion. Gunfire erupted from the nearby tangles. Both Pat Craighead and Earl West answered with a deafening crescendo of their own, letting bullets penetrate the night at unseen and unknown targets. Though it must have seemed an eternity, in but a few heartbeats Constable West was knocked out of the fight, severely wounded, a bullet tearing though his right arm, shoulder, and exiting though his back leaving a ragged and gaping hole as a memorable souvenir. With Earl West down and wholly incapacitated, the hidden snipers turned their full attention to Private Craighead. Clearly this was another instance when cheap talk about one Ranger, one Riot was utterly ridiculous, a cliché fully discernible to Craighead, all alone, at night, the number of assailants unfixed, and three bleeding comrades before him on the ground. Prudent was Ranger Pat Craighead's decision to implement an abrupt one-eighty and go for help.

The choice to retreat was sensible—downright smart under the circumstances. The good judgment would not hold. What had sounded reasonable in planning conversations, morphed into fiasco of the first order. In a state of understandable near panic, Ranger Craighead set his mental compass and finally managed to negotiate through the chaparral, attaining footing on the San Benito Road. Hearing the ginning of an approaching Ford, Pat Craighead pointed the muzzle of his Winchester skyward and by design let loose with a round—in his mind, a prearranged signal of distress and indicator of geographical positioning. The auto's occupants indeed were civilian possemen rushing to the forefront, but adequately attuned to the deliberate rationale of the rifle's fire-belching crack they were not. Bandits or smugglers or goddamn lowdown bushwhackers had opened up on them, they summarily supposed. They returned the compliment.[22]

Caught in the fusillade as the relief squad opened up with every available weapon in their arsenal, Ranger Craighead collapsed, not intentionally; a rifle ball had passed through his left thigh, pellets from a charge of buckshot adding weight to his right leg. His wounds were severe. When the shooting stopped, the mistake was discovered: Friendly fire had snuffed the fight out of Pat Craighead.[23] Embarrassed and remorseful remarks were plentiful, but irrevocable damage had already been done to pride and person. While first-aid was being administered to Ranger Craighead, others rushed to the real crime scene, finding the deceased deputy, the wounded constable, and the near-dead Ranger alive but not kicking. *Mal hombres*? There were none. With haste the critically injured lawmen, Carnes, West, and Craighead, were rushed to the nearby residence of Fred Wedegartner, Water Superintendent for the San Benito Land & Water Co. Doctors were summoned. There, the next morning at nine o'clock Texas Ranger Private Quirl Bailey Carnes closed his eyes and slipped to the other side.[24]

While Carnes had been putting up his desperate fight to outwit the Grim Reaper under medical supervision at Wedegartner's house, after daybreak, others returned to the scene intent on recovering the dead body of Benny Lawrence. While poking about trying to recon-

struct the previous night's affair, a gruesome and revealing discovery was made: The lifeless body of Pablo Treviño. Pablo's cold dead
hands were yet clutching his cold-barreled Winchester, jammed with
a cartridge—his last—partially protruding from the loading gate.
A malfunction, mechanical or human blunder was irrelevant. The
rifle had been made useless. Easily it was determined the direction
accomplices had taken. Footprints leading to the Rio Grande were
indisputable clues.

Not surprisingly the fact that Pablo Treviño had been on the
scene, rifle in hand, fueled speculation, rumor, and gossip. Had he
been playing the role of a double agent? Had he actually informed
on his relatives and friends? Was he, all along, a part of the plot to
kill Robertson? Had it been from the get-go a convoluted scheme
to off Texas Rangers and other area Anglo lawmen? Writing for
the *San Antonio Daily Light*, at least one newspaperman thought
he had it locked down tight: "The rangers were in pursuit of a murderer, Jacinto Trevino, and were led into an ambush by a cousin of
Trevino, who had made a pact with the officers to lead them to where
they could capture Trevino. The rangers were led to a lonely spot in
the road, where they were fired upon by the Mexicans...."[25] There yet
remains a niggling question, one that should give pause to dutiful
historians and maybe vex folklorists swimming the river of political correctness. Who now could even prove—with unimpeachable
creditability—that Jacinto Treviño was even on Texas soil when the
murderous fireworks erupted? Probabilities are high, but so too is
the hurdle of hearsay testimony—in most instances inadmissible.[26]

Certainly justice of the peace for Cameron County's Third Precinct, Justice Corkill, acting in the role of coroner, didn't have satisfactory and conclusive answers. By law he was obligated to conduct
an Inquest and render decisions. Judge Corkill concluded: "Pablo
Trevino was killed by Deputy Sheriff Lawrence and Ranger Carnes,
while trying to stop a plot to kill Sam Robertson, and that Lawrence
and Carnes were killed by Pablo Trevino and other parties unknown."
Somewhat astonishingly coming from a judicial bench, even if one
at the lower court level was Corkill's opinion of the all-civilian witnesses' testimony "that at the time, their excitement was so great
that they really did not know exactly what did happen."[27]

What did happen was a manhunt. A local militia unit, the
Brownsville Rifles, was called out by order of the adjutant general.
Sheriff William L. "Will" Wright from Wilson County, the home turf

of Ranger Carnes, rushed to Cameron County with seven heavily armed deputies. From Harlingen, Captain Frank Johnson and all of his available Rangers were on scene, as well as Captain John Hughes then stationed at Amarillo, who sent Company D Sergeant Herff Carnes, Quirl's brother, and Private Charles Craighead, Pat's brother, to San Benito.[28] Captain Bailey came from Marfa.[29] The story, though sad, was rich for Cameron County journalists. Raring to go newsmen for the *Brownsville Daily Herald* made note: "A considerable number of armed men, including rangers and deputies, have been beating the brush along the river in search of Jacinto Trevino or his confederates since Sunday morning."[30] Somewhat surprisingly in light of his future criticisms of Rangers overstepping their authority, State Representative J. T. Canales was the driving force behind Governor Campbell's reward proclamation: $500 for the arrest and conviction of each person responsible for murdering Private Carnes and Deputy Lawrence.[31] Although Captain Frank Johnson crowed to a reporter that "We have the country fully covered and expect no further trouble" there was an additional hard truth unspoken by Texas Rangers in the field, but the front office was practical: "The adjutant general's department.... believes the Mexicans participating in the attack have recrossed the Rio Grande and will probably not be captured."[32] Predictions coming out of Texas Ranger headquarters at Austin were spot on: Jacinto Treviño was never arrested, extradited, imprisoned—or shot!

The body of Private Carnes was removed to Floresville where it was reverently interred.[33] Benny Lawrence was buried in the cemetery at Alice.[34] Pat Craighead suffered the amputation of his leg, remained in Texas Ranger service for awhile, ultimately becoming the elected sheriff in Jim Hogg County (Hebbronville), Texas. Larkin Earl West, after recovering from his wounds, went on to become a U.S. Mounted Customs Inspector, and later chief of police at McAllen (Hidalgo County), Texas.[35]

Crowning Jacinto Treviño with a halo of heroism may provide a degree of satisfaction within the mindsets of certain subgroups, and such must have been the case in the naming of a now-defunct community college at Mercedes (Hidalgo County), Texas. If 1970s reporting in the *Corpus Christi Caller-Times* was accurate, the students "said they know of Trevino only as a Mexican-American folk hero who had killed a Ranger."[36] Somewhat a bizarrely distinguishing honor, it would seem! As educator Américo Paredes pointed out in *With His Pistol in His Hand: A Border Ballad and Its Hero*, the story of Jacinto Treviño—or more correctly a version of the story—has been preserved in a *Corrido*, a Mexican narrative folk song.[37] Mistaking melodic verse for historical truth may now and again result in a sour note. If Dr. Paredes is right, based on what someone told him in 1928, Jacinto Treviño died of "old age."[38]

Gauging any heroic status Jacinto Treviño may have been awarded uproots questions of less than tortuous logic. Is heroism actually calculated by waylaying someone in the dark? Or is it weighed by killing a man leisurely walking to work? After the San Benito episode did Jacinto Treviño ever set foot in Texas again? Or, was he even at San Benito in the first place? And if not, was taking false credit and puffing more appealing than owning up to the truth? *¿Quíen Sabe?*

Chapter 15

Grover Scott Russell
1913

Seesawing back to the other end of the Texas/Mexican border is where another sad story will in due course play out. Stephenville, Erath County, Texas, was the birthplace of Grover Scott Russell, popularly known as Scott, but he would earn Ranger pay in faraway West Texas, primarily scouting along Lucifer's Line in El Paso County.

Samuel Nicholas "Sam" Russell and Clara May (Chastain) Russell were proud parents of eight, Scott being the second child and the first-born son, greeting the world on the second day of December 1887.[1] Sam Russell was a full-time farmer and part-time deputy for Erath County Sheriff John Chesley Gilbreath. Somewhat later he gave up his deputyship and was elected to the position of Erath County Constable.[2] Reportedly, Sam went about his law enforcement duties armed with a long-barreled six-shooter once belonging to the notorious Bloody Bill Longley, the self-promoting Texas rascal hanged at Giddings, Texas, on October 11, 1878. According to family lore Sam Russell won the revolver as result of a bet with a political rival over who would land the constable's job.[3]

The county seat was Stephenville more or less dead center in the survey carving Erath County from Bosque and Coryell Counties during 1856, the same year it was formally organized.[4] As she grew to maturity, like many early day Texas cities, Stephenville's past would be recounted with shushed tones by genteel ladies engrossed with politeness and niceness and social standing. Be assured though, Stephenville was no sarsaparilla sippin' town. For a period of time it was no secret: Stephenville was "the wildest little town in Texas."[5]

Constable Sam Russell's law-enforcing duties were typical: he tracked a man wanted for assaulting a fellow with a knife, found him at a dance at Morgan Mill north of Stephenville, arrested him and pitched him in the Erath County calaboose; Sam latched on to two women of questionable virtue who refused to give their last names, but Fannie and Lillie were charged with Vagrancy anyway and each fined $1.00; Kate Morse was charged with Keeping a Disorderly House as a result of the constable's February 24, 1900, arrest, pleading guilty before the court; and Sam Russell arrested the thrice-married Annie Williams for stabbing and killing Austin King, editor of Stephenville's gossiping rag *The Erath Appeal*.[6] Constable Sam Russell's authenticated history as a frontier peace keeper was enviable, earning praise from one newspaper reporter as being "a splendid record of service."[7] Layperson psychoanalysis in the historical context is knotty, but suggesting Scott Russell's career choice was influenced by his father's sterling reputation as a lawman is not an overreach.

At the age of twenty-four years and ten months, on the first day of October 1912, Scott Russell enlisted in the Texas Rangers. Private Russell was assigned to Company A, which after having undergone bureaucratic reshuffling was now under command of Captain John Reynolds Hughes. The five-foot, ten-inch, brown-eyed rookie Ranger reported for scouting duty at Fort Stockton, Pecos County.[8] Scott Russell busied himself learning the ropes, much of the time working hand-and-glove with an ex-Ranger, Pecos County Sheriff Dudley S. Barker, who was in the midst of clearing up a murder investigation.[9] It was a turbulent place and time, the borderland country. Mexico was ablaze with political upheaval, the Mexican Revolution intrigues and bloodletting were ongoing. Events taking place along the Rio Grande below El Paso would all too soon impact the life of Ranger Scott Russell.

During early February 1913 armed revolutionary forces from Mexico attempted to breach the border, firing on two Rangers and an El Paso County deputy sheriff scouting the river. Company A Sergeant Charles Robert "C. R." Moore, Private Charles H. Webster, and Deputy William Henry Garlick reined their horses to a standstill, withdrew Winchesters from saddle scabbards and in harmony squeezed triggers, emptying three Mexican saddles. Finding the temperature of the Rio Grande rather hot, the surviving insurgents turned tail, splashed out of the river, making a hasty retreat back into the Mexican state of Chihuahua, frantically abandoning a battle flag. The dropped banner was recovered and later sent to the Texas adjutant general with a note affixed from Sergeant Moore: "I don't think our rebel would be in shape to again use the Mauser carbine we got off his saddle."[10] After reading John R. Hughes' recap of the incident, Governor Oscar B. Colquitt voiced his hearty approval and then issued the captain a standing and unequivocal order: "you and your men keep them [Mexican revolutionaries] off of Texas territory if possible, and if they invade the State let them understand they do so at the risk of their lives."[11]

Sergeant Moore would continue risking his life as a lawman, but not as a Texas Ranger. The gutsy Moore had accepted appointment as a Deputy U.S. Marshal for the Western District of Texas on April 5, 1913. In anticipation of the upcoming manpower vacuum at Ysleta, Captain Hughes had transferred Private Russell to Company A headquarters in late March. From there he worked with Deputy Garlick on investigations of mutual interest and/or joint jurisdiction, that is, when he wasn't dispatched hither and yon throughout the Big Bend Country of West Texas.[12]

Geographically the territory Company A was responsible for was mindboggling: From El Paso to Del Rio. Naturally, navigating the twists and turns along the Rio Grande and through the mountainous canyons was a difficult task on horseback, and dangerous, too! True there were Mexican nationals and sympathizers committed to principle and patriotism, but there were also the chameleons, bandits hiding behind revolutionary skirts of idealism; they were desert pirates plundering for profit. Mix in Anglo scalawags, murderers, smugglers, cow thieves, gun runners, and fugitives from justice advantaging the region's proximity to Mexico as protection from any extradition and the picture is clear. Private Grover Scott Russell was in a position to know.

Earlier that year, downriver from El Paso and above Candelaria in Presidio County, in some truly remote country, two U.S. Mounted Customs Inspectors and an investigator for what would become the Texas & Southwest Cattle Raisers Association had ridden into an ambuscade orchestrated to liberate a Mexican bandit they had arrested. One of the federal men was killed, while the other two lawmen were severely wounded, but luckily they survived—for the time being. Along this stretch of the river hiding behind boulders and hurling bullets not rocks was but par business for desperadoes fixed on freeing their pals from an officer's custody.[13]

In another instance that same year Ranger Private Jefferson Eagle Vaughn and the deputized Jesse Woodson "Buck" Pool were ambushed while transporting a prisoner from the river to Marfa. Mexican bandits were, once again, trying to free their *amigo*. During the gunfight there was a net loss all the way around. The lawmen were forcefully deprived of their prisoner. The bandits reversed course, hightailing for security of the river. And, the alleged horse thief lay dead on the ground. *La ley de fuga*? Suicide? Friendly fire from unfriendly Mexican banditos? In this instance the latter scenario seems most likely. The lawmen hotfooted to Shafter, notified Presidio County Sheriff Milton Chastian, who in the company of Texas Ranger Ira Cline rushed to their aid. When the news reached Captain Hughes at Ysleta he immediately ordered the Company's 1st Sergeant and Private Scott Russell to lend a helping six-shooting hand. Somewhat later forty stolen horses and mules were rounded up and a quartet of Mexican thieves and an Anglo cohort were ensconced in the hoosegow at Marfa.[14]

The real drama in Private Scott Russell's life would play out not in the wild reaches of the Big Bend Country but closer in. Aside from revolutionary forces trying to unseat this or that president in Mexico City, workers at the American Smelting and Refining Company on the outskirts of El Paso were likewise embroiled in acrimony—a labor dispute. Upwards of 3,000 employees at the plant, the overwhelming majority tracing roots of Mexican ancestry, were on strike. The management team and labor leaders were at loggerheads, unwilling to compromise, unable to affably settle. Sheriff Peyton Edwards, in whose jurisdiction Smeltertown, the nearby raucous and tough civilian community, lay, had insufficient manpower to maintain order and protect lives. A call went out for Rangers.[15] Russell was detailed to Smeltertown. His duty plain: Do what a Ranger was supposed to do.

On April 22, 1913, Ranger Russell was on assignment at the smelter when strikers grabbed the rifle of a company guard. Facing superior numbers Scott Russell resorted to the helpmate in his holster. Before the Winchester could be wrestled away from the man, Ranger Russell shot a belligerent in the leg, an act that quickly disbursed the crowd but guaranteed enmity from many in the Spanish-speaking communities living along both banks of the river.[16]

Within that ethnic assemblage there was a subgroup of suspicious and treacherous characters, and Scott Russell earned their hatred, too. More specifically he drew ire of the Guaderrama family, operators of the *Eje del Barrio Libre* corrals, a combination grocery and butcher shop, with an attached tavern. By most folks' best reckoning, mixed with gossip and rumor, the broad consensus was that the Guaderramas's facility near Smeltertown was undisputed headquarters for a band of local livestock thieves.[17] To be blunt, in one newspaper account it was mentioned that "the general reputation of the Guadarrama [sic] boys was not good...."[18]

Skepticism and trepidation swirling about the Guaderramas— some of the Guaderramas—was not misplaced. One of the boys, Abelino, had been arrested in connection with a boxcar burglary. Before trial the district attorney's star witness against Abelino undertook swimming across the Rio Grande, a heavy wagon wheel chained around his neck. A prosecutable suspect for the murder was never identified. At varying times Guaderrama brothers would rack up arrests for theft of ore from the smelter, actual gun running, and conspiracy to smuggle arms.[19]

An assertion that at least a few of the Guaderrama boys were shady characters is somewhat borne out by Rangers Russell and Webster, accompanied by Deputy Garlick, filing a sworn Complaint with Justice of the Peace James J. Murphy and obtaining arrest warrants for Sabino Guaderrama, L. Dominguez, and an Anglo, William "Willy" Hill, for stealing cattle from the Nunn & Latham Cattle Company on the mesa outside of town. An *El Paso Morning Times* newspapermen inked that the lawmen were "making it warm" for the "gang" of cow thieves after the prospective defendants had been placed in jail.[20] Attorneys for Nunn & Latham promptly filed a Writ of Sequestration forbidding the removal of any live cattle then standing in the corrals at *Eje del Barrio Libre*.[21] Deputy Garlick testified at the Preliminary Hearing, and the local magistrate found Probable Cause to forward the case to an El Paso County grand jury. The trio of detainees posted bond and were released from custody pending return of an Indictment. Particularly mad was Juan Guaderrama, Sabino's brother: He threatened to "get" those officers involved in the arrests. The message did not go unnoticed by Texas Ranger Russell, but it went unheeded; because although he feared the clan might kill him, it would be a back-shooting and of that, he could do nothing.[22]

On the afternoon of June 23, 1913, Scott Russell and Henry Garlick were on duty near the smelter. About two o'clock they encountered Sergeant J. H. Shirks, C Troop, 13th Cavalry, U.S. Army, responsible for overseeing a military patrol in response to any supposed collateral turmoil from Mexico's enduring political upheaval spilling into America. The two lawmen asked the noncom if he had seen a particular Guaderrama brother, and were politely advised that he had not. Later in the afternoon, again in a conversation with Sergeant Shirks,

Russell and Garlick mentioned that they were headed to the *Eje del Barrio Libre* to purchase tobacco at the grocery.[23] Their entry into the store is a sure thing, as will be their exit, but events transpiring in between are draped behind mystery and supposition, so much so, an unconstrained newspaper scribe laconically but equitably tendered: "What actually took place within the adobe walls of that smelter settlement store, saloon and rendezvous of Mexican border men will probably never be known."[24] Well, Juan Guaderrama knew what was about to happen. After being forewarned that lawmen Russell and Garlick were approaching the store—maybe with more arrest warrants, but more likely to inspect corralled cattle under instructions of Sheriff Edwards—Juan Guaderrama remarked to a boy standing nearby, that "he was going to kill those sheriffs."[25] Purportedly, Juan's angry mother, Marina, also piped up: "Here come those sons of bitches."[26]

Reconstructing a crime scene is doable—at least in part and by varying degrees of probability. It this instance, it seems, when appraised that Russell and Garlick were on the march toward his family's business, Juan began loading a pistol—by some reports a German Luger. Meanwhile Marina Guaderrama grabbed an axe-handle, held it by her side obscurely wrapped behind pleats of her colorful floor-length skirt. Scott Russell purchased a package of tobacco, rolled a cigarette and took a lung-filling drag. Exhaling, he remarked to Juan that the tobacco was pitiably stale, in fact, downright nasty. Garlick and Russell face-to-face with Juan, directed one hundred percent of their attention to his response. Inattentively standing inside an enemy's stronghold was a major blunder. Undetected, Marina raised the axe-handle high overhead and swung downward with all her strength, right on top of Garlick's head, and with another reenergized blow knocked Russell senseless. While both lawmen lay on the floor bloodied and stunned Juan jumped into action shooting and shooting and shooting some more. Seemingly he was drunk on gunpowder. In his state of hysteria when the pistol ran dry Juan reloaded and once more continued the bloodlust frenzy—a few bullets going wild. Then grabbing a hatchet he made sure his handiwork was complete—dead sure.[27] With echoes of gunshots yet in the room, and the stench of burnt powder hanging heavy, a touch of reality—soberness—reentered the grocery. Realizing the firing-pin had struck a cap one too many times, Juan Guaderrama shrieked in unimaginable horror: "Oh, God, I've killed my mother." And he had! Plus a Ranger and a deputy sheriff.[28]

Outside, Sergeant Shirks had distinctly heard at least nine gunshots. Dutifully responding, he rushed inside the *Eje del Barrio Libre* complex and saw Scott Russell's and Henry Garlick's prostrate forms, lifelessly reposed in pools of their own and each other's blood. Shirks boldly confronted Juan. Sharply the gutsy sergeant queried: "Who killed Garlick?" Juan, unthinkingly and unashamedly yelped, "I did."[29]

With aid and approval of his commanding officer, Lieutenant Prince, Sergeant Shirks placed a military blockade around the whole Guaderrama multiplex, insuring no ingress, no egress—not until civil law enforcing authorities could be summoned to the scene.[30] From the standpoint of apprehending guilty parties the cordon was a not unwise tactic, though corralling buildings from the outside did allow for mischief and skullduggery and tampering with items on the inside, a criminal investigator's worst nightmare from an evidentiary perspective. Sheriff Peyton Edwards was in California on a prolonged visit and fundamental responsibility for the investigation and the apprehension of perpetrators—one or several—fell on the shoulders of Chief Deputy Stanley Good. He ordered the arrests, perhaps with good cause, of nine folks within the complex, four of whom were Guaderrama brothers: Juan, Sabino, Jesus, and Adolfo, no Anglos in the gaggle.

That Texas peace officers and judicial stewards were on the march—albeit a slow march—to criminal investigative professionalism is evidenced by Chief Deputy Good and the El Paso County Attorney, Perry Riley Price, summoning a photographer and having permanent images made of the crime scene and corpses.[31] Interestingly and incriminatingly, Ranger Russell's and Deputy Garlick's Colt's six-shooters were nowhere to be found, as if they had somehow melted into nothingness.[32] Unfired weapons, had they been recovered, would have accelerated belief that the two lawmen had been foully murdered by means of a premeditated scheme. The state's top lawman in the area offered his two cents' worth of political incorrectness and racial insensitivity relating to the missing revolvers:

A third theory which is given by Capt John R. Hughes of the rangers is that some of the Mexicans who were in the store took the guns from the natural inclination of a Mexican to steal a six-shooter, wherever it could be found.[33]

Captain Hughes' stereotypical characterizations were the coin of the realm in many Texans' schema of thinking. The sharp horn of bigotry cut both ways, though. Many were the Mexicans and *Tejanos* who absent good reason damned every act of a *rincher*, any armed Anglo Texan wearing a badge, be it a policeman's shield, a sheriff's star, or a Texas Ranger's handcrafted *cinco peso*. The sentiment that Russell and Garlick had earned their just deserts was not scarce:

> After the killing Monday afternoon, a number of the strikers expressed themselves as highly satisfied with what had taken place... a striker told one of the Americans at the smelter that the Mexicans could shoot as well as the *"gringos"* and they would be able to care for themselves should the Americans start anything.[34]

There was in fact overblown talk in the barrooms and bragging in bordellos about storming the El Paso jail and issuing extralegal justice—but it died on the tobacco-stained floors and in the rumpled linens. The Blind Mistress of Justice won out. Alleged killers would have their first judgment day in a courtroom; one in the Hereafter would be postponed. The State of Texas also had some unfinished business. Adjutant General Henry Hutchings wired Captain Hughes:

> His Excellency, the Governor deeply regrets the death of Ranger Russell in the line of duty and directs the body be prepared for burial and returned to his former home in Erath County for interment, should such be the desire of his nearest kin, accompanied by a member of your command, if the public service will possibly admit. All reasonable expense will be met by the State.[35]

Grover Scott Russell's body was returned to Stephenville, where after the reverent funeral service he was buried in the city's East Memorial Cemetery. His time in the Texas Rangers measured in months, not years. The body of William Henry Garlick, the married father of five, was removed to the cemetery at Valentine and laid peacefully to rest.[36]

The wheels of legal justice turn slow, but they grind nevertheless. During the first trial, after 116 ballots the jury reported it was hopelessly deadlocked. There had been kinks of sorts, ones fully exploited by smart defense attorneys. And they revolved around the dead mother, Marina.

Jurors had tackled the best they could two disquieting conundrums. If mama Guaderrama had, indeed, gratuitously murdered Ranger Russell and Deputy Garlick, how on God's green earth could her son Juan be convicted of heartless killings, when the two lawmen were already dead? It was more or less common knowledge after medical examination of the two deceased lawmen: "Both men would have probably died from injuries inflicted by the blunt instruments, according to the belief of the physician."[37] Furthermore Doctor L. G. Witherspoon confirmed that the "wound found on Russell's head could have been made with a hand ax."[38] True, the two official Death Certificates would list the cause of demise as result of gunshot wounds, but to conscientious jurors, Beyond Reasonable Doubt—the required standard of proof—had crept into their decision-making efforts. As an alternative, since the lady was killed—no doubt by run-amok lawmen, as the defense lawyers were claiming, wasn't it but reasonable to think Juan would go for his under-the-counter pistol, trying to prevent his mother's annihilation? Jurymen had set their personal convictions in concrete—none would budge. The judge ruled a Mistrial.

Reasonable Doubt is tricky. Though two years had passed, with other hard-fought trials and different juries, in the end all but one of the now well-known Guaderrama brothers were found not guilty. Juan Guaderrama was convicted of Murder in the second degree and caught a nickel (five-year prison sentence) for his part in the deaths.[39] Patience may be a golden virtue. Revenge is best served cold, it's said, but along Lucifer's Line the goblets are filled with blood—not wine.

Chapter 16

Eugene B. Hulen
1915

The native Texan warranting a spot in this coverage of bloodshed along the Rio Grande was product of a border county—just not a Mexican border county. Eugene B. Hulen had been born in Cooke County (Gainesville) adjacent to the Red River, the dividing line separating Texas and Oklahoma. Eugene's parents, Harvey and Frances "Fannie" Hulen, could rightly be proud of their family's contribution to Lone Star State history. Their first-born, John Augustus Hulen, would serve for a time as the adjutant general of Texas, the Rangers headman, and as brigadier general of the National Guard. During 1879 the month of March blew in with the breath of a proverbial lion and made her exodus leaving behind the gentleness of a lamb's bleat—and baby Eugene, seven years junior to his oldest brother.[1]

Eugene would grow to manhood topping out at a middling five-foot, nine-inches, underneath a crop of light brown hair. Unlike so many fellows heretofore profiled, Eugene was not a career cowboy shielding his fair complexion and blue-grey eyes from beneath a wide-brimmed hat, spending long days and longer nights in a slick-forked Texas stock saddle. Nope, Eugene Hulen was for the biggest portion of his allotted time as an adult, a "contractor."[2] Contracting for what is left unanswered, and for the unwinding episode at hand, really not too significant. There is, however, a critical point demanding explanation and consideration.

For whatever the reason Eugene Hulen, at thirty-six years of age, wanted to strap on a Colt's six-shooter and be a Texas Ranger. Regrettably he had not a lick of law-enforcing experience. Opportunely his older brother was a most influential fellow. Even more conveniently, Eugene's vocational desire coincided perfectly with a gloomy, but nevertheless out-and-out public service dynamic: Texas was rife with cronyism and political corruption. James E. Ferguson, who would later be removed from office, was the state's chief executive and bane of the Ranger Force.[3] Ferguson was, conceivably, the "crookedest governor in Texas history. The advent of Ferguson was a disaster for the Rangers. Ferguson had political debts to pay, and Ranger commissions to bestow."[4] Not all of Governor Ferguson's appointments were doled out to misfits and/or ne'er-do-wells, but the patronage and payoffs portended dark days for the Texas Rangers. There is not reason, not even slight reason, to suggest the Hulen boys were anything less than first-rate and honest, but it is a surefire fact the former adjutant general exercised his influence in prompting Ferguson to plug a vacancy on the Ranger muster roll with his brother's name.[5]

On the twenty-ninth day of March 1915 at Austin, Texas, Eugene B. Hulen completed the required paperwork, took his oath of office, and became a Ranger private in Company C. The assignment to Company C was but administrative expediency based solely on where Hulen had enlisted. Within days Private Hulen received traveling instructions from the front office. He was to report to Captain James Monroe Fox, Commander of Company B at Marfa, far West Texas.[6]

Part of the Presidio County territory Captain Fox's Rangers were responsible for scouting lay west of Marfa to the Rio Grande. On the face of a topographical map or as the crow flies the distance appears moderate, easy, and uncomplicated. On the ground, however, covering the distance was not painless, but torturous. The Sierra Vieja Rim was the culprit interdicting any trouble-free travel. "From the Rim Rock, all of the country drains toward the Rio Grande, a constant succession of canyons, cliffs, and ridges terminating at the river.... In all of this area only two roads cross the Rim Rock from towns inland to the river, one from Marfa via Brite's Ranch to Candelaria, and the other from Marfa to Presidio through Pinto Canyon. And in 120 miles, only two passable trails cross the Rim Rock toward the river.... On both sides of the thick bosque there is a well-beaten trail that follows the river. The one on the Mexico side, called the 'San Antone' Trail, runs from Pilares through San Antonio del Bravo and down to Ojinaga."[7]

Not only was the country tough, but so too were the people inhabiting the remote settlements scattered at varying points beside the river, usually but a very few "houses or jacales" built by erecting ocotillo poles, cracks filled in with copious handfuls of mud. Many—most—because of the intense summertime heat had a *ramada*, poles supporting a yet attached open-air covering which provided a wel-

come shade.[8] Upright folks found respite under those canopies block-
ing sunlight, as did an assortment of not-so-nice folks. It was bandit
country. One quick story bears repeating: as illustration and because
it plays directly into Ranger Hulen's biographical narrative.

Joseph Russell Sitter, an ex-Texas Ranger, had forsaken the lesser
paying job and signed on as an Inspector with the U.S. Mounted
Customs Service on May 1, 1899, doubling his monthly salary.[9] Joe
Sitter was one hard *hombre* and a career lawman with years spent
in the saddle chasing after Mexican bandidos and Anglo brigands
from Del Rio to the Upper Rio Grande area. He was noted throughout the Southwest in law-enforcing circles as one helluva of tracker
and manhunter.[10] It's been written, and perhaps it does escalate
above the anecdotal, that because of personnel reforms in the federal government Joe Sitter was booted out of Customs due to his
inability to pass a written Civil Service examination. True, he seemed
but semi-literate, telling Western writer Zane Grey in 1913 that the
Texas-Mexico borderlands were "most as bad an' wild as ever!"[11] All
so soon, however, the pointed-headed bureaucratic pencil-pushers
in Washington, D.C. learned that fellows, even though well-meaning
and enthusiastic, recruited from big cities in the East were not suited
for a work-life outdoors up and down the winding Rio Grande, sometimes living like a wolf, and carrying six-shooters and Winchesters.
The emphasis on hiring "cattlemen, hunters, trappers, and so forth"
and men who had "lived in the open" returned, replacing the theoretical nonsense.[12] Joe Sitter was rehired.[13]

Also working with Joe Sitter as a mounted Customs Inspector
was John Simpson "Jack" Howard, a former real-deal cowboy and a
combat veteran of the Spanish-American War. Howard was just the
kind of man cut out for federal law enforcing along the river. Jack
made doubly sure prospective hiring officials at U.S. Customs were
aware of his practical know-how:

> I have been a cowboy, Wagon boss, trail boss and have worked
> at the cow business since I was 12 years old.... I naturally had to
> read brands readily.... and can classify and read them as well as
> anyone.... I can ride anything I ever tried to, broken or unbroken
> horses, having been raised on a ranch. I am perfectly familiar with
> all the work of same. Can ride an ordinary cow-pony on the round
> up, encircle and cutting out work around the herd.... I have han-
> dled firearms all my life and am considered a fine shot, both at

moving objects and targets, can shoot horseback as well as upon ground. I use a .30-30 rifle and Colt's .45. I used a Krag-Jorgeson going up San Juan Hill.[14]

Much of the U.S. Customs work along the river dealt with smuggled livestock. Working in tandem with federal officers throughout the state and especially along the Rio Grande, were another class of bona-fide lawmen: livestock detectives employed by the cattle raisers' associations, special interest organizations with inordinately powerful political clout in Texas. For the near inaccessible country below the Sierra Vieja Rim patrolled by Customs Inspectors Sitter and Howard, thirty-four-year-old James Adam "Ad" Harvick from San Saba County held title as the cattle association's Field Inspector.[15]

Connecting the relevancy of Ranger Eugene Hulen's story is this. On the morning of February 10, 1913, under the Rim Rock at tiny Pilares, Texas, Sitter, Howard, and Harvick started out for Marfa with a prisoner in tow, the notorious borderland bandit Francisco "Chico" Cano, whom they had arrested the previous day. Having progressed not much more than a mile from Sabino Hernandez's village store, the taken aback lawmen were ambushed. Once again, the familiar borderland story was playing out: friends and relatives were liberating their *compadre* from custody with bullets—not bail bonds. Chico Cano atop a surefooted mule escaped during the gunfire. Lady Luck was not with the lawmen. Though their wounds would not prove mortal, Joe Sitter and Ad Harvick were knocked from saddles, incapacitated and in serious need of medical attention. Jack Howard not only suffered a horrific bullet wound, but was injured severely when his wounded horse fell dead, pinning him underneath.[16] Two days later, Jack Simpson Howard died.[17] Yes, U.S, Customs Inspector Sitter was dead right; the Rio Grande borderlands were "most as bad, an' wild as ever!"

Two years later, when Private Eugene Hulen reported for duty in Presidio County, situational violence was still a part of a border lawman's expectation; the landscape and losers had not changed. Inspector Joe Sitter was yet on the job, working closely with fellow U.S. Customs comrade Charles Archer Craighead, a veteran of borderlands law enforcing with at least one cut on his notch-stick.[18] It may also be noted, Charley was brother of Pat Craighead the Ranger wounded at San Benito five years earlier. Chico Cano was on the loose, not forgotten or forgiven by Texas and federal lawmen. In fact,

John Harris Rogers, the former Ranger Captain, but now the United States Marshal for the Western District of Texas, had the Chico Cano band pegged: "This gang, for the most part stay in Mexico just across the river from the scene of this unfortunate affair [Howard's death], occasionally coming to the American side on some lawless expedition."[19] Livestock smuggling and banditry and arms trafficking were widespread in that generic labeled Big Bend Country, especially underneath the Sierra Vieja Rim.

Somehow, from somebody, either Inspector Joe Sitter or Charley Craighead received confidential information that a herd of smuggled horses were being held somewhere in the vicinity of Pilares.[20] Joe Sitter not unwisely tried to hedge his bet, sending a spy to ferret out actionable intelligence: "I had been sent by Joe Sitter there to locate the said bandits."[21] In another account, it's alleged that Inspector Sitter and Ranger Hulen, "captured a man who could tell him Cano's whereabouts, and the two officers 'roped, dragged and put through the 3rd degree a Mexican,'" eliciting the criminal intelligence they were seeking.[22] That an allegation of brutality was based on hearsay is not just cause for dismissing it outright—maybe it's true, maybe not. The lawman not growing a crop of detractors is possibly not doing his job; arrestees, their kinfolks, and their pals are normally not enchanted with peace officers. Generally speaking, an academician of Ranger doings reports, Joe Sitter was "well respected" and though a "good man" was sometimes "excoriated unfairly during these provocative years."[23] Withholding crucial information from a grizzled and seasoned gunfighting border man like Joe Sitter would not have been smart, with or without a dose of rough treatment. Regardless, for historical purposes there is a quantifiable record of what happened next.

On the twenty-first day of May 1915, U.S. Mounted Customs Inspectors Sitter and Craighead, accompanied by Texas Rangers Eugene Hulen, Harris C. "Harry" Trollinger, and twenty-eight-year-old Arthur P. "Sug" Cummings, a native of Haskell, Haskell County, at the eastern edge of the Texas Panhandle, departed Valentine, Jeff Davis County. The horseback trip would take them across the Rim Rock, thence into Pilares.[24] On the night of the twenty-second the lawmen camped near Pilares. At that point they were told by "some of Villa's soldiers" where some Mexican bandits were hiding in the mountains on the Texas side of the river.[25] The next morning, picking up what they considered a viable trail, they continued their scout after suspected smugglers and the herd of illicitly imported horses. By late evening, in the distance, they espied three outriders overseeing a band of horses. The men making up the mini-task force closed with the supposed enemy at the gallop. The suspected horse thieves vamoosed at the gallop, firing shots over their shoulders. The Rangers answered with their Winchester .30-30s. No damage was done. Fast approaching dusk shielded the outlaws' escape.[26] Rather than foolishly chase after ghosts in the darkness, the haggard lawmen went to bed-ground, camping near a windmill, their nearest source for potable water.[27]

At the crack of dawn, the Rangers and U.S. Customs men were up, making ready to recover horses and capture Mexican bandits. They hobbled their pack horses and stepped into stirrups of saddle horses. With good luck this twenty-fourth day of May they would wind down the chase and lock up border-jumping lawbreakers. In but short order they located some of the smuggled horses, and more or less had them corralled in a box canyon, "up against a bluff." Naturally, due to law enforcement seniority and time spent living near the Rio Grande Joe Sitter was in command, unofficially, but in charge nonetheless. He detailed Inspector Craighead and Rangers Trollinger and Cummings to gather the horses, while he and Ranger Hulen worked their way to the top of a crest to "get a view of the surrounding country," and keep an eye out for Mexican bandits.[28]

After "riding up this Ravine a little ways they [Craighead, Trollinger, and Cummings] decided to turn out of it; as they rode out, up on the bank, Rangers Cummings being in the lead, they were fired upon by Mexicans who were not over forty yards away. They dismounted and under a heavy fire, retreated into the ravine. Seeing a large rock near, they made a dash for it, but were met by a heavy fire from behind it. They could then see Inspector Sitters [*sic*] and Ranger Hulen, who had ridden out on a very small hill, motion to them to get back and go back down the ravine the way they had come. Being cut off from their horses they went down the ravine under a heavy fire while Sitters and Hulen opened up on the Mexicans to cover their retreat. After circling several times, trying to get to Sitters and Hulen, and finding it impossible, they gained the top of the canyon and started to where they had left their Pack train that morning, a distance of about eight miles. As they went out of the canyon they could still hear Sitters and Hulen shooting, they thought they were getting away as they still had their horses."[29]

Geographically pinpointing the site of the ambuscade is illustrative of how peace officers in the wild and woolly border country had nobody to rely on but themselves should the situation turn "Western." United States Marshal John Harris Rogers spotlighted just how isolated was the crime scene: "about 8 miles east of Pilares, near the Rio Grande, in Presidio County, and about 40 miles in a southerly direction from Valentine and about 60 miles in a westerly direction from Marfa."[30] Time elapsing between being notified of an emergency and actually arriving at the scene in the lexicon of twenty-first century police work is "Response Time." During 1915 in Presidio County the Response Time was measured at the best in hours, at worst in days.

After marching over rough country for somewhere between 15 and 20 miles, Craighead, Trollinger, and Cummings made it to the Bill McGee Ranch. From there they messaged for help: backup. Deputy U.S. Marshal W. B. Matthews, stationed at Marfa, received notification an hour before midnight, but jumped into action immediately summoning help. The automobile cavalcade went as far as it could go, then at the John Pool Ranch, about thirty miles short of their destination, the fifteen-man posse mounted horses for the last leg of their rough country journey. There's no room for doubt, the men riding to the rescue were wishing for the best, hoping to encounter Sitter and Hulen making their way to the ranch, but fearing the worst as the gaps between the Pool Ranch and McGee Ranch and the McGee Ranch and Pilares closed tighter.[31]

Finally, about three o'clock in the afternoon, beneath a broiling sun, the posse pussyfooted along the canyon rim where Sitter and Hulen had last been seen, cutting for sign and on guard lest they be ambushed by lurking assassins. Disgustingly they found what they were looking for. On the ground before them lay the lifeless bodies of Joe Sitter and thirty yards further on (ten feet in a separate report), Eugene Hulen.[32] Both had been horribly mutilated, their faces near battered beyond recognition by the pounding from heavy rocks. Numerous bullet wounds in Sitter's body were mute testimony to the cause of his death; sixty spent cartridge casings surrounding his corpse was indication he had gone down fighting.[33] And even while bleeding and down they had showed he owned grit and guts:

He [Apolonio Valdez] confessed to me as follows: He said "We (alluding to the said bandits) killed Sitter; that Manuel Zapata did most of the shooting at Sitter, while the other three shot mostly at Hulen; that after Sitter was down and supposed to be dead, the said Manuel Zapata started in to mutilate his (Sitter's) body. Sitter, then dying, raised his pistol and shot the said Zapata in the face, marking him for life....[34]

Ranger Private Eugene Hulen also succumbed to gunshot wounds.[35] Purportedly, because there was but one ejected rifle cartridge casing by his body, it was surmised—maybe correctly, maybe not—that Eugene Hulen had been "killed early in the fight."[36] Crime scene reconstruction is normally not an easy task, nearly always leaving room for further probing. This instance is par. "Frozen from fear" is an assertion appropriately predicated with "probably" and "might have" when intimating Texas Ranger Hulen "performed poorly" in his "first and last shootout."[37] With eight bullet holes in his body, who now—or then—could proffer how long Hulen lasted on the battlefield?[38] Did he employ his Colt's six-shooter, emptying it, before putting his carbine to work? Was he wholly incapacitated—knocked out of the fight—with the first or the eighth of the bushwhackers' shots? Could any of those sixty spent cartridge casings have been from Hulen's Winchester, ejected while the two lawmen were pinned down together, but before Eugene readjusted his spot of concealment in a frantic effort to upgrade target acquisition? The hard fact is this: Inspector Joe Sitter and Ranger Eugene Hulen were murdered, killed in the line of duty.

With great difficulty bodies of the slain officers were strapped onto pack mules for removal back across the Sierra Viejo Rim to Valentine. There Joe Sitter was buried. From Houston where he was employed as a business executive, John A. Hulen instructed that the family's wish was to have Eugene's body shipped to Gainesville, Cooke County, for burial.[39] The thirty-six-year-old bachelor, a Texas Ranger with but fifty-seven days' service as a lawman, was in due course laid to rest in Fairview Cemetery.[40] Rookies could not expect undue sympathy while riding Lucifer's Line.

Texas Rangers Trollinger and Cummings couldn't either. Their conduct, leaving the scene of the fight, was not well-received at headquarters. Excoriation would measure as mild terminology. Both were fired! Though it makes for an interesting sidebar, that drama and its repercussions and reinstatements are best saved for another time, another story.[41]

Was Chico Cano hiding behind those rocks cocked Winchester in hand when the doomed lawmen broached the Rim? Evidence—and that's what washes away doubt—is scant, though if he wasn't on hand, he's usually credited, then and now, with masterminding the killings.[42]

For all of his crimes, and undoubtedly there were many, Francisco "Chico" Cano skated on paying any debts to the criminal justice system on America's side of the Rio Grande. Mentioning just one of Chico's deplorable acts puts him at the Devil's right hand. After polishing off a bottle or two of fiery *sotol* the rascally and drunken Chico thought target practice was in order. He took a frightened child—petrified child may be more accurate—placed a long-necked bottle on the kiddo's head, stepped back several paces and took aim with his wobbling six-shooter. Chico squeezed the trigger. The bullet missed the bottle. The little boy died.[43]

Cano was remorseful for awhile—a little while. In the end he retired to his cattle *rancho* in the Mexican state of Chihuahua, giving up the ghost due to natural causes on August 28, 1943.[44]

Sometimes the good boys die young. Sometimes the bad men don't.

Chapter 17

Robert Lee Burdett
1915

Hardly had two weeks passed since the murders of Ranger Hulen and Inspector Sitter when more appalling news would break along the river. And it, too, would bear sad tidings for the Texas Rangers of Company B, the unit captained by James Monroe Fox headquartered at Marfa. Yes, the Grim Reaper works his timetable, not the Texas Rangers, not even the ones who would charge Hell with a bucket of water, despite the hurdles and hazards—and hyperventilated prattle.

Austin, Texas, is a pretty place. Austin girls are pretty, too. And they darn sure were in 1880. In fact a newspaperman writing for the *Austin Daily Statesman* thought the city owned bragging rights when it came to those attractive and petite young thoroughbreds:

> Austin has more pretty school girls between the ages of eight and eighteen of any other city of its size on the globe. Our healthy, clear atmosphere develops pretty girls just as bluegrass and lime-stone water in Kentucky develops the finest horses in the world.[1]

Sam Burdett didn't want to brag about anything. It seems Sam and a black man, Lewis Bedford, on one side, and an unidentified person or persons got into a heated row in a Red River Street store operated by Emelie Sckerls.[2] The proprietor, standing alone, is an interesting Old West character herself. Three years before, Emelie had suffered a gunshot wound due to another's recklessly mishandling a six-shooter at her place of business. Closer in, time-wise, Emelie found herself under arrest for Disturbing the Peace. The following month, October 1880, there was another quarrel at the store, one in which an emotionally charged Emelie had right fast "emptied her five-shooter at a negro."[3] Following this dustup by a day or two was the ruckus involving Sam Burdett and Lewis Bedford. It must have been a hot time.

Sam and Lewis ended up in jail answering charges for Assault to Murder and using Abusive Language. Bedford was forced to languish in the calaboose, while Burdett posted his $700 appearance bond and was turned out onto the city's brick streets. To his utter astonishment Sam Burdett was rearrested for unlawfully carrying a handgun in his back pocket, the charge to be prosecuted in Austin's municipal court. A $50 bond freed him, the second time.[4]

As a gossipy sidebar: Emelie would find her name in print again the following year, 1881. She would be arrested at Austin in the company of a genuine gunfighter, James Madison Brown, the then sheriff of Lee County (Giddings). The arrest would come at the hands of another gunman, the legendary Ben Thompson who was serving his stint as Austin's police chief. Emelie had been traveling with Sheriff Brown incognito, dressed in a man's attire and openly wearing a gunbelt and six-shooter: Intent of the disguise was clear from the get-go. Brown, a colorful and very well-known fellow throughout Texas, could ill afford publicity about slipping into town with a woman "notorious for dealing out the ardent."[5] At the time such cross-dressing was a flagrant violation of an Austin city ordinance. As would be expected, the city newspapermen had a field day exposing the masquerade and implying that the deception reeked with immorality on the part of Sheriff Brown.[6]

Returning to the story at hand, on October 7, 1880, at Mayor's Court, after changing his plea to guilty, Sam reluctantly paid a $25 fine for the weapons violation and was legally free to go home to his expectant wife Elizabeth, popularly known as "Lizzie." Finally there was something for Sam to puff his chest about, the birth of his son, Robert Lee Burdett arriving at the family farm near Walnut Creek on the ninth day of June 1881.[7] Growing up near the tiny community of Sprinkle just northeast of Austin the boy in this narrative shed his first name, going by his middle name. Lee Burdett, who would later become a Texas Ranger, owned something many of his fellow lawmen did not: an education.

Peeking down on the city of Austin proper, with an almost eerie but graceful expression of majesty, is St. Edwards University: A Catholic institution of gemstone quality with examples of exquisite architecture. Combine that with an excellence exhibited by its teaching cadre and the college was then and is now one of Austin's cherished treasures. For a period of time as a strapping teenager Lee Burdett was a student, reflected in St. Edwards' *Catalogue of Students*.[8] Lee

Burdett was an athlete too, a hard-throwing and hard-hitting centerfielder for the school's Excelsiors, one of the youthful scholars' baseball teams.[9]

In Lee's case the apple didn't fall far from the family tree. In some form or fashion Lee Burdett found himself tangled up with another. The brouhaha, after the filing of offsetting Complaints, resulted in dismissal of the twin cases, but did not wipe Lee's December 27, 1905, arrest from the Austin Police Department's blotter.[10] Lee could swing hard when he needed to, or thought he needed to. Also hard-hitting was Lee's first cousin, William Jesse "Will" Morris, the city's police chief.[11] How much that influenced Robert Lee Burdett's eventual career choice is unknowable, but it may be reported that the six foot brown-haired boy's head was turned toward policing.

On October 6, 1911, Lee Burdett, with some type of "peace officer" experience already under his gun-belt, enlisted in the Texas Rangers at Austin, assigned to Company C under the leadership of the aforementioned J. M. Fox, former Austin city detective and an elected Travis County constable. Fox had just been promoted to Texas Ranger captain the day before.[12] Company C had been reactivated thanks to an influx of federal funds designed to beef up borderland security and prevent spillage of bloodshed on Texas ground as result of the then storming Mexican Revolution. "For the only time in the history of the United States the federal government agreed to subsidize a state police force to defend the American border." Robert Lee Burdett was one of the thirteen privates, answering to a 1st Sergeant, rounding out the revamping of Company C, all thanks to Uncle Sam.[13]

Private Lee Burdett's appointment was rather short-lived, the federal subsidy played out, and even the adjutant general noted that Company C "has practically mustered itself out by resignation," which begs the questioning of Captain Fox's overall competency and managerial skills, in spite of a paucity of the Ranger outfit's financial wherewithal.[14] Certainly Lee Burdett was not riding the lonesome trails in faraway West Texas or slapping at mosquitoes in the tropical Lower Rio Grande Valley as he chased after Mexican Bandits or Anglo cow stealers. The 1912 *City Directory* for the city of Austin, after the untimely death of his father in 1890, indicates Lee was living with his mother, his barbering brother Frank, and his sister Mary, a "trained nurse," in their home at 209 W. 8th Street.[15]

During the routine shenanigans of Texas politics, Captain Fox had maintained a foothold, commander of a company of one—himself. During reshuffling in the Ferguson administration Captain Fox was shifted to be the headman for Company B, temporarily stationed at Valentine, Jeff Davis County, at the top of the Big Bend Country in West Texas, then later repositioned to Marfa, Presidio County. On the first day of February 1915 after a three-year hiatus, at age thirty-two Lee Burdett reenlisted with the Rangers, this time with Company B.[16] He was posted at Fabens, downriver from El Paso and upriver from Fort Hancock.

The following month, on March 15, another thirty-two-year-old signed on with Company B. Charles Pryor "Charley" Beall, born in Live Oak County at Oakville, then the county seat (later George West), had decided a shift from humid South Texas to dry West Texas was the ace in his hand of career cards.[17] The actual depth of the friendship between Ranger Privates Lee Burdett and Charley Beall is yet to be plumbed, but with assurance they were affable working partners from time to time, scouting in tandem across very treacherous ground.

An armchair assertion that *mal hombres* pulling triggers yesterday influenced borderland Rangers' behavior on the morrow is but logical—and sustainable. During May of 1915 Mexican bandits crossed the Rio Grande in the Big Bend Country and ruthlessly murdered Pablo Jiménez by "shooting him and beating him."[18] Ranger Hulen and Inspector Sitter had been killed on May 24, 1915. The river was running red that May of 1915, or so it seemed to borderland lawmen. Private Lee Burdett penned a letter to his now-widowed mother, making sure she would be aware of his taking out a life insurance policy so that he could "make especial provision" for her and his sister should he be killed, purposely or accidently. But two days after the deaths of Hulen and Sitter, Lee submitted payment to the North American Accident Insurance Company for Policy No. 983363, and pocketed the Post Office receipt.[19] Had he an ominous premonition?

During the early afternoon hours of June 8, 1915, Privates Burdett and Beall were on duty at Fabens, patrolling, keeping the peace, and staying attuned to any news about revolutionary fellows crossing the river—without or without smuggled livestock—or abettors hustling toward the nearby Rio Grande with arms and ammunition destined for Mexico. Their duties were by definition multifaceted. Whether somewhat emboldened by the recent deaths of a Customs Inspector and Texas Ranger, or just plain stupid is indeterminate, but five unruly and no doubt inebriated "Mexicans" were creating quite a stir. Purportedly the hooligans were part of "a gang of Mexicans from Fort Hancock."[20] They, repeatedly, were driving their hack up and down Fabens' main—and only—thoroughfare "creating considerable excitement by yelling and cursing."[21] Not the least intimidated, the two lawmen advised the drunks to knock it off, settle down or they would find themselves staring out from behind jailhouse bars. Perhaps the Rangers' admonishment and warning had been delivered offensively, crustily. Maybe the words had been spoken with the tenderness of a mother's love. Regardless the bottom line is this: the rowdy yahoos were not arrested, but given a second chance to straighten up and fly right. The blitzed guys departed, no doubt cursing under their sour breaths, but nonetheless they cleared off of the street.[22] Fabens returned to normal, if there ever was a normal along the Rio Grande.

As Burdett pulled out his gold-plated pocket watch he noted it was half past seven o'clock. These Texas Rangers had made another day. Then, in a heartbeat, the world turned upside down. The five scalawags were back on Fabens' street, this time purposefully jeering as they walked, wobbled, and stumbled past Privates Burdett and Beall in the fading twilight. They were, it seemed, patently looking for trouble, even hallooing insults at the lawmen. Then as if by some premeditated design they vanished from the road, disappearing into a darkened alley. Eyewitness testimony is always iffy, but either Ranger Burdett or Ranger Beall was overhead to say: "I think they have guns, and I think we ought to go and search them."[23] That said, there was naught to do but search them.

Forthrightly, in the alleyway, Burdett and Beall rounded up three of the fellows. What of the other two? Well, they were not there, not seen, perhaps they had gone on ahead knowing they would be accosted by the Rangers if they dared tarry. Private Charley Beall stepped back. He would stand as the covering officer. Ranger Lee Burdett stepped in. He would perform the hands-on searching—the pat down for unlawfully concealed weapons. It was dark. It was dangerous. It was obligatory—they were Rangers.[24]

At first the mechanical protocol was coming off without a hitch. Then, one of the detainees began to physically resist. In a jiffy the fight was underway. Looking back the breaking into fisticuffs was but a marker. Taking his cue, from behind a woodpile a fellow stood up and fired his six-shooter. The blast reverberated putting Fabens on notice: Something was amiss.

"The shot was evidently the signal for the commencing of the battle that occurred between the rangers on the one side and the Mexicans on the other."[25] There were not neutral eyewitnesses to the actual shooting in the alleyway, and quite naturally versions and bullet-counts varied. The *El Paso Morning Times* reported "something like thirty or forty shots were fired," while the *Alpine Avalanche* and the *El Paso Herald* pared the number down to twenty.[26] If truth be told for on-the-ground Rangers, one was too many. That's not the card they were dealt and had to play, however. The close-range gun battle waxed hot, a scorcher, each side scrapping tooth and toenail—until their Colt's revolvers spun dry. When the cylinders were empty, thankfully, the gunfight was over. The "Mexicans" ran out the far end of the alley and were gone, presumably racing for safety the Rio Grande could allow.

There's little doubt Charley Beall breathed a sigh of relief: he had come through the ordeal unscathed, no numbness, no pain, not leaking any blood. Lady Luck had smiled for Private Beall. She had looked the other way for Ranger Lee Burdett, though. He was lifelessly reposed on the dirty alley's floor, a gaping bullet wound in the upper part of his chest, just below the neck, blood pooling beneath his head and shoulders. He was dead.[27] According to one newspaper his Colt's was empty, not a live round in the wheel. He'd gone down fighting. There was speculation based on sound reasoning that at least one of the gutless assailants had suffered a hit, wounded but not immobilized, still able to move about belching fire and spitting misery from a six-gun's muzzle.

When the news broke at El Paso, the county sheriff, Peyton J. Edwards, quickly notified Doctor L. G. Witherspoon, deputy sheriffs J. B. Kilpatrick and Jim Fulgham, a former Texas Ranger, and Ranger Oscar W. "Doc" Goodwin, Company B. Without delay they left for Fabens. With the aid of soldiers from the U.S. Army's 15th Cavalry a cordon was thrown around the little border town, corralling those within city limits. No ingress. No egress. Lawmen followed a blood trail to a house on the outskirts of town. There they learned a man had tried to enter the adobe home, but was refused admittance by the owner upon seeing the bleeding man was angrily clutching a six-shooter and looked scary. The injured man moved on.[28] He was heading for the Rio Grande. Unfortunately for lawmen the blood trail finally petered out. During the course of an intensive investigation and manhunt—and the searching of houses—three fellows who had not run for the river were taken into custody by the sorrowful squadron of Lone Star lawmen: Venobla Pena, Ponciano Gonzales, and Luciano Lopez.[29] Three days later Rangers arrested two more alleged gang members, Luz Gandero and Isidoro Cadena. They, too, were taken to El Paso and placed in the county jail.[30] True, the suspects had been rounded up at Fabens in real short order; however on the Company B Monthly Return it appears they were charged with Disturbing the Peace, not Murder.[31] Lacking specificity as just who had pulled which trigger that had sent the death shot on its way, homicide charges could not be sustained beyond that necessary standard of Reasonable Doubt.

Though characterizing it as ambulance chasing may be an easy overreach, an undertaker from El Paso's Nagley & Kaster Funeral Home was hot on the sheriff's heels, also arriving in Fabens. The funeral parlor man assumed custody of Lee Burdett's remains and his personal property, carefully making an inventory.[32] One day after his death, Robert Lee Burdett's body was escorted by "Texas rangers, deputy sheriffs and other peace officers" to El Paso's Union Station and placed on a train destined for Austin.[33] Dipping into his pocket and knowing—or believing—he would be reimbursed, Ranger Private Andrew Charles "Andy" Barker had forked over $20.95 due the station agent for transportation costs.[34] Advising interested readers that Burdett's body would arrive at the depot about midnight, the *Austin Daily Statesman* also noted that Lee Burdett would be returning home to Travis County on his birthday.[35]

Captain Fox who was already in Austin when he received news of Lee Burdett's death was interviewed by a reporter about conditions along the Rio Grande. Fox did not mince words: "the Texas border is infested with Mexicans of a desperate character. The rangers have been actively engaged recently in an effort to check cattle thieving and other depredations along the border and in the Big Bend country."[36] Though his rhetoric was of a gentler tone Adjutant General Henry Hutchings in his Biennial Report acknowledged that "conditions along the border" had fostered a beefed-up Ranger presence; buildup "an absolute necessity" in certain sectors.[37]

On June 10, 1915, while his mother Lizzie and his sister Mary wept, and brother Frank was in Mexico, the earthly remains of Ranger Robert Lee Burdett were peacefully lowered into space 8, lot

310, section E, at Austin's Mt. Calvary Cemetery.[38] There was no wife to grieve, no widow demanding justice for killers somewhere roaming the borderlands, footloose and fancy free, unrepentant.

Near a week later, Austin Chief of Police Will Morris delivered and released Lee Burdett's inventoried property to his mother, advising Adjutant General Hutchings: "Have just delivered to Mrs. Burdett effects of her son Lee. She asked me to thank you for your kindness in her trouble and I wish to say that our entire family shall ever remember your aid in this deplorable affair."[39]

In regards to Lee Burdett's murderers there had been no Judge Lynch imprudence—not while those suspects were in custody—on the Texas side of the line! There was, however, after their release a seamy side to the story. Pancho Villa's raid on Columbus, New Mexico, was months into the future. Before he completely fell from grace, certain borderland lawmen were wheeling and dealing with Pancho for good reasons—and bad. One of whom, at this point in time, was purportedly Jefferson Eagle "Jeff" Vaughn, Texas Ranger. Vaughn and Ranger Ivy R. Fenley, it's been written, tipped Villa off about the diplomatic importance of apprehending Burdett's murderers, especially if they were being shielded across the river somewhere in Chihuahua.[40] In another rendition of the same story, it was Captain Fox who connived with Pancho Villa for a solution.[41] Villa obliged. After some sleuthing he found two fellows, allegedly had them identified by Vaughn and Fenley, then Villa stood the hapless fellows in front of an adobe wall—facing a firing squad. On that day, according to one account, Pancho "saved the State of Texas the cost of a trial."[42] Case closed!

Not closed, though, is the book enumerating Texas Ranger deaths along the Rio Grande.

Chapter 18

William P. Stillwell
1918

More so than any other, 1918 would prove to be the deadliest year for Rangers scouting the Texas-Mexico border. Adhering to the earlier pledge that this volume would focus on Rangers dying with their boots on, there will not be chapter-length digressions focusing on three who passed plagued with coughs, fever, wheezing, or sprints to outhouses as a result of influenza and dysentery. Their law-enforcing work history should not be downplayed, but conditions surrounding their demise fall outside the promised parameters of this storyline, though when chronologically fitting their deaths will earn mention.[1] Their ultimate sacrifices, though not dramatic in a Wild West context were laudable and sad nevertheless; they went where they were sent, doing what they were supposed to be doing—dying on the job carrying Ranger commissions.

John Stillwell was a wandering man. Along the way he picked up a wife, Emily Kay, marrying her in 1859 at Kempers Bluff, Texas. Although originally from the Vicksburg, Mississippi, area, John would seek his fame and fortune throughout the Lone Star State and across the Rio Grande, once even joining a colony trying to chisel out an existence near Tampico, Mexico. Retuning to Texas, John and Emily eked out a living freighting along the Rio Grande near Brownsville. Leaving the Lower Rio Grande Valley behind, John moved closer in toward Corpus Christi, for awhile settling at San Patricio, before moving his growing brood to Oakville, then to nearby Lagarto, both in Live Oak County. There John and Emily ranched and operated a general merchandise store.[2] And it was in Live Oak County that William P. Stillwell was born on February 24, 1870.[3] At home and by family he was dubbed "Will" but later in adulthood many associates and colleagues would opt for the short version of William calling him "Bill."

When Will was ten years old, the family moved again, this time to Bee County taking up residence on the Rountree Ranch, ten miles from Beeville. There they stayed—for four years. During 1884 John uprooted the clan for another sojourn in Mexico, this time across the river twenty-nine miles south of Dryden, Terrell County, upriver from Del Rio. "John Stillwell while ranching there had his share of trouble from Mexican outlaws and cattle thieves." Simply stated that section of the river was just too tough for family life, and the Stillwells before the year was out migrated northwest, eventually settling in Marathon, Brewster County, geographically the largest county in Texas. A homestead at Marathon would lessen threats of banditry and better access seven of his nine children to the classroom.[4]

The Stillwells had finally found a home base for Emily and the school-age kids. Until his death from natural causes in 1909, John Stillwell "ran his cattle over the vast open spaces without the obstacle of a single fence...."[5] Part of those vast open spaces, according to Hallie Stillwell who later married into the family, was in Mexico and the senior Stillwell had "built a barge that would carry horses, supplies, and travelers across the river and anchored the barge to the bank after each crossing.... The crossing where the barge was placed became known as Stillwell Crossing, a name still used today."[6] Not unexpectedly cattle knew no boundary and wandered back and forth across the Rio Grande when it wasn't a raging torrent—which was not often. Chasing after those cattle for roundups, branding, and screwworm doctoring was Will Stillwell, a top-hand cowboy in his youth, a respected stockman in maturity.

Also not too surprisingly, when the Stillwells tried to cross their cattle back across the river into Texas for shipment from the nearest railway connection at Marathon, Mexican soldiers and/or border guards "always found some legal technicality or reason" to sequester the herd—it was, after all, land of the *mordida*. Circumspectly, oftentimes it became a game of "cat and mouse" if the Stillwells were to cross their cattle and avoid the financial bite.[7] Conveniently, though unspoken of course, is the fact cattle coming into Texas were supposed to stand clearance by U.S. Customs—the obfuscation of same being a clear-cut case: Smuggling.

Purportedly, and it does come from a secondhand account, during one exhilarating adventure Will Stillwell and his brother Roy, along with cowboy Punch Roberts, made a midnight trip across the Rio Grande in an effort to repossess horses and saddles taken from them by Mexican soldiers—or opportunistic revolutionists. The Texans were daring and sneaky and moderately successful: recovering their horses but not the saddles.[8]

Will was a cowman for damn sure, but he sheepishly asked for the hand of Meddie Bennett. The nuptials were performed at Alpine, the county seat, on June 5, 1897. Will was twenty-seven; Meddie was twenty-one. Two children would issue from this union: Bernice and Willie Jack.[9]

By any reckoning Will Stillwell wasn't inclined to being a six-shootin' borderland lawman. He was content playing his role as a Big Bend Country ranchman, a well-respected ranchman. Besides his own interests Will was foreman for the Piedras Blancas Ranch.[10] The topsy-turvy Mexican Revolution would upend the best laid plans of Mr. William P. Stillwell, however.

A series of borderland events would significantly impact Stillwell and his sense of duty. Though a chronological skip backwards is necessary, the stopovers will be short, recaps skeletal. During January 1916 near Santa Ysabel, Chihuahua, Villistas stopped a train carrying eighteen American mining engineers: they were summarily executed. American outrage was widespread. Another of the precipitator episodes would have its origin in New Mexico. The overspill would douse the Big Bend with blood. During the night of March 9, 1916, Mexican raiders under the direct command structure of Pancho Villa struck hard and fast across the international line hitting Columbus, New Mexico, with a stinging vengeance. After a battle with U.S. Army personnel Villa's marauders scooted back across the border leaving seventeen lifeless civilians and soldiers, torched buildings, and several of their own dead to serve as fuel for the settling of scores by Americans with a vulgar funeral pyre. A few live Mexican prisoners would not be burned at the stake, but were later hanged at Deming.[11] Subsequent to the raid at Columbus and a somewhat helter-skelter Punitive Expedition directed by Brigadier General John J. "Black Jack" Pershing, the geographical scene for revolutionists morphing into banditry shifted to the southeast: below the Rio Grande in the vicinity of Ojinaga/Presidio, underbelly of the Texas Big Bend Country.[12]

On that far-flung Texas-Mexico border the motives of replacing dictators with democracy took a backseat to thievery and murder: "More than the Sediciosos of South Texas, the Big Bend raiders deserved the label 'bandit.'"[13] On May 5, 1916, the Big Bend Country suffered its "worst raid." The Mexican bandits, at least a few whom were known as the "fiercest outlaws in Mexico" augmented by *amigos* from the Texas side of the river, under cover of darkness pre-positioned themselves for striking the remote hamlets of Glenn Springs and Boquillas in that secluded country where the Rio Grande really does make its big bend.[14] Glenn Springs, nestled in the foothills of the striking Chisos Mountains, was home of the wax factory operated by C. D. Wood and W. K. Ellis, which employed "50 Mexicans." There was a small general store to meet local families' needs.[15] Garrisoned at Glenn Springs because of the erratic Mexican Revolution was a detachment of U.S. Army soldiers, consisting of a 1st Sergeant and eight privates armed with 1903 Springfield rifles, .30-06 caliber, and newfangled Colt .45 auto pistols. Further to the east about twelve miles, around the river's bend, was a tiny spot on the map, Boquillas, Texas, a near mirror's image of Boquillas del Carmen, state of Coahuila, Mexico, on the Rio Grande's opposite bank. An aerial tram operated by Jesse Deemer facilitated the crossing of silver ore from the Mexican side to the Texas side for transshipment to the railhead at Marathon, as well as commissary items from Jesse's small store going the other way to hungry villagers and American mining executives in Boquillas, Mexico. Mexican bandits had an affinity for stores.[16]

Shortly before midnight the brunt of the gang, numbering between 80 and 125, splashed across the river and attacked Glenn Springs, while a smaller unit, 75 in one retelling that may well be overblown, struck out for Boquillas.[17] At Glenn Springs, Sergeant Charles Smyth was taken unawares. He and half-dozen privates were wholly surrounded and forced to barricade themselves inside a crude building—such as it was—with a thatched roof. Two soldiers managed to hide out, undetected. Gunfire was intense. The fight was lopsided. When bandits pitched a torch on the roof of the soldiers' lair, the conflagration drove them from cover, barefooted and yet in their underclothes.[18] Three died: Privates William Cohen, Steven Coloe, and Hudson Rogers, all cut down by bullets. In a private home, bandits killed a child:

> Little Garnett Compton, four years old, had been killed by shots through his chest, abdomen, and leg, but his six-year old brother, who was deaf and dumb, was walking about the battle scene

unharmed. This happened because some Mexicans are extremely superstitious about harming a deaf mute.[19]

Superstitious or not, Mexican bandits busied themselves looting the store, taking everything except the sauerkraut thinking its distinctive odor an indication of rot. Then they fled, leaving one dead bandit behind on the battlefield.[20]

At Boquillas the other set of bandits didn't meet with armed resistance; Jesse Deemer and his black clerk, Monroe Payne, had seen the wisdom in submitting, not shooting. When the bandits crossed the river into Mexico, loaded with booty, they were accompanied by an unwilling Jesse and Monroe. On the Mexican side of the Rio Grande, at the sliver mine, after looting and pillaging, the hardhearted yahoos made off with piles of goods and a bonus—six more prisoners. Disorganized would be kind terminology for the gangsters' competency in making a clean getaway. After trickery and deception by the American prisoners, the tables turned and several kidnappers found themselves being hustled back to Boquillas, across the Rio Grande, and into the handcuffs and leg-irons of the Brewster County sheriff, J. Allen Walton, and his deputy Jim Shoemaker. The lawmen, after learning of the attacks, had been accompanied to the river by sixty heavily armed citizens from Alpine and Marathon, part of the Stillwell clan among them.[21]

Needless to say, citizens of Brewster and Presidio Counties were outraged. Will Stillwell was tough, yet a peaceable fellow hard to rile. For the Big Bend Country there was a short respite in the raids by Mexican bandits. The breather was just that, impermanent, not a truce. While 1917 was coming to a close it seemed bandolier-wearing thugs were competing amongst themselves, seeing how much damage could be inflicted on West Texas *gringos*. The first day of December they struck the J. F. Tinger ranch, driving stolen cattle across the Rio Grande, and ultimately killing his foreman, Justo González. American military responded, chasing the thieves into Mexico and doing battle at Buenavista with the loss of one killed, one wounded. Thirty-five Mexicans paid with their lives for the indiscretion. Making use of the tiny Mexican hamlet of Los Mimbres as sanctuary and shield, on December 3 bandits fired across the river at U.S. soldiers, wounding a trooper. American military response was decisive: Twelve Mexican bandits were killed, and the villages of Los Mimbres and Buenavista, "known to the Rangers and mounted Customs inspectors as a nest of bandits," were burned to the ground. During mid-month, a sniper from the Mexican side tried to kill the U.S. Army's Captain Leonard Matlack. The bandit's bullet missed; Matlack's didn't.[22] Cowman Will Stillwell began mulling over what role he could or would play; the Big Bend Country he knew was aflame with murder, thievery, and dread.

Another border country episode would make any man's blood boil. On December 25, 1917, most folks in Texas were celebrating Christmas. Mexican bandits, forty-five strong, opted to spend their holiday at Luke Brite's ranch, thirty-odd miles southwest of Marfa. The carefully orchestrated attack came, as planned, when the ranch owner and his family were away, rejoicing with dinner guests at their well-appointed Marfa home. The ranch was so large and had so many employees scattered far and wide that it too had a store and post office, one with an official designation as noted by fifteen year ranch employee and a future Texas Ranger, La Fetra E. "Lee" Trimble:

> Brite's ranch, you see, had a store, and it was Brite's ranch and post office. You could write a letter—Brite, Texas—that's where it would go—Brite, Texas. And they carried, every other day, the mail from Candelaria, to Brite, Valentine, Valentine back to Brite, to Candelaria.[23]

The only folks at ranch headquarters per se were ranch foreman Trevaniel Tul "Van" Neill and his family, plus his father Samuel H. "Sam" and his wife. After the initial exchange of gunfire, wherein the elder Neill had shot the gang's nominal leader out of the saddle, the bandits soon found they could not dislodge the enemy, and the Neills realized they could not extricate themselves from jeopardy or call for help, the telephone wire having been cut: It was a real siege, a Mexican Standoff.[24]

Fortuitously the bandits caught a stroke of good luck. They made a hostage—or supposed hostage—of Mexican "chore-man" José Sanchez. He would serve as the bandits' go-between. José carried the message: if foreman Neill would give over keys to the store and outbuildings, the bandits would be satisfied without drawing blood.[25] They lied. Van Neill complied. As had postmaster Pierre Guyon when he was handed a message to fork over mail-bag keys—or else! Unbeknownst to postman Mickey Welch, driving the mail-hack and accompanied by two Mexican passengers, Demetrio Holguin and Ernesto

Juarez, the trio drove into the maelstrom uncorking at Brite's Ranch. Bandits killed the two passengers outright. Then, turning their attention to the mailman, they strung Mickey Welch upside down to an overhead beam, cut his throat and gutted him.[26] After plundering the store and stealing ranch horses the bandits fled toward the river. Belatedly the alarm was spread.

Pursuing soldiers and ranchmen and Rangers failed to overhaul the bandits, except for some long-range sniping which netted minimal result—unless one were the Mexican Bandit killed or wounded in the lobbing bombardment. Had that military and civilian posse been more successful Texas Ranger history might stand a rewriting—a dark and sinister chapter erased.

Even an apologetic massaging cannot set straight what happened at Porvenir, however. Rangers misbehaved, murderously so. Bending to popular Anglo ranchmen's urgings that the 150 residents of Porvenir, Presidio County, on the river just below the Sierra Vieja Rim, were nothing short of a nest of bandits and accomplices of bandits and spies for bandits, Ranger Captain James Monroe Fox acted, dispatching a detachment of Rangers to Porvenir.[27] The long and the short of the story is simple—but not too nice. Though what actually happened may be clouded with excuses and face-saving finger-pointing, when the Texas Rangers and a handful of perturbed ranchers rode out of Porvenir during the wee morning hours of 28 January 1918, a month after the murders at Brite, an end result was calculable: fifteen dead Hispanics aged sixteen to seventy-two. Or, as an erudite historian uncovered, "The Rangers orphaned forty-two children that night."[28]

There, too, is a quantifiable consequence regarding these Rangers, and it's a story meriting inspection, but for this narrative it must be shelved. Suffice to say Company B would be formally disbanded and Captain Fox would resign under protest. Dark as it was, the incident at Porvenir did not lessen the need for Texas Rangers—good Rangers—in the Big Bend Country. Standing backstage watching his homeland more-or-less deteriorate before his eyes was the curtain-call for a middle-aged guy who would rather ranch than ranger, but his sense of duty was crying out.

On the fifteenth day of February 1918 at Marathon, Will Stillwell, age forty-seven, enlisted in the Ranger Force, Company F, commanded by Captain James Carroll Bates.[29]

Will Stillwell, although wholly inexperienced as a lawman, was the type of Ranger any captain assigned the Big Bend Country would want. Will was thoroughly familiar with the geography between Marfa and Alpine on the north, and the Rio Grande near 100 miles below all the way southeast to Langtry. He had cowboyed and overseen ranching operations in Texas and Mexico. As a lifelong borderlander Stillwell had acquired the ability to speak Spanish fluently, an asset not to be undervalued when compelled to scout along the Rio Grande with its hidden canyons and winding smugglers' trails leading to and from the river; accosting non-English speakers.

While Company B headquarters was Marfa, further to the east was the jurisdictional domain of Company F, theoretically based at Marathon because of the luxury of a railway connection. The real work for the company, however, was south along the river: "Bates maintained camps at Rio Grande Canyon, Santa Elena, and Lajitas. Each detachment patrolled the river nine miles each way from its camp on a daily basis."[30] Will Stillwell knew the river crossings well.

Another Ranger was up to crossing the river—an embarrassment to the service and to his company. Captain Bates, obviously miffed, reported to Adjutant General James A. Harley that Private John C. Palmer had "turned out bad." It seems Private Palmer, a forty-five-year-old Oklahoman, had been writing hot checks, sold his rifle and saddle, was AWOL from the Ranger camp, and by the grapevine it was rumored he was "going to Mex." He had been offered a "Captain's Command" by one side or another. Absconder Palmer's Ranger days were history forthwith.[31]

Hardly had Will Stillwell signed on as a Ranger when another Mexican bandit raid captured headlines and broke a Presidio County ranchman's heart. Ranch owner Edwin Watts "Ed" Nevill was in Van Horn (Culberson County) obtaining supplies and visiting with his wife and three youngest children where he had moved them after the Brite Ranch raid. His oldest son Glenn, eighteen, had remained at the ranch. In the city Ed Nevill was posted about the seemingly credible rumors of an impending raid. He hurried back to the ranch. Surging across the river raiders struck the Nevill Ranch on the night of March 25, 1918. Perhaps it was revenge for Porvenir or maybe it was banditry for banditry's sake. The firefight was uneven, seventeen against two, Ed and Glenn. A Mexican employee managed to slip away undetected leaving his wife, the cook, and their small children behind as he went in search of help. Ed Nevill, trying to reposition himself and tactically improve his field of fire, raced for an arroyo outside. Alas, Glenn and Rosa Castillo stayed put. After killing Glenn and ransacking the house, the bandits left their calling card: "The Mexican woman sat propped against the wall in her room, a bullet in the head and another in the chest. A stick had been rammed up her vagina, and a severed breast lay on either side—possibly a warning to Mexicans who consorted with Anglos. The children had witnessed the barbarity but had not been otherwise harmed."[32] Oral history versions vary about the mutilation.[33]

Following the Nevill Ranch raid, a U.S. Army detachment chased after the bandits, crossing the Rio Grande, following them past and then back to the Mexican settlement of Pilares where the pursuers and the pursued locked up tight. Thirty or so Mexicans died in the gunfight. During searches American soldiers reportedly found a "substantial cache of weapons, and ammunition, including German-made rifles" and personal property that could be traced both to the Brite and Nevill Ranch raids. The soldiers torched Pilares and scooted back to Texas and controversy.[34]

The Big Bend Country was afire with hot feelings. A writer for the *El Paso Times* didn't water down his words with lily-livered verbiage: "Cattlemen from all parts of the Big Bend district will attend the meeting. According to tentative plans, home guard units of cowboys and ranchers who can ride and shoot will be formed to co-operate with the military authorities in patrolling the border.... While depredations have been going on for a long time, the recent raid on the Nevill ranch and the killing of young Nevill has resulted in the ranchers banding themselves together for mutual protection."[35] Yes, Will Stillwell was Rangering in tough and merciless country, the Big Bend of 1917–1918.

Less than two months after enlisting, Private Stillwell was called on by Captain Bates. The captain had been notified on April 2, 1918 that the ranch of John Daniels had been raided by Mexican bandits. They had stolen a band of horses and driven them across the river. The Ranger captain learned rather quickly from a Mexican informant that the chief suspect was Pablo Dominquez, a noted thief, "the terror of this side and the other.... leader of one of the hardest gangs along the river."[36] Two years earlier, along that same forbidding section of the Rio Grande, Texas Rangers had engaged members of the Dominquez clan in a gunplay, killing Francisco Dominquez while they were attempting to serve arrest warrants for murder committed on the Texas side of Lucifer's Line.[37] Pablo's reputation was that of a desperado, but also a survivor caught between rivaling revolutionary factions, "furnishing both with beef and horses." According to Co. F's Captain Bates, Dominquez had "figured in most of the raids and all of the stealing, [and] was Commander at the Glenn Spring's Raid." At one time there was a governmental price tag for the head of one Mr. Pablo Dominquez: $500. Short on handy manpower, Captain Bates turned to the U.S. Army for help. Eight soldiers either volunteered or were assigned to assist Captain Bates and Private Stillwell. At daylight the posse cut for sign, picked up the trail, and undauntedly crossed the Rio Grande into Mexico.[38] By their reasoning it was a legit hot pursuit.

It was clean work, uncomplicated and not too taxing or time consuming. The headquarters village of Dominquez was not a closely held secret. Though the Rangers and soldiers probably should have suspected it for self-preservation's sake, the river-jumping thugs were outfitted with firearms equivalent to what the lawmen were carrying, their guns being "all new and plenty of ammunition."[39] The posse swept through Mexico's countryside with a purpose: righting wrongs. Then they were there. Unceremoniously, Captain Bates reports "we surrounded the village."[40]

There is slight discrepancy as what came to pass, but not too much. The outcome is unaltered. From prior knowledge or intelligence slyly gained at the moment, Pablo Dominquez's home was spotlighted for the Rangers' inquiry and/or a dynamic entry. Approaching the residence of suspects targeted for arrest is always a dangerous proposition. The lawman's helpless exposure a hazard of not just shooting into the house willy-nilly and hoping bullets find the right mark. Frequently in such naked but necessary approaches it is the peace officer who wears a bulls-eye. Due to his fluent Spanish, Private Stillwell was cast in the role of spokesman. Riding up to the doorway of Dominquez's residence Will Stillwell was met by an apprehensive Mexican woman. Will's inquiry was direct and pointed: "*¿Esta Pabalo?*" Will Stillwell had spoken his last words. Pabalo was standing in the shadows six-shooter in hand. In the blink of an eye Dominquez eared back the hammer on his revolver. Hearing the all-so-recognizable clicks as the six-shooter was staged to full cock, his wife ducked for cover while Pabalo let bullets fly. From atop his gyrating horse the Ranger managed to pop two .45 rounds toward the entryway, but both went wide. Pabalo's luck held for a moment, but just a moment: one of his bullets toppled Will from the saddle. The Grim Reaper looked down at Ranger Stillwell's lifeless body and then jokingly winked at Captain Bates and the soldiers standing by: Their fusillade knocked Pabalo evermore into the abyss of eternity. Widow Dominquez wept.[41]

Cognizant of their untenable situation and geographic positioning, the Ranger captain and the soldiers strapped Will's body to his horse, departing the Mexican village before more fireworks erupted. As quickly as he practically could, after making it back across the Rio Grande, Captain Bates telegraphed Austin posting Adjutant General Harley about the April 3, 1918, shooting: "Bill Stillwell was killed in fight with Mexicans this morning."[42]

Upon arriving in Alpine, Captain Bates sent a second message, no doubt making doubly sure the AG knew where the fight had actually taken place—not in Texas:

Pabalo Dominguez [the] terror of this country and Mexico came over and drove off four horses used in camp near Santa Helena Tuesday night[.] Wednesday we trailed him into Mexico where he barricaded in a house which we surrounded[.] When he began the shooting Stillwell was killed early in the fight as was Dominguez[.] Letter following[.][43]

Adjutant General Harley apparently was not overly concerned at the time as to which side of the line hosted a gunfight, though later cross-border incursions would be scrutinized and supervised more closely to ward off indignant complaints from Mexican diplomats. His first concern on April 3, appropriately so, was an appearance of respect. Even though the fallen Ranger had only seen service with the Lone Star State for less than two months, Harley telegraphed Captain Bates to have Will Stillwell buried; the state of Texas would pick up the tab.[44]

At Alpine, with several fellow Texas Rangers acting as pallbearers, William P. Stillwell was buried under the auspices of the Knights of Pythias and Woodsmen of the World. According to Captain Bates, the memorial service, with Stillwell's wife and children present, after all business houses had deferentially closed, "was one of the largest attended funerals ever attended in Alpine...."[45] Perhaps a single sentence, simple as it is, encapsulates honorable eulogy for Ranger Will Stillwell: "his friends were numbered by his acquaintances."[46]

The day following Will's death a snippet in the *El Paso Times* echoed the sentiment of many West Texas borderland folks: "He [Stillwell] is well known in this district and feeling is bitter against Mexican raiders throughout the Big Bend district."[47] And why wouldn't it be? That very same day, Texas Rangers of Company F had a gunfight with fifteen Mexican interlopers ninety miles south of Alpine at Santa Helena, the site of the horse theft that led to Stillwell's death.[48] Captain Bates, thankful that he had not lost another man, updated the adjutant general by wire: "Two Mexicans left on ground. Wounded carried away. No Rangers wounded."[49]

Wounded or not on-the-ground Rangers of Company F were expecting additional trouble. Captain Bates may have had his faults, as all men do, but in this case he was not analytically far off base, not while particularizing cause and effect generated by the near-decade-long Mexican Revolution: "Conditions are sure bad here now and no prospects of them getting better, as the Mex. are worse than poverty stricken and everything has been destroyed across the river that would sustain life, in many places they are eating burro meat and go for days without meat or flour, under these conditions I don't see much chance for the raids to cease."[50]

On the seventeenth day of May 1918, a month after the incursion into Mexico and Stillwell's death, all Ranger captains were put on notice. They were not to cross the river absent specific criterion. If the trail was hot Rangers could charge into Mexico if their purpose involved "the rescue of American citizens who have been captured by the bandits." Likewise an exemption would be in place for other instances wherein a "responsible Mexican commander" agreed the sortie was jointly suitable. Rangers were instructed not to even fire across the river, unless as a last measure of self-defense. Furthermore: "Individual Mexicans entering the United States from Mexico at unauthorized points will not be fired upon when it is possible to capture them; and unarmed Mexicans who have crossed the line from the United States into Mexico will not be fired upon, unless there is good reason to believe that they are guilty of a crime against the United States and their capture is otherwise impossible." Clearly the last caveat broadened—diluted—the full force of the order, leaving open to individual interpretation what in fact constituted a "good reason to believe" that a crime had been committed and an apprehension was "otherwise impossible."[51] Whether or not Captain Bates stewed over the clearly diplomatically inspired order goes unrecorded:

He was, in fact, living in real time, on the real ground—charged with daily scouting Lucifer's Line. Company captains had to comply with orders from headquarters, but good ones had to also look out for the rank and file; Mexican bandits and/or revolutionists weren't raiding up and down Austin's Congress Avenue where bureaucracy sat.

Asking for a bit of insurance from headquarters, the Ranger captain specifically asked for a supply of "steel point bullets as the soft point don't work good in the guns we have and I don't want any of my men killed without a fighting chance."[52] Nineteen-eighteen was not yet half gone.

Chapter 19

Joe Robert Shaw
1918

The day after Independence Day 1918 twenty-eight-year-old Joe Robert Shaw laid aside his leggings and catch-rope, intent on shifting career gears from cowboy to cop: A Texas Ranger. What his wife thought about the switch would be but guesswork, but there's little doubt she, as the mother of two, vacillated between pride and apprehension. Joe Robert was on the right side. Flipping the coin, she also knew Joe Robert's posting in the Lower Rio Grande Valley near the southern tip of Texas would not be a cakewalk.[1]

Joe Robert Shaw's reporting to Company G headquarters in Hidalgo County would be a genuine eye-opener for the young Ranger-to-be. Butting up against the Rio Grande the locale was far different from the rolling hills interspersed with live oaks where he had grown up. There were no palm trees, seagulls, sharks, and salty Gulf breezes in that interior Texas country drained by the Guadalupe, Navidad, and Lavaca Rivers. Where Joe Robert actually had first seen the light of day has not been historically nailed down. However, geography he tramped over and rode horses across as a youngster and into manhood is not worthy of nitpicking dispute. Joe Robert Shaw, when asked where he was from declared he hailed from Yoakum, Lavaca County—but not that part of Yoakum in adjoining DeWitt County. Cowmen in Lavaca County when registering their hot-iron marks went to the courthouse at Hallettsville, those ranchmen in DeWitt County traveled to Cuero for recording their earmarks and brands.[2] If the price to pay for Joe Robert Shaw quitting the cow chasing and beginning the crook chasing was but relocating a home address, so be it.

Although Shaw was green as a gourd in this business of enforcing the law, his captain wasn't. Captain Charles F. Stevens had quite a résumé. Ancestrally his Ranger roots were deep, his father Edward A. Stevens having seen state service during the 1840s before Texas

Rangers were institutionalized as a law enforcing entity. Thereafter, the elder Stevens had stood for election at San Antonio for several terms, earning the voters' trust as sheriff of Bexar County.³ Previous to the administration of Joe Robert's oath, Charles Stevens, primarily based in Bexar County, had already been a deputy constable, elected constable, deputy sheriff, chief deputy sheriff, and U.S. Deputy Marshal for the Western District of Texas.⁴ By any measure Stevens was a veteran cop.

On November 27, 1917, Charles F. Stevens had been commissioned captain of Company G, assigned to represent the Ranger Force in the Lower Rio Grande Valley.⁵ The area of watch for Company G reached west upriver to the vicinity of Los Ebanos and downriver to Point Isabel (now Port Isabel) and the pretty white sands country that is now known as South Padre Island. Subsequent to fits and starts, Captain Stevens established Company G headquarters at Mercedes, just inside the eastern Hidalgo County line. Right across that line was Cameron County and its thriving borderland city of Brownsville, directly opposite Matamoros on the Mexican side of the Rio Grande.

Age does not necessarily grow wisdom, but Captain Stevens, at forty-seven and with years of practical experience under his belt, brought two character traits with him to the Lower Valley. First he opted to interview applicants for Texas Ranger positions face to face, making his own assessment rather than relying on partisan recommendations made at the behest of political and/or personal interests. Commendably he wanted to x-out cronyism. Second, Stevens believed in professionalism, as reflected in a 1918 order issued not long before Joe Robert enlisted:

> As to your work on the river do nothing but what the law authorizes you to do. Treat all law abiding citizens with courtesy and give all good citizens the full protection of the law, either rich or poor, white or black. Keep a close lookout for all lawbreakers and try your best to apprehend all criminals.... Don't jump at conclusions so fast and when you know you are right then go ahead.⁶

Captain Stevens was no martinet. He did believe, though, that unchecked tomfoolery, public drunkenness, abusive and insulting language to men or women were not wholesome examples of professional conduct and were grounds for dismissal. Particularly known at

headquarters for making personal notations on pre-printed enlistment forms, Captain Stevens did seem to entertain high hopes for
Private William Scott, the son of a former Texas Ranger captain, jot-
ting: "Has had considerable experience with horses, a good rider, and
speaks spanish [*sic*] fluently."[7] Nevertheless, the twenty-six-year-old
Private Scott had not followed Ranger guidelines, ignoring the pro-
hibitions regarding alcohol. The oversight or disobedience or stupidity cost him his job. Another Ranger was impolitely ushered out of
Company G for "making unwanted advances to two young Anglo
schoolmarms."[8]

Less than six months after making his presence known in the
Lower Rio Grande Valley, Captain Stevens had whipped Company
G into shape not only earning accolades from the citizenry at large,
but several (not all, see following chapter) of the local lawmen and
military commanders at Brownsville's Fort Brown as well. Working
closely with most other law enforcing components, building public
trust, and upholding the best of Texas Ranger tradition was a hallmark of Captain Charles Stevens's leadership style, from a charitably
uncorrupted perspective. Many residents from the native Spanish-
speaking community were more than thoroughly convinced that
Company G Rangers overstepped legality's line, frequently shredding
guarantees benchmarked in the U.S. Constitution's Bill of Rights, and
did so with the unbending and unapologetic championing of Captain
Stevens.[9]

There's not wiggle room to doubt that when Joe Robert Shaw
sat down before Captain Stevens for that orientation interview, no
negotiation as to what would be expected of him was permitted.
When asked if he understood, Joe Robert probably cocked his head,
tilting that mop of brown hair and with uncompromising blue eyes
and somber deportment said he was up to the task. Unquestionably
Captain Stevens supposed Joe Robert would be an okay Ranger, pen-
ning his evaluation at the bottom of the printed form: "This man is
a good man."[10]

Due to Stevens' overall assessment that "soldiers do very little
patrolling on the river and most all of the trouble which is done, is
carried on along the river, and in about a radius of fifteen miles North
of the river" the captain rethought how best to position his limited
manpower. By his way of thinking, since the U.S. Army tactics along
the river were inadequate, and the fact "local County Officers absolutely do nothing" he had decided to keep the Company G Rangers

deployed "in small numbers and keep them scattered out." For the most part Captain Stevens subdivided the company by twos. There was a pair of Rangers at Mission and at Harlingen, as well as Santa Maria, thirty miles west of Brownsville, at La Palma fifteen miles closer in, and at the Piper Plantation eight miles east of Brownsville, where Joe Robert Shaw was stationed. Those not thus deployed caught their enforcement and scouting assignments working out of company headquarters at Mercedes.[11]

From the best evidence at hand it seems Mrs. Shaw had said goodbye to Joe Robert's parents John and Hattie, and moved with the two children to Harlingen, not far above Brownsville, to be closer to her beloved husband.[12] With work on the river so intense, and the law-enforcing demands so strong, Joe Robert was seldom at home.

Also working—more or less as Joe Shaw's law-enforcing partner—was a thirty-three-old San Antonio native, Sebastian T. "S. T." Chávez. Private Chávez held seniority with the Texas Rangers by about six months, but he was much better acclimated than Joe Robert regarding the twists and turns and terrors of the Lower Rio Grande. Ranger Private Chávez had seen honorable service with the U.S. Army and had been a federal employee working out of Remount Station No. 3, "attending stock and riding fence for Government." Not surprisingly Ranger S. T. Chávez was a fluent speaker of Spanish. Though small in physical stature at five-foot two inches, S. T. Chávez was wrapped tight like a stick of dynamite: short but formidable.[13]

One of the hot spots along the river west of the Piper Plantation in want of near constant patrol was Tomate Bend, long a crossing for smugglers and fugitives. Tomate Bend had earned not overblown status as a sadistic piece of ground. Though technically sited within the sprawling Brownsville city limits, the riverfront location "had always been a thorn in the side of peace and border patrol officers," at least so said a newspaperman writing for the *Brownsville Herald*.[14] More particularly and more hyperbolic was an ex-Texas Ranger's depiction of Tomate Bend; "that sinister curve near Brownsville.... the Rio Grande's most bloodstained spot.... Here numerous *contrabandistas* plied their nocturnal trade and did not hesitate to shoot when anybody attempted to stop them.... The shadows provided by this river bottom jungle have made it a favorite rendezvous for smugglers since the treaty of Guadalupe Hidalgo was signed in 1848."[15]

U.S. Mounted Customs Inspectors J. C. Adkins and Fred Tate weren't overawed with finer points of agreed diplomatic niceness during a previous century—they were living in real time. And real time equated to summertime 1918 at Tomate Bend when the federal officers were shot at: "The bullets came so close that dirt was sprinkled on their clothing."[16] Captain Stevens did not turn a blind eye to the dangers of scouting the Lower Rio Grande, noting that gunfire emanating along Lucifer's Line was no anomaly: "Of late, the River Guards have been fired on several times from the direction of the river."[17]

Thanks to due diligence of modern-era researchers and writers Drs. Harris and Sadler a normally neglected borderland detail is brought to the forefront, and it plays into Joe Robert's story. The United States was at war in Europe and the military draft was in place. Although it somewhat dilutes the Kool-Aid typically guzzled while serving an entrée of Ranger mythology, some men were on the payroll out of a sense of purpose, not principle—avoiding the draft.[18]

Also ducking conscription were not just a few Mexican-Americans living in South Texas. Amid rumors that the Ranger Force would be upwardly staffed to about 800 to guard the border from machinations by agitating German evildoers, Hispanics "were fleeing to Mexico in droves, fearing not only the Rangers but mainly the prospect of being drafted into the American Army."[19] To staunch such hemorrhaging of the able-bodied workforce of cheap labor Lower Rio Grande Valley farmers relied on, Governor Ferguson stepped in: Issuing a proclamation intended to assuage their worries of either being executed by a run-amok Ranger or killed on a trans-Atlantic battlefield.[20] Because actual decisions concerning conscriptions and deferments were left up to whims of local Draft Boards, which many Hispanics didn't trust, the governor's proclamation garnered but lukewarm reception.[21] There were several ways to skin the cat, and Company G's Captain Charles Stevens posted his Austin headquarters' hierarchy regarding one method of dodging the draft:

> Most all of these young Mexicans who are born on the American side try to evade Registration, on the ground of being Mexican citizens. The custom of Mexicans who are born on the American side, most all are baptized on the Mexican side of the river, and they try to claim exemption from the draft, by getting a certificate from the church of their baptism, stating they were baptized.[22]

So, with *contrabandistas* and bandits daily crossing the river to the Texas side and federal neutrality law violators running guns across into Old Mexico just ahead of the fugitives and draft dodgers, there was plenty to do for lawmen working the Lower Rio Grande Valley.

Owing to the fact rookie lawmen are more often than not enthusiastic it's not unrealistic to suggest that Joe Robert, hurriedly latching on to his scattergun, was raring to go that night of August 21, 1918. Due to its wetness—close to the Gulf —Tomate Bend was fertile warm ground for a medley of semi-tropical plants, accentuated by impenetrable undergrowth giving way to clearings and crisscrossing trails. Scouting Tomate Bend horseback unsheathed the double-edged sword: From atop, the border lawmen had an aerial view, surveying the tangles before them; at ground level, smugglers concealed in snarls had clear view of their targets. Regardless, mounted or afoot it was a close quarter catch-as-catch-can game. Day or night there is a handy tool for self-defense or proactive apprehensions in tight spots—shotguns.

Rangers Shaw and Chávez were tasked with scouting in the general vicinity of Tomate Bend. More specifically they, horseback, were crossing a small strip of farmland owned and operated by Teófilo Solís. Sudden movement in the darkness put them on high-level alert. The partnered Texas Rangers weren't the only folks on the ball that summer night. They had been spotted, too! Either the good guys or the bad guys were aware of the simultaneous detections. Both troupes began mapping a nighttime battlefield strategy.

After a quick huddle Privates Shaw and Chávez began executing their plan. Chávez would flank the shadowy figures, slip to the river putting it to his back, and stand ready to holler the challenge. Shaw would advance toward the half-dozen fellows who would break for the river. Cut off on the north bank of the Rio Grande between shotgun-wielding Rangers, the *mal hombres* would be snared and they would be forced to surrender—that was the plan.

Francisco Solís and his brother Manuel, along with their *amigos*, also had devised a plan. Carefully hide, and when the first man—obviously a lawman—came by, kill him. Then, with the advantage of overwhelming numbers, surround and kill the second officer. After that? Well, just cross the river and merge into Matamoros anonymity.

Shortly after separating from his mounted partner, Joe Robert advanced, scouting the brush. Francisco stayed still—deathly still. The distance closed. Camouflaged by profuse stands of uncultivated shrubbery the unseen gunmen's hearts pounded. The distance closed. The bladder of patience could stand it no more; it ruptured. Francisco quietly nudged his comrades a warning and quickly jumped up. Raising his Winchester to shoulder Solís snapped a shot—the first shot. His pals followed suit. A hot steel ripped into Joe Robert's torso, directly under the nipple of his left breast, spinning him in the saddle, while another tore into the right side of his back. Reeling he managed to discharge his shotgun a split-second prior to it being near halved by a "rifle ball." Joe Robert tumbled to the ground, dying where he fell.[23] Francisco Solís had screamed in pain when pellets from Joe Robert's shotgun blast peppered his head, face, and neck—with birdshot. In an act of abject neglect the young Ranger had not smartly charged his weapon with buckshot prior to scouting the river, otherwise "the way he shot the Mexican, it would have torn the Mexicans [sic] head off."[24]

Not surprisingly the booming reports of gunfire attracted attention from two quarters, but not the townsmen of Brownsville, a scant two miles west of the battle-site. Teófilo Solís scampered out of his farmhouse looking for an explanation and the whereabouts and well-being of his sons. Ranger S. T. Chávez, still mounted, had heard the shots and saw "three Mexicans run and he fired at them." Not knowing outcome of his marksmanship Chávez dismounted and waited in the stillness. The silence was deafening. Private Chávez had none but a general idea of where his colleague Joe Robert might be, and absolutely no clue as to whether he was wounded, killed, or safely lying low. Nor did the Ranger know if his rounds had connected, killing or injuring one or more human tigers hiding in the river valley's darkness, now ready to pounce at his next movement. Prudence overrode any foolish notion of blindly stumbling and bumbling in the dark, all alone. No, this was not a one-Ranger one-riot job. Remounting his horse, Private Chávez raced to Brownsville for backup. Meanwhile, Teófilo found Francisco, bleeding badly from Texas Ranger Shaw's birdshot barrage, Manuel Solís kneeling by his side. The body of Joe Robert, lifeless, was sprawled on the ground nearby, just fifty feet or so. At the near bank of the Rio Grande scared to death fellows removed footwear, and swam that river of lackluster extraditions. On the outskirts of Matamoros they emerged, dripping with notions of stirring up an alibi. Teófilo carried his wounded son inside, and then left for Brownsville to fetch a doctor. Manuel gathered up the guns, three rifles and a shotgun, concealing them, as it turned out not very well, "in an old hole in the field."[25]

At Brownsville two men were bent on summoning help. Ranger Chávez quickly rounded up two federal River Guards to accompany him back to the Solís farm. Teófilo, too, made contact with a medical man, but failed to mention that out in his pasture a man, somebody, lay doornail dead. All parties soon converged at the Solís residence. And very soon two were being escorted back to the city of Brownsville: the lifeless Joe Robert Shaw in a makeshift ambulance, the under-arrest Manuel Solís in handcuffs.[26]

When notified of Ranger Shaw's death, Captain Stevens rushed to Brownsville, then to the scene of the crime, arriving at shortly before three o'clock in the morning. By daylight Stevens, too, had executed a two-pronged feat: he found the secreted firearms and he placed Teófilo Solís under arrest. Then, at Brownsville, Captain Stevens sent a telegram to Adjutant General Harley: "Private Joe Shaw killed last night two miles east of Brownsville by smugglers. One smuggler wounded. I have three men under arrest. All quiet."[27]

The Company G captain was right, but only partly right. On the night of August 21, 1918, the Solís clan was not engaged in any smuggling activity, not if Captain H. M. Harrison, District Intelligence Officer for the U.S. Army was correct. One of his informants, Confidential Agent No. 2 to be precise, had passed along the following details which he in turn passed to Stevens:

> Four brothers and their father, by the name of Solis, were at the Tomates last night, August 21st, 1918, for the purpose of crossing the river to avoid the Draft. A Ranger tried to stop them and one of the brothers fired at him and killed him. One of the Solis brothers was wounded, but this is not the one that killed the Rangers. That one got across to the other side.[28]

Subsequent to preliminary undertaking protocols at the Morris Funeral Parlor in Brownsville, the remains of Joe Robert Shaw were to be removed from the city: "the murdered officer will be sent to his family in Harlingen for interment."[29] Widows grieve and there's little doubt Joe Robert's wife searched her innermost soul questioning how unfair life was in that Lower Rio Grande Valley: the killing of a Ranger with less than two months' service. Ten days later *déjà vu*!

On August 31, 1918, another widow mourned. Alice, the wife of U.S. Mounted Customs Inspector Fred Tate, lost her husband, cut down by smugglers near Tomate Bend.[30] There were no exemptions—federal, state, local. Riding Lucifer's Line anyone might pay the sacrificial toll.

Chapter 20

Lenn T. Sadler
1918

Another Company G Ranger serving in the Lower Rio Grande Valley commanded by Captain Charles F. Stevens was Lenard Tillman "Lenn" Sadler, geographical product of Pearsall, Frio County, Texas and genealogical issue of James Kaine Sadler and his wife Mary.[1]

Lenn Saddler's arrival on July 23, 1884, was welcomed not only by delighted parents but also by George Sadler, his two-year-old brother, the couple's firstborn.[2] Just as James and Mary would claim pride in their growing family, Frio County owned her share of historic legacy. Situated southwest of San Antonio, bisected by the Frio River, the landscape during its earlier days had hosted travel over a King's Highway between Saltillo, Mexico, and Spanish settlements in East Texas, before there was a Texas. Later, Santa Anna and his army plodded through what would become Frio County on their march to teach hard lessons to those damn Texian upstarts at the Alamo. After Texas wrested herself away from Mexico, stumbled through beleaguered days as a free-standing Republic, survived Secession and Reconstruction, and was re-inducted into the United States, Frio County was finally organized on July 20, 1871. The county's first seat of government, Frio Town, was knocked off the map due to the coming of the International-Great Northern Railroad. The hamlet of Pearsall, a small station on the railway line, grabbed shiretown honors during 1883 and has clutched them tightly from then to now.[3]

Frio County was ranch country and the Sadlers were ranchmen, increasing their land holdings and livestock numbers by the most basic of basics, generating a genetic numerical advantage in cows and kinsmen. Ranchmen they were, owing to the reproductive fact mama Sadler had been busy—rhythmically in sync—producing sons. Lenard Tillman's birth had been followed by that of John W. (1886), William D. (1889), and Thomas H. (1891). The significance for this narrative is this: in addition to all five brothers referencing a work history as a "ranchman" or a "stockman" they would—one and all—perform law-enforcing duties as Company G Texas Rangers.[4]

At age twenty-three Lenn Sadler took a wife, eighteen-year-old Lula Ellen Long, marrying at Jourdanton, Atascosa County, on the fifteenth day of July 1908. The bride's sister, Letha Avis Long, followed suit, marrying into the family six years later when she accepted the proposal of Lenn's younger brother John.[5] Pitch into a genealogical mix the other Sadler sisters, Rebecca, Minnie Ollie, Cora Lee, and Eva, along with their husbands and in-laws, and the picture comes clear—in concert these folks could swing a precinct election or field a major league baseball team.

Relating with precision all of the causative factors pushing the Sadler brothers toward signing on with the Rangers is, at this late date, unworkable. It may be said with clarity, however, that after Charles Stevens' commissioning as the Company G's captain in mid-November 1917, two of the Sadlers, George and Tom, were standing in the wings willing and ready to go, enlisting on December 18, 1917.

Subsequent to the holiday season winding down, the Rangers of Company G went to work. In addition to the typical workload of investigating crimes and apprehending wanted fellows, other dynamics acted as multipliers. The coming of a new year seemed to foster an uptick in the cow stealing taking place along the river in the Lower Rio Grande Valley. One of the reasons for the surge, at least according to Captain Stevens' reasoning, was that many of the "slackers" who had crossed into Mexico could not find legitimate work. Resultantly the draft dodgers, afraid of honest work in Texas with a possibility of conscription, turned to crime and "were doing quite a bit of this cattle stealing."[6] The borderland has always harkened nightmarish troubles for law enforcers but the near pandemic escalation of cattle theft, coupled with the real and imagined fears of subversive German agents fomenting plots of invasions, intrigues, and downright espionage were keeping federal, state, and local lawmen awake at night—literally. Hardly could they catch up or catch a break or catch forty winks.

The Rangers were proactively conducting sweeps through the Lower Valley, making arrests and confiscating weapons. Gauging the reasonableness of obligatory Probable Cause for their seizures and detentions is open-ended. No doubt sometimes they were right; at other times they most likely were wrong. Hispanics of Cameron

County, the predominate population, were complaining that a Ranger overreach was—since they were Americans—depriving them of safeguards as spelled out in the United States Constitution. Local sheriff William T. "Will" Vann was not blindly immune to concerns of his constituency. He was, after all, an elected official. Sheriff Vann thought Rangers owed him clarifications, legally justifying some of their recent enforcement actions. One of those concerns promulgated by the sheriff weaves a Sadler into the web. Either George or Tom Sadler, the records are not first-name specific, confiscated firearms belonging to or in possession of Pedro Lerma. Captain Stevens thought the seizure perfectly justified: "these people have these guns to give to any bandit along the river on either the American or the Mexican side."[7] Believing and spinning excuses and defending his Ranger, Stevens notified the assistant adjutant general that Private Sadler "took these guns for the safety of the people in this Valley." Captain Stevens felt not an iota of obligation to update the sheriff about anything. Even more unsettling, Captain Stevens, in writing, communicated to Ranger headquarters that he did not consider Sheriff Vann "a safe officer."

Certainly Sheriff Vann did not think finding oneself in Ranger custody a safe proposition. Florencio García, a Mexican national, had been a Ranger prisoner—for a little while. Florencio García's supposed bones, but definitely his bullet-riddled hat and clothes, had been found near Point Isabel. Shortly before he went missing Florencio had been in custody of Company G Rangers George Sadler, John Baptist Sittre, and A. P. Lock.[8] The Rangers claimed they had turned Florencio loose to act as an informant, gathering crucial intelligence that would ultimately lead to the arrest of a cow-thieving kingpin. The Hispanic community, by and large, thought that story was fishy, a rotten scheme masking the odor of coldblooded murder. Captain Stevens would have nothing of it: "These Rangers are all good men, and I do not think that they are guilty."[9] Stevens was particularly miffed at the way Sheriff Vann handled the situation, requiring the three Rangers to post $3,000 bonds rather than just allowing the Cameron County Grand Jury to either indict or not indict Sadler, Sittre, and Lock based on steadfast proof.[10] Knowing that headquarters would need to be in the know Captain Stevens messaged: "They absolutely have no evidence against these men to hold them, but you understand how some lawyers are, they want a fee."[11] Stevens was parked on shaky legal and political ground.

For whatever the reason—or reasons—Lenn Sadler had decided it was past time to join his brothers in the Lower Rio Grande Valley. Traveling to Mercedes he met with Captain Stevens. Standing tall, the six-foot, thirty-three-year-old Lenn Sadler became a private in Company G on May 27, 1918. The captain noted on his paperwork: "L.T. Sadler will make a good ranger."[12]

Though it happened away from the Rio Grande, the whole Ranger Force was shaken to its knees after being posted about the death of a comrade, and there was a lesson affixed: Arresting deserters and draft dodgers was not to be taken lightly—it was man's work, not child's play. Thirty-nine-year-old John Dudley White, son of R. Emmett White, former sheriff of Travis County (Austin), and another Ranger, Walter Ivory Rowe, twenty-eight, were working as partners in East Texas, assigned to apprehend two U.S. Army deserters. During July 1918 near Broaddus in San Augustine County they were ambushed by the fugitives, two cousins. Ranger White died at the scene; Rowe recovered after treatment at a Beaumont (Jefferson County) hospital.[13] The following month was when that message had been hard-driven home for Company G Texas Rangers: Private Shaw had been murdered.

Still mourning the pitiable loss of law-enforcing comrade Joe Robert Shaw three days earlier, Company G Texas Rangers yet again were involved in a desperate gunplay in the Lower Rio Grande Valley. Once more, it too would take place in familiar territory, in the neighborhood of that well-known citrus farm, the Piper Plantation. The Sadler boys, Lenn, George, and John, along with fellow Rangers Othello Edward Walters and John Sittre were scouting the river when trouble, serious trouble, erupted. Daytime of August 24, 1918, was about gone, the window of twilight fast giving way to nighttime along the crisscrossing river trails. Without warning bullets rained down on the Rangers, an ambuscade originating on the American side, but also a starting signal for shooters on the Mexican side of the river. The Rangers answered with bullets. After a hot fight with supposed smugglers, and the expenditure of fifty-odd rounds of Ranger ammo, silence enveloped the scene—real quiet for the "four or five dead Mexicans on a sandbar in the river and on the river bank."[14] What was not silent was the political hollering about Company G Rangers' involvement in yet another shooting incident. Ranger detractors were furious about quick-triggered state lawmen. Ranger supporters were thankful the fight had not fostered more officer funerals. The racket was causing a not-insignificant number of *Tejanos* to slip across the Rio Grande into Mexico, some bent toward avoiding U.S. military conscription, others thinking it was but an act of self-defense from zealous—overzealous—itchy fingered Texas Rangers with bad attitudes and big Colt's .45 six-shooters. The noise was loud and it was heard at Austin. Politicos have good ears.

Two days later, swaying to the political pressure for putting a new face on the Ranger Force stationed deep in the heart of the Lower Rio Grande Valley, Governor William P. Hobby acted, ordering Adjutant General James A. Harley to make the personnel adjustments. Special Order No. 30 was straightforward:

> Captain Charles F. Stevens, Company "G" will proceed at once with his command to Sanderson, Texas overland, which will be his station.[15]

Hearing specious rumors that the Company G transfer order had been countermanded, State Representative J. T. Canales sent a telegram to the adjutant general in support of removing Captain Stevens and his Rangers from the Lower Rio Grande Valley. According to Canales, if the relocation was not carried forward it would "cause a great exodus of Mexican laborers.... We have stopped the trouble by assuring them Captain Stevens was going to be transferred but if this is not true I am afraid we will not have many laborers left inside ten days."[16] The order held.

Sanderson was a lonesome piece of West Texas real estate. Located in Terrell County between the settlements of Del Rio on the east and Marathon on the west, the town was not positioned directly on the border, but was several tortuous miles above the Rio Grande. Cut by numerous canyons and out-of-the-way hiding spots, with its southern borderline hugging the river, Terrell County was ideal stomping ground for smugglers and/or insurrectionists to interlace their conspiracies and circumventions of American law. The county was not an open range model for efficient cattle production, but it was good sheep and goat country—and good train robbing country, too, thanks to the Galveston, Harrisburg & San Antonio Railway (Southern Pacific) tracks traversing its remoteness.[17]

Scarcely had three weeks passed before Company G Rangers were yet involved in another shooting incident. This gunplay, though, would not result in the downfall of a desperado, but it reeked with overtones of idiocy.

Although exact positioning is indistinct, somewhere in the vicinity of the Devils River north of Del Rio in Val Verde County, a Company G detachment established a subcamp, at least temporarily. Two of the several Rangers scouting from this encampment were Privates Lenn Sadler and A. P. Lock. Just shy of his fiftieth birthday, Lock was no greenhorn in the policing business, having served as a peace officer in DeWitt County prior to enlisting with Company G on March 18, 1918. He, too, was one of the three Rangers arrested in Brownsville by Cameron County Sheriff Will Vann as a suspect in the disappearance and murder of Florencio García; and one of the lawmen two grand juries failed to indict for a lack of creditable evidence, more especially since the body could not be positively identified and there were no eyewitnesses—at least not any eyewitnesses with admissible testimony—or persons with an inclination to chance testifying against Rangers.[18] Yes, the Rangers had been the last known persons to see Florencio García alive, but that does not a guilty verdict make.[19] It does, however, lead to provocative but unanswerable questions. Perhaps the enigmatic difficulty even ropes in Private Lenn Tillman Sadler who was not even a Texas Ranger the day Florencio García breathed his last.

Captain Stevens had lagged behind in the Lower Valley while the Company G Rangers had moved west. There he visited around, hobnobbing with some of the Anglo movers and shakers of the area. Clearly it was face-saving doings before his departing for Sanderson:

> I went to McAllen, Mercedes, Harlingen and San Benito. I saw most of the prominent citizens and explained to them that I was not removed from that territory for any political cause, and that no one had me removed from that territory, but that Gen. Harley needed my Service in the Big Bend Country.[20]

There are, as with many Texas Ranger tales, sometimes two, or even more versions of a tragedy. To be certain in Captain Steven's absence camp life on the Devils River exploded—imploded! One account asserts Ranger Sadler had been forewarned of carrying his Colt's revolver in the waistband of his trousers rather than a scabbard, and, too, that it was ill-advised for him to keep all six chambers loaded, the firing pin resting on a cartridge's primer. After acquiring particular criminal intelligence, the Rangers decided to stake out a river crossing waiting for smugglers. Surprisingly the tip proved good. The smugglers were spotted. As the Texas Rangers were mounting their horses to give chase and make arrests, Private Sadler's six-shooter fell from his pants, landed wrong, and discharged. The bullet punched through the Ranger's mid-section, inflicting severe damage.[21]

Another standard and oft-repeated story is this: During the evening of September 15, 1918, at about 7:30, Ranger Lock was sitting on the ground, wiping off his personal arsenal of firepower arrayed on a tarp before him. For an undisclosed reason Private Lenn Sadler slipped up behind Lock and in the spirit of "horseplay" grabbed Lock's ears. It has been written with charitable logic on Sadler's behalf that Lock was in a "grumpy mood." Maybe it's true. In any case, Ranger Lock picked up his Colt's six-shooter, thumbed the hammer to full-cock, pressed the trigger, letting fly a round over his shoulder without even glancing back. The bullet entered Private Sadler's stomach region, ranged upward, exiting through a shoulder and then losing its decelerating momentum somewhere along the river.[22]

In any event, quickly the wounded Texas Ranger was rushed to Del Rio where he was hospitalized. Ranger George Sadler after sending the below cited telegram to Adjutant General Harley at Austin, rushed to his brother's bedside at the city's Southwestern Hospital:

> Notify Capt. Stevens L. P. Sadler shot on Devils River seven thirty this PM accidently. In hospital Del Rio.[23]

Ostensibly if Private Sadler had been shot by a fellow lawman the most likely wording of Ranger George Sadler's telegram might have been akin to: "L. T. Sadler accidently shot by A. P. Lock." One might think George Sadler's telegram donates more weight to the gun-dropping assertion than the alternative. On the downside, with a Ranger-involved shooting, accident or otherwise, customarily there are by and large a smattering to a hopper full of retrievable primary source documents. In this case the dearth of records seems to speak volumes.[24] A gateway to speculation is thrown open. Abstract thinking might reasonably give rise to an intriguing rhetorical question: Was there something said in camp embarrassing to the Texas Ranger public relations image, a trifling unpleasantness warranting a cover-up? Situations wherein a Ranger killed another Ranger, while not unheard of, were always awkward to explain, upsetting for those trying to uphold an image. Did Private Lenn Sadler, even if he did pull on Lock's ears, accompany the gesture with a rude and incriminating remark—or dire warning—associated with his brother's involvement or lack of involvement in the apparent execution-style killing of Florencio García? *¿Quíen Sabe?*

There is an unbendable truth. On the sixteenth day of September 1918 Ranger Lenn Tillman Sadler died as result of the unfortunate gunshot wound.[25] The State of Texas was billed $26.05 by the hospital for Ranger Sadler's medical treatment and overnight stay, an obligation promptly settled by H. M. Johnson, Quartermaster, Ranger Force.[26]

Although the death of John Dudley White in East Texas and the spectacularly controversial Captain Henry Lee Ransom, killed at Sweetwater (Nolan County), had both taken place during 1918, it was Texas Rangers riding the Rio Grande who were dancing with the devil, numerically: April, William P. Stillwell; August, Joe Robert Shaw; September, Lenn T. Sadler. Nineteen-nineteen may have been forthcoming, but Lucifer had Texas Rangers on his dance card leftover, the clock had not yet struck midnight for 1918.

Chapter 21

Delbert "Tim" Timberlake
1918

Wilson County, as has been noted, produced more than her fair share of Texas Rangers. Edgar Timberlake was one. Delbert "Tim" Timberlake, Edgar's younger brother, was another. Born on the twelfth day of September 1884 Tim Timberlake aspired to the life of a South Texas cowboy. And so he was. At age twenty-one, for whatever reason, he corrected course, setting his sights on a career in law enforcement. And so that was. Riding a $75 horse, the solidly built, five-foot nine-inch, brown-eyed cowboy reined in at Floresville on January 14, 1905. There, as if by prearrangement, he took his oath of office, becoming a private in Ranger Company A.[1] Certainly Tim Timberlake had known his try at drawing state wages would not end in rejection, his brother Edgar apparently having already greased the skids for Tim with Captain J. A. Brooks.

Before his month of enlistment was out, Ranger Tim Timberlake, in company of another Ranger, was busy scouting hither and yon throughout Webb County (Laredo), paying particular attention to any unruliness or criminality near the coal mines. The following month Tim assisted a U.S. Mounted Customs Inspector with the arrests of two smugglers, and, on a train trip to the city of Laredo was obliged to place a passenger under arrest, charged with a misdemeanor, Disturbing the Peace. Frequent were his scouts through Webb, Encinal, and Zapata Counties, sometimes venturing northwest into Dimmit County, and as late as June 1905 Private Timberlake made a scout to the Texas Hill Country at Rock Springs (Edwards County).[2] Specifically delving into his workaday assignments is doable, but not necessary for moving Timberlake's story forward. His first Ranger enlistment was a whirlwind of activity. Law enforcing he found to his liking, but perhaps not so much moving about. Timberlake tendered his state commission.[3]

Shortly he made two acquisitions: wife Annie and a deputyship with the Galveston County Sheriff's Office.[4] Two years on the Gulf

Coast was about all Deputy Timberlake could stomach. He was better suited for scouting a zigzagging river and its offshoot canyons, than the coastal bays and swampy inlets. Tim Timberlake moved to Val Verde County (Del Rio) where he had acquired livestock interests.[5] To maintain law-enforcing authority and the legality of daily carrying a Colt's .45 six-shooter Timberlake once more enlisted with the state, becoming a Special Ranger without pay on the ninth day of March 1916.[6]

John W. Almond was serving his third term as sheriff of Val Verde County when he called on Rangers for a touch of help. Hispanic whores at a Del Rio brothel were under siege; Drunk and disorderly black soldiers of the U.S. 24th Infantry were trying to break into the establishment and rape the working girls, or so the gals asserted. Ranger Willie Lee Barler—future Ranger Captain—and Special Ranger Tim Timberlake assisted Sheriff Almond, but found the hormone-charged khaki-clad boys had already moved on. Rangers Barler and Timberlake were posted at the whorehouse as a preventative measure should the soldiers return. Sure enough, back they came, this time throwing rocks, cursing a blue streak, making threats, and proclaiming they would fast gain entry through a front gate or climb over the back fence. One riot, two Rangers! That the drunken hubbub morphed into a full-blown riot is not overstatement. During a desperate hand-to-hand struggle, fighting for his life, Ranger Barler was compelled to employ deadly force, shooting an irrationally behaving soldier, killing him on the spot. A Hispanic deputy sheriff was made a hapless prisoner. Black troopers were indiscriminately firing into this, one of the city's several sin palaces. Texas Rangers Barler and Timberlake, once they had secured their Winchesters, were tasked with evacuating the prostitutes to safer quarters at the Val Verde County Courthouse. Eventually white troops from a nearby camp were sent to quell the riot and restore order, patrolling the city's downtown district: "The citizens of Del Rio were furious at this rampage by black soldiers, whose presence they had resented all along. The army was embarrassed by the breakdown in discipline and bowed to the clamor of demands that the blacks be withdrawn. Soldiers of the 24th Infantry were transferred to duty with General Pershing's Punitive Expedition in Mexico."[7] Barler and Timberlake, through it all, had stayed hitched.

Relinquishing the commission as a Special Ranger, Timberlake drew a much heftier workload by becoming the paid city marshal at

Del Rio. One particular incident stands out and warrants repeating. Marshal Timberlake and a pal, Special Ranger George Washington Newberry, crossed to Ciudad Acuña, Del Rio's sister city on the Mexican side. While there they found themselves entangled in a beef with the collector of customs. The brouhaha netted the Texans wasted time in a Mexican jail and seizure of their saddle horses. Subsequent to taking their figurative lumps Timberlake and Newberry scooted back across the river, wiser men but unforgiving men. Unfortunately for the Mexican Customs Collector, Señor Rivera, the lumps he took were literal. He had crossed into Texas on October 8, 1916, a fact fast noted by one Del Rio city marshal and his Special Ranger buddy: "Timberlake and Newberry spotted him and gave him a world-class beating." The outcry from the Mexican Counsel across the river was loud. Sheriff Almond went though the motions of arrests. Officers Timberlake and Newberry motioned themselves right out of the Val Verde County jailhouse after posting—or seemingly posting bond.[8]

Roughly a year later breaking news from Houston registered with Timberlake about just how lucky he'd been during the whorehouse dust-up in Del Rio. At Houston, on August 23, 1917, black soldiers, again from 24th Infantry, ran amok. Rumors had spread that one of their corporals, Charles W. Baltimore, had been arrested and mistreated by local policemen—some gossip even circulating that he had been killed. Infuriated soldiers from nearby Camp Logan raided the supply tent where arms and ammunition were being stored. Armed with Springfield rifles with bayonets affixed the black military men went on a rampage—a bloodbath. In the end, after order was at long last restored, the body count was tabulated: eleven dead and thirty wounded Harris County civilians, five Houston police officers in the morgue, four 24th Infantrymen dead, and one of the ringleaders, Sergeant Vida Henry, dead from suicide rather than face sentencing imposed by a court martial. During trial seven soldiers traded immunity for testimony and talked their comrades-in-arms straight into the guardhouse: "One hundred ten of the mutinous soldiers were found guilty of at least one charge. Nineteen of them were hanged, and sixty-three of them received life sentences."[9]

From the best information at hand, Tim Timberlake let the city marshal's job at Del Rio go after eighteen months, moving southeast to Laredo, Webb County. There, for a little while, Timberlake carried a deputy sheriff's commission, but the lure and mystique of the Texas Rangers was too strong. Taking advantage of the opportunity,

Timberlake reenlisted, this time at Laredo, on the twenty-seventh day of June 1918. He was thirty-four years of age, assigned to Company I, which was really a short-lived slot, due to the fact he was transferred and promoted to 1ˢᵗ Sergeant Company F during September of that same year.

After the several shootings embroiling Company G Rangers and that involuntary transfer to Sanderson meant to mollify Hispanic public opinion and cauterize the hemorrhaging of Mexican-American farm laborers from Texas, a replacement was named. The Lower Rio Grande Valley became the Ranger bailiwick of Captain William Walter Taylor and a reactivated Company F. The exodus of cheap labor may have been somewhat stemmed, but deep South Texas along the river was still bleeding violence. Rotating the field deployments of specific companies may have put a new face on individual Texas Rangers in the Lower Valley, but six-shooter fireworks were yet slated for 1918's scorecard.

Captain Bill Taylor's personal relationship with Cameron County Sheriff Will Vann at Brownsville was much more attuned to cooperation than that of his predecessor. Captain Stevens and Sheriff Vann, seemingly from the get-go, due to personality and/or philosophical differences, had been at loggerheads. Sheriff Vann and Captain Taylor sometimes shared law enforcing secrets and, correspondingly, shared the potential glories—and the interrelated risks.

One of the numerous borderland outlaws of the Lower Valley causing heartburn for area lawmen—local, state, and federal—was Encarnación Delgado, who himself was a captain of sorts, the headman for "a gang of dangerous Mexican smugglers."[10] There were numerous though unconfirmed reports that it was Encarnación who acted as the chief triggerman during the gunfighting imbroglio wherein Ranger Shaw had been killed on the Teófilo Solís farm.[11]

Regardless, criminal intelligence had been developed by Sheriff Vann that Delgado and crew had plans to smuggle *mescal*—in quantity—across the river below Brownsville somewhere near Tomate Bend, most certainly after dark and most likely on October 10. Sheriff Vann did not sit on the informant's hot tip, intent on hogging the laurels sure to follow Encarnación Delgado's arrest. He mutually disclosed the information to state and federal counterparts.[12] Despite the fact that not two months had expired since the nighttime bushwhacking of Ranger Joe Robert Shaw, Lower Valley lawmen made plans for a joint venture interdiction, hazardous as it might be. Today it would be dubbed a Task Force operation. Then it was simply inter-agency teamwork.

The Texas Rangers would be represented by Captain Taylor, Com-pany F 1ˢᵗ Sergeant Tim Timberlake, and Private Francis Augustus "Frank" Hamer, who had just recently rejoined the Ranger Force after another of his intermittent absences from the outfit's Muster and Payroll. Standing in for Cameron County would be Sheriff Will Vann and his stalwart deputy Fred Winn. Joining this quintet would be two U.S. Customs officers, trustworthy men.

Downtime prior to embarking on a stakeout—one with arrests as the aim—is mentally tricky. Maintaining an outward show of com-posure while one's mind is literally racing with flashing contingences of what might happen, what will go right—or could go wrong—is challenging. Once action breaks there's not time for dillydallying or over-thinking, events supersede worry.

By most accounts Ranger Timberlake was anxious during that emotional buildup between daytime posturing and nighttime engage-ment. He had a premonition—an ominous premonition. Sergeant Timberlake was not at all reluctant to share his innermost thoughts, "freely discussing this foreboding with his comrades and said he knew his number was up."[13] Notwithstanding his gloominess Ranger Timberlake did what a good Texas Ranger was supposed to do; he bucked up, answering the call to duty and self-respect. Purportedly, when asked by Private Hamer why he intended on carrying a short-barreled shotgun for the takedown, Sergeant Timberlake replied: " 'Well, Pancho'—which is Mexican for Frank—'the way I feel tonight, one gun will do me about as much good as another. I have a feeling I'll get mine any way you take it.' "[14]

Pancho and Sheriff Will Vann also had a pre-arrest discussion. If the writings are to be taken at face value, it seems while planning their positioning on the river Private Hamer's battle tactic proposi-tion was to shoot first, then say "hands up" or "freeze" or something along those lines. Sheriff Vann took exception. The sheriff wanted to have nothing to do with taking a chance on killing an innocent man, woman, or child. Sometimes true professionalism calls for risk tak-ing. Private Hamer countered that innocent folks wouldn't be any-where near Tomate Bend at night. Captain Taylor and Sheriff Vann overruled Private Hamer's entreaty.[15] If the smugglers—or anyone else—crossed the river a verbal challenge would be hurled first, to be followed by bullets and buckshot only if there was non compliance to the order of stop and standstill.

The snitch had laid the smugglers' plans in Sheriff Vann's lap. Before the main body of men and contraband entered the river, a *guia* (guide) would cross first making sure the coast was clear. Once that was satisfied the *guia* would signal his *amigos* by mimicking the bleating of a goat. The spy had done his part. Now, the border lawmen could do theirs.

Selecting what they deemed as the most likely trail leading from the river, the law enforcing platoon secreted themselves amid the Rio Grande's jungle of tangles—uncomplainingly waiting. Sergeant Timberlake, wearing his faded brush jacket made of ducking, squatted with his eyes cast toward the river, straining, peering into darkness. There was not need to repeatedly glance at his pocket-watch. Smugglers worked their own timetables, especially those working up nerve drinking *mescal* or smoking dope—as *guias* might do before breeching the river and stepping into the uncertain.[16] For these border lawmen, surveillance would end at daybreak—or before.

After noting that there seemed to be nothing suspiciously drawing attention on the Texas side, shortly after nine o'clock Encarnación Delgado like a phantom slipped into the river. Guarding against wetness and complacency Delgado carried a cocked Colt's six-shooter in one hand, near a dozen .45 cartridges clutched tight in the other. Encarmación had not only to be on the lookout for lawmen. Amongst lawbreakers anywhere, and especially along the river, there was no honor owned by thieves and crooks and smugglers. Mexican bandits and/or Texas gangsters weren't opposed to highjacking other owlhoots' payload. Smuggling was dangerous business, damned dangerous. When he gained America's bank Delgado saw naught, heard naught, and suspected naught. The coast was clear! Facing the river crossing Encarnación replicated the bleating of a goat: Then the smuggler turned and walked inland thirty feet content to stand by while his wily coconspirators crossed the contraband *mescal* valued at $.75 a quart in Mexico, $40.00 a gallon in Texas.[17] Encarnacion may have been blind to the presence of concealed lawmen, but they were not oblivious to his whereabouts.

Sheriff Will Vann—it can be argued prematurely—shouted "*Alto!* Stop! Hands up!" Trying to draw first blood Encarnación Delgado snapped a pistol shot toward the noise. Such was suicide. Will Vann let loose with his two-barreled shotgun and Ranger Private Frank

Hamer with his semi-automatic rifle, which was spitting fire like a "pear burner," the blowtorch type instrument used for eradicating cactus. Encarnación Delgado was eradicated that night, precisely at 9:27 p.m. And at that exact point in time a gang of scared smugglers reversed course, abandoning their pricy load of *mescal*, and emerged from the Rio Grande on the Mexican side thankful not to own perforated hides.[18] A deathly stillness swept over the battlefield—momentarily. The silence was broken by Sergeant Timberlake. Delgado's bullet had—though haphazardly fired—done its damage. There may be room for dispute whether the bullet ricocheted or flew straight, but its chart through Sergeant Tim Timberlake is undisputed; into his left hip, through his abdomen, then colliding with and stopping the timepiece in the Ranger's right pant's watch pocket. The wound was serious. Any adulation for tapping out Encarnación Delgado's running lights was dimmed by the auto's headlights rushing Sergeant Timberlake to the hospital at Brownsville.

Exploratory surgery was revealing. The prognosis was dismal. There would be no recovery. Doctors could alleviate pain with drugs, but they could not undo the lethal internal destruction. Time would take Tim Timberlake—he had but hours. At 7:30 a.m. on October 11, 1918, Doctor B. O. Works pronounced Ranger Timberlake dead as a result of "hemorrhage & shock" from the nasty bullet wound puncturing his intestines in "several places."[19]

Sergeant Timberlake's body was transferred to Uvalde (Uvalde County), Texas, where his father was then living, at all times accompanied by an honorary Texas Ranger escort, namely Captain Taylor, and Privates Lee Moser (Mosley), John Milos Cooper, and John Henry Long.[20] On the thirteenth day of October 1918 Texas Ranger Sergeant Delbert Timberlake was peacefully interred in Uvalde's City Cemetery.[21]

Weight given to an assertion that if the lawmen had but fired first at Encarnación Delgado, not gifting him with any warning whatsoever, that Ranger Timberlake's life would have been spared has appeal in the fictional world of melodrama and movie-script writing and pumping heroic hot air. Even in 1918 and even along the troublesome Rio Grande, good law enforcing protocol cried for issuance of verbal notice before any shooting.

Within a week after Sergeant Timberlake's death the Brownsville Board of City Development took stock of what was happening in their neighborhood and passed the following resolution for public consumption, specifically instructing it be passed on to the local press:

> The tragic and untimely death of three of our peace officers, including two rangers [Joe Shaw and Delbert Timberlake] and one customs official [Fred Tate], which have occurred within the last few weeks, while these officers were engaged in the faithful performance of their duties; has called to our attention, in a most forceful way, the extreme hazard involved in connection with preserving law and good order on this border.
>
> This body, therefore, desires to give evidence of its moral support to our Rangers and other peace officers entrusted with the enforcement of the law and to express its respect for and confidence in the men who are thus engaged. We furthermore call upon all law-abiding people to co-operate in every way possible with these men to the end that their duties may become less hazardous, which will mean a more peaceful era for the entire citizenship of our community.[22]

Yes, lawmen working the Texas-Mexico border were facing extreme hazard, the optimistic anticipation of a more peaceful or healthful era was but a good laugh for Lucifer: He had plenty of 1918 time! The very next day after Timberlake's death another on the Texas Ranger payroll gave up the ghost. At El Paso on October 12, 1918, Spanish Influenza claimed the life of a hard-drinking and hard-fighting and seemingly ever-controversial Texas Ranger from Bell County, Benjamin L. "Ben" Pennington, formerly a city marshal and constable at Holland, Texas.[23] Three days later Ranger Robert Ernest Hunt, thirty-six, a former cowboy from Tom Green County (San Angelo) was mortally victimized by the same malady. Pennington and Hunt had been sent to the Pass of the North to assist Health Inspectors with quarantine regulations.[24] Just a few months prior to the deaths of Pennington and Hunt, Private Thomas Carlyle "Charlie" Hyde had mortally succumbed to amoebic dysentery due to unhygienic drinking water in the well at the Clint (El Paso County) campsite, where a Company L detachment was stationed.[25] Although all three Rangers would have probably chosen to go down for the count during a hail of gunfire, fighting for their lives with Colt's six-shooters in hand, that choice was not an option. There was not a badman's bullet with their names on it, but each had drawn the black bean.

Chapter 22

T. E. Paul Perkins
1918

Jessie and Nannie Perkins were the proud parents of two sons: James Clark, the youngest, and T. E. Paul, more affectionately known as Ellzey. The boys could claim status as native Texans, born not along the international border but in Milam County, not too terribly far south of Waco in Central Texas. Both boys would become Texas Rangers.[1]

The Perkins home was near the Yarrellton community.[2] The county seat was Cameron, where "the Steamboat *Washington* had once landed with a shipment of sought after merchandise from Washington-on-the-Brazos to J. W. McCown and Co.... The first, last, and only steamboat to navigate the Little River."[3] The Perkins brothers would, too, be navigating along a river, the twisting Rio Grande cutting itself south through El Paso County. They would not be under command of a riverboat captain like the *Washington's* Basil M. Hatfield, but would answer to Captain William W. "Will" Davis, Company L, Ranger Force, headquartered at Ysleta.

Scouting the borderlands and river was best—in spades—yet accomplished by horseback. However, it's relevant to make mention even the fêted Texas Rangers were being overhauled by racing technology. The days of the motor car were upon them, even if the roadways in many spots were primitive and near untraceable ruts, especially the surfaces leading from ranch to ranch, or between the intermittent and remote river crossings. Illustrative of many Rangers' unfamiliarity with the gasoline gizmos is reflected in a report submitted by Captain Davis: "Captain [Henry L.] Ransom took his man back home with him as they came overland in an Automobile and he did not know enough about the machine to make the trip alone."[4] Making it unconditionally clear to Texas Ranger headquarters that he was not trapped behind the eight-ball of twentieth-century progress Captain Davis penned his dispatch: "I have my Automobile here and one at Fabens at my disposal...."[5] Yes, Rangers were on the cusp of change. There was one dynamic, however, that would not and has never changed for lawmen: Bad men are bad.

Although he was younger by about six years, J. C. Perkins was the first of the brothers to enlist, initially assigned to Company C on August 25, 1917. During January 1918 the twenty-seven-year-old Ranger private transferred into Company L. If J. C. Perkins was hunting a little action he had managed to be at the right place—and just in the nick of time.

Captain Will Davis in a March 3 update apprised the adjutant general that "The Mexicans are sniping across the river nearly every day at soldiers but so far have not bothered my boys."[6] All too soon the Ranger boys would be bothered. Hell popped on the morning of March 22.

Eyeing a perceived weakness about twelve miles downriver from Fabens the "Mexican river guard crossed the river .... and attacked a patrol of eight [U.S] soldiers. The soldiers ran away, some of them lost their rifles and some their ammunition."[7] Scouting in the vicinity were three Company L Rangers and a U.S. Mounted Customs Inspector. Naturally gunshots attracted their attention, and they raced to investigate. To their utter dismay they were fired on too by the intruding Mexicans, which numbered about fifteen. The three Texas Rangers and the U.S. Customs man "got four of the [U.S.] soldiers and ran the bunch across the river, where there was about 300 Carranza soldiers" standing as backup for their interloping brethren. For awhile the exchange of gunfire waxed hot between the Rangers and Customs man on one side, and the Mexican pot shooters on the other. From nearby Fabens a contingent of U.S. soldiers feinted a reinforcing maneuver. But, according to Captain Davis, the military commander "had great difficulty in doing any thing with his men. Could only [get] five or six up to the river bank where the fighting was.... The soldiers acted might[y] badly and their Captain 'who is a brave man' says he is going to send a bunch to Leavenworth." All in all the lawmen suffered not a scratch, but their grit and marksmanship did not go unnoticed by the shocked Mexicans they unhorsed or the Texas Ranger captain they worked for: "I do not know exactly how many Mexicans were Killed. Reports say from eight to twelve. I know that eight were killed for they were in plain sight. About fifteen Mexican horses were Killed and one U.S. horse. The Mexican Commander sent a flag of truce and took away his dead & wounded and asked for a peace talk the next morning at 9 o'clock but he never showed up...."

Ranger Private J. C. Perkins had acquitted himself well, notching his scorecard rather handily, a fact duly acknowledged by his boss: "I think Ranger Perkins Killed at least five of them, the other Rangers & River Guard probably got the rest."[8] Purportedly the U.S. Army's 5th Cavalry captain was so outraged at some of his faint-hearted subordinates' lackluster performance he caused the guardhouse population to increase by twenty, brought up on charges for "cowardice."[9] After posting headquarters that his Rangers had positively been in the right since the Mexicans had breeched the Rio Grande, Captain Davis polished the apple by sending a souvenir to the adjutant general: "I send you by parcel post a pair of Mexican bridle bits that was taken off the horse of the Mexican Major who was killed."[10]

Will Davis had a lot of ground to cover and few men to accomplish the task. His manpower deployment strategy was thus: Four men at Clint, three privates and the 1st Sergeant at Fabens, and the captain and three Rangers at Ysleta.[11]

One of the banes of effective personnel management is turnover. The Rangers were not exempt. In fact the nightmarish task of following particular Rangers on the merry-go-round of enlistments, resignations, reenlistments, promotions, and intra-company transfers is well-nigh a mindboggling chore for Texas Ranger researchers, writers, and historians. In this instance there is a bit of good luck. Company L's 1st Sergeant was thirty-seven-year-old Albert Franklin Gholson, for a little while. Not surprisingly for a good Ranger, he could find better paying work. Sergeant Gholson tendered his resignation. He had accepted appointment as a U.S. Mounted Customs Inspector, stationed in Presidio County.[12] Stepping into the noncom vacancy was that Milam County fellow with a dead-shot reputation, James C. Perkins.[13] Working from the company's subcamp at Fabens, Sergeant Perkins had more than a plateful of law enforcing gristle before him. The feelings between Americans and Mexicans were "getting worse here all the time."[14] Adding to that pesky little nuisance was the fact the Company L Rangers had no confidence in the U.S. 5th Calvary any longer, as "the bunch are not much force."[15] The overworked and underpaid Texas Rangers were particularly miffed at the U.S. Army's timidity at scouting the river after dark, coming in at 9 o'clock, while they were "working nearly every night."[16] If the country along the river south of El Paso wasn't headache enough, there was also plenty of work for a lawman twenty miles above the city at Canutillo near the Texas state line. There "five or six saloon men" were fixing to spike the little wide-spot's reputation by circumventing liquor laws and setting up shop, even though the town was already well known as "a tough hole any way."[17] Perhaps Sergeant James Perkins thought his company could use another good hand, a topnotch fellow in his mind, like his older brother Ellzey.

At Ysleta on September 1, 1918, T. E. P. Perkins shed his identity as a workaday cowboy. At age thirty-four years and six months Ellzey unlimbered his six-foot-plus frame, fixed his grey eyes to the front, held up his right hand before El Paso County Notary Page Kerry, and became a private in the Ranger Force, Company L.[18] With no wife behind in Central Texas and nothing but prospects of exciting activity on the near horizon along the border, Ellzey Perkins was fixed.

Also well fixed—financially—were the dubious men of both Anglo and Mexican extraction immersing themselves in the lucrative business of smuggling arms and munitions across the Rio Grande. The appetite for firepower on the south side of the river was—and remains—insatiable. Decent men and dishonest men have paid with their lives simply due to the greed of gunrunning. Although it plays directly into Ranger Ellzey Perkins' short story, this is not the format for untangling the intrigues—with an overview emphasis—of the shady business of Neutrality Act violations, others have handled that assignment admirably.[19]

There is a core for unscrambling myths and leaving palatable facts in the historical skillet. How they had become cognizant of the criminal intelligence is somewhat iffy, but the fact that Private Ellzey Perkins and a working partner, Special Ranger Joseph Thomas "Joe" Place, thirty-one and an Arizona native, were hot on the trial of an alleged arms trafficker is cooked.[20] They were after Belen (Ben) Anaya. Purportedly Hipoliti Villa, Pancho's brother, was running up and down the border on the Mexican side carrying an alluring supply of silver bullion, the aroma of quick profit wafting across the river. Ben Anaya was a close associate of smuggler George Holmes, an arms trafficking kingpin of no little repute, and a fellow well capable of trading Hipoliti Villa's high-quality ordnance for highly refined ore. Purportedly, if reports be right, Rangers had even gone so far as to search the home of Ben Anaya, "on the island near Fabens," a well-known "haven for smugglers."[21]

The island was where Captain Frank Jones had been killed years before; little had changed. Captain Davis noted its geographical description and accessed its population and hinted of its dangers in a letter to Adjutant General James A. Harley:

> My men stay in quarters very little but are out on the river most of the time. The Island is twelve miles by three, "and is the worst place on the entire border" and some the men are over there all the time. There is practically no other officers in the valley and the rangers are called in all cases.... and we have to make a great many night calls. We also watch the river crossings at night quite often, as the Customs Guards will not go out without rangers.[22]

During the earlier raid the Rangers had been looking for a clandestine cache of weapons, but had struck a dry hole. Thinking they might have acted too quick—prior to a shipment actually being offloaded at Anaya's farm—the riverfront location was targeted for intermittent but frequent spot surveillances, a technique common in lieu of an exhaustive twenty-four and seven setup.

As the sun began going down on the night of November 7, 1918, Rangers Ellzey Perkins and Joe Place teamed up. Piling into an automobile, the pair left Fabens and drove to the general vicinity of Anaya's piece of Pirate Island ground. Whether by unfortunate happenstance or as a planned ruse, the Rangers' auto overheated, necessitating a stop for replacing a radiator hose. As chance would have it, the mishap was conveniently close—for observation purposes—to Anaya's property on the island.[23] Joe Place began working to fix the problem—or at least acting like it. Ranger Ellzey Perkins standing close by acted as eyes and ears for the lawmen's presence. Down along the river it was ever dangerous. Watchfulness was smart.

Private Perkins detected movement in a nearby irrigation canal and spoke his warning to Joe Place in sync with the lurking assassins voicing their serenade with rifle bullets. Not having time to grab his rifle from the backseat, Private Perkins went for the Colt's six-gun at his hip, popping three quick rounds at the shadowy figure advancing, someone also with a ready pistol in hand. The Ranger's handiwork was exceptional. Anaya went down, three searing .45 slugs spiraling into his heart; he was a dead man falling. In but a heartbeat Ranger Perkins, too, caught a bullet—one to the stomach, staggering him backwards. Whether it was a gritty conscious act of self-preservation or simply spontaneous movement is unknowable—and extraneous. Perkins had been carrying his Colt's six-shooter in the safest mode, five cartridges in the cylinder, and so he stumbled into the darkness with two to go.

Meanwhile, at the automobile Special Ranger Joe Place was captured. For reasons that at first blush seem unfathomable he was not executed to keep a witness quiet , but was placed on a horse by the courtesy of eight or nine owlhoots and told to skedaddle. He arrived in Fabens breathless and worried at half-past eight o'clock.

Unnerving developments were playing out in harmony. At Fabens the alarm had been sounded. A posse began gathering arms and making preparations to rush to the aid of Perkins, whom Joe Place had last seen alive and stumbling into the chaparral. The race to get medical aid to the wounded Ranger was launched.

Ben Anaya's father was racing too. Blood lust filled his vengeful heart; he was hot on the blood trail left by the man who had killed his son. The elder Anaya would cross the finish line ahead of the posse. Somewhere in the brush, about a mile from the Anaya farm, Perkins and Anaya met, though the Ranger—with two rounds yet in his revolver—probably remained unaware of the introduction. If he had been conscious surely he would have fired, once or twice. He didn't. No doubt finding his target an easy mark, the senior Anaya clubbed Ranger Perkins to death.[24] Then he mutilated the body, his primordial thirst for revenge yet quenched. When he did return to a modicum of level-headedness the real seriousness of his merciless crime sank in. He had murdered a lawman, a Texas Ranger at that! Had he but watched and waited the Ranger might have died anyway, and if not Anaya could have easily helped him along by standing on his neck for a minute or two and none would be the wiser. Rage had drowned rationality.

At the same time Anaya was rushing across the Rio Grande to escape, Captain Davis and helpmates were rushing towards the river. They could not find any worthwhile clues in the darkness. Next morning the search for Ellzey Perkins continued and, at last, about ten o'clock, when responding to the yelping of overwrought dogs, frantic searchers found Ranger Perkins' horribly bludgeoned corpse. Captain Davis notified headquarters by telegram:

> Ranger T. E. Perkins and Special Ranger Joe Place ambushed on the Island last night. Perkins Killed. Perkins killed one Mexican.[25]

Acknowledging receipt of Captain Davis's telegram with bureaucratic flair, Samuel Donelson Warren "Sam" Low, who was sitting in the acting position for Adjutant General Harley, after asking for a "full report" incredulously expounded with a typical from behind-the-desk opinion: "killings are becoming entirely too frequent on the border and some steps must be taken at once in the matter."[26] Really? Any worth-his-salt Ranger posted on the border could have—would have—seconded that blather!

It was no deep dark secret who had murdered Ellzey Perkins. And it was not a mystery as to the killer's whereabouts. Captain Davis, from his own pocket, offered Mexican river guards $100 if they would but latch on to Anaya and deliver him to the Texas side. It never happened.

Brokenheartedly Sergeant Perkins had his brother's body removed to the McBean, Simmons & Harford mortuary. There the earthly remains of T. E. P. Perkins were prepared for shipment back to Milam County and interment.[27] Ranger Perkins accompanied his brother's body by rail to Cameron, personally delivering it to the home of one of their uncles, J. M. Eplen. After the formality of a small funeral at Mr. Eplen's residence, the body was removed to the North Elm Cemetery where a burial spot had been made ready.[28]

Maybe it was true: Pirates did live on Pirate Island.

Chapter 23

William M. Alsobrook
1919

Historically tracking outlaws commonly opens wide the doorways to unanswered questions. Poking around in Ranger files pertaining to William M. Alsobrook likewise conjures up more room for query than it does backstopping clear-cut resolution.

James Garland "Jim" Alsobrook and Frances Fern "Fannie" White were equally proud of their birthplace, Manchester (Red River County), Texas.[1] Manchester, pleasantly spotted just below the Red River, was rich farm country. The region was fruitful not only with the luxuriant production of foodstuffs and fiber, but with budding romances as well. Jim Alsobrook bet the farm that his tying the knot with Fannie would brighten his immediate future, plus amplifying his contentment during life's twilight years. And so it was. The happily married couple embarked on their lives raising crops and children. The firstborn son was Sims, arriving at the homeplace during 1880. Four years later, on the twenty-third day of August 1884, Jim's and Fannie's second child came into the northeast Texas world, the subject of this vignette. Though formally named William M., the fair complected grey-eyed baby boy would make the progression through childhood, adolescence, and adulthood simply known by the short version and common nicknames of Will or Willie.[2]

Will Alsobrook was a farmer, not a cowboy. Although it seems obvious Will didn't own the traits of rambunctiousness typically associated with those young men following the festive cow, he did cleave unto himself a taste for adventure and public service. Those innate desires were served by Will becoming, at age twenty-nine, the elected constable for Red River County's Precinct 1, at Clarksville.[3] Perhaps there was a stitch of law-enforcing thread pulling Will into that line of work. His older brother Sims had earned practical policing experience while serving as a Red River County deputy sheriff.[4] Unfettered by responsibilities owed a wife and children, Will set to work serving legal papers and occasionally making arrests, lodging his prisoners in the three-story stone jailhouse adjacent to the Red River County courthouse. Structurally the building was substantially sound, almost a fortress—except for the bars on outside windows, "they were so soft that they could be filed with a fingernail file."[5] Escapes were commonplace. Not all of the fleeing jailbirds were rounded up, but Will Alsobrook's first-rate reputation was never a fugitive with Clarksville folks.

America's embroilment in World War I and an ever sputtering but reliably bloody Mexican Revolution then underway, coupled with reports that a clandestine network of German agents and/or sympathizers was stirring—or alleged to be stirring—the pots of local discontent and disloyalty throughout the Southwest's borderlands spilled over yet another convenient threshold, that of bureaucracy-building. A unique class of Texas Rangers came into being: Loyalty Rangers.

Like their affiliated brethren the Special Rangers who carried commissions as Texas peace officers but who drew their paychecks from cattle raiser's associations, railroad corporations, or other capitalistic conglomerates—or were just allowed to carry six-shooters as payback for political favors—Loyalty Rangers were a distinct subspecies of the Ranger Force.

Full-scale real Rangers they were, but unpaid: no sucking sweet milk from the public's teat. Numerical distribution of the outfit called for assignment of three Loyalty Rangers per county. The reason for their being was clearcut: "to act as a secret service department for the State and to work in conjunction with all Federal, State, county and municipal officers in the execution of all State laws" most especially breaches of the recently enacted Hobby Loyalty Act.[6] Alsobrook enlisted as a Loyalty Ranger June 1, 1918, stationed at Clarksville.[7]

Absent sound reason to the contrary, speculation that Will's enlistment was anything other than patriotically sponsored is fitting. In fact, when enrolling he pledged: "I am only too glad to help in any way I can."[8] Will Alsobrook had joined the lines with 476 other fellows, all operating under the command of Captain William Martin Hanson headquartered in Austin. Official orders to rank-and-file Loyalty Rangers were explicit. After assuring the new recruits that they were entitled "to all the rights and privileges given any peace officer in the State of Texas, with reference to the execution of the State laws" the orders further read, in part:

> You are to serve only in your county, and will not be called out, unless something extraordinary happens....appointments are made mainly for the purpose of assisting our local officers in the execution of the "Hobby Loyalty Act," and for the further assisting our government in every way possible, especially during this war. You are not expected to, in any way, execute local laws unless called upon by your local officers to do so. You are not expected to make arrests, but are supposed to work under cover as much as possible and in a secret capacity, and report all disloyal occurrences to this office for instructions.[9]

Occasionally it's suggested that all appointments of Loyalty Rangers were predicated on blind political affiliation. For the overall schema that's true. That said, it does not mindlessly follow that persons in opposing political parties are wholly incompetent or untrustworthy or morally corrupt. Perhaps, in this regard, it is important to take note and remember a twenty-first-century truth. Even today, in 2012, the United States Attorneys and the United States Marshals serve at the president's pleasure. When political parties are upended and there is change in the White House's Oval Office, the dominos of personnel adjustments fall. The USA's and USM's are replaced with persons of like political persuasion. Assistant USAs and Deputy USM's may remain on post since their spots are considered career, not political positions; but at the top it's a merry-go-round based on Democratic or Republican Party loyalty—or professed loyalty.

Will Alsobrook's voluntary tenure with the state was short-lived. World War I finally came to a close and so, too, did need or perceived need for Loyalty Rangers. Alsobrook's honorable service ended in February 1919.[10] Another Texas Ranger's service ended during February, and his exiting the stage was a newsmaker—a public relations nightmare for Ranger management.

A quartet of partying Rangers were making a day of February 7, 1919, in the Capital City. For sure they were drinking. Likely is the assertion they were barhopping and gambling in Austin's underground vice dives and, perhaps, its even true as the day wore on they stopped off for a visit with ladies of, well, gals of questionable virtue. There's no room for doubt "they got pretty well drunk."[11] An auto tour and target shooting were put on the late afternoon agenda.[12] Outside the city of Austin by three miles, yet traveling in the car, thirty-six-year-old Ranger Private Bertram Clinton "Bert" Veale and

Ranger Captain Kinlock Faulkner Cunningham, traded words—real hot words. The gasmobile came to a brake-squealing and tire-screeching stop. Out jumped the two aforementioned Texas Rangers, and their bleary-eyed speech-slurring traveling companions of that mild winter day, Captain Harry M. Johnston, of the Headquarters Company, and Ranger Sergeant Walter E. Mayberry, also of the Headquarters Company, formerly a Special Ranger and stockman from Coryell County (Gatesville).[13] Two other items came out, too: Forty-five caliber pistols, one in the hand of Ranger Veale, one in the hand of Captain Cunningham. These Ranger boys weren't fooling and were playing for keeps. The hurricane blew past the breakwaters! When the shooting stopped Cunningham was alive, but leaking blood; Veale was just plain dead.[14] Aside from the humiliating embarrassment for top-level Ranger officialdom, as would be expected, the disciplinary dominos fell rapidly.[15]

For whatever the reasons ex-Loyalty Ranger Alsobrook made his mind up not to sever his working relationship with the State of Texas. He fancied being a fulltime—paid—Texas Ranger. Before the month of February ended civilian Will Alsobrook penned a personal letter to Adjutant General James A. Harley: "in the event there is any changes in the regular force I would be glad to have a place...."[16] And a few places there would be, all due to that just-cited February misbehavior, though the sifting and shifting would take a month or two or three.

Will Alsobrook was summoned to Ranger Headquarters. Indeed there was a spot of the roster awaiting him. After traveling to Austin at his own expense, on June 16, 1919, thirty-five-year-old Will Alsobrook accepted appointment as a paid Texas Ranger, Company D. The company designation was but for pencil-pushing expediency.[17] Private Alsobrook was, within the month after enlisting, assigned to Captain William Matthew Ryan's reorganized Company C, headquartered at Laredo in Webb County. Ranger Private Alsobrook was pleased with both the deployment and his new boss, writing to the newly appointed Quartermaster, Captain Roy Wilkinson Aldrich: "I sure want to thank you for sending me to Capt. Ryan. I like it fine and am getting along fine."[18] Private Alsobrook had reported for duty with Captain Ryan brandishing a good attitude and a brand new $28.50 Winchester, one he was scheduled to reimburse the state for. Alsobrook's pleasing demeanor and near contagious affability did not go unnoticed by Captain Ryan who updated headquarters: "Captain

Ryan was here a few days ago and told me [Captain Aldrich] that you were getting along fine."[19]

Details of the personal familiarity between Captain Aldrich and Private Alsobrook are sketchy, but the fact Texas Rangers' management team thought him trustworthy and reliable is rock solid. According to the voice of Captain Roy Aldrich, he had already favorably known Will Alsobrook in "Clarksville long before he joined the force, and in fact [I] took up this matter of his joining myself."[20] No doubt factoring in Will's previous law enforcing service as constable, he was not stationed at Laredo under tight supervision, but fifty-odd miles due east at a subpost in Hebbronville (Jim Hogg County).[21] Many of the Hebbronville denizens took notice, agreeably so: a dandy Texas Ranger had come to town.

Jim Hogg County was a late addition on the macro blueprint for building Texas counties, surveyed and organized during 1913, with Hebbronville as county seat.[22] Spotted below the Nueces River and at a near center point between the Rio Grande at Laredo on the west and the Gulf of Mexico to the east, Hebbronville was tough South Texas real-estate. The county's second sheriff, James Patterson Nelson "Pat" Craighead, in office when Private Will Alsobrook was sent to Hebbronville, was one tough *hombre*, too! It was Pat Craighead who had lost a leg as result of the 1910 Lower Rio Grande Valley shootout when Ranger Quirl Bailey Carnes was murdered.[23] Crutches and a peg-leg didn't bend the sheriff's backbone—or his gun hand.

An ingredient for part of the drama touching Private Alsobrook's law-enforcing life sprouted not in his jurisdictional realm in South Texas, but in West Texas, on the outskirts of Marfa.

Marfa had long been a gateway—due to a railroad connection—for folks jaunting down to the international line. Travelers from El Paso or San Antonio stopped at Marfa, detrained, next traveling south sixty miles overland to the Rio Grande and the border towns of Presidio/Ojinaga. During the Mexican Revolution era, 1910–1920, Mexican Army officers sometimes jumped off at Marfa, heading due south with soldiers' pay. If such was ever a secret, it was an open secret. On occasions the Marfa National Bank even received and disbursed funds to the "Mexican Federal Paymaster." Once, during 1913, a Mexican military courier feared robbery and hid himself and the $101,000 under a bed in an adjoining room at the St. George Hotel. His deception panned out. Perhaps saving the money had also saved his appearance before a firing squad.[24] Shortly after Private Will

Alsobrook had become a Ranger stationed in Hebbronville a similar story took a somewhat different twist.

Arriving in Marfa on July 30, 1919, was Mexican military paymaster Captain Palma. He and his minimal escort, carrying $22,600, were destined for the army's encampment at Ojinaga. They were in need of transportation from Marfa to the border. Ex-Texas Ranger Andrew C. "Andy" Barker stepped to the forefront offering to drive the fellows to Presidio, for remuneration of course, where they could then cross the bridge into Mexico. The deal was struck. After dark the party started on the automobile trip. Hardly had they reached the outskirts of Marfa before the dirt roadway was blocked by a Ford motorcar and three heavily armed highjackers. One of the masked highwaymen was remarkably fluent in Spanish, and at gunpoint the message was made clear to both driver Barker and paymaster Palma—fork over the loot or die. There was not room for argument. The robbers hightailed it into the dark, richer by $22,600. Andy Barker and Captain Palma rushed back to sleeping Marfa where the story broke—indeed a headliner, a newsmaker of international implication.[25] To most Big Bend Country folks the whole dubious episode oozed with rancid aroma—an inside job if they were to place a bet: "It is the generally accepted opinion that the American escorts were in cahoots with the hold-up men."[26]

There was a theory that Andy Barker had tipped off three comrades, all ex-Texas Rangers also, and that they were the actual gun-wielding robbers. The three *alleged* musketeers making off with the funds were Presidio County Constable Charles Craighead, Jim Hogg County Sheriff Pat Craighead's brother; Alexander Glenn Beard, the city marshal at Marfa; and James Boone Oliphant, an ex-Ranger who seemed between jobs, a bona fide rough and tough borderlander. Charley Craighead was bilingual, fluent in Spanish—remarkably so. The robbers' physical descriptions meshed rather well with the suspects. Aside from the touchiness of Craighead being related to a sitting South Texas sheriff was the thorny fact Andy Barker, the suspected chauffeur and tip-off man, was the nephew of a popularly elected West Texas lawman too, Pecos County (Fort Stockton) Sheriff Dudley Snyder "Dud" Barker, himself an ex-Ranger. Due to possible international repercussions, the feds also became entangled in the Mexican payroll robbery investigation.[27] Sergeant Jefferson Eagle Vaughn, Ranger and future sheriff of Presidio County, would also later report that he had been "working on a robbery case in which some ex rangers are supposed to be implicated."[28] Clogging up the investigative mess even further was the fascinating little fact that another ex-Ranger, Albert Henry Woelber, was on the sly acting as a confidential informant for federal investigators. One of the chief U.S. agents working the case was Gus T. Jones, himself a Texas Ranger of days past, and in the interworking of his mind the payroll robbery wasn't a whodunit, but rather a how-do-we-prove-it?[29]

One of the several approaches for making the case, in the eyes of Agent Jones, was to employ the use of an undercover operative. Gus Jones also noted, however, a cold hard fact of life: "These suspects are all more or less men of considerable experience as officers and any under cover men that go to Marfa would have to be very careful of their identity as this bunch of men would not hesitate to use violence to prevent any evidence being used against them."[30]

As luck would have it, just two weeks later Captain Roy Aldrich penned two letters to Ranger Private Will Alsobrook at Hebbronville, both on the eighth day of September 1919, but one was clearly marked: "<u>Private & confidential</u>" and in closing it carried explicit instructions: "and destroy this after you have read it." The not secret missive dealt with routine Ranger business and cordiality. The classified letter (which obviously was not destroyed) as we now know dealt with robbery of the Mexican paymaster at Marfa. Such specificity, however, was not passed to Private Will Alsobrook in the letter from Austin. The orders, in truth, were vague—real vague. The Ranger's official instructions were to check into someone's spending habits, a fellow in Hebbronville visiting his brother: "Captain Jerry Gray of Marfa wants a report on Charlie Craighead, who is now, or has been, at your town. Have you noticed him spending money, or showing a 'roll'?"[31] Alsobrook's September 13 reply to Captain Aldrich about the visitor to Hebbronville was short, noting Charles Craighead "was here several days but wasn't around us much and I don't know any thing about what he had as I didn't see him with any money .... he said he was going from here to Marffa [sic] when he left .... if you want us to make inquire [sic] about this matter let us know."[32] A hint of criticism that Ranger Private Will Alsobrook's investigation was somewhat lackluster might be justified had he been brought up to full speed on the robbery in Marfa and just who the prime suspects were in the first place, but such is not in evidence. The criminal investigation was on a strictly need-to-know basis and, apparently, Ranger Will Alsobrook didn't need to know—everything. He surely knew when asked to make a discreet inquiry concerning the sheriff's own brother that there was some thin ice to be skated across. Too, temperature between Sheriff Craighead and Ranger Alsobrook could have been dropping, perhaps a little frosty—maybe?

Some of the movers and shakers in Hebbronville and throughout Jim Hogg County were pushing for Will Alsobrook to make a political challenge for the sheriff's job: "he was well liked by the best people of Hebbronville," said Ranger Ben Tumlinson, Jr. from Alice.[33] And, according to Captain Aldrich, word he was receiving via the grapevine touted that Ranger Will Alsobrook was a near shoo-in when the time came, and was almost guaranteed to be "the next Sheriff there [Jim Hogg County]."[34] An editorial writer for the *Laredo Times* went so far as to say of Alsobrook, that since he was held in such high esteem the people of Hebbronville "were desirous of making him sheriff of Jim Hogg county at the next election" and that he could, most probably would be, "elected by almost unanimous vote, as it is believed he would have no opposition."[35] That is, if his good fortune held.

There is a tad of geographical confusion as to exactly where the next chapter in the life of Ranger Will Alsobrook plays out, but authenticated technicality pushes him across a county line, qualifying him for inclusion in *Riding Lucifer's Line.*

During the afternoon of December 8, 1919, Private Will Alsobrook boarded a South Texas train. Lady Luck, standing on a platform at the depot, waved him goodbye. At some point on the line near Crestonia in the southern reaches of Duval County, not too terribly far from Hebbronville, a Colt's .45 barked and the bullet bit into Alsobrook's midsection, flooring him to the aisle between the coach's seats.[36] Not unexpectedly the wound was serious. Whether or not Ranger Alsobrook remained conscious is indistinct, as are details as to how the gunshot damage was actually inflicted.[37] Clinging to life, Ranger Will Alsobrook, via a special train, was rushed to Webb County where he was admitted to Laredo's Mercy Hospital. The night was long, the prognosis was guarded. On December 9 doctors anesthetized Will and performed surgery. For awhile, a short while, physicians and nurses were ecstatic, Alsobrook was breathing on his own. Sadly, the downturn was unpredicted; the end result was irreversible. Before the clock struck midnight Texas Ranger Will Alsobrook had relapsed, slipping to the other side.[38]

Notified of his son's untimely death, Jim Alsobrook at Clarksville sent his oldest son to Laredo.[39] There, after contacting mortician

H. L. Jackson, Sims Alsobrook and Ranger Captain Ryan reverently accompanied Will's body back to Clarksville where it was taken to the home of Charles McDonald, the fallen Texas Ranger's brother-in-law.[40] After a memorial service, the body of William M. Alsobrook was interred in Clarksville's cemetery. The Red River County community wept.

Hardcore details of Ranger Will Alsobrook's death remain murky. If there were eyewitnesses to the tragedy their testimony has—to this point in time—been lost or misplaced or expunged. Such a deficit is history's loss to be sure. Generally it is accepted and, scant newspaper coverage is in accord for the most part, that Ranger Will Alsobrook's demise was result of an unfortunate accident. Whether he dropped his Colt's .45 and the six-shooter discharged or whether someone else irresponsibly touched off a hot round goes unsaid. An unverified family history typescript deposited with the Red River County Public Library suggests Will was "accidently shot while trying to separate two friends, who were fighting, at Hebronville [*sic*], Texas."[41] There is a tantalizing thread of mystery postulated by a contemporary journalist that an arrest would be forthcoming, but as of this writing such has been swept into the abyss of uncorroborated conjecture.[42] Interestingly, on the legal shuck's front side of Will Alsobrook's Oath of Members Ranger Force paperwork is a thought provoking notation: "Shot Dec. 8th; Died Dec. 9th 1919 In line of duty."[43] And though it necessitates reading between the lines, a one-page letter received by Captain Aldrich from Ranger Ben Tumlinson, Jr. regarding Alsobrook's death is curious in the fact one sentence says: "If any thing of importance ever happens here I will let you know at once."[44]

At face value it does seem the shooting may have been accidental. While raising rhetorical questions of a conspiratorial nature might be intriguing, the evidence, meager as it might be, is what we have—and that's what counts. Raw accusations, to have legal meaning, must come off of the courtroom's spit well-done, not oozing the pinkness of undercooked conjectural thinking. Assuredly the gooses of Charley Craighead, A. G. Beard, Andy Barker, and Boone Oliphant were not cooked. Besides Ranger Will Alsobrook's death in a Texas border town there are two worthy-of-note sidebar bottom-lines. The underhanded Marfa payroll heist was then unsolved, now being euphemistically pigeonholed in Presidio County's "cold case" files.[45] And, the gutsy one-legged Pat Craighead was reelected sheriff of Jim Hogg County.[46] If there were any deep dark secrets maybe they were cremated amid the fire and brimstone of Lucifer's Line.

Chapter 24

Joseph B. Buchanan
1921

Joseph Benjamin Buchanan was a Bosque County boy of sorts, tracing his earliest roots to the tiny community of Iredell, northwest of the county seat at Meridian, Texas.[1] His parents and several older siblings had made the migration from Virginia to Central Texas traveling first by train, then with two wagons and a buggy. Joe Ben was born on the first day of May 1890, but fond memories about swimming and fishing in the nearby North Bosque River were not to be. George Craig Buchanan and his wife Sallie Columbia (Gillespie) were fated to move further west while little Joe Ben was but three. The family eventually settled on farmland in Scurry County about six miles east of Snyder, the county seat.[2]

Although to some, chiefly non-Texans, it might have a ring of— "Hell, you say?"—the state is subdivided into 254 separate counties. Fifty-four of them, encompassing the Texas Panhandle, were created by the 1876 state legislature in one fell swoop. Such was a cost-cutting measure. Most of these counties hardly had sufficient population for formal organization and installation of county officeholders at the time. However the astute politicos at Austin knew ever expanding railroad lines and liberal land policies would bring new faces and hopeful dreamers to a region once occupied solely by nomadic Comanche and their allies, along with millions of shaggy buffalo. As a point of interest, grazing within that migrating Southern herd of buffalo, and inside the confines of what would become Scurry County, was a legendary and seldom seen white buffalo. The atypical trophy—considered magnificent at the time—was brought down by the ever industrious and thoroughly hard-working hidehunter J. Wright Mooar, who later delighted in displaying the handsomely tanned hide.[3]

What J. Wright Mooar didn't appreciate were some folks' misconceptions about the role buffalo hunters played in clearing the way for making Texas' Panhandle and Caprock Country inhabitable for future generations, those easy-living whippersnappers with such newfangled amenities as windmills, barbed-wire fences, "airtights" (canned food)—and indoor plumbing. Mooar's take was frank:

> Buffalo hunting was a business and not a sport; it required capital, management and work, lots of hard work, more work than anything else. Many magazine and newspaper articles claim the killing of the buffalo a national calamity and accomplished by vandals. I resent their ignorance.[4]

Scurry County was one of these farsighted on-paper creations. Starting as but a trading post for wandering buffalo hunters, Snyder, west of Rath City and further west of rip-roaring Fort Griffin, didn't go by the wayside as the threat of Indian raids neutralized and proficient hide hunters worked themselves right out of a job. The Sharps .50s quit booming but Snyder was booming with activity—primarily cattle ranching activity—and Scurry County organized during June 1884.[5] William W. Nelson was the county's first sheriff.[6] And clearly Scurry County was in need of a sheriff, as one early day complaining Complainant, a lawyer, noted:

> I am a good deal exercised in my mind whether to move for a change of venue in the case. Snyder is a very hard place to get a conviction against anyone....the only way to get a conviction there is for the prisoner to go in with you and plead guilty, and even then the jury may say the prisoner is a liar and does not know what he is talking about, and turn him loose.[7]

Joe Ben's older and married brother had also relocated to Scurry County. Charles Russell Buchanan notched a favorable name for himself in both local and state politics. At various times the eldest Buchanan boy served as the Scurry County Clerk and several terms as the Scurry County Judge, as well as a stint in Austin as a state senator.[8] Senator C. R. Russell was a powerhouse player in the world of rough and tumble Texas politics, an arena sometimes comical, sometimes corruptible, but at all times a darn good show. When it came time to get shed of a governor, Joe Ben's older brother was one of the senators writing the Bill of Impeachment leading to Governor Ferguson's undoing.[9]

On the first day of August 1900 at Snyder, Frank Courtney Mellard had married into the Buchanan family, taking the hand of Joe Ben's sister Helen. After a series of moves throughout the Texas Panhandle and no little hard work, the Mellards finally had the financial wherewithal to satisfy their mutual and long sought dream. In 1908 the couple began tending their own mama cows on a ranch 20 miles south of Marfa.[10] The Mellards settling in Presidio County would play into the saga of Joe Ben Buchanan's law enforcing life.

Sometime and somewhere along the timeline—exactness is elusive—Joe Ben Buchanan took a wife, Lucille. By the best information currently at hand the happy couple located to the ranching vicinity of Joe Ben's brother-in-law and sister in Presidio County.[11] Exactly how he finagled it is imprecise, perhaps his older brother's political clout was a factor, or maybe he was just particularly popular with Presidio County cowmen, but in any event Joe Ben made a specially arranged trip to the state's capital. On the 7th day of December 1917 in Travis County [Austin] Joe Ben Buchanan received his commission as an unpaid Special Ranger. Examination of the official paperwork reveals no particular company designation.[12] What he did receive however was a Warrant of Authority and Descriptive List, his official credentials for making lawful arrests for the State of Texas.[13] Although it must fall short of conclusiveness, the best guess is that Special Ranger Buchanan—living in Presidio County—was legally carrying a six-shooter and trying to catch cow thieves at the behest of Big Bend Country ranchers, before the beeves were herded across the border. Joe Ben's next move is sealed tight.

Shy of his thirty-first birthday by a couple of months, Joe Ben Buchanan enlisted in Captain Jerry Gray's Company A Ranger Force, then headquartered at Marfa.[14] He was no longer a Special Ranger—now he was drawing monthly pay from the state. Due to a paucity of Ranger records for this time-period, tracking Ranger Private Joe Ben Buchanan's day by day movements is problematic. A sporadic paper trail reveals that for Rangers scouting the border it was yet tough duty—even in the Lower Rio Grande Valley, too. Captain Roy Aldrich updated Ranger Sergeant L. E. Trimble, stationed in the Big Bend Country at Candelaria:

> Just had a letter from one of the boys down in the Valley advising me that a Mexican jerked the gun out of Howard Craig's holster and shot a constable who had him under arrest. Craig got the

Constable's gun and they buried Mr. Mexican next day. Craig is an ex-Ranger and is some other kind of an officer now.[15]

Although it cannot be put forth with finality it is not unreasonable to suggest that Private Buchanan was one of the Rangers getting the call regarding the transportation of a "cold blooded murderer" from Marfa to Alpine. The Brewster County Sheriff, E. E. Townsend, a former Texas Ranger and later the customarily acknowledged Father of the Big Bend National Park, had ask of Ranger Force headquarters that "Capt. Gray and five or six men be ordered to accompany me and to stay here [Alpine] as long as it may be necessary to keep the accused here.... I desire to have these men in order to avoid any chance of violence being done to the prisoner."[16]

Institutionally the Texas Rangers had hurdled 1920's mark. Practically speaking however, for many lonesome spots along the Rio Grande and far West Texas is was as if time stood still: Many men—and some women—still buckled on a Colt's six-shooter or tucked a .45 autoloader into their waistband as a matter of due course. The practice of Selective Enforcement gave them the wink and nod of approval. The county seats may have been relatively safe, but there was a population outside those towns, and not all those folks were real nice guys—or girls.

One of the border hotspots needing a little Ranger attention once and awhile was Polvo—in close proximity to present day Redford—on the river downstream from Presidio. From the geographical perspective this stretch of the Rio Grande is scenic to be sure, in large part due to its ruggedness. From the lawman's viewpoint—then or now—its sheer isolation portends a nightmarish truth: Backup is always faraway.

Some of the local folks at Polvo were yet celebrating the Christmas Holidays of 1921, as the December 25th *baile* (dance) continued well past bewitching hour. During the wee morning hours two "Mexicans" made an appearance, strangers to the revelers. Ranger Joe Ben Buchanan, doing his job, was on duty at the shindig keeping the peace and keeping any drunken nitwits from hurting themselves—or each other. Unfamiliar faces, there and at that time of night were an oddity. Good lawmen are curious. Private Joe Ben Buchanan was a good lawman. Although the two party-crashers had yet done no perceptible wrong, Ranger Buchanan wanted to clarify who they actually were: Fugitives or fun-lovers, sly smugglers or sloshed partygoers?

At least a cursory interrogation—at a minimum—was obligatory. When Private Buchanan asked if they knew them, even the locals were stymied; having never—ever—seen the two fellows before they swaggered into the makeshift dancehall.

There's no reason of record to indicate that Joe Ben Buchanan was an overbearing or randomly abusive Texas Ranger. In fact, due to his brother's election successes in Scurry County, it might suggest Joe Ben was well attuned to a realization that interpersonal pleasantries were necessary for developing critical intelligence and garnering cooperation from the population at large. That bit of conjecture said, apparently the two interlopers fancied themselves ten feet tall and bullet proof—or invisible—a not scarce psyche self-appraisal for folks with bloodstreams diluted by too much spirituous liquor. Standing tall, all six foot and one inch, Joe Ben Buchanan approached the strangers. The Ranger's query was but routine: "Who are you, and where are you from?" One spoke, snarling it was "none of his damned business." Both yahoos went for their guns. Undoubtedly, not for an instant, visualizing their resort to six-shooters as a reply, Joe Ben failed to get there. His was a second place finish. While reaching for his holstered Colt's .45, a bullet ripped into Joe Ben's right shoulder causing him to drop his revolver. Wholly unarmed the solitary Texas Ranger was at their mercy—helpless. The "Mexicans" continued firing, eight more rounds tearing into Joe Ben Buchanan's staggering frame.[17] The Ranger fell facedown on the dance floor—dead.[18] The shooters ran out the door, splashed across the river and dashed to sanctuary inside Mexico's line.

Immediately upon notification, Captain Jerry Gray and other Texas Rangers responded, not content one little bit to let the international border interfere with their police business: "We trailed the Mexicans into Mexico and up the river about one-half mile, where they crossed back to this side. Ranger [George Calvin] Brown and two men are trailing them through the mountains and I am trying to cut them off by going to Lajitas."[19]

At Ranger headquarters Captain Aldrich was distraught over the paucity of news coming from the Big Bend Country. He messaged the Presidio County Sheriff, Jefferson Eagle Vaughan, a former Texas Ranger: "I wish you would send me a copy of the Marfa paper giving the full details of the killing of Ranger Buchanan. I want it for my record. It was a bad affair and we regret it very much. I hope that his murderers will be captured but I fear that you boys will have a hard job to catch them...."[20] Unfortunately Captain Aldrich's guesswork was right; this manhunt proved fruitless.[21] As did the one after New Year's Day, when Captain Gray was on the river at Presidio, and even instigating cross-border inquiries "to San Carlos, Mex. To see if I can locate the Mexicans that Killed Buchanan."[22] Captain Jerry Gray couldn't and didn't round up the suspects: Score another one for *mal hombres*.

Ranger Buchanan's body had been transported to Marfa. There, with his brother-in-law Frank Mellard acting as informant for Doctor Church's completion of a Death Certificate, the routine legal duties attendant to death had been completed.[23] The cemetery internment was sad, the new widow Lucille Buchannan grieved. Ranger Joe Ben Buchannan had not been a winner. Along Lucifer's Line second place was last!

Afterword

Fortunately, in a bizarre fashion, the killing of Joe Ben Buchanan was—at least to date—the last Texas Ranger death on the line. Regrettably, murdering lawmen up and down the Texas-Mexico border continues to this day. Why is such a statistic so heavily weighted against the Texas Rangers for years, and then radically tapers off? The answer is not elusive. And it damn sure is not due to peacefulness and goodwill of borderland criminals.

Although the Mexican Revolution and the several wholesale bandit incursions had gone by the wayside, the hard lesson had not been lost in Washington, D.C. The Texas-Mexico border was a trouble spot, an ever-festering hotbed. Recognizing responsibility at the federal level a new outfit was birthed and an existing one doughtily beefed up. On May 28 legislators passed the Labor Appropriations Act of 1924, formally launching the U.S. Border Patrol. Federal funds were set aside and a staffing model made room for hiring 450 Patrol Inspectors. Their work assignment on a piece of paper was simple: secure America's borders between Ports of Entry. In practice, as we now know, it's a near undoable and yet dangerous—and often thankless job. Nonetheless the new recruits—not just a few ex-Rangers in the lot—furnishing their own horses and saddles received postings along the border. As well as a monthly salary of $140—much higher than Ranger pay—the new Border Patrol Inspectors were furnished with a shiny new badge, a government-issued revolver, and feed for their horses.[1] They were not, however, awarded a free pass from getting killed while working the borderline. U.S. Border Patrolmen trading spots with Rangers netted a disheartening but measurable result: they now hold the first place distinction for officers' making that ultimate sacrifice along the border, followed by U.S. Customs officers.[2] Border Patrolmen—and women—now number 21,500. That recruitment sculpting number, by itself, exposes truth: the borderlands yet own trouble.[3]

Too, it must be mentioned—and not forgotten—though not highlighted in this particular narrative, while this set of Rangers were being killed in the Rio Grande country, other intrepid Rangers were paying the ultimate price within the state's interior.[4] Deployment of the Border Patrol Inspectors and the increased staffing patterns of the U.S. Customs Service had cleared the way for headquarters personnel to refocus the workaday efforts of in-the-field Texas Rangers. And there was need for an adjustment, some overdue fine-tuning. For Texas Rangers enforcing laws during the so-called "boom town" and "gangster era" much of the hot action took place away from the Texas/Mexican border. The call for Rangers stationed away from the border was at a fever pitch. Factoring in their peace-keeping assignments in the oil boomtowns and obligations pursuant to labor unrest, and the picture comes even clearer. Just because they were not being killed on the border does not mean they were not being murdered in the line of duty: Quite the contrary. It's yet a chancy business, factoring in the contemporary Texas Ranger's everyday work of chasing home-invasion robbers, rescuing kidnapped kids, looking into public corruption cases, security assignments, responding to riots, solving serial killings, busting druggies, dealing with fanatical religious zealots with a barn full of under-aged "wives" and arresting other modern-era desperadoes of the deepest dye—and complying with bureaucracy's mountain of rules and paperwork demands.

Today warring narco cartels are literally at each others' throats—lopping off heads. The dope and death spilling into Texas, together with risks from would-be wacko suicide bombers slipping across the line, guarantees a Ranger presence is again, thankfully, felt on the border. Rangers are there: Now![5] Scouting the river is, always has been, trouble. The take away is this: All lawmen live in real time, where at any given moment conditions can go haywire in a heartbeat!

Endnotes

Notes to Preface:

1. For an insightful examination of modern day violence along the United States/Mexican border the reader is referred to Ed Vulliamy's 2010 *AMEXIA: War Along the Borderline* and Charles Bowden's *Murder City: Ciudad Juárez and the Global Economy's New Killing Fields*. Particularly focused in the Texas Big Bend Country is Terrence E. Poppa's excellent treatment *Drug Lord: The Life & Death of a Mexican Kingpin*. For a gripping account of a drugster so rich and powerful he made *Forbes* magazine listings [amid considerable controversy] see *The Last Narco: Inside the Hunt for El Chapo, The World's Most Wanted Drug Lord* by Malcolm Beith. A compelling primer for the reader interested in exploring background material for the rise of Mexican based drug trafficking, U.S policy infighting, political corruption, and the murder of an American DEA Special Agent is Elaine Shannon's *Desperados: Latin Drug Lords, U.S. Lawmen, and the War America Can't Win*. Also recommended is the outstanding study by Ioan Grillo, *El Narco: Inside Mexico's Criminal Insurgency*. The foregoing accounts are written by print media journalists; one and all are dandy—and enlightening reads. No less readable and attention grabbing are two volumes researched and penned by professors, Howard Campbell's *Drug War Zone: Frontline Dispatches From the Streets of El Paso and Juárez* and George W. Grayson's *Mexico: Narco-Violence and a Failed State?*

2. Leon C. Metz. *Border: The U.S.-Mexico Line*, 406.

3. Assistant Director DPS-Chief Texas Rangers, Kirby W. Dendy to author Sept. 25, 2012.

4. Malcolm Beith, *The Last Narco*. "In September 2006, five heads were rolled on to a dance floor in the central state of Michoacan. By late 2007, beheadings had become commonplace, barely even making the evening news....There were more than 300 beheadings in Mexico in 2009 alone; there are still no signs of the violence ebbing," xvii; Ed Vulliamy, *AMEXIA: War Along the Borderline*. "Four decapitated seventeen-year-olds are among twenty-one people killed in Tijuana during the first week of the year [2009]," 15. And, "His [Hugo Hernández] torso is in one location, his severed arms and legs boxed in another place, and his skull found in another. His face has been flayed, left near the city hall of Los Mochis, sewn to a soccer ball," 16.

5   Don Graham, *Kings of Texas: The 150 Year Saga of an American Ranching Empire*, 17–18.
6   Hallie Crawford Stillwell, *I'll Gather My Geese*, 12.
7   Charles H. Harris III and Louis Ray Sadler, *The Texas Rangers and the Mexican Revolution: The Bloodiest Decade, 1910–1920.*
8   C. L. Sonnichsen, *Tularosa: Last of the Frontier West*, 3
9   Roy R. Barkley and Mark F. Odintz, eds., *The Portable Handbook of Texas*, 725.
10 Two significant studies of the Rio Grande for the general reader are Paul Horgan's two-volume treatment, *Great River, The Rio Grande in North American History* and Metz's *Border: The U.S.-Mexican Line*. Also see, John Busby McClung, "Texas Rangers Along the Rio Grande, 1910–1919," Ph.D. dissertation, Texas Christian University, Fort Worth, 1981.
11 Walter Prescott Webb, *The Texas Rangers: A Century of Frontier Defense.* First part of quotation, 495; second part, 508. Along the Rio Grande in the Big Bend Country even store personnel carried guns. See, Diane Garner, *Letters From the Big Bend: Legacy of a Pioneer*: "Secondly, I [James Robert "Jim" Landrum] am not only a good pistol shot, but am known to be and always go armed (a wise percausion [*sic*] here.)," 112.
12 J. C. Cameron, Secretary/Actuary, Great Southern Life Insurance Company, to Texas Adjutant General James A. Harley, Dec. 10, 1917, Texas State Library and Archives, hereafter TSA. Clearly staking out a section of real-estate and declaring it the most perilous spot in Texas, in a law enforcing context, could arguably be injudicious: Individual perspective does matter. Texas State Police lost four officers in a single day (March 14, 1873) as result of gunfire inside and outside Jerry Scott's saloon at Lampasas; was it the most dangerous place in Texas? The Bosque County sheriff may have thought his county was toughest of the tough after losing three deputies in 1874. Texas prison administrators, after burying three correctional officers killed in three separate episodes during 1890, might have reasonably postulated patrolling the prison yard and walking the cell blocks was the most risky place in the state. Perhaps families and friends of the four Galveston police officers losing their lives on the same day during a 1900 hurricane would suggest the island was the most dangerous site in Texas. Or, was Fort Worth, during her formative years, the most hazardous town in Texas for guys sporting tin stars, twirling police batons, and wearing a gun—or guns? Certainly authors Richard F. Selcer and Kevin S. Foster make a good case for their city in the two-volume treatment *Written in Blood: The History of Fort Worth's Fallen Officers*. But, the mother of Ben J. Hill, the city marshal of Blossom (Lamar County) would have likely declared on October 19, 1902, that

her son's city had the gold-star for meanness, even though as of this writing he has been the municipality's only fallen officer. And even later into the twentieth-century five officers from the Houston Police Department were killed on August 23, 1917, during a race riot involving black soldiers of the U.S. Army's 24th Infantry. The salient point is: Law enforcement is dangerous work—anytime, anywhere. *Riding Lucifer's Line* but highlights the lives and deaths of one group policing across a narrowly defined stretch of ground. Those lawmen making the supreme sacrifice elsewhere in Texas should not be forgotten, their stories should not be dropped into the cubbyhole of obscurity. History owes them a fair shake—Texas owes them thanks!

13   Walter Prescott Webb, "Texas Rangers In Eclipse," *The State Trooper*, January 1926. "They [Texas Rangers] are used in time of trouble, abused in time of peace. That is the history of the force," 13.

14   Harris and Sadler, *The Texas Rangers*, 3.

15   Adalberto Aguirre, Jr. and Jonathan H. Turner, *American Ethnicity: The Dynamics and Consequences of Discrimination*, 150.

16   Frank Richard Prassel, *The Western Peace Officer: A Legacy of Law and Order*, 158; Bob Alexander, *Winchester Warriors: Texas Rangers of Company D, 1874–1901*, 231-232.

17   Robert J. Casey, *The Texas Border And Some Borderliners*, 313.

18   Ibid. Although in *Mexico: Narco-Violence and a Failed State?* he is speaking of Tijuana on the Mexican/California border, Professor George W. Grayson somewhat confirms the vivid remarks of Casey's uncle: "Nevertheless, one sector continues to flourish, the funeral industry—to the point that parlors are short of morticians.... Tijuana now suffers from plummeting tourism, even while its mortuaries thrive because of shootouts and gangland mutilations," 1. Moving west the scholar addresses "zones of impunity" of which the Texas/Mexican border is one: "....neighborhoods in cities along the U.S. Mexican border where cartel thugs carve up judges, behead police officers, and disappear journalists who incur their wrath...," 271; Professor Howard Campbell in *Drug War Zone* picks up on reality, politically incorrect as it may be for chamber of commerce spokesmen: "Tourists ceased going to Juárez [opposite El Paso]. Foreign investors avoided the city after seeing news reports about a decapitated body hung from a bridge, severed heads left on sidewalks ...," 268.

19   Charles Bowden, *Juárez: The Laboratory of Our Future*. Throughout this fascinating—yet disturbing—volume, the author highlights, with many photographs, the violence taking place in Juárez. For the death of Nuevo Laredo's police chief, see, Beith, *The Last Narco*, 115.

20   Bob Alexander, *Rawhide Ranger, Ira Aten: Enforcing Law on the Texas Frontier*, 76.

21   Elmer Kelton, "Generational Chauvinism," *West Texas Historical Association Yearbook*, 1991, 133.

Introduction to Part I: The Frontier Battalion Era, 1874–1901

1   Stephen L. Moore, *Savage Frontier: Rangers, Riflemen, and Indian Wars in Texas*, four Volumes.

2   Gregory Michno, *The Settler's War: The Struggle for the Texas Frontier in 1860s*. "Actually, Europeans were in the present-day boundaries of Texas before their future adversaries, the Comanches...," 1. In this work, and others by Michno, the author adheres strictly to the factual side of history, "without moralizing or portraying the protagonists as good or evil," allowing that the "characters' actions will define them."

3   Ed Carnal, "Reminiscences of a Ranger," *Frontier Times*, December 1923, 20.

4   Henry W. Barton, "The United States Cavalry and the Texas Rangers," *Southwestern Historical Quarterly*, April, 1960, 495–510.

5   Ann Patton Baenziger, "The Texas State Police Under Reconstruction: A Reexamination," *Southwestern Historical Quarterly*, April, 1969, 475; *San Antonio Daily Herald*, September 11, 1870; William Curtis Nunn, "A Study of the State Police during the E. J. Davis Administration," MA thesis, University of Texas, Austin. 1931. A book-length study of the Texas State Police may be found by referencing a recent release of the late Barry A. Crouch and his writing partner Donaly E. Brice, *The Governor's Hounds: The Texas State Police, 1870–1873*. For article-length assessments the reader is referred to Donaly E. Brice's paper, "Finding a Solution to Reconstruction Violence: The Texas State Police" as contained in Chapter Six of *Still the Arena of Civil War: Violence and Turmoil in Reconstruction Texas, 1865–1874*, Kenneth W. Howell, ed.; also, David Bowser, "Reconstruction State Police Not Entirely Evil, Says Archivist," *Livestock Weekly*, May 24, 2012.

6   Carl H. Moneyhon, *Edmund J. Davis: Civil War General, Republican Leader, Reconstruction Governor*. Author Moneyhhon asserts that operations of the State Police were "particularly successful." At a mini-mum two factors should be added regarding an overall assessment of the State Police's success. The outfit's first Chief of Police, James Davidson, *allegedly* embezzled $37,434.67 before fleeing to New Zealand, and one State Police captain, John Marshall "Jack" Helm, a man described as "the most noted brigand since the days of Quantrill," a full-fledged terrorist and killer, was kicked off the police force for summarily executing prisoners. See Alexander, *Winchester Warriors*,

6–7; also, Chuck Parsons, *The Sutton-Taylor Feud: The Deadliest Blood Feud in Texas*, 77–106.

7   *Dallas Daily Herald*, April 22, 1873.

8   H. P. N. Gammel, comp., *The Laws of Texas, 1822–1897*, Ten Volumes, Vol. 8, 86.

9   Harold J. Weiss, Jr., "Western Lawmen: Image and Reality," *Journal of the West*, January 1985, 28.

10 Robert M. Utley, *Lone Star Justice: The First Century of the Texas Rangers*. "Administratively, it became known as the Frontier Battalion. Its personnel, however, called themselves Texas Rangers. So did the newspapers, and so did the people," 145–46.

11 Chuck Parsons and Marianne E. Hall, *Captain L. H. McNelly, Texas Ranger: The Life and Times of a Fighting Man*, xii.

12 Mike Cox, *The Texas Rangers: Wearing the Cinco Peso*: "….McNelly and his men showed up in South Texas wearing what they wanted to. A militia company on paper, in appearance and function they rode as Rangers," 242.

13 Utley, *Lone Star Justice*: "The men regarded themselves as Rangers, and so did the public….McNelly's Rangers," 158; Robert Draper, on the other hand, in "The Twilight of the Texas Rangers," for the February 1994 edition of *Texas Monthly* opts for rigorously strict interpretation: "His [McNelly's] troops were structurally and budgetarily set apart from the six companies making up the separately legislated Frontier Battalion of Texas Rangers," 82.

14 Governor Richard Coke to Captain L. H. McNelly, July 9, 1875, TSA.

15 Interview by author with Byron A. Johnson, Executive Director, Texas Ranger Hall of Fame & Museum, Waco, Texas, hereafter TRHF&M, July 28, 2012. See also the 2011 TRHF&M publication, *Your Guide to the Official Historical Center of the Texas Rangers*: "Nominees and Inductees are chosen by the Texas Rangers from deceased Rangers who significantly contributed to the development of the Service or gave their lives under exceptional circumstances," 4.

16 Ronald G. DeLord, *The Ultimate Sacrifice: Trials and Triumphs of the Texas Peace Officer, 1823–2000*, 51; Program, *The Thirteenth Biennial Texas Peace Officer's Memorial Services. May 1–2, 2011*, 66, Texas State Capitol, Austin, Texas.

17 For a critical and complete analysis of the contributions John B. Jones made to Texas and Texas Ranger history the reader must consult the University of North Texas Press' 2012 publication of Rick Miller's *Texas Ranger John B. Jones and the Frontier Battalion, 1874–1881*.

18 Alexander, *Winchester Warriors*, 18–38.

19 Captain Frank Jones, Company D, Frontier Battalion, to Texas Adjutant General Woodford Haywood Mabry, March 1, 1892, TSA.

20 General Order Number 2, Frontier Battalion, May 6, 1874, TSA.
21 Ibid.
22 Alexander, *Winchester Warriors*, 19.
23 AG Steele to Captain L. H. McNelly, Adjutant General Correspondence, Letterpress Book, April 5–9, 1875; Undated Letter, TSA; Erik T. Rigler, "A Descriptive Study of the Texas Rangers: Historical Overtones on Minority Attitudes," MA thesis, Sam Houston State University, Huntsville, Texas, 1971.
24 Utley, *Lone Star Justice*, 145–46.
25 Gammel, *The Laws of Texas*. Vol. 8, 86-91; Frederick Wilkins, *The Law Comes to Texas: The Texas Rangers, 1870–1901*, 28.
26 For seminal exploration of all facets of this feud, the reader is referred to the outstanding research and investigative work of David Johnson, as reflected in *The Mason County "Hoo Doo" War, 1874–1902*.
27 Major John B. Jones, Frontier Battalion to AG Steele, October 28, 1875, TSA.
28 Lieutenant Dan Roberts, Frontier Battalion, Company D, to Major Jones, February 16, 1876, TSA.
29 Private H. B. Waddill, Frontier Battalion, Company C, to Major Jones, February 27, 1877, TSA.
30 Major Jones to AG Steele, May 6, 1877, TSA. For an in-depth look at the Kimble County Roundup, see Peter R. Rose, *The Reckoning: The Triumph of Order on the Texas Outlaw Frontier*.
31 General Order Number 10, Frontier Battalion, August 25, 1876, TSA; Utley, *Lone Star Justice*, 152;
32 Alexander, *Winchester Warriors*, 114.
33 Captain L. P. Sieker, Frontier Battalion, Company D, to AG King, February 13 and 20, 1885, TSA; Alexander, *Winchester Warriors*, 272.

Chapter 1: Sonny Smith, 1875

1 Clifford R. Caldwell and Ron DeLord, *Texas Lawmen, 1835–1899: The Good and the Bad*, 331. The authors place Smith's age at the time of his death as between 16 and 18 years, particularly noting, "The city of Brownsville Record of Interments indicates that he was seventeen." That Smith was yet a teenager at the time of his death is undisputed; Jerry Thompson, *Cortina: Defending the Mexican Name in Texas* writes that Smith was seventeen years old, 226. Regardless, the salient point remains unaltered: Smith was the youngest Ranger and correspondingly the youngest full-time Texas lawman ever killed in the line of duty.
2 DeLord, *The Ultimate Sacrifice, 1823–2000*, 51; Chuck Parsons, *"Pidge": A Texas Ranger From Virginia*, Appendix A, 125. For an opposing

view that Smith was not a Texas Ranger at the time of his death see, John C. Rayburn and Virginia Kemp Rayburn, *Century of Conflict, 1821–1913: Incidents in the Lives of William Neale and William A. Neale Early Settlers in South Texas,* "….Berry Smith, Jr. who was not a Ranger but followed his father…," 121. Primary source records in the form of State of Texas Certification of Payment Due unalterably refute any claim that L. B. Smith was not a Ranger in McNelly's company. See Voucher dated March 31, 1875, signed by McNelly, TSA.

3 Telegram, Captain L. H. McNelly to Governor Coke, June 12, 1875, as cited in *Galveston Daily News,* June 13, 1875; George Durham, *Taming the Nueces Strip: The Story of McNelly's Rangers.* Durham adds to the name confusion of young Smith by referring to him as Febe, 14.

4 Captain L. H. McNelly to Adjutant General William Steele, June (??), 1875, Courtesy, TRHF&M; Affidavit and Personnel File (L. B. Smith) for Texas Peace Officers Killed in the Line of Duty, Courtesy Ronald G. DeLord, Executive Director, Combined Law Enforcement Associations of Texas, (CLEAT); Parsons and Little, *Captain L. H. McNelly,* 201; Luke Gournay, *Texas Boundaries: Evolution of the State's Counties,* 92. For a thumbnail sketch of Lee County, see Julia Jones, "Brief History of Lee County," in the January 1942 edition of *Frontier Times,* 143–44.

5 Parsons and Little, *Captain L. H. McNelly,* quoting Austin's *Daily State Journal,* October 11, 1872, 165; Charles M. Robinson III, *The Men Who Wear The Star: The Story of the Texas Rangers,* 190.

6 Bob Scott, *Leander McNelly, Texas Ranger: He Just Kept On Keepin' On.* With an effort to highlight border violence, the author cites a battle between Texas Rangers and Mexicans. Unfortunately the author places the incident a decade too early. For a thorough examination of the incident the author chronologically transposed erroneously, see Alexander's *Rawhide Ranger: Ira Aten,* 71–89. The particular gunfight, in an abbreviated format, is also found in Chapter Five of this volume.

7 Gournay, *Texas Boundaries,* 52; T. C. Richardson, "Corpus Christi: 'Naples of the Gulf,'" *Frontier Times,* June 1939, 390-395; Jerry Thompson, *A Wild and Vivid Land: An Illustrated History of the South Texas Border,* 39.

8 Coleman McCampbell, "Romance Had Role in Founding of Corpus Christi," *Frontier Times,* September, 1933, 569; Mary Jo O'Rear, *Storm Over the Bay: The People of Corpus Christi and Their Port,* 12; Thompson, *A Wild and Vivid Land* brands Henry Lawrence Kinney's trading post, which would later become Corpus Christi, "A haven for smugglers," 39.

9 Betty Dooley Awbrey and Claude Dooley, *Why Stop? A Guide to Texas Historical Roadside Markers,* 112.

10 Durham, *Taming the Nueces Strip,* 25.

11 William M. Hager, "The Nuecestown Raid of 1875: A Border Incident," *Arizona and the West*, Autumn 1959. Quoting the *Galveston Daily News* of May 9, 1873, 258.

12 Cox, *Wearing the Cinco Peso*, 246.

13 Barkley and Odintz, *The Portable Handbook of Texas*, 625; Julian Samora, Joe Bernal, and Albert Peña, *Gunpowder Justice: A Reassessment of the Texas Rangers*, 47.

14 Leopold Morris, "The Mexican Raid of 1875 on Corpus Christi," *Texas Historical Association Quarterly*, July 1900, 128. In *The Tejano Community, 1836–1900* author Arnoldo De León makes sure the reader is aware that the Corpus Christi raiders were Mexican nationals and not *Tejanos*, 19.

15 Thompson, *Cortina*, 223.

16 *Galveston Daily News*, March 27, 1875; *Dallas Daily Herald*, April 3, 1875.

17 *Galveston Daily News*, March 28, 1875.

18 *Dallas Daily Herald*, April 2 and 3, 1875; Parsons and Little, *Captain L. H. McNelly*, 167.

19 Coleman McCampbell, *Texas Seaport: The Story of the Growth of Corpus Christi and the Coastal Bend Area*, 54.

20 Ruth Dodson, "The Noakes Raid," *Frontier Times*, July 1946, 180.

21 J. B. (Red) John Dunn, *Perilous Trails of Texas*, 95.

22 *Galveston Daily News*, March 30, 1875; Arnoldo De León, *They Called Them Greasers: Anglo Attitudes Toward Mexicans in Texas, 1821–1900*, 99.

23 Thompson, *Cortina*, 223.

24 Michael G. Webster, "Intrigue on the Rio Grande: The Rio Bravo Affair, 1875," *Southwestern Historical Quarterly*, October 1970, 152.

25 N. A. Jennings, *A Texas Ranger*, 65; Hager, "The Nuecestown Raid," 267.

26 *Austin Daily Democratic Statesman*, April 13, 1875.

27 Adjutant General William Steele to Captain L. H. McNelly, April 5–9, 1875, TSA; Rigler, "A Descriptive Study of the Texas Rangers: Historical Overtones on Minority Attitudes."

28 *San Antonio Daily Herald*, May 6, 1875; *Galveston Daily News*, May 4, 1875.

29 Parsons, *Pidge*, 71. Quoting the *Daily Express* of May 8, 1975.

30 T. R. Fehrenbach, *Lone Star: A History of Texas and the Texans*, 576.

31 Durham, *Taming the Nueces Strip*, 38; Frederick Wilkins, *The Law Comes to Texas*: "Callicott, like Durham, was quite frank about the fate of any prisoners," 91.

32 Douglas V. Meed, *Bloody Border: Riots, Battles and Adventures Along the Turbulent U.S.-Mexican Borderlands*, 48.

33   Cornelus C. Smith, Jr., *Emilio Kosterlitzky: Eagle of Sonora and the Southwest Border*, 101.

34   Ibid., 105. For a comprehensive look at the *Rurales* the reader is referred to Paul Joseph Vanderwood's Ph.D dissertation "The Rurales: Mexico's Rural Police Force, 1861–1914," University of Texas, 1970. The author discusses the policy of *la ley de fuga* throughout, and specifically 105–11.

35   Durham, *Taming the Nueces Strip*, 40; Harold J. Weiss, Jr., "Organized Constabularies: The Texas Rangers and the Early State Police Movement in the American Southwest," *Journal of the West*, January 1995, 30; Utley, *Lone Star Justice,* questions the assertion: "....McNelly turned these particular spies over to the sheriff of Cameron County (Brownsville), and it may be doubted that Casuse [Jesús Sandoval] ended his interrogations with a rope very often, if at all," 162.

36   Ibid., 44–45.

37   Ibid., 18; Thompson, *Cortina*, 224.

38   Ibid.

39   Ibid., 19; Ben Proctor, *Just One Riot: Episodes of Rangers in the 20ᵗʰ Century*, 3.

40   Parsons and Little, *Captain L. H. McNelly*, 174, 335 n.32

41   McCampbell, *Texas Seaport*, 56.

42   Graham, *Kings of Texas,* 136.

43   Durham, *Taming the Nueces Strip*, 20–21; Mike Cox, "The Ranger From Washington County," *Round Top Register*, Fall 2011, 8.

44   Ibid.

45   Ibid., 30–33. Terminology describing a horse's stamina as "bottom," is commonplace with cattlemen and horse folks. Also see, *Western Words: A Dictionary of the Old West* by Ramon F. Adams, 16, and Peter Watts's *A Dictionary of the Old West,* 43.

46   Jane Clements Monday and Frances Brannen Vick, *Letters to Alice: Birth of the Kleberg-King Ranch Dynasty*, 17.

47   Herbert Molloy Mason, Jr., *The Texas Rangers*, 96–98.

48   Jane Clements Monday and Frances Brannen Vick, *Petra's Legacy: The South Texas Ranching Empire of Petra Vela and Mifflin Kenedy*, 231.

49   Mary Margaret McAllen Amberson, James A. McAllen & Margaret H. McAllen, *I Would Rather Sleep in Texas: A History of the Lower Rio Grande Valley and the People of the Santa Anita Land Grant*, 330.

50   Walter Prescott Webb, *The Story of the Texas Rangers*. This Texas Ranger treatment by Webb is much shorter and published much later than his epic *The Texas Rangers: A Century of Frontier Defense*. Webb, in this later version, is not indefinite in defending McNelly's extralegal executions, 46.

51 Any assertion that Jesús Sandoval was not a Ranger, but rather a civilian spy or scout, is belied by primary source documents, as but one example the Muster Roll for McNelly's company, dated 26 July 1876, TRHF&M.

52 Amberson, McAllen and McAllen, *I Would Rather Sleep in Texas*, 315–16; Thompson, *Cortina*, 225. Fehrenbach, *Lone Star*, reports that in one contract with Cuban marketers Cortina was to furnish 18,000 head of cattle at $18 apiece, 579.

53 C. L. Douglas., *The Gentlemen in the White Hats: Dramatic Episodes in the History of the Texas Rangers*, 108.

54 Chuck Parsons, *John B. Armstrong: Texas Ranger and Pioneer Ranchman*, 14.

55 Webb, *The Story of the Texas Rangers*, 42; Thompson, *Cortina*, 225–26; Mrs. G. C. Mayfield, "Interesting Narrative of Capt. W. L. Rudd, Ex-Ranger," *Frontier Times*, December 1932, 124.

56 Captain McNelly to AG Steele, June (??) 1875, TRHF&M.

57 J. Frank Dobie, *A Vaquero of the Brush Country*, 68.

58 *San Antonio Daily Herald*, June 14, 1875; Affidavit and Personnel File (L. B. "Sonny" Smith) For Texas Peace Officers Killed in the Line of Duty. Courtesy, Ronald G. DeLord, Executive Director, Combined Law Enforcement Associations of Texas (CLEAT).

59 *Galveston Daily News*, June 13, 1875.

60 Calliott as quoted in Webb's *The Story of the Texas Rangers*, 51.

61 Parsons and Little, *Captain L. H. McNelly*, 198.

62 *San Antonio Daily Express*, June 14, 1875; Richard B. McCaslin, *Fighting Stock: John S. "Rip" Ford of Texas*, 226; Sammy Tise, *Texas County Sheriffs*, 86.

63 Affidavit of Joseph P. O'Shaughnessy for the U.S. District Court, Eastern District of Texas, June 16, 1875, TSA; *Galveston Daily News*, June 16, 1875; Monday and Vick, *Petra's Legacy* records the deceased's name as Billy McMahan, but do not shy away from a central issue, the brutality: "In November a popular and 'inoffensive' American schoolteacher, Billy McMahan, was captured north of Brownsville. The desperados tortured him by cutting off his fingers, toes, wrist, and ears, and finally 'severed his legs from his body and left him lifeless,'" 228.

64 Dudley G. Wooten, ed., *A Comprehensive History of Texas, 1685–1897*. 2 Vols. Texas Adjutant General W. H. King contributed a chapter: "The Texas Ranger Service and History of the Rangers, With Observation on Their Value as a Police Protection." The quotation in this text may be found in Vol. 2, 350.

65 Captain McNelly to AG Steele, June (??) 1875, TRHF&M.

66 Fehrenbach, *Lone Star*, 578.

67 D. R. Smith to Sarah P. Smith, June 15, 1875, courtesy Ron DeLord, CLEAT.

68 Walter Prescott Webb, *The Texas Rangers: A Century of Frontier Defense*, 251; McCaslin, *Fighting Stock*, 226.

69 Captain McNelly to AG Steele, June (??) 1875, TRHF&M.

70 Spencer J. Adams to Sarah P. Smith, June 15, 1875. Courtesy Ron DeLord, CLEAT.

Chapter 2: John E. McBride & Conrad E. Mortimer, 1877

1 Gournay, *Texas Boundaries*, 26, 60.

2 Barkley and Odintz, *Portable Handbook of Texas*, 309.

3 Bob Alexander, *Desert Desperadoes: The Banditti of Southwestern New Mexico*, 91.

4 Charles Frances Ward, "The Salt War of San Elizario—1877," MA thesis, University of Texas, Austin, 1932, 10.

5 Ibid., 8

6 United States House of Representatives Executive Document 93, 45th Congress, 2d Session, 1878, El Paso Troubles In Texas (HR-ED 93 EPT): Statement of Ward B. Blanchard, 93.

7 HR-ED 93 EPT, Statements of Charles Kerber, Sheriff, El Paso County and Edmund Stine; C. L. Sonnichsen, *Pass of the North: Four Centuries on the Rio Grande,* 179–80; Ward, "The Salt War of San Elizario," 30; Harriot Howze Jones, ed., *El Paso: A Centennial Portrait*, Chapter Five; Marjorie F. Graham and Otilia Goode, "Schools of El Paso." "At first, attendance was poor and parental opposition was great...," 98.

8 C. L. Sonnichsen, *The El Paso Salt War*, 5.

9 Leon Claire Metz, *The Shooters*, 217.

10 Wayne R. Austerman, *Sharps Rifles and Spanish Mules: The San Antonio—El Paso Mail, 1851–1881*, 33.

11 Alexander, *Desert Desperadoes*, 102; Paul Cool, "J. A. Tays: The Frontier Battalion's Forgotten Officer," *Texas Ranger Dispatch*, Summer 2004; James B. Gillett, *Six Years with the Texas Rangers, 1875–1881*; Wilkins, *The Law Comes to Texas*, 137.

12 Ibid., 95.

13 Robinson, *Men Who Wear the Star*, 223.

14 Report, Adjutant General, State of Texas, Fiscal Year Ending August 31, 1878: "The [Guadalupe] salt lakes in question were discovered in 1862 or 1863 by United States troops, while engaged in scouting and there is no evidence to show that any salt was ever taken from them or anything ever known of their existence, prior to that time," TSA, HR-

ED 93 EPT; Statements of Caleb B. Miller 105 and Ward B. Blanchard, 69; Leon Metz, "Gunfighters of the Old West—Texas Posse Stuns New Mexican Wagon Train in Opening Round of 'Magoffin's Salt War,'" *El Paso Times*, February 17, 1974; J. Morgan Broaddus, *The Legal Heritage of El Paso*, 58.

15   Alexander, *Desert Desperadoes*, 97; Paul Cool, *Salt Warriors: Insurgency on the Rio Grande,* suggests that eight *salineros* were either killed or seriously wounded, 13; Broaddus, *The Legal Heritage of El Paso* makes no mention of anyone being killed, and the author's enumeration of the criminal cases filed by New Mexican authorities does not include a charge for Murder, 57–58.

16   HR-ED 93 EPT, Statement of Sheriff Charles Kerber. Refer to Paul Cool's "Salt War Sheriff: El Paso's Charles Kerber," in the January–March 2003 edition of the *National Outlaw/Lawman History Association Quarterly* (NOLA) for a well-documented and well-written biographical profile of Friedrick Sperfechter, aka Charles Kerber.

17   HR-ED 93 EPT, Statement of Albert J. Fountain, 127–29;

18   HR-ED 93 EPT, Statements of Ward B. Blanchard, 69 and Maximo Aranda, 101.

19   Rick Hendricks and W. H. Timmons, *San Elizario: Spanish Presidio to Texas County Seat*: "Cardis saw an opportunity to champion Mexican interests and increase his own political following," 87.

20   Alexander, *Desert Desperadoes*, 99; HR-ED-93 EPT, Statement of G. N. Garcia, 106.

21   HR-ED 93 EPT, Statement of Sheriff Charles Kerber, 118.

22   Sonnichsen, *The El Paso Salt War*, 27.

23   HR-ED 93 EPT, Statements of Juan N. Garcia, 96, Benjamin S. Dowell, 54, and Wesley Owens, 59.

24   *Waco Daily Examiner*, October 16, 1877.

25   C. L. Sonnichsen, *Ten Texas Feuds*, 138.

26   Harris and Sadler, *The Texas Rangers and the Mexican Revolution*, 2.

27   Oath of Office, Frontier Battalion, Company C, El Paso Detachment, TSA.

28   Muster Roll, Frontier Battalion, Company C, El Paso Detachment, TSA.

29   Paul Cool, *Salt Warriors,* 82.

30   Muster Roll, Frontier Battalion, Company C, El Paso Detachment, TSA.

31   Telegram, Major Jones to AG Steele, November 20, 1877, TSA; Owen P. White, *Out of the Desert: The Historical Romance of El Paso*, 106; Alexander, *Desert Desperadoes*, 106.

32   HR-ED 93 EPT, Statement of Vidal Garcia, 73; Jacqueline Meketa, *From Martyrs to Murderers: The Old Southwest's Saints, Sinners, and Scalawags*, 124; Cool, *Salt Warriors*, numerous citations to Atkinson.

33   Sonnichsen, *The El Paso Salt War*, 42

34   HR-ED 93 EPT, Statement of Allen Blacker, Judge, Twentieth Judicial District of Texas, 126.

35   W. W. Mills, *Forty Years at El Paso, 1858–1898*. Mills casts the conflict as a feud, 149.

36   Report, Adjutant General, State of Texas: Fiscal Year Ending August 31, 1878, TSA; Mills, *Forty Years at El Paso:* "some to fight....some to steal...," 157.

37   Sonnichsen, *The El Paso Salt War*, 49–58; Bob Alexander, *Lawmen, Outlaws, and S.O.Bs*, 38.

38   Cool, *Salt Warriors* for "looting everything not tied down," 196.

39   Miller, *Texas Ranger John B. Jones*, 176.

40   Jack Shipman, "The Salt War of San Elizario," *Voice of the Mexican Border*, January 1934, 214; Alexander, *Desert Desperadoes*, 109; Cool, *Salt Warriors*, 166–71.

41   Affidavit and Personnel File [Conrad E. Mortimer] For Texas Peace Officers Killed in the Line of Duty. CLEAT; *Washington Post*, December 21, 1877; Caldwell and DeLord, *Texas Lawmen*, 332–34; Muster Roll, Frontier Battalion, Company C, El Paso Detachment. "C. E. Mortimer.... Killed Dec. 13th 1877," TRHF&M.

42   HR-ED 93 EPT, Statement of Wesley Owens, 59.

43   *Washington Post*, January 5, 1878.

44   Owen P. White, *Lead and Likker*: "The besieged men were guaranteed safety if they surrendered," 36; Caldwell and DeLord, *Texas Lawmen*: "despite guarantees not to harm them," 333.

45   For most histories of the area and time period, the native Spanish-speaking population figures along both banks of the Rio Grande are given as 5,000 on the American side, 7,000 on the Mexican side. Checking the best available primary source estimates, the so-called El Paso Salt War mob measured at the top end about 500, although it sounds much larger when written—which it frequently is—as "half a thousand." If, indeed, these numbers are reasonably correct, the correlation is enlightening. From the twenty-first century armchair ascribing conclusive motives for cultural behavior in the nineteenth-century is at best problematic, but a mathematical accounting does suggest that 95.8% of the native Spanish-speaking population of El Paso's Rio Grande Valley opted to sit out any overt participation—whatsoever— in demonstrating, extorting , rioting, kidnapping, looting, and/or murdering and/or extralegal executions. This factual dynamic would not peel away any veils shielding a deep-rooted and understandable

affirmation of tacit sympathy with their more aggressive brethren, but a sweeping majority of the majority population chose, for one reason or another, not to participate in criminality. Their restraint is laudable.

46   Barkley and Odintz, *The Portable Handbook of Texas*, 309.
47   Amberson, McAllen, and McAllen, *I Would Rather Sleep in Texas*, 316.
48   Miller, *Texas Ranger John B. Jones*, 178.
49   Sonnichsen, *Pass of the North*, 209; HR-ED 93 EPT, Statement of Mary Antonio Cooper, 74.
50   Affidavit and Personnel File [John E. McBride] for Texas Peace Officers Killed in the Line of Duty, CLEAT; Cool, *Salt Warriors*, 196; *Washington Post*, December 21, 1877; Caldwell and DeLord, *Texas Lawmen*, 332–34; Muster Roll, Frontier Battalion, Company C, El Paso Detachment, "J. C. [*sic*] McBride .... Killed Dec. 17, 1877," TRHF&M.
51   Cool, *Salt Warriors*, 196, 211.
52   Sonnichsen, *The El Paso Salt War*, 61.

Chapter 3: Samuel "Sam" Frazier, 1878.

1   Muster Roll, Frontier Battalion, Company C, El Paso Detachment, TRHF&M.
2   HR-ED 93 EPT, Statements of H. O. Matthews, 112 and John W. Hughes, 86.
3   HR-ED 93 EPT, Statement of John K. Ball, 102.
4   Chapters specifically devoted to McDaniels may be found in Alexander's, *Lawmen, Outlaws, & S.O.Bs*, "Adrenaline, Alcohol and Attitude," 29–47, and Paul Cool's "The Many Lives and Suggested Death of Jim McDaniels" in *Revenge! And Other True Tales of the Old West,* 21–39, edited by Sharon Cunningham and Mark Boardman. Most recent mentions of McDaniels may be found in Clifford R. Caldwell's revised 2nd edition, *Dead Right: The Lincoln County War*, check index; Alexander, *Desert Desperadoes* for "as black a picture...," 210, and reference is made to Philip J. Rasch's *Desperadoes of Arizona Territory*, Robert K. DeArment, ed., for a chapter-length analysis of Pony Diehl's life of crime, 33–40. As a sidebar there is in certain quarters spirited argument as to whether Evans' first name is spelled with or without the "i" and such debate is spoken to in the December 2009 edition of *Wild West Magazine*. Fred Nolan champions "Jesse" while the United States Marshal's Service Historian, David S. Turk, cites primary source documents signed by Evans as "Jessie." Likewise Evans' biographers Grady E. McCright and James H. Powell in *Jessie Evans: Lincoln County Badman,* clearly opt for "Jessie." For mentions in this volume Evans will be cited as "Jessie," the most likely correct choice.

5   Muster Roll, Frontier Battalion, Company C, El Paso Detachment.
    TSA.
6   Ibid., TRHF&M.
7   Cool, *Salt Warriors*, 211; Rasch, *The Desperadoes of Arizona Territory*,
    134–41. Rasch makes no mention of Barton being a Texas Ranger
    in his biographical profile; however, the time gap in Rasch's research
    meshes with Barton's dates of service to the State of Texas;
    Scott L. Nelson, "Trailing Jerry Barton," NOLA *Quarterly,* January–
    March 2002, likewise does not identify Jerry Barton as a Texas
    Ranger, but like Rasch, the timeframe wherein Barton's Arizona
    Territory footprints temporarily disappear fits with time spent in the
    Texas Rangers, 36–42.
8   Cool, "J. A. Tays: The Frontier Battalion's Forgotten Officer";
    Alexander, *Desert Desperadoes*, 131–32.
9   Joyce Aros, *The Cochise County Cowboys: Who Were These Men?* 72.
10 Monthly Return, Frontier Battalion, Company C, El Paso Detachment,
    September 1878, TSA; Petition recommending promotion of M.
    Ludwick to the rank of lieutenant for the El Paso detachment of
    Company C, December 17, 1878. McMaster is one of the Ranger signa-
    tories, TSA; Peter Brand, "Sherman W. McMaster(s): The El Paso Salt
    War, Texas Rangers & Tombstone," *Western Outlaw-Lawman History
    Association Journal* (WOLA) Winter 1999; Dan L. Thrapp, *Encyclopedia
    of Frontier Biography*, Vol. 2, 921; Bob Alexander, "Square Deals and
    Real McCoys," WWHA *Journal,* June 2011, 32–52; Steve Gatto, *The
    Real Wyatt Earp*, 174; Casey Tefertiller, *Wyatt Earp: The Life Behind the
    Legend*: "By Wyatt Earp's own admission, he shot a man begging for
    his life," 27; Dave Johnson, *John Ringo, King of the Cowboys: His Life
    and Times From the Hoo Doo War to Tombstone*: "Florentino Cruz was
    shot ten or twelve times, all in the back," 252.
11 Frontier Battalion, Special Order Number 110, TSA.
12 *El Paso Times*, June 25, 1916.
13 Barkley and Odintz, *The Portable Handbook of Texas*, 309.
14 Esther Darbyshire MacCallum, comp., *The History of St. Clement's
    Church, El Paso, Texas, 1870–1925*. 28.
15 *Galveston Daily News*, December 26, 1877.
16 Ibid. January 6, 1878.
17 Sonnichsen, *The El Paso Salt War*, 58.
18 Ward, "The Salt War of San Elizario," 122.
19 Bob Alexander, "Tucker x Texas =Trouble," *Wild West History
    Association Journal* (WWHA) June 2008, 5–16; Bob Alexander,
    Dangerous Dan Tucker: New Mexico's Deadly Lawman; Robert K.
    DeArment, *Deadly Dozen: Twelve Forgotten Gunfighters of the Old West*,
    66–80.

20   Cool, *Salt Warriors*, 214. Unfortunately, in a chronologically jumbled and agenda-driven account, John Kinney is erroneously awarded the position as sheriff of El Paso County, a distinction he never had. See, Andrés Tijerina, "Foreigners in Their Native Land: The Violent Struggle between Anglos and Tejanos for Land Titles in South Texas during Reconstruction," in *Still The Arena of Civil War: Violence and Turmoil in Reconstruction Texas, 1865–1874*, ed. Kenneth W. Howell, 322.

21   Alexander, *Desert Desperadoes*, 117; HR-ED 93 EPT, Statements of Meregildo Montez, Gavino Villaneuva, and Pablo Mejillo, 103.

22   Special Order Number 110, Frontier Battalion, Company C, El Paso Detachment, TSA.

23   Ibid.

24   HR-ED 93 EPT, Statement of J. W. Campbell, 84; Alexander, *Desert Desperadoes*, 114; Cool, "Salt War Sheriff," 26.

25   HR-ED 93 EPT, Statement of Colonel Edward Hatch, 87.

26   HR-ED 93 EPT, Statement of Mariana Nuñez, 84.

27   Ward, "The Salt War of San Elizario," 127.

28   HR-ED 93 EPT, Statement of Charles Kerber, 79

29   *El Paso Times*, August 15, 1931.

30   Alexander, *Desert Desperadoes*, 116–17.

31   Cool, *Salt Warriors*, 233.

32   *Grant County Herald*, January 26, 1878.

33   HR-ED 93 EPT, Minority Report submitted by Major John B. Jones, Frontier Battalion, 22, 28.

34   *Grant County Herald*, January 12, 1878.

35   Cool, "Salt War Sheriff," 26.

36   HR-ED 93 EPT, Statement of H. O. Matthews, 112.

37   Hr-ED 93 EPT, Statement of John K. Ball, 102–3.

38   HR-ED 93 EPT, Statement of H. O. Matthews, 112.

39   HR-ED 93 EPT, Statement of John W. Hughes, 86; Miller, *Texas Ranger John B. Jones*, 181.

40   HR-ED 93 EPT, Statement of John K. Ball, 102.

41   Sonnichsen, *The El Paso Salt War*, 59. The author places Frazier's death on New Year's Day, 1878; however the Muster Roll, Frontier Battalion, Company C, El Paso Detachment is explicit: "Frazier, S. .... Died Jany 31st," TRHF&M.

Chapter 4: George R. "Red" Bingham, 1880.

1   Pecos County Sheriff Harry Ryan to Adjutant General John B. Jones, January 26, 1880, TSA.

2   Clayton W. Williams, *Texas' Last Frontier: Fort Stockton and the Trans-Pecos, 1861–1895*, 253.

3   Ed Bartholomew, *Jesse Evans: A Texas Hide-Burner*, 32.

4   Rasch, *Warriors of Lincoln County*, 33.

5   Clifford Casey, *Mirages, Mysteries and Reality: Brewster County, Texas, the Big Bend of the Rio Grande*, 25.

6   Virginia Madison, *The Big Bend Country of Texas*, 45–46.

7   McCright and Powell, *Jessie Evans: Lincoln County Badman*, 184; Bartholomew, *Jesse Evans*, 33; Chuck Parsons, "An Incident in West Texas: The Jesse Evans Gang and the Death of Texas Ranger George R. Bingham," WOLA *Journal*, Winter 2006, 21.

8   Robert W. Stephens, *Texas Ranger Captain Dan Roberts: The Untold Story*, 174.

9   Monthly Return, Company D, Frontier Battalion, May 1880, TSA.

10 Robert W. Stephens, *Texas Ranger Sketches*, 142; Bob Alexander, *Winchester Warriors: Texas Rangers of Company D, 1874–1901*, 152.

11 Telegram, G. M. Frazer, County Judge, Pecos County to AG Jones, June 3, 1880, TSA,

12 Sergeant L. B. Caruthers, Company E, Frontier Battalion to AG Jones, June 14, 1880, TSA,

13 Sergeant E. A. Sieker, Company D, Frontier Battalion to AG Jones. June 15, 1880, TSA.

14 Telegram, Frazer to Jones, June 16, 1880, TSA.

15 Alexander, *Winchester Warriors*, 155.

16 Sergeant Caruthers to AG Jones, June 14, 1880: "their agent here is Capt Tyson, his real name is John Selman, who I find is Ind. [indicted] in Shackelford Co. I think from what I can learn that he is Chief of the gang and as he was getting very scary, I had him appointed Depty. Sheriff and Jailer as the Jailer had just resigned for fear that if Carr was brought here that the band would attack the jail to rescue him, as they are evidently strong enough to take the jail from any posse that the Sheriff could gather...."

17 Lucy Miller Jacobson and Mildred Bloys Nored, *Jeff Davis County, Texas*: "Caruthers's plans were foiled when 'Old ' Presidio County Sheriff T. A. Wilson got drunk and blabbed the whole story," 99; Madison, *The Big Bend*: "Then the day before the play was to come off, the sheriff went on a bender," 43; Chuck Parsons, "The Jesse Evans Gang and the Death of Texas Ranger George R. Bingham," *Journal of Big Bend Studies* 20, 2008, 83.

18 J. Marvin Hunter, ed., "Texas Rangers on the Border," *Frontier Times*, April 1924, 18; Alexander, *Winchester Warriors*, 157.

19 Cliff Caldwell, "Davy Thomas 'Tom' Carson, Texas Ranger," WWHA *Journal*, June 2009, 44; J. Marvin Hunter, ed., "Texas Rangers Battle With Outlaws in 1880," *Frontier Times*, August 1927: "No better Ranger ever lived than Tom Carson," 1.

20 Parsons, "The Jesse Evans Gang," 76–77.

21 Madison, *The Big Bend*, 44.

22 Sergeant Sieker to AG Jones, June 12, 1880. In point of fact, this is a copy of Sieker's July 8, 1880, report detailing the event, but sent to AG Jones by Captain Dan Roberts, Company D, Frontier Battalion, with notation: "Genl. You may have received this report ere this, but I send it anyway," TSA. Interested readers may also find a copy of this report in the August 1927 edition of *Frontier Times*; also reprinted in Jacobson and Nored, *Jeff Davis County, Texas*, 99–100.

23 Ibid.; Affidavit and Personnel File [George R. Bingham] For Texas Peace Officers Killed in the Line of Duty, CLEAT; Monthly Return, Company D, Frontier Battalion, July 1880, TSA.

24 Ibid., Recapitulation of Arrests: "Jesse Evans, Chas' Graham, John Gross—Robbery—Presidio County—Lodged in Jail at Ft. Davis," TSA.

25 Sergeant Sieker to AG Jones, June 12, 1880, TSA.

26 Ibid.

27 Parsons, "The Jesse Evans Gang," 85.

28 Sergeant Sieker to AG Jones, June 12, 1880, TSA.

29 Dan W. Roberts, *Rangers and Sovereignty*, 114.

30 Telegram, Captain Neal Coldwell to AG Jones, July 7, 1880, TRHF&M.

31 Parsons, "The Jesse Evans Gang," 86.

32 Telegram, Captain Coldwell to AG Jones, July 7, 1880, TRHF&M.

Chapter 5: Frank Sieker, 1885.

1 Stephens, *Texas Ranger Sketches*, 142–47.

2 Ibid.

3 Monthly Return, Company D, Frontier Battalion, September 1884, TSA.

4 Gournay, *Texas Boundaries*, 71, 107.

5 Monthly Return, Company D, Frontier Battalion, December 1884, TSA.

6 Monthly Return, Company D, Frontier Battalion, January 1885, TSA.

7 Ibid.

8 Monthly Return, Company D, Frontier Battalion, February 1885, TSA.

9 Captain L. P. Sieker to Adjutant General William King, February 28, 1885, TSA.

10   Ira Aten to J. Evetts Haley, February 1928, 59, Haley Memorial
     Library and History Center, Midland, Texas. Hereafter HML&HC.
11   Alexander, *Rawhide Ranger*, 58.
12   Alexander, *Winchester Warriors*, 202.
13   Adolph Petree to J. Evetts Haley, July 26–27, 1941, HML&HC.
14   Captain Sieker to AG King, February 13 and 20, 1885, TSA.
15   Monthly Return, Company D, Frontier Battalion, March 1885, TSA.
16   Lieutenant Frank Jones' supplemental report for Monthly Return,
     Company D, Frontier Battalion, November 1884, TSA.
17   Captain Sieker to AG King, May 31, 1885, TSA.
18   Aten to Haley, 1928, 52, HML&HC.
19   Ira Aten to J. Evetts Haley, Earl Vandale, and Hervey Chesley, July
     1941, 28, HML&HC.
20   Ibid.
21   Alexander, *Rawhide Ranger*, 76; Aten to Haley, 1928, 53, HML&HC;
     Aten to Haley, Vandale, and Chesley, 1941, 28, HML&HC.
22   Affidavit and Personnel File [Frank E. Sieker] For Texas Peace Officers
     Killed in the Line of Duty, CLEAT; Monthly Return, Company D,
     Frontier Battalion, June 1885, TSA.
23   Aten to Haley, 1928, 53, HML&HC.
24   Sergeant Lindsey to Captain Sieker, July 10, 1885, TSA.
25   *El Paso Daily Times*, June 4, 1885.
26   *Dallas Daily Herald*, June 3, 1885.
27   *Corpus Christi Caller*, June 7, 1885.
28   Aten to Haley, Vandale, and Chesley, 1941, 42, HML&HC.
29   Unidentified newspaper clip titled "Webb County Grand Jury,"
     HML&HC; Darren L. Ivey, *The Texas Rangers: A Registry and History*
     asserts that the shooting actually took place in Maverick County,
     243. Admittedly the incident occurred close to county lines, but it
     was a Webb County grand jury that returned indictments against the
     Rangers.
30   *Galveston Daily News*, June 19, 1885, a story picked up from the *San
     Antonio Daily Express*.
31   Ibid.
32   Sergeant Lindsey to Captain Sieker, July 10, 1885, TSA.
33   Ibid.
34   Aten to Haley, 1928, 58–59, HML&HC.
35   AG King to Captain Sieker, July 22, 1885, TSA.
36   Aten to Haley, Vandale, & Chesley, 1941, 33, HML&HC.
37   *El Paso Times*, June 4, 1885; Utley, *Lone Star Justice*. The author dis-
     cusses the two opposing perspectives, 245.

Chapter 6: Charley Fusselman, 1890.

1 Robert W. Stephens, *Bullets and Buckshot in Texas*, 172,
2 Awbrey and Dooley, *Why Stop?* 356.
3 Chuck Parsons, "Charles H, Fusselman," *Texas Ranger Dispatch*, Summer 2004.
4 Monthly Return, Company D, Frontier Battalion, May 1888, TSA.
5 Gournay, *Texas Boundaries*, 108.
6 Captain Frank Jones to AG King, May 21, 1889, TSA; Robert W. Stephens, *Walter Durbin: Texas Ranger and Sheriff*, 77; Alexander, *Winchester Warriors*, 224.
7 Tise, *Texas County Sheriffs*, 65.
8 Corporal Charles Fusselman to AG King, June 5, 1889, TSA.
9 Inquest Finding: Death of Donaciano Beslanga, Executed by Justice of the Peace J. R. Dawson, Precinct 1, Brewster County, Texas, written on letterhead of Sheriff J. T. Gillespie, TSA.
10 For discussion of Ranger policy regarding involuntary assignment of undercover roles, see Alexander's *Rawhide Ranger*, 108.
11 Corporal Fusselman to Captain Sieker, July 3, 1889, TSA.
12 U.S. Marshal Paul Fricke, San Antonio, to AG King, Austin, December 12, 1889, TSA; Robert Ernst, *Deadly Affrays: The Violent Deaths of the US Marshals,* reports that Fusselman also carried commission as a Presidio County deputy sheriff, 97. For further discussion of U.S. Marshals and the policy of cross-deputation with local or state peace officers, the reader is referred to Larry D. Ball's *The United States Marshals of New Mexico and Arizona Territories, 1846–1912*, and *Desert Lawmen: The High Sheriffs of New Mexico and Arizona 1846–1912.* Though specifically focused on New Mexico and Arizona, this practice was applicable in Texas also.
13 Captain Jones to AG King, December 16, 1889, TSA.
14 Alexander, *Rawhide Ranger*, 206–7.
15 Stephens, *Bullets and Buckshot*, 172
16 Sergeant Fusselman's enforcement activity as Company D's 1st Sergeant may be examined by review of Monthly Returns, August 1889 thru April 1890, and Ranger Correspondence Files for the same period, TSA.
17 U.S. Marshal Fricke to AG King, July 3, 1889, TSA; *The National Police Gazette*, May 3, 1890, "during his [Fusselman's] career as a ranger, made many notable arrests and done good service towards breaking up the lawless bands of horse thieves and desperadoes in the Lone Star State."

18   An unidentified newspaper clip suggests, "Chas. H. Fusselman, com-
     mander of the Presidio county rangers, who was in the city in atten-
     dance on the U. S. court...," TRHF&M.

19   Ibid.; *El Paso Times*, April 18, 1890.

20   Rick Miller, *Sam Bass and Gang*, 373.

21   Unidentified newspaper clip, TRHF&M

22   *El Paso Times*, April, 18, 1890; *Arizona Daily Star*, April 17, 1890.

23   Antonio Croce, "In The Line of Duty," *The Texas Gun Collector*, Fall
     1996, 13; Bob Alexander, *Fearless Dave Allison: Border Lawman*, 44.

24   *El Paso Times*, April 19, 1890.

25   Unidentified newspaper clip, TRHF&M.

26   Affidavit and Personnel File [Charles Henry Vanvalkenburg
     Fusselman] For Texas Peace Officers Killed in the Line of Duty, CLEAT.

27   *El Paso Times*, April 19, 1890.

28   Unidentified newspaper clip; thought to be *El Paso Times*, TRHF&M.

29   *San Antonio Daily Express*, April 19, 1890.

30   Captain Frank Jones to AG King, April 19, 1890; Ranger John R.
     Hughes to Captain L. P. Sieker, April 18, 1890; Captain Frank Jones to
     Captain L. P. Sieker, April 22, 1890, TRHF&M.

31   Telegram, Captain Jones to Ranger John R, Hughes, TSA.

32   Ernst, *Deadly Affrays*, 98; Karen Holliday Tanner and John D. Tanner,
     Jr., *Directory of Inmates: New Mexico Territorial Penitentiary (1884–
     1912)*, 37, 53.

33   *El Paso Times*, September 26, 1965; *Sundial Magazine*, Byline, Joe
     Parrish, "Ranger Killed in Gun Battle Gave Fusselman Canyon Name."
     On May 3, 2003, Fusselman Canyon was officially recognized with
     placement of a Texas Historical Marker; see *Fussleman Canyon Texas
     Historical Marker Dedication Program*, TRHF&M.

34   Ibid.

35   *San Antonio Daily Times*, April 19, 1890.

36   Captain Frank Jones to AG King, May 2, 1890, TRHF&M.

37   Ranger John R. Hughes to M. A Dolan, May 17, 1890, TSA.

38   Unidentifed newspaper clip, TRHF&M; *Dallas Morning News*, April 20,
     1890.

39   *El Paso Times*, April 29, 1890.

40   Stephens, *Bullets and Buckshot in Texas*, 175.

41   Douglas V. Meed, "Daggers on the Gallows: The Revenge of Texas
     Ranger Captain 'Boss' Hughes," *True West*, May 1999; Alexander,
     Winchester Warriors, 301–3; Caldwell and DeLord, *Texas Lawmen*,
     347–48; Chuck Parsons, *Lone Star Ranger: Captain John R. Hughes*,
     162–66.

Chapter 7: John F. Gravis, 1890.

1 Gournay, *Texas Boundaries*, 61.
2 T. Lindsay Baker, *Ghost Towns of Texas*, 134–36.
3 Henry E. McCulloch to Governor L. S. Ross, October 27, 1889: "the men are paid off at the end of the Month, and most of them spend their money here [Shafter]. Consequently it is a place where gamblers, roughs and lewd women routinely congregate...," TSA.
4 Captain Frank Jones to Captain L. P. Sieker, October 28, 1890, TSA.
5 Ranger John R. Hughes to Captain L. P. Sieker, April 18, 1890, TSA.
6 Private Calvin G. Aten to Captain L. P. Sieker, April 22, 1890, TSA.
7 Corporal C. H. Fusselman to Captain L.P.Sieker, July 20, 1889, TSA.
8 Captain Frank Jones to AG William King, June 30, 1890, TSA.
9 Sergeant Fusselman to AG King and/or Captain L. P. Sieker, November 16, 1889, TSA; Sergeant Fusselman to Captain Sieker, February 2, 1890, TSA.
10 Descriptive List, John F. Gravis, Private, Company F, Frontier Battalion, February 24, 1890, Encinal, Texas, TSA. The fact that the Descriptive List, for the space captioned "Enlisted Where" is significant; it is specifically filled in, "Encinal Texas" rather than Encinal County, which had been formed from present day Webb County in 1856 but never organized, and abolished on March 12, 1899, a timeframe applicable to the date of Gravis' enlistment with the Rangers; see, Gournay, *Texas Boundaries*, 74. Confirming that he swore his oath at Encinal, Texas, is the signature of W. S. Cobb, Ex-Officio J. P., La Salle County, Texas; Paul N. Spellman, *Captain J. A. Brooks, Texas Ranger*, 70.
11 Alexander, *Winchester Warriors*, 232; Monthly Return, Company D, Frontier Battalion, March 1890, TSA.
12 Although it is not conclusive, an examination of Company F Monthly Returns for February, March, and April 1890 do not identify Gravis by name. His transfer into Company D is duly noted in the Monthly Return for May 1892, TSA .
13 Ed Blackburn, Jr., *Wanted: Historic County Jails of Texas*, 206.
14 William Warren Sterling, *Trails and Trials of a Texas Ranger*, 307; Spellman, *Captain J. A. Brooks,* 32.
15 Monthly Return, Company D, Frontier Battalion, April 1890, TSA.
16 Monthly Return, Company D, Frontier Battalion, May 1890, TSA.
17 Monthly Return, Company D, Frontier Battalion, June 1890, TSA.
18 Ibid.
19 Petition from citizens of Presidio County requesting deployment of Texas Rangers to Shafter, TSA.

20 Sergeant C. H. Fusselman to Captain L. P. Sieker, November 29, 1889, TSA.
21 McCullogh to Governor Ross, October 27, 1889, TSA.
22 Casey, *The Texas Border and Some Borderliners*, 298. The reader will have to accept or reject this version at face value as the author provides no source citations. It should be noted, however, that a later newspaper edition makes reference to the "lynching of a Mexican" as being the cause of the subsequent street fight.
23 Report of the Adjutant General: State of Texas, 1889–1890, TSA.
24 Parsons, *Captain John R. Hughes*, 283.
25 Monthly Returns, Company D, Frontier Battalion, May 1887; October 1889; January 1890, TSA.
26 Casey, *The Texas Border and Some Borderliners*, 298.
27 Descriptive List. John F. Gravis. February 24, 1890, TSA.
28 Petition of James Walker, and others, to Governor Ross, May 3, 1890, TSA.
29 Wilkens, *The Law Comes to Texas*, 294.
30 Affidavit and Personnel File [John F. Gravis] For Texas Peace Officers Killed in the Line of Duty, CLEAT; Monthly Return, Company D, Frontier Battalion, August 1890; "J. F. Gravis Killed in Action Aug. 4th 1890," TSA.
31 *Galveston Daily News*, August 5, 1890.
32 *El Paso Times*, August 6, 1890.
33 *Brooklyn Daily Eagle*, August 5, 1890.
34 Casey, *The Texas Border and Some Borderliners*, 299.
35 Report of Adjutant General: State of Texas 1889–1890, 25, TSA.
36 *Luling Signal*, August 7, 1890.
37 Captain Jones to Captain Sieker, August 9, 1890, TSA.
38 Monthly Return, Company D, Frontier Battalion, August 1890, TSA; Parsons, *Captain John R. Hughes*, 64.
39 Ibid.
40 *Dallas Morning News*, September 27, 1890.

Chapter 8: Robert E. Doaty, 1892.

1 Affidavit and Personnel File [R. E. Doaty] For Peace Officers Killed in the Line of Duty, CLEAT. An instructional notation is a permanent part of the file: "There is name confusion in this case. The Texas Ranger enlistment reports his name as Robert E. Doaty as does the Texas Ranger Hall of Fame and Museum. Historians report his name as E. E. or Robert Doaty. Contemporary newspaper accounts and the 1880 census report his name as Robert Doughty. While his real name is probably Doughty, he enlisted as Doaty and that is how he should be

listed on the memorial." And, for this narrative, the name Doaty will be used in deference to the name inscribed on memorials.

2   *Dallas Morning News*, March 25, 1892.

3   Federal Census, 1880, San Diego, Duval County, Texas.

4   *Dallas Morning News*, March 25, 1892.

5   Paul N. Spellman, *Captain John Rogers, Texas Ranger*, 68; Elliott Young, *Catarino Garza's Revolution on the Texas-Mexican Border*, 42–43. Spellman and Young are at odds regarding Garza's attainment of the Mexican Counsel position at St. Louis; De León, *They Called Them Greasers*, 60.

6   Ibid.; Cox, *Wearing the Cinco Peso*, 342.

7   Captain Jones to AG King, December 9, 1887, TSA.

8   Captain Jones to AG King, May 19, 1888, TSA; Monthly Return, Company D, Frontier Battalion, May 1888. The notation is clear: Dillard killed Abraham Recéndez, TSA; Alexander, *Winchester Warriors*, 354, n. 42.

9   Ibid.: "District Court is in session in Starr County and the matter will be fully investigated. I am confident that Dillard will be exonerated."

10 Cox, *Wearing the Cinco Peso*, 342.

11 Alexander, *Winchester Warriors*, 221–22; Charles M. Robinson, *Frontier Forts of Texas*: "The reservation was purchased and declared, and the post, which up until now [1867] had been Ringgold Barracks, received the permanent designation of 'fort,'" 28.

12 Cox, *Wearing the Cinco Peso*, 343; Parsons, *Captain John R. Hughes*, 43. Interestingly it was Ranger Private John Hughes who made the arrest, and not surprisingly in light of the brewing tempest, it was not an example of solo police work. Hughes had a Texas Ranger helpmate. See, Monthly Return, Company D, Frontier Battalion, August 1888. "Aug 19—Prvt Hughes and one man arrested C. E. Garza in Realitos wanted in Starr County for Criminal libel…," TSA.

13 Stephens, *Walter Durbin: Texas Ranger and Sheriff*, 69.

14 Utley, *Lone Star Justice*, 255; Louis Ray Sadler to author April 21, 2012: "the Federal Records Center in Fort Worth has 600 case files/indictments of Catarino Garza supporters"; as would be expected, Elliott Young's psychosexual dissections applied within a framework of differentiating between ethnicities, cultures, and/or work assignments as highlighted on pages 47 and 237 in *Catarino Garza's Revolution* are impotent, rather than compelling.

15 *Dallas Morning News*, March 25, 1892.

16 *The Knoxville Journal*, January 3, 1892.

17 *Dallas Morning News*, February 2, 1892.

18 Cox, *Wearing the Cinco Peso*, 352–53.

19 Caldwell and DeLord, *Texas Lawmen*, 386–87.

20   Interview with Ron DeLord by author, September 25, 2011; Gravis' family genealogical records; Charles H. Harris III, Frances E. Harris, and Louis R. Sadler, *Texas Ranger Biographies: Those Who Served, 1910–1921*, 130–31.

21   *Dallas Times Herald*, March 24, 1892.

22   State of Texas: Certificate of Pay, Frontier Battalion. "R. E. Doaty, mustered into the State Service on the 1st day of March 1892," TSA.

23   *Dallas Morning News*, February 2, 1892.

24   *Dallas Times Herald*, March 24, 1892.

25   *Dallas Morning News*, March 25, 1892.

26   Ibid.

27   DeLord, *The Ultimate Sacrifice*, 63

28   *Dallas Times Herald*, March 24, 1892. Looking at a current Texas state map one might legitimately wonder how Ranger Bob Doaty's sketch fits within the predesigned parameters of this work. After noting that Brooks and Jim Hogg Counties were twentieth-century creations, 1912 and 1913 respectively, it is clear that the northern edge of Starr County bordered the southern boundary of Duval County in 1892. The newspaper citation, as quoted, made reference to the fight taking place "on the line of this [Duval] and Starr counties." See, Gournay, *Texas Boundaries*, 117, 119.

29   *Dallas Morning News*, March 24, 1892.

30   *Omaha World Herald*, March 24, 1892; Caldwell and DeLord, *Texas Lawmen*, 349.

31   *Dallas Morning News*, April 7, 1892. In the newspaper account Will Shely correctly identifies the deceased Ranger as Doughty; likewise, Cox, *Wearing the Cinco Peso* makes a proper identification, 353, as does Elliott Young, *Catarino Garza's Revolution*, 183.

32   *Dallas Times Herald*, March 24, 1892.

33   Louis Ray Sadler to author April 21, 2012. "There is a tantalizing interview by a federal agent in South Texas in the second decade of the 20th century of an individual purporting to be Garza."

34   State of Texas: Certificate of Pay, Signed, "Mrs. Frank C. Gravis, $22," TSA.

Chapter 9: Frank Jones, 1893.

1   Petition of El Paso County Grand Jury to Governor James S. Hogg, January 31, 1893, TSA.

2   Sheriff F. B. Simmons, El Paso County, to AG Mabry, February 1, 1893, TSA.

3   George W. Baylor to AG Mabry, February 15, 1893, TSA.

4   Candice DuCoin, *Lawmen on the Texas Frontier: Rangers and Sheriffs*, 124.
5   Ibid.; Tom Bailey and Ralph J. Weaver, "The Nine Lives of Captain Frank Jones," *Frontier Times*, Spring 1960, 38.
6   Captain Jones to AG Mabry, January 25, 1893; Jones to Mabry, June 2, 1893, TSA.
7   Captain Jones to AG Mabry, April 16, 1893, TSA.
8   Captain Jones to AG Mabry, June 11, 1893, TSA; Alexander, *Winchester Warriors*, 256.
9   Ibid.; Captain Jones to AG Mabry, December 20, 1892. "If you have no objection I would like to visit Austin about the 6th of January on some business connected with my candidacy for the Marshal's office. I am very anxious to meet some parties who will be in Austin when the Legislature convenes," TSA. The position of United States Marshal was given to former Ranger and ex-sheriff of Mitchell County (Colorado City) Richard Clayton "Dick" Ware.
10 Captain Jones to AG Mabry, June 2, 1893, TSA.
11 Captain Jones to AG Mabry, April 16, 1893, TSA.
12 Captain Jones to AG Mabry, February 17, 1893, TSA.
13 A recap of at least three of Jones' gunplay involvements may be complied from these sources: DuCoin, *Lawmen on the Texas Frontier*: "Frank and four other privates scoured the countryside throughout the night in search of him. After a shootout and running him into the river, [Jim] Goodman decided surrendering was a favorable alternative to the freezing temperature of the water," 114; Alexander, *Winchester Warriors*: "Then in Frank Jones own words, the outlaw 'caught for a pistol he had in his pants and wheeled his horse and ran. We killed the horse and it thought fatally wounded the man [G. C. Neeley],'" 215. For Jones' participation in chasing train robbers and the resultant fight, see, Jeffrey Burton's seminal study *The Deadliest Outlaws: The Ketchum Gang and the Wild Bunch*, 71–72. Also Alexander's, *Lawmen, Outlaws, and S.O.Bs*, 10–28, as well as Frank W. Doughtery's "Las Vegas de los Ladrones and the Flynt Gang," *Journal of Big Bend Studies*, 1991. Furthermore there is a fascinating written account by one of the players, Joe Sitter. Refer to "Joe Sitter's Account of the Trailing and Capture of the Train Robbers," statement of Joe Sitter as recorded by Harry Warren. Harry Warren Papers, Archives of the Big Bend (ABB), Sul Ross University, Alpine, Texas.
14 Captain John Hughes to AG Mabry, September 6, 1893, TSA.
15 Stephens, *Texas Ranger Sketches*, 68.
16 George Wythe Baylor, *Into the Far, Wild Country: True Tales of the Old Southwest*, ed. Jerry D. Thompson, 30.

17   George Baylor to AG Mabry, July 9, 1893, TSA; Parsons, *Captain John
      R. Hughes*, 82.

18   Ibid.; Captain John R. Hughes to AG Mabry, September 4, 1893, TSA.

19   Stephens, *Texas Ranger Sketches*, 33. Occasionally writers neglect to
      award Ed Bryant status as a Texas Ranger during this scout, assert-
      ing that he was an El Paso County deputy sheriff. True the possibil-
      ity exists that he was dually commissioned at the time, but author
      Stephens is blunt: "In 1892 Bryant became a Deputy Sheriff in El
      Paso County but again became a Ranger on June 23, 1893, when he
      enlisted in Captain Frank Jones's Company D at Ysleta"; Monthly
      Return, Company D, Frontier Battalion, June 1893, supports
      Stephen's aver somewhat, the enlistment with Company D actually
      taking place on June 26, 1893, three days before the scout to Pirate
      Island began, TSA.

20   George Baylor to AG Mabry, July 9, 1893, TSA.

21   Ibid.

22   Ibid.; Monthly Return. Company D, Frontier Battalion, June 1893,
      TSA; Douglas, *The Gentlemen in the White Hats*, 150.

23   Ibid.; Affidavit and Personnel File [Frank Jones] For Texas Peace
      Officers Killed in the Line of Duty, CLEAT; The direct quotation attrib-
      uted to Jones may also be found in the Company D Monthly Return
      for June 1893, TSA.

24   Corporal Carl Kirchner to AG Mabry, July 2, 1893, TSA.

25   George Baylor to AG Mabry, July 9, 1893, TSA.

26   Telegram, Corporal Kirchner to AG Mabry, June 30, 1893, TSA.

27   Corporal Kirchner to AG Mabry, July 2, 1893, TSA.

28   Frank B. Simmons, Sheriff, El Paso County, to Governor James S.
      Hogg, July 7, 1893, TSA. Touching on the near systemic Mexican
      problem of corruptible lawmen, Andres Oppenheimer in *Bordering
      on Chaos: Mexico's Roller-Coaster Journey Toward Prosperity* reiterates
      an all-too-familiar tall story: "If you get mugged on the street, don't
      yell: You may attract the police!" 305. Also see, Gary Cartwright, *Dirty
      Dealing: Drug Smuggling on the Mexican Border and the Assassination
      of a Federal Judge*: "out of that money they are expected to bribe the
      various Mexican customs officials, who survive on bribes, or *la mordida*
      ('the bite')." 13.

29   Telegram, Corporal Kirchner to AG Mabry, July 1, 1893, TSA.

30   Corporal Kirchner to AG Mabry, July 2, 1893. Appropriately C. L.
      Sonnichsen in *Pass of the North: Four Centuries on the Rio Grande*,
      awards the proper credit to Sheriff Simmons for the recovery of Frank
      Jones' body, 315. Interestingly, after leaving the Ranger service Carl
      Kirchner operated the Silver King Saloon, and after purchasing an
      interest in the El Paso bottling plant was nicknamed the "Coca Cola

Cowboy." See the insightful work of Martha Deen Underwood and Hamilton Underwood in *Concordia Cemetery, El Paso: A Walking Tour*, 22.

31 As of this writing (2012) Frank Jones' pocket watch, badge, and rifle are a part of the Donald and Louise Yena collection, San Antonio, Texas, and are currently being exhibited at the TRHF&M, Waco, Texas.

32 James A. Browning, *Violence Was No Stranger: A Guide to the Grave Sites of Famous Westerners*, 125.

33 Corporal Kirchner to AG Mabry, July 2, 1893, TSA.

34 Governor J. S. Hogg to AG Mabry, August 22, 1893, TSA.

35 Frontier Battalion, Special Order No. 105; Captain John R. Hughes, Company D, Frontier Battalion, to AG Mabry, July 8, 1893, TSA.

36 Captain Hughes to AG Mabry, July 26, 1893, TSA.

37 Special Ranger Ernest St. Leon, to AG Mabry, July 1, 1893, TSA.

38 John L. Davis, *The Texas Rangers; Their First 150 Years*, 76.

39 *El Paso Herald*, September 1, 1898.

40 Douglas' *The Gentlemen in the White Hats* was first published in 1934, while Webb's *The Texas Rangers: A Century of Frontier Defense* came out the following year. Douglas carries the summary execution story forward; Webb omits it altogether.

41 Parsons, *Captain John R. Hughes*, quoting the *El Paso Herald-Post* of May 13, 1938, 95.

42 Clifford Alan Perkins, *Border Patrol, With the U.S. Immigration Service on the Mexican Boundary 1910–1954*, 42.

43 Utley, *Lone Star Justice*, 342, n.33.

44 Captain Jones to AG Mabry, August 25, 1893.

45 AG Mabry to Captain Hughes, August 16, 1893; AG Mabry to Ernest St. Leon, August 22, 1893; Certification of Pay, Ernest St. Leon from September 1, 1893 thru April 1894; Appraisement of Horses, Company D, September 6, 1893; Monthly Returns, Company D, Frontier Battalion, September 1893 thru February 1894, TSA.

46 Captain Jones to AG Mabry, July 26, 1893, TSA. Noteworthy is the fact that this is just four days before he enlisted Ernest St. Leon as a private in Company D.

47 *El Paso Herald*, September 1, 1898.

Chapter 10: Joseph McKidrict, 1894.

1 Captain Hughes to AG Mabry, January 14, 1894, TSA; Hughes to Mabry, January, 26, 1894, TSA. Not surprisingly the mishap is not mentioned in *Texas Ranger's Diary and Scrapbook*, edited by Ann Jensen, nor is it highlighted in *The Rest of the Diary and Scrapbook of Alonzo Van Oden*, edited by George L. "Jack" Richards, his grandson.

2 Captain Hughes to AG Thomas Scurry, March 14, 1901: "I had bought me a new pistol 38 cal Smith& Wesson that has a safety notch in the hammer and I thought it was perfectly safe to carry all six chambers loaded but last night I went to buckle it on and it slipped out of the scabbard and the hammer hit the floor and shot me through the right foot from the inside," TSA; Alexander, *Winchester Warriors*, 309–11.

3 Stephens, *Texas Ranger Sketches*, 91; *El Paso Daily Times*, April 8, 1894.

4 Parsons, *Captain John R. Hughes*, 283.

5 Monthly Return, Company D, Frontier Battalion, July 1893, TSA; Caldwell and DeLord, *Texas Lawmen*, 353.

6 Monthly Return, Company D, Frontier Battalion, August 1893, TSA.

7 Ibid.

8 Alexander, *Winchester Warriors*, 269–70; Captain Hughes to AG Mabry, August 25, 1893, TSA; Captain Hughes to Captain G. A. Wheatly, November 4 and 12, 1893, TSA. Quite interestingly, Lon Oden, in *Texas Ranger's Diary and Scrapbook* avers that the person killed by Private Fulgan [*sic*] was J. R. Burris rather than Charles Carroll, 64.

9 Monthly Return, Company D, Frontier Battalion, October 1893, TSA.

10 Monthly Return, Company D, Frontier Battalion, November 1893, TSA.

11 Captain Hughes to AG Mabry, December 1, 9, 31, 1893, TSA. For an insightful profile of Frank McMahan, see Doug Dukes' "Frank McMahan: In Custody," WWHA *Journal*, August 2009, 36–39.

12 Monthly Return, Company D, Frontier Battalion, January 1893, TSA.

13 Robert K. DeArment, *George Scarborough: The Life and Death of a Lawman on the Closing Frontier*, 61; Leon Claire Metz, *John Wesley Hardin: Dark Angel of Texas*, 222; Richard C. Marohn, *The Last Gunfighter: John Wesley Hardin*, 214–15; Bob Alexander, *John H. Behan: Sacrificed Sheriff*, 236.

14 *El Paso Daily Times*, April 6, 1894.

15 Leon Claire Metz, *John Selman: Texas Gunfighter*, 131.

16 *El Paso Daily Times*, April 7, 1894.

17 Alexander, *Winchester Warriors*, 253.

18 Walter Durbin manuscript, copy in author's possession courtesy Robert W. Stephens.

19 Oden, *Texas Ranger's Diary and Scrapbook*, 40.

20 Ibid., 10.

21 *El Paso Daily Times*, April 6, 1894.

22 H. Gordon Frost, *The Gentlemen's Club: The Story of Prostitution in El Paso*, 72.

23 Captain Hughes to AG Mabry, April 6, 1894, TSA.

24 Metz, *John Selman*, 147.

25 Captain Hughes to AG Mabry, April 6, 1894, TSA; Frank Collinson, *Life in the Saddle*, ed. Mary Whatley Clarke, 98–99; Ed Bartholomew, *The Biographical Album of Western Gunfightrers*, Alphabetical listings.

26 *El Paso Daily Times*, April 6, 1894; *Austin Daily Statesman*, April 6, 1894.

27 Affidavit and Personnel File [Joseph W. McKidrict] For Texas Peace Officers Killed in the Line of Duty, CLEAT; Monthly Return, Company D, Frontier Battalion, April 1894, TSA.

28 *El Paso Daily Times*, April 6, 1894; Eugene Cunningham, "Bass Outlaw," *Frontier Times*, January 1928, 145–46.

29 Alexander, *Winchester Warriors*, 276; Telegram, Captain Hughes to AG Mabry, April 6, 1894, TSA.

30 Captain E. B. Outlaw to AG Mabry, April 16, 1894, TSA.

31 Interview with Dr. Deen Underwood, October 11, 2011.

32 Metz, *John Wesley Hardin*.

33 DeArment, *George A. Scarborough*.

34 Captain Hughes to Captain G. A. Wheatley, May 12, 1894, TSA; *El Paso Daily Times*, April 8, 1894.

35 James A. Browning, *Violence Was No Stranger*, Volume 2, 79.

Chapter 11: Ernest St. Leon, 1898

1 *San Antonio Daily News*, September 1, 1898; Stephens, *Texas Ranger Sketches*, 147–48. Confusion abounds regarding St. Leon's date and place of birth. Some chroniclers cite 1859 for the DOB, and variously list his POB as Canada or France. For the purposes of this narrative primary source documents, executed by Ernest St. Leon himself, will be utilized. In two separate applications for the position of Special Texas Ranger, one in 1892, the other in 1894, Ernest states he was born in San Antonio, Texas, and reported his ages at the time as 24 and 28 years, respectively, TRHF&M.

2 Ibid.; *El Paso Daily Times*, September 1, 1898.

3 Ibid.

4 Monthly Return, Company D, Frontier Battalion, September 1890, TSA; Certificate of Pay, Ernest St. Leon, September 1, 1890 thru November 30, 1890, TSA; physical description taken from latter application for the position of Special Ranger, TRHF&M. A report in the *Galveston Daily News*, September 1, 1898, suggests St. Leon served as a Texas Ranger ten years earlier under "Colonel Baylor's company of rangers...." A check of Texas Ranger records archived at Austin does not support a contention that St. Leon served under Baylor: Donaly Brice, TSA, to author, October 12, 2011.

5 *Los Angles Times*, August 31, 1898.

6   *El Paso Daily Times*, September 1, 1898.
7   State of Texas Certificate of Death, Maria de Jesus Ornellas de St. Leon. That Mrs. St. Leon was illiterate is evidenced by her "X" as signature on official Texas Ranger documents, TRHF&M.
8   Captain Jones to John F. Camps, June 28, 1891, TSA.
9   Monthly Return, Company D, Frontier Battalion, January 1891, TSA; Alexander, *Winchester Warriors*, 241.
10   Captain Jones to AG Mabry, June 26, 1891; Monthly Return, Company D, Frontier Battalion, June 1891, TSA.
11   Leon Claire Metz, *The Encyclopedia of Lawmen, Outlaws, and Gunfighters*, 233–34; *Los Angeles Times*, August 31, 1898; *El Paso Daily Times*, September 1, 1898.
12   Monthly Return, Company D, Frontier Battalion, January 1892: "Matilde Carrasco, Jose Villeto, and Quinlino Chaves—Killed while resisting arrest," TSA; Dane Coolidge, *Fighting Men of the West*, 147.
13   Captain Jones to AG Mabry, January 15, 1892, TSA.
14   *Los Angles Times*, July 3, 1892.
15   Corporal Hughes to AG Mabry, January 15, 1892, TSA.
16   Captain Jones to AG Mabry, March 9, 1892, TSA.
17   Coolidge, *Fighting Men of the West*, 144; Alexander, *Winchester Warriors*, 257.
18   Special Ranger St. Leon to AG Mabry, September 16, 1892, TSA.
19   Special Ranger St. Leon to AG Mabry, July 1, 1893, TSA.
20   Alexander, *Winchester Warriors*, 266–69.
21   Monthly Returns, Company D, Frontier Battalion, January and February 1894; Official Appraisal and Description of Company D Rangers' horses, TSA.
22   Captain Hughes to AG Mabry, April 30 and May 23, 1894, TSA; Monthly Returns, Company D, Frontier Battalion, May and July 1894, TSA; *El Paso Daily Times*, September 1, 1898.
23   Captain Hughes to AG Mabry, September 10, 1894, TSA.
24   Application for Position as Special Ranger, May 1, 1896, Ernest St. Leon, TSA.
25   Monthly Returns, Company D, Frontier Battalion, May, June, and July 1897, TSA.
26   Monthly Return, Company D, Frontier Battalion, October 1897, TSA.
27   Monthly Returns, Company D, Frontier Battalion, November and December 1897, TSA.
28   Monthly Returns, Company D, Frontier Battalion, January and February 1898, TSA.
29   Monthly Return, Company D, Frontier Battalion, January 1898, TSA.

30   Captain Hughes to Adjutant General A. P. Wozencraft, August 31, 1898, TSA; *El Paso Daily Times*, August 31, 1898; *Galveston Daily News*, August 31, 1898.

31   Alexander, *Winchester Warriors*, 298–301; *El Paso Daily Times*, August 31, 1898; *Los Angeles Times*, August 31, 1898.

32   Captain Hughes to AG Wozencraft, August 31, 1898, TSA.

33   Monthly Return, Company D, Frontier Battalion, August 1898, TSA; Alexander, *Winchester Warriors*, 300; Parsons, *Captain John R. Hughes* opts to forgo mentioning Hughes' participation in the St. Leon and Dr. Breaux shooting incident.

34   *Galveston Daily News*, August 31, 1898; Alexander, *Winchester Warriors*, 298–301; Tise, *Texas County Sheriffs*, 172.

35   *Galveston Daily News*, September 1, 1898.

36   Captain Hughes to AG Wozencraft, August 31, 1898; *El Paso Daily Herald*, September 1, 1898; *San Antonio Daily News*, September 1, 1898; Affidavit and Personnel File [Ernest St. Leon] For Texas Peace Officers Killed in the Line of Duty, CLEAT. Unfortunately Ivey in *The Texas Rangers: A Registry and History*, places the shooting of Ernest St. Leon near Socorro, New Mexico, rather than Socorro, Texas.

37   *Dallas Morning News*, September 2, 1898.

38   Ibid.

39   Caldwell and DeLord, *Texas Peace Officers*, 355; Captain Hughes to AG Wozencraft, November 3, 1898, TSA.

40   Captain Hughes to AG Wozencraft, September 15, 1898, TSA; Alexander, *Winchester Warriors*, 300.

41   Underwood and Underwood, *Concordia Cemetery*, 52.

42   Certificate of Pay for Ernest St. Leon from June 1, 1898–August 31, 1898, TRHF&M.

43   Underwood and Underwood, *Concordia Cemetery*, 52; Metz, *Encyclopedia of Lawmen, Outlaws, and Gunfighters*, 234.

44   Caldwell and DeLord, *Texas Lawmen*, 354.

Introduction to Part II: The Ranger Force Era, 1901–1935.

1   Harold J. Weiss, Jr., *Yours to Command: The Life and Legend of Texas Ranger Captain Bill McDonald*, 200–1.

2   J. Evetts Haley, *Jeff Milton: A Good Man with a Gun*, 49.

3   Miller, *Texas Ranger John B. Jones*, 289–91; Alexander, *Winchester Warriors*, 167–69; Stephens, *Texas Ranger Captain Dan Roberts: The Untold Story*, 205.

4   Weiss, *Yours to Command*, 202–3.

5   Gammel, *The Laws of Texas*, Volume 8, 86–91.
6   Mike Cox, *Time of the Rangers: Texas Rangers from 1900 to the Present*, 19–21; Alexander, *Winchester Warriors*, 306–8; Utley, *Lone Star Justice*, 271–73; Wilkins, *The Law Comes to Texas*, 345.
7   Weiss, *Yours to Command*, 204–5.
8   Captain Hughes to AG Scurry, June 2, 1900; Sergeant Wood Saunders to AG Scurry, May 29, 1900; Lieutenant Wood Saunders to AG Scurry, June 3, 1900; J. C. Hudson to AG Scurry, June 2, 1900, TSA.
9   Alexander, *Winchester Warriors*, 308.
10 Compilation of Company D Monthly Returns, June–December 1900, January–March 1901, TSA.
11 Weiss, *Yours to Command*, 210.
12 Joel Samaha, *Criminal Law*, 7; Robert M. Bohm and Keith N. Haley, *Introduction to Criminal Justice*, 36.
13 Harris and Sadler, *Texas Rangers and the Mexican Revolution*, 210–12.
14 Ibid. Chapter 17 deals in detail with Canales' motives, allegations, and the subsequent hearings, 427–61.
15 Robert M. Utley, *Lone Star Lawmen; The Second Century Texas Rangers*, 166–78.
16 Ibid.; Cox, *Time of the Rangers*, 165–85.

Chapter 12: W. Emmett Robuck, 1902.

1   J. Marvin Hunter, ed., *The Trail Drivers of Texas*, 32.
2   Ibid., 687.
3   Donaly E. Brice, *The Great Comanche Raid: Boldest Indian Attack of the Texas Republic*, 27–48; Moore, *Savage Frontier*, Volume 3, 101–28.
4   Victoria Dunnahoo Daywood and Peggy White Engledow, *The Bad Boys of Caldwell County, Texas: Book One, Murders in the 1800s*, 86.
5   Descriptive List, W. E. Robuck. July 9, 1901, TRHF&M.
6   Appointment of W. E. Robuck to 2nd Lieutenant, Frontier Battalion: Signed by J. N. Browning, Lt. Gov. & Acting Governor, State of Texas, TRHF&M.
7   Monthly Return, Ranger Force, Company A, September 1902, TSA; Gournay, *Texas Boundaries*, 117.
8   Alexander, *Winchester Warriors*, 306–8; Utley, *Lone Star Justice*, 272; Captain J. A. Brooks, Ranger Force, Company A to Adjutant General Thomas Scurry, September 18, 1902, TSA. In this correspondence and the previously cited Company A Monthly Return for September 1902, Ranger Emmett Robuck is clearly referred to as Private Robuck, not Lieutenant Robuck. Although it has been written that the Monthly Returns were done away with as result of disbandment of the Frontier Battalion and creation of the Ranger Force, such is not the case. As

an example the interested reader is referred to the Monthly Returns
for Company D, Ranger Force, for the years 1902, 1903, 1904, 1905,
1906, 1907, 1908, 1909, 1910....1918 etc, TSA.

9   Paul N. Spellman, *Captain J. A. Brooks, Texas Ranger*, 141.

10 Special Report of Adjutant General Thomas Scurry to Governor
    Joseph D. Sayers, November 11, 1902, TSA. The document records the
    testimony from individual witnesses and participants, hereafter cited
    as SRAG followed by last name of affiant. In this instance the citation
    is SRAG-Wallis. Occasionally Harry J. Wallis is inadvertently confused
    with Hayes Moore Wallis (02-18-1891 to 09-13-1957). See, Harris,
    Harris, and Sadler, *Texas Ranger Biographies*. Also see, Harris and
    Sadler, *The Texas Rangers and the Mexican Revolution*, 55–56.

11 Andrew R. Graybill, *Policing the Great Plains: Rangers, Mounties, and
    the North American Frontier, 1875–1910*. The author unhesitatingly
    acknowledges Ramón de la Cerda was "illegally branding a steer" but
    somehow leaves an impression mitigating overt criminality by sug-
    gesting the cow thief was "an opponent of King Ranch expansion,"
    105. Setting aside the fairness or unfairness of King Ranch manage-
    ment practices, proffering such a defense for an admitted act of "illegal
    branding" seems somewhat anemic.

12 SRAG-Raymond, TSA.

13 Sterling, *Trails and Trials of a Texas Ranger*, 323.

14 SRAG-Wallis: "We released Reyes Silguero about 10 o'clock that morn-
    ing"; Spellman, *Captain J. A. Brooks, Texas Ranger* asserts that Reyes
    Silguero was "later carted off to jail," 142.

15 Report of the Adjutant General: State of Texas, 1901–1902, 34, TSA;
    Dallas Morning News, September 11, 1902. "Robuck and Baker were
    arrested last spring for killing Ramon Cerda while attempting to arrest
    him."

16 Robert J. Kleberg to AG Scurry, Not dated, TSA.

17 John B. Armstrong to AG Scurry, November [??] 1902, TSA.

18 Américo Paredes, *With His Pistol in His Hand: A Border Ballad and Its
    Hero*, 24.

19 Graham, *Kings of Texas*, 199.

20 Harris and Sadler, *The Texas Rangers*, 57.

21 Monthly Return, Ranger Force, Company A, September 1902, TSA.

22 Webb, *The Texas Rangers*, 464.

23 Monthly Return, Ranger Force, Company A, September 1902: "he
    knowing the boatman who crossed those of the guilty party to this
    side of the Rio Grande...," TSA.

24 Sterling, *Trails and Trials of a Texas Ranger*, 322–25; *Brownsville Daily
    Herald*, September 10, 1902.

25 Ibid., 323; Spellman, *Captain J. A. Brooks*, 144.

26 Monthly Return, Ranger Force, Company A, September 1902. "Prvt. W. E. Robuck was waylaid and killed Sept. 9, 1902 near Brownsville," TSA; Affidavit and Personnel File [W. E. Robuck] For Texas Peace Officers Killed in the Line of Duty, CLEAT; *Galveston Daily News*, September 11, 1902: "The weapons used by the assassins were shotguns loaded with buckshot.... Indications showed that five parties composed the waylayers, three of whom did the shooting."

27 Ibid.; SRAG-Brooks, TSA.

28 *Brownsville Daily Herald*, September 10, 1902. For this rendition it was reported that Emmett Robuck and Jesse Miller had traded horses and it was Robuck's horse that was killed.

29 Telegram, Captain Brooks to AG Scurry, September 10, 1902, TSA; *Houston Chronicle*, September 10, 1902.

30 *Brownsville Daily Herald*, September 10, 1902; *Corpus Christi Caller*, September 12, 1902.

31 Ibid., September 11, 1902; Telegram, Captain Brooks to AG Scurry, September 11, 1902. "Will ship body to Lockhart by order of his father," TSA.

32 Ibid.

33 Captain Brooks to AG Scurry, September 10, 1902, TSA.

34 Captain Brooks to AG Scurry, September 12, 1902, TSA.

35 Captain Brooks to AG Scurry, September 18, 1902, TSA.

36 Monthly Return, Ranger Force, Company A, TSA; Telegram, Captain Brooks to AG Scurry, September 11, 1902. "Jesse Miller was with them. Enlisted him yesterday," TSA.

37 SRAG-Brooks, TSA.

38 Monthly Return, Ranger Force, Company A, September 1902, TSA; Report of the Adjutant General, State of Texas, 1901–1902, 34, TSA; *Dallas Morning News*, September 11, 1902.

39 Captain Brooks to AG Scurry, September 12, 1902, TSA.

40 Monthly Return, Ranger Force, Company A, September 1902, TSA.

41 SRAG-Scurry, TSA; Report of the Adjutant General, State of Texas, 1901–1902, 34, TSA.

42 Harris and Sadler, *The Texas Rangers in the Mexican Revolution*, 57–58.

43 SRAG-Brooks, TSA.

44 Monthly Return, Ranger Force, Company D, December 1902, TSA.

45 Webb, *The Texas Rangers*, 465; Alexander, *Fearless Dave Allison*, 80.

Chapter 13: Thomas Jefferson Goff, 1905.

1 Unfortunately but understandably, John E. Sparks in "Tom Goff, Texas Ranger" for the December 1987 edition of *True West* reports Goff was born in Keytesville, Missouri, 14. There is now a Keytesville,

Missouri, located in Chariton County. However, primary source documents associated with Goff's enlistments with the Texas Rangers clearly state he was born in Keatsville, Barry County, Missouri. Keatsville, Missouri, no longer exists, having been renamed Washburn, Missouri, yet in Barry County. Clarification was graciously furnished by Amber Wilson, Barry County Museum, Cassville, Missouri, to author December 16, 2001.

2   J. Wright Mooar, as told to James Winford Hunt, *Buffalo Days: Stories From J. Wright Mooar*, ed. Robert F. Pace, 74. Mr. Mooar refers to the elder Goff as "John" rather than "James."

3   Warrant of Authority and Descriptive List, T. J. Goff, TRHF&M; Don McAlavy and Harold Kilmer, eds., *High Plains History; 100 Years of History of East Central New Mexico*, 135.

4   Newton Josephus Jones to J. R. Webb, March 15, 1947, 5, J. R. Webb Papers, Rupert Richardson Research Center, Hardin-Simmons University, Abilene, Texas. For geographical orientation of this section, refer to Lester W. Galbreath, *Fort Griffin and the Clear Fork Country: 100 Years of History, 1850–1950, on 25 Miles of the Clear Fork of the Brazos River*.

5   Gournay, *Texas Boundaries*, 82.

6   Loyd M. Uglow, *Standing in the Gap: Army Outposts, Picket Stations, and the Pacification of the Texas Frontier, 1866–1886*, 9–10; Paula Mitchell Marks, *In a Barren Land: American Indian Dispossession and Survival*, 125.

7   McAlavy and Kilmer, *High Plains History*, 135.

8   Tise, *Texas County Sheriffs*, 490; Sallie Reynolds Matthews, *Interwoven: A Pioneer Chronicle*, 149.

9   Don Hampton Biggers, *Shackelford County Sketches*, ed. Joan Farmer, 29.

10   Robert K. DeArment, *Bravo of the Brazos: John Larn of Fort Griffin, Texas*, 88–89.

11   Baylor County Historical Society, *Saltpork to Sirloin: The History of Baylor County, Texas From 1879-to 1930*, 98.

12   Jan Devereaux, *Pistols, Petticoats, and Poker: The Real Lottie Deno, No Lies or Alibis*. 97.

13   Baylor County Historical Society, *Saltpork to Sirloin*, 98.

14   Tise, *Texas County Sheriffs*, 490; McAlavy and Kilmer in *High Plains History* report that James M. Goff "became tax collector...." 135. At the time, in many Texas counties the political title was "Sheriff and Tax Collector."

15   Sparks, "Tom Goff, Texas Ranger," 14.

16   John H. Rogers, quoted in *The Waco Times-Herald*, September 19, 1905.

17   Sparks, "Tom Goff, Texas Ranger," 14.
18   Ibid. Fort Morgan, Colorado, is located a rough 100 miles northwest of Denver in Morgan County. For absorbing details of this particular cattle drive, see, Phin W. Reynolds to J. R. Webb, May 1936 and April 1938, Webb Papers, Hardin-Simmons University.
19   Ibid. For biographical sketches and recounts of frontier-era history along the Clear Fork of the Brazos River, see, *Tracks Along the Clear Fork: Stories From Shackelford and Throckmorton Counties*, Lawrence Clayton and Joan Halford Farmer, eds .
20   Ibid. This portion of Sparks' story in *True West* is not disputed, but thus far has not been confirmed by corresponding primary source documents in Texas Ranger service records, which are voluminous. The author John E. Sparks (now deceased) was Tom Goff's grandson, no doubt obtaining much of his information from family oral history, but somewhat atypically, he makes primary source documents and period photographs a part of his piece; Spellman, *Captain John H. Rogers, Texas Ranger*, 72–73.
21   Ibid. For warfare with Indians and horseback outlaws it was widely accepted as preferable to shoot the horse first, dismounting the adversary. See, Martin Blumenson, ed., *The Patton Papers, 1885–1940*. "I [Patton] started back, when I saw a man on a horse come right in front of me, I started to shoot at him but remembered that Dave Allison had always said to shoot at the horse of an escaping man and I did so and broke the horse's hip, he fell on his rider," 333.
22   Ibid. After the death of his first wife, James Meadow Goff married Susan Howard. In the late 1890s the couple relocated from Throckmorton County, Texas, to Hobart, Kiowa County, Oklahoma. See, McAlavy and Kilmer, *High Plains History*, 135.
23   Monthly Return, Company E, Ranger Force, December 1893: "Tom J. Goff enlisted Dec. 10th 1893," TSA; Certificate of Pay, Thomas J. Goff, TSA; Spellman, *Captain John H. Rogers, Texas Ranger*, 75.
24   Ibid., Report of Scouts and Arrests, TSA.
25   Oath of Office, Tom J. Goff, April 27, 1894, "Casa Blanca, Texas," TRHF&M.
26   Application for Commission as Special Ranger, April 27, 1894, TSA; Activity Report of Special Ranger, May, June, and August, 1894, TSA; Certificates of Pay [regular Ranger] February, March, August, November, 1895, TSA; Application for Commission as Special Ranger, August 13, 1896, TSA; Descriptive List [regular Ranger] August 25, 1896, TSA. By November 1896 Goff is again filing reports as a Special Ranger, TSA.
27   *Austin Daily Statesman*, September 16, 1905.

28 Interview, November 15, 2011, with Dody Fugate, Curator of Archeological Research, Libratory of Anthropology, Santa Fe, New Mexico. Ms. Fugate is Thomas Jefferson Goff's great-grandniece.

29 Sparks, "Tom Goff, Texas Ranger," 17–18.

30 Walter Prescott Webb, "Rangers Reorganized," *The State Trooper*, July 1927, 13.

31 Oath of Service, Ranger Force, T. J. Goff, May 1, 1905; Warrant of Authority and Descriptive List, T. J. Goff, May 1, 1905, TRHF&M; Monthly Return, Company C, Ranger Force, May 1905; "T. J. Goff enlisted May 1st 1905," TSA.

32 Spellman, *Captain John H. Rogers, Texas Ranger*, 130; Report of Scouts and Arrest, Company C, Ranger Force, June 1905. Entry for June 23 places Private Goff at his new duty station, Big Bend, a community with post office in the Terlingua Mining District, TSA.

33 Gournay, *Texas Boundaries*, 108.

34 Baker, *Ghost Towns of Texas*, 161–64.

35 *Alpine Avalanche*, September 14, 1951, Sixteenth Anniversary Edition.

36 State of Texas Reward Notice for the Arrest of Augustine Garcia: "Address all information to J. H. Rogers, Capt . Rangers, Alpine, Texas," TRHF&M.

37 R. W. Simmons to Captain Rogers, September 14, 1905, TRHF&M.

38 Report of Scouts and Arrests. Company C, Ranger Force, July 1905, TSA.

39 Captain Rogers to Adjutant General John A. Hulen, September 16, 1905, TRHF&M.

40 *The Alpine Times*, September 20, 1905; Curren Rogers McLane, ed., *The Rogers Family Genealogy*, 27.

41 Captain Rogers to AG Hulen, September 16, 1905, TRHF&M; *Waco Times-Herald*, September 19, 1905.

42 *The Alpine Times*, September 20, 1905.

43 R. W. Simmons to Captain Rogers, September 14, 1905, TRHF&M.

44 Telegram. Captain Rogers to AG Hulen, September 14, 1905, TRHF&M.

45 *Houston Chronicle*, September 16, 1905.

46 AG Hulen to Captain Rogers, September 19, 1905, TSA; *The Alpine Times*, September 20, 1905; Affidavit and Personnel File [Thomas Jefferson Goff] For Texas Peace Officers Killed in the Line of Duty, CLEAT.

47 Captain Rogers to AG Hulen, September 16, 1905, TRHF&M.

48 Captain Rogers to AG Hulen, September 22, 1905, TRHF&M.

49 Thomas Jefferson Goff is buried in the Throckmorton City Cemetery, Throckmorton, Texas.

50 Report of the Adjutant General of Texas for the Period Ending December 31, 1906. 32, TSA.

Chapter 14: Quirl Bailey Carnes, 1910.

1   Maude T. Gilliland, *Wilson County Texas Rangers, 1837–1977*, 104;
    Tise, *Texas County Sheriffs*, 547.
2   Harris, Harris, and Sadler, *Texas Ranger Biographies*, 53–54; Alexander,
    Lawmen, Outlaws, and S.O.Bs, Chapter 14, 255–76, is devoted to
    sketching the biographical profile of Herff Alexander Carnes.
3   Gilliland, *Wilson County Texas Rangers*, 46; Harris, Harris, and Sadler,
    Texas Ranger Biographies, 54. Both of the sources cite the birthplace
    of Carnes as Wilson County. Somewhat inexplicably the enlistment
    papers for Carnes dated September 4, 1908, in two separate spaces,
    have "Atascosa" as the place of birth, TSA; Atascosa County joins
    Wilson County on the western side.
4   Ibid., 2.
5   Louise Stadler, *Wilson County History*, 43; Alexander, *Lawmen,
    Outlaws, and S.O.Bs*, 5.
6   Enlistment, Oath of Service, and Description, Ranger Force for Q. B.
    Carnes, Company B, Stationed at Alice, Texas, signed by Captain Tom
    M. Ross, TSA; Monthly Return, Company B, Ranger Force, September
    1908, TSA.
7   Harris and Sadler, *The Texas Rangers*, 27.
8   Enlistment, Oath of Service, and Description, TSA
9   Harris and Sadler, *The Texas Rangers*, 30–31.
10 Christina Stopka, Director, Texas Ranger Research Center, TRHF&M,
    "Partial List of Texas Ranger Company and Unit Commanders."
11 Ibid.; Monthly Return, Company B, Ranger Force, January 1909;
    Monthly Return, Company A, Ranger Force, January 1909, TSA;
    Tise, *Texas County Sheriffs*, 378; Harris, Harris, Sadler, *Texas Ranger
    Biographies*, 202.
12 Harris and Sadler, *The Texas Rangers*, 38.
13 Harris, Harris, and Sadler, *Texas Ranger Biographies*, 74.
14 Harris and Sadler, *The Texas Rangers*, 41.
15 *Brownsville Daily Herald*, August 1, 1910.
16 Ibid.
17 *Brownsville Daily Herald*, August 2, 1910.
18 *Brownsville Daily Herald*, August 1, 1910.
19 Ibid.
20 Ibid.
21 *Brownsville Daily Herald*, August 2, 1910; Affidavit and Personnel File
    [Henry B. Lawrence] For Texas Peace Officers Killed in the Line of
    Duty, CLEAT.
22 *The Floresville Chronicle-Journal*, November 25, 2004; *Brownsville Daily
    Herald*, August 3, 1910.

23   Harris and Sadler, *The Texas Rangers*, 42. Maude T. Gilliland in
     *Horsebackers of the Brush Country: A Story of Texas Rangers and Mexican
     Liquor Smugglers* incorrectly asserts that Ranger Pat Craighead was
     wounded by "Mexicans bandits," 79.

24   Biennial Report of the Adjutant General of Texas For the Period
     Ending December 15, 1910, TSA; Affidavit and Personnel File [Q. B.
     Carnes] For Texas Peace Officers Killed in the Line of Duty, CLEAT.

25   *San Antonio Daily Light*, August 1, 1910.

26   Harris and Sadler, *The Texas Rangers*. The authors report that
     Brownsville City Marshal Joe Crixell made a discreet investigation
     in Mexico and was told that on the night of the San Benito episode
     Jacinto Treviño in company of Benjamin Estrada and an *amigo* named
     Loya had been seen heading toward the Rio Grande, 43.

27   *Brownsville Daily Herald*, August 2, 1910.

28   Monthly Return, Company D, Ranger Force, August 1910, TSA.

29   Telegram, Acting Adjutant General Phelps to Captain M. E. Bailey,
     July 31, 1910, TSA; Captain M. E. Bailey to Adjutant General J. O.
     Newton, July 31, 1910, TSA.

30   *Brownsville Daily Herald*, August 2, 1910; *San Antonio Daily Light,*
     August 1, 1910; *Dallas Morning News*, August 2, 1910; *Brownsville
     Daily Herald,* August 3, 1910.

31   *Dallas Morning News*, September 7, 1910.

32   *San Antonio Daily Light*, August 2, 1910. In fact Ranger Alfred
     Randolph Baker was critical of Captain Johnson's resolve in bringing
     the killers of Carnes and Lawrence to bay, writing to Captain John H.
     Rogers: "Capt. Johnson and his men have gone back to Harlingen....
     Capt. Johnson don't seem to take the interest he should. He has never
     conferred with us [Rangers Herff Carnes, Charley Craighead, and A. R.
     Baker] in regard to the matter." Baker to Rogers, August 8, 1910, TSA.

33   DeLord, *The Ultimate Sacrifice*, 73.

34   *The Alice Echo*, August 4, 1910.

35   Harris, Harris, and Sadler, *Texas Ranger Biographies*, 74, 399.

36   *Corpus Christi Caller-Times*, February 28, 1971, in a story picked up
     from the *Mercedes Enterprise*. Also see, Gilliland, *Wilson County Texas
     Rangers*: "School Honors Folk Hero," 44.

37   Paredes, *With His Pistol in His Hand*, 223, 234.

38   *Corpus Christi Caller-Times*, February 28, 1971.

Chapter 15: Grover Scott Russell, 1913.

1   Patti Russell to author, May 29, 2001.

2   Ibid.; Tise, *Texas County Sheriffs*, 176.

3   Alexander, *Lawmen, Outlaws, and S.O.Bs*, 87, 99 n. 14. The defini-
     tive biography of Bill Longley is Rick Miller's *Bloody Bill Longley: The
     Mythology of a Gunfighter.*
4   Gournay, *Texas Boundaries*, 69.
5   James Pylant, *Sins of the Pioneers: Crimes and Scandals in a Small Texas
     Town*, 12-19.
6   Ibid., 44, 61, 64, and 79. Author Pylant creates an enlightening
     portrait of the routine and not-so-routine criminality and scandals,
     surgically exposing the underbelly of Stephenville's raunchy and racy
     and sometimes perilous past.
7   *The El Paso Herald*, June 24, 1913.
8   Warrant of Authority and Descriptive List, Scott Russell, October 1,
     1912, TRHF&M.
9   Tise, *Texas County Sheriffs*. 410; Harris and Sadler, *The Texas Rangers,*
     124.
10   Sergeant Moore to Adjutant General, February 5, 1913, TSA.
11   Governor Colquitt to Captain Hughes, February 3, 1913, TSA.
12   Captain John R. Hughes to Adjutant General, April 8, 1913. "Sergt.
     Moore has quit and has been appointed Deputy U.S. Marshal at El
     Paso," TSA; Harris and Sadler, *The Texas Rangers,* 124.
13   Glenna D. Kieffe, "Finis: The Final Entry," *Customs Today*, Fall 1990.
14   Captain Hughes to Adjutant General, April 18, 1913, TSA;Harris and
     Sadler, *The Texas Rangers,* 123.
15   El Paso County Sheriff Peyton J. Edwards to Captain Hughes, April
     19, 1913, TSA; Harris and Sadler, *The Texas Rangers,* 50; Alexander,
     Lawmen, Outlaws, and S.O.Bs, 88. Award-winning author David
     Dorado Romo's estimation of Texas Ranger manpower strength at the
     time is quite liberal, and perhaps historically overstated in *Ringside
     Seat to a Revolution: An Underground Cultural History of El Paso and
     Juárez, 1893 – 1923*, 209. A breakdown of available Ranger manpower
     for 1913 may be found in Harris and Sadler, *The Texas Rangers*, 114–16
     and numerous Texas Ranger records archived at TSA.
16   Captain Hughes to Adjutant General, April 23, 1913. Captain Hughes
     makes reference to Private Russell's shooting incident as "his little
     difficulty at the smelter," TSA; *El Paso Herald*, June 24, 1913. The story
     was also carried in the *El Paso Times* for three successive days; Bob
     Alexander, "Hell Paso," *NOLA Quarterly*, April–June 2002, 7–8.
17   *El Paso Morning Times*, June 24, 1913. The name is variously spelled
     "Guadarrama" and "Guaderrama."
18   *El Paso Herald*, June 9, 1915.
19   Harris and Sadler, *The Texas Rangers,* 125.
20   *El Paso Morning Times*, June 24, 1913.
21   Ibid.

22   Alexander, *Lawmen, Outlaws, and S.O.Bs*, 91.

23   Captain Hughes to AG Henry Hutchings, June 24, 1913. According to Hughes' official report Ranger Russell and Deputy Garlick had in hand an arrest warrant for Manuel Guaderrama. "There was a bullet hole through the warrant in Garlick's pocket.... The newspaper that I sent you this morning has a very good account, except that the Reporter was not told of the warrant for Manuel Guadarrama [sic], as it has not been served yet, and we don't want it to get out," TSA.

24   *El Paso Herald*, June 24, 1913.

25   Ibid., June 11, 1915: "Sheriff Peyton J. Edwards, on the stand, testified that he had instructed deputy sheriff Garlick to inspect all cattle brought into the corral at the Guadarrama place"; *El Paso Morning Times*, June 12, 1915: "go to the Guadrrama [sic] corrals every time cattle were taken there and inspect them."

26   Ibid., January 16, 1914.

27   *El Paso Herald*, June 11, 1915; Harris and Sadler, *The Texas Rangers*, 125.

28   Telegram, Captain Hughes to AG Henry Hutchings, June 23, 1913, TSA; Affidavits and Personnel Files [Scott Russell and W. H. Garlick] For Texas Peace Officers Killed in the Line of Duty, CLEAT; Texas Department of Health, Bureau of Vital Statistics: Death Certificate Number 12950, Scott Russell, June 23, 1913. Cause of Death: "Gunshot wounds, murder." Death Certificate Number 12986, William H. Garlick, June 23, 1913. Cause of Death: "Gunshot wound, murder."

29   *El Paso Morning Times*, June 24, 1913

30   Alexander, *Lawmen, Outlaws, and S.O.Bs*, 93.

31   *El Paso Herald*, June 11, 1915; Broaddus, *The Legal Heritage of El Paso*, 226.

32   Alexander, *Lawmen, Outlaws, and S.O.Bs*, 94.

33   *El Paso Herald*, June 24, 25, 1913.

34   Ibid.

35   Telegram, AG Hutchings to Captain Hughes, June 24, 1913, TSA.

36   Alexander, *Fearless Dave Allison*, 163; *Stephenville Empire-Tribune*, April 1, 2001.

37   *El Paso Morning Times*, June 24, 1913.

38   Ibid., June 12, 1915.

39   *El Paso Herald*, June 18, 1915.

Chapter 16: Eugene B. Hulen, 1915

1   Enlistment, Oath of Service, and Description, Ranger Force, E. B. Hulen, dated March 29, 1915, TSA; The U.S. Federal Census 1900,

Cooke County, Texas, lists Hulen as a "Stock Raiser" but gives his age as 24.

2 Ibid.

3 Webb, "Texas Rangers In Eclipse," 14.

4 Harris and Sadler, *The Texas Rangers,* 189.

5 John A. Hulen to Adjutant General Henry Hutchings, May 27, 1915: "My brother E. B. Hulen wants to be in the Ranger service. He is 36 years old, sober, steady and reliable. Although he has never served as a Peace Officer he will satisfactorily fill the bill as a Ranger. I would be pleased indeed if you could take care of him," TSA.

6 Alexander, *Lawmen, Outlaws, and S.O.Bs,* 200, n. 95.

7 Robert Keil, *Bosque Bonito: Violent Times Along the Borderland During the Mexican Revolution,* ed. Elizabeth McBride, 4–6.

8 Ibid.

9 Monthly Return, Company D, Frontier Battalion, May 1899, TSA; Joyce E. Means, *Pancho Villa Days at Pilares,* 171; Dorothea Magdalene Fox, "Marked for Death!" *Frontier Times,* March 1965: "When a chance came to go into the Customs Inspection work, Dad [Joe Sitter] chose that because the salary was more, twice as large, I believe," 20.

10 *El Paso Herald,* May 26, 1915: "Captain Hughes says.... [Sitter] was one of the best trailers he had ever known and was one of the men who trailed and arrested the train robbers at Samuels siding on the G. H. many years ago..."; Kevin Michaels, "Tracker," *Great West,* September 1974, 22; Wayne T. Walker, "Joe Sitters: The Best Damn Tracker in Texas," *Oldtimers Wild West,* December 1978, 29–31, 48.

11 Mike Cox, *Texas Ranger Tales: Stories That Need Telling,* 136.

12 T. P. Love, Senior Patrol Inspector, *Sign Cutting,* Training Document, United States Department of Justice, Immigration and Naturalization Service, September, 1936, 4. Courtesy Don and Louise Yena collection.

13 Cox, *Texas Ranger Tales,* 138.

14 Application for Employment as Inspector, U.S. Mounted Customs Service, for Jack Howard, December 21, 1901, Courtesy Charles L. Wright, Assistant Port Director, U.S. Customs and Border Protection, El Paso, Texas.

15 The Crockett County Historical Society, *A History of Crockett County,* 310; *The Cattleman,* June 1914, 17; *The Cattleman,* July 1953, 66; Texas and Southwestern Cattle Association listing of Field and Market Inspectors, courtesy Susan Wagner, Editor, ret., *The Cattleman.*

16 Harry Warren, who visited with the injured men at Pilares, later wrote his remembrances of the event, herein quoted in part: "The bullet Joe Sitter received had barely grazed the left side of his head without breaking the skull; Ad Harvick was shot in the leg, the bullet passing clear through; 'Jack' Howard was struck in the breast. The first two

[Sitter and Harvick] I found resting quietly—Harvick even joking me when I asked him about his wound, but Jack was very restless and suffering intensely, yet emitting no moans or other expressions of pain—a small man with nerves of steel...." Harry Warren Papers, ABB.

17   J. A. Harvin, Collector of Customs, Eagle Pass, Texas, to Secretary of Treasury, Washington, D.C., February 14, 1913, and Deputy Collector of Customs Luke Dowe to Collector of Customs, Eagle Pass, Texas, February 15, 1913, National Archives [NA]; Charles L. Wright, "A Western Tragedy," *Customs Today*, Fall 1992, 6–9; Alexander, *Lawmen, Outlaws, and S.O.Bs*, 185–87. Innocently, but unfortunately, Kenneth B. Ragsdale in *Big Bend: Land of the Unexpected* reports that Joseph Russell Sitter was killed during this 1913 confrontation, 244, n. 21. Indeed, Sitter would die violently as an offshoot of the Chico Cano affair, but it would be two years later during 1915.

18   Monty Waters, "A. G. Beard: West Texas Law Officer," Unpublished draft manuscript prepared by and in possession of Ranger Alexander Glenn Beard's grandson, Monty Waters, 46.

19   John H. Rogers, United States Marshal for the Western District of Texas, Austin, to United States Attorney General, Washington, D. C., May 29, 1915, NA.

20   Captain J. M. Fox to Adjutant General Henry Hutchings, May 27, 1915, TRHF&M. For her article in the April 4, 1996, edition of the *Jeff Davis Mountain Dispatch,* Nessye Mae Roach says that the tipoff about smuggled horses came from some of Pancho Villa's soldiers.

21   Sworn statement of Evans Means before an unnamed notary public on May 21, 1925, handwritten by Harry Warren, Harry Warren Papers, ABB. This document, made ten years after the fact by a partisan, should not be dismissed out of hand, but must be utilized with reasonable and workable skepticism—and caution if not corroborated independently.

22   Harris and Sadler, *The Texas Rangers,* 190.

23   Paul N. Spellman, "Dark Days of the Texas Rangers, 1915–1918," *Journal of South Texas Studies* 12, Spring 2001, 85, 92; Alexander's *Lawmen, Outlaws, and S.O.Bs* particularly profiles the life of Sitter, covering his law-enforcing career as a deputy sheriff, Texas Ranger, and U.S. Mounted Customs Inspector.

24   Captain Fox to AG Hutchings, May 27, 1915, TRHF&M; Harris, Harris, and Sadler, *Texas Ranger Biographies*, 78, 381–82. Unfortunately due to oversight or typographical errors Webb in both *The Texas Rangers* and *The Story of The Texas Rangers*, Robinson in *The Men Who Wear the Star* and Glenn Justice in *Revolution on the Rio Grande: Mexican Raids and Army Pursuits, 1916–1919* place the date of this episode in 1916 rather than the correct 1915, and intimate

Ranger Eugene Hulen was the son, rather than the brother of John A. Hulen, the former Texas Adjutant General. Pointing this date discrepancy out should not be misinterpreted as gratuitous nitpicking; it is not. Events during 1915, subsequent to those occurring in this chapter, including the death of another Texas Ranger, must be appropriately examined in chronological order. The scenarios playing out in real time were being identified with by borderlanders and lawmen in real time, an important distinction for rationally studying cause and effect. What actually happened to colleagues yesterday might influence actions and/or reactions of tomorrow.

25 Jack Shipman, "The Killing of Ranger Hulin [*sic*] and Inspector Sitters [*sic*]," *Voice of the Mexican Border*, Centennial Edition, 1936, 66.

26 Ibid. For this article Shipman quotes verbatim the remembrances of Ranger Sug Cummings.

27 Alexander, *Lawmen, Outlaws, and S.O.Bs*, 190.

28 Ibid., 191; Jacobson and Nored, *Jeff Davis County, Texas*, 209.

29 Captain Fox to AG Hutchings. May 27, 1915, TRHF&M. The headline in the May 25, 1915, edition of the *El Paso Herald* was: "Mexicans Fight River Guards."

30 U.S Marshal Rogers to U.S. Attorney General, May 29, 1915, NA.

31 *Dallas Morning News*, May 29, 1915; The headline in the May 27, 1915, edition of the *El Paso Herald* was: "Mob Leaves To Avenge Killings." In this edition it was reported that in addition to other mutilations of Sitter's and Hulen's bodies, that their "ears had been cut off."

32 Captain Fox to AG Hutchings, May 27, 1915, TRHF&M; Al Ritter, "Death on the Rio Grande," *DPSOA Magazine*, March/April 1996, 54. DPSOA is acronym for Texas Department of Public Safety Officers Association.

33 Ibid.; Shipman, "The Killing of Ranger Hulin and Inspector Sitters," 66.

34 Warren Papers, Statement of Evans Means, ABB.

35 Death Certificate, E. B. Hulen, May 24, 1915: "Gunshot by bandits"; Affidavit and Personnel File [E. B. Hulen] For Texas Peace Officers Killed in the Line of Duty, CLEAT.

36 Shipman, "The Killing of Ranger Hulin and Inspector Sitters," 66.

37 Harris and Sadler, *The Texas Rangers*, 191.

38 Captain Fox to AG Hutchings, May 27, 1915: "Inspector Sitters [*sic*] had been shot about ten times and his head beaten with rocks, his horse was found shot and his guns had been taken. Ranger Hulen was found about ten feet from Sitters, he had been shot about eight times and his head beaten in a pulp with rocks, the Mexicans taken his guns, searched his pockets and taken the boots off of his feet. His horse and saddle were also missing," TRHF&M.

39   Telegrams. AG Hutchings to John A. Hulen, May 26, June 2 , and June 4, 1915, TSA; *Dallas Morning News*, June 6, 1915. Death Certificate notation: "to Gainsville, Tex."

40   Personnel File, E. B. Hulen, CLEAT.

41   McClung, "Texas Rangers and the Rio Grande, 1910–1919," 72.

42   Tony Cano and Anne Sochat, *BANDIDO: The True Story of Chico Cano, The Last Western Bandit*: "Cano had succeeded in baiting them into the canyon…. and the three that got away couldn't positively swear that Chico was at the scene, even though all evidence indicted he was present," 77–80. In *Lawmen, Outlaws and S.O.Bs*, Volume 2, Alexander devotes a chapter, "Feared, hated, and hunted," to the life and mis-adventure of Chico Cano. There was one element not garnering any debate: this bushwhacking was the foul work of the border's best *bandito*, Chico Cano! 277. U.S. Marshal Rogers to U.S. Attorney General, May 29, 1915: "It is the general opinion that this crime was committed by what is known as the Cano gang of outlaws…," NA; Harris and Sadler, *The Texas Rangers*: "And then a week later Cano carried out his ambush of the Customs inspectors and Rangers," 193.

43   Alexander, *Lawmen, Outlaws, and S.O.Bs*, vol. 2, 280; Cano and Sochat, *BANDIDO*, 231.

44   Harris and Sadler, *The Texas Rangers*, 336.

Chapter 17: Robert Lee Burdett, 1915.

1   *Austin Daily Statesman*, October 6, 1880.

2   Ibid.; Interview with Doug Dukes, nonfiction writer and historian of the Austin, Texas police department, December 5, 2011.

3   *Austin Daily Democratic Statesman*, July 6, 1877 and October 5, 1880, as quoted in *James Madison Brown: Texas Sheriff, Texas Turfman* by Chuck Parsons, 97.

4   *Austin Daily Statesman*, October 6 and 7, 1880.

5   Doug Dukes. *Ben Thompson: Iron Marshal of Austin*, 22.

6   Parsons, *James Madison Brown*, 87–108.

7   *Austin Daily Statesman*, October 7, 1880 and July 9, 1915; Alexander, *Lawmen, Outlaws, and S.O.Bs*, 119; Harris, Harris, and Sadler, *Texas Ranger Biographies*, 47.

8   Catalogue of Students 1895–1896, St. Edwards University, Austin, Texas. Courtesy Ingrid Karklins, University Archivist.

9   Ibid.; photographic copy of the Excelsiors baseball team, courtesy St. Edwards University, is shown on page 121 of Alexander's *Lawmen, Outlaws, and S.O.Bs*.

10   Austin Police Department Arrest Records for Lee Burdett, December 27, 1905, courtesy Doug Dukes.

11   *Austin Daily Statesman*, June 9, 1915; William Jesse "Will" Morris' mother, Alameda [Burdett] Morris, was the sister of Sam Burdett, Robert Lee Burdett's father: Doug Dukes to author, December 6, 2011.

12   Enlistment, Oath of Service, and Description Ranger Force, Robert Lee Burdett, October 6, 1911, TSA; Al Ritter and Chick Davis, "Captain Monroe Fox and the Incident at Porvenir," *Oklahoma State Trooper*, Winter, 1996, 36.

13   Harris and Sadler, *The Texas Rangers,* 75–76.

14   Ibid., 105. Quoting AG Hutchings to Governor Colquitt, October 4, 1912.

15   *Austin City Directory*, 1912, page 90; *Austin Daily Statesman*, June 9, 1915; Doug Dukes to author, December 6, 2011; Sam Burdett, Lee's father, died during December 1890.

16   Enlistment, Oath of Service, and Description Ranger Force, Robert Lee Burdett, February 1, 1915, TSA.

17   Enlistment, Oath of Service, and Description Ranger Force, C. P. Beall, March 1, 1915, TSA.

18   Ronnie C. Tyler, *The Big Bend: A History of the Last Texas Frontier*, 163.

19   *Austin Daily Statesman*, June 9, 1915; AG Hutchings to Will J. Morris, Chief of Police, Austin, Texas, June 12, 1915, TSA.

20   *Alpine Avalanche*, June 10, 1915; *El Paso Herald*, June 8, 1915: "Monday a gang of Fort Hancock Mexicans went to Fabens."

21   *El Paso Morning Times*, June 9, 1915.

22   Alexander, *Lawmen, Outlaws, and S.O.Bs*, 124.

23   *El Paso Morning Times*, June 9, 1915. That Ranger Burdett had a gold pocket watch is reflected in an inventory of personal property in his possession and recovered at the time of death. See, AG Hutchings to Chief W. J. Morris, June 14, 1915, TSA.

24   Alexander, *Lawmen, Outlaws, and S.O.Bs,* 124.

25   *El Paso Morning Times*, June 9, 1915; *Austin Daily Statesman*, June 9, 1915.

26   Ibid.; *Alpine Avalanche*, June 17, 1915; *El Paso Herald*, June 8, 1915.

27   AG Hutchings to Governor Ferguson, June 8, 1915, TSA; Monthly Return, Company B, Ranger Force, June 1915. "Burdett killed June 8, 1915," TSA; Affidavit and Personnel File [R. L. Burdett] For Texas Peace Officers Killed in the Line of Duty, CLEAT.

28   *El Paso Morning Times*, June 9, 1915.

29   *El Paso Herald*, June 11, 1915.

30   Ibid., June 14, 1915.

31   Monthly Return, Company B, Ranger Force, June 1915, TSA. The names of suspects listed in the newspapers correspond—more or less—phonetically with names carried in the Monthly Return, but not verbatim.

32 Earl Mayfore, Nagley & Kaster Undertaking Company to AG Hutching, June 9, 1915, TSA.

33 *El Paso Herald*, June 9, 1915.

34 AG Hutchings to Captain Fox, June 10, 1915, TSA; Harris, Harris, and Sadler, *Texas Ranger Biographies*, 17.

35 *Austin Daily Statesman*, June 9, 1915.

36 *El Paso Herald*, June 11, 1915, picking up a story datelined Austin.

37 Biennial Report of the Adjutant General of Texas, from January 1, 1915 to December 31, 1916, TSA.

38 Paul A. Zielinski, Director, Assumption Chapel Mausoleum & Cemetery, Austin, Texas to author, July 3, 2002.

39 Adjutant General Hutchings to Chief Will Morris, Austin Police Department, June 14, 1915; Chief Morris to AG Hutchings, June 15, 1915, TSA.

40 Cox, *Texas Ranger Tales*, 127. Cox identifies Vaughn's Ranger partner as Ivey Findley; Harris, Harris, and Sadler, *Texas Ranger Biographies* have an entry for Ivy R. Fenley, serving as a Regular Ranger from June 8, 1915 to June 30, 1916. Interestingly, Fenley's EOD is the same day Ranger Robert Lee Burdett was murdered, 109.

41 DeLord, *The Ultimate Sacrifice,* 78.

42 Douglas, *The Gentlemen in the White Hats* devotes several pages to the account of Pancho Villa ordering the apprehension and execution of Ranger Burdett's killers, subsequent to an interview with ex-Ranger Captain J. M. Fox, 168; Cox, *Texas Ranger Tales,* 127. Somewhat bolstering Douglas' aver that Rangers and Villia sometimes had a working relationship is the letter from Ranger Winfred Finis Bates to AG Hutchings, May 31, 1915. Although Bates will soon become embroiled in interagency Ranger politics, he did write, only one week after Burdett's death: "and owing my acquaintance with some of Villa leaders they have agreed to furnish me every assistance toward returning the cattle," TSA.

Chapter 18: William P. Stillwell, 1918.

1 Donaly Brice, TSA, to author, December 13, 2011; Enlistment, Oath of Servcie, and Description Ranger Force, Ben L. Pennington: "Died of Spanish Influenza Oct. 12, 1918," TSA; DeLord, *The Ultimate Sacrifice*, 83; Harris, Harris, and, Sadler, *Texas Ranger Biographies*; 193, 304; Harris and Sadler, *The Texas Rangers*, 345.

2 *Alpine Avalanche*, June 28, 1962, Diamond Jubilee Edition.

3 Enlistment, Oath of Service, and Description Ranger Force, W. P. Stillwell, February 15, 1918, TSA; Harris, Harris, and Sadler, *Texas Ranger Biographies*, 362.

4   *Alpine Avalanche*, June 28, 1962.

5   Ibid.

6   Stillwell, *I'll Gather My Geese*, 14–16.

7   Ibid., 18.

8   Ibid., 19.

9   Harris, Harris, and Sadler, *Texas Ranger Biographies*, 362.

10 Ibid.

11 Charles H. Harris III and Louis R. Sadler, *The Border and the Revolution: Clandestine Activities of the Mexican Revolution, 1910–1920*, 7; Barkley and Odintz, *The Portable Handbook of Texas*, 372; Christopher Lance Habermeyer, *Gringos' Curve: Pancho Villa's Massacre of American Miners in Mexico, 1916*, 64–69; James W. Hurst, *The Villista Prisoners of 1916–1917*; Dr. Roy Edward Stivison (as told to Tom Bailey), "Night of Terror," *Old West*, Summer 1974: "we saw military wagons gathering up the bodies of the bandits. These were taken to the edge of town, placed in a pile, saturated with kerosene, and burned. It was a grisly sight but we were glad to know that these particular men would no longer be a menace in the peace of the border," 43.

12 Jack Shipman, ed., "Villa Takes Ojinaga," *Voice of the Mexican Border*, Centennial Edition 1936, 67.

13 Robert M. Utley, *Lone Star Lawmen: The Second Century* of the *Texas Rangers*, 53.

14 Raht, *The Romance of the Davis Mountains and Big Bend Country*, 352–51.

15 Ronnie C. Tyler, "Notes and Documents: The Little Punitive Expedition in the Big Bend," *Southwestern Historical Quarterly*, January 1975, 277.

16 Tyler, *The Big Bend*, 165; Justice, *Revolution on the Rio Grande*, 11.

17 *Alpine Avalanche*, September 14, 1951, Byline Cas Edwards, "Story of Glenn Springs Raid Is Told from Eye Witnesses of Border Murders"; Louis Ray Sadler to author April 21, 2012, downgrades these numbers by as much as twenty percent.

18 Sergeant Charles E. Smyth, Troop A, 14th Cavalry, Report of Incident as quoted in Raht, *Romance of the Davis Mountains and Big Bend Country*: "Also please send shoes and clothes, as we all fought in our underclothes, except the two men on guard, they had their clothes on at the time," 357.

19 Edwards, "Story of Glenn Springs Raid…."; Elton Miles, *Stray Tales of the Big Bend*, 96.

20 Tyler, *The Big Bend*, 165.

21 Edwards, "Story of the Glenn Springs Raid…."; Tise, *Texas County Sheriffs*. 65.

22 Harris and Sadler, *The Texas Rangers*, 336.

23   Lee Trimble, "The Oral Memoirs of Lee Trimble," *The Texas Ranger Annual*, vol 1, 1982, 39.

24   Justice, *Little Known History of the Big Bend*, 141–47. This is, perhaps, the most authoritative and comprehensive account on the Brite Ranch Raid; Harris, Harris, and Sadler, *Texas Ranger Biographies*, 267–68.

25   Trimble, "The Oral Memoirs of Lee Trimble," 141.

26   Utley, *Lone Star Lawmen*: "they took Welch inside, hanged him to a rafter, slit his throat, and gutted his torso," 58; W. D. Smithers, "Bandit Raids in the Big Bend Country" as contained in *Pancho Villa's Last Hangout: On Both Sides of the Rio Grande in the Big Bend Country*: "There they hanged him by his feet to the rafters and cut his throat. It is presumed that Mickey and the two passengers were killed because they recognized some of the band," 76; Waters, "A. G. Beard: West Texas Law Officer," 26; Miguel A. Levario writing the chapter "The El Paso Race Riot of 1916" contained in *War Along the Border*, Arnoldo De León, ed., tries to obliquely endorse criminality it seems: "Ranch raids caused great distress among Anglo property owners living along the border on the U.S. side. Some of these attacks were the work of individuals who, driven by need and the opportunity to retaliate for past wrongs, sought justice through banditry," 140. Readers may judge the degree of lameness to award the statement.

27   Al Ritter, "Captain Fox's Colt," *Handguns*, February 1997. Quoting Big Bend ranchman Raymond Fitzgerald: "Their standing as thieves, informers, spies and murders has been well known in this section for two or three years. They used this El Porvenir ranch as headquarters.... but stayed in Mexico during the day and occasionally came over at night," 48.

28   Justice, *Little Known History of the Big Bend*, 151. Noticeably, but not surprisingly or unpredictably, Richard Ribb's contribution to *War Along the Border*, edited by Arnoldo De León, "La Rinchada: Revolution, Revenge, and the Rangers, 1910–1920," rightly castigates Texas Rangers for involment in the mass murders at Porvenir, but somewhat conveniently it would seem, wholly chooses to omit mentioning the precursor Mexican raids and murders carried out at Glenn Springs and Brite Ranch in the Big Bend Country of West Texas shortly before.

29   Enlistment, Oath, and Description Ranger Force, W. P. Stillwell, TSA.

30   Harris and Sadler, *The Texas Rangers*, 357.

31   Captain Carroll Bates, Company F, Texas Rangers to Adjutant General James A. Harley, April 6, 1918, TSA. Interestingly this letter written on Company F letterhead stationery is marked "Texas Rangers" rather than "Ranger Force"; Harris, Harris, and Sadler, *Texas Ranger Biographies*, 298.

32   Utley, *Lone Star Lawmen*, 64–65.

33   Justice, *Unknown History of the Big Bend*, 161.

34   Cox, *Time of the Rangers,* 82.

35   *El Paso Times*, April 4, 1918.

36   Captain Bates to AG Harley, April 6, 1918, TSA.

37   *El Paso Herald*, June 2, 1916; *El Paso Morning Times*, June 2, 1916. Newsclips courtesy Monty Waters.

38   Captain Bates to AG Harley, April 6, 1918, TSA; DeLord, *The Ultimate Sacrifice,* 82. Based on faulty newspaper reporting there has been confusion as to exactly who assisted Captain Bates and Private Stillwell, U.S. Customs or U.S. Army personnel. Captain Bates is not indistinct in his report to the adjutant general: "I was short of men so borrowed eight soldiers from a nearby camp...," TSA.

39   Ibid.

40   Ibid. Again, newspaper reports erroneously place the fight at Santa Helena, Texas, where the horses were stolen from instead of across the Rio Grande in Mexico where the actual shooting took place, and where Texas Ranger William P. Stillwell's death occurred.

41   Affidavit and Personnel File [W. P. Stilwell] For Texas Peace Officers Killed in the Line of Duty, CLEAT; *El Paso Times*, April 4, 1918; *Beaumont Enterprise*, April 4, 1918; Harris, Harris, and Sadler, *Texas Ranger Biographies*, 362; Death Certificate, "Will P. Stillwell. Gunshot Wound—Homicide."

42   Telegram, Captain Bates to AG Harley, April 3, 1918, TSA.

43   Telegram, Captain Bates to AG Harley, April 4, 1918, TSA; Casey, *Mirages, Mysteries and Reality Brewster County, Texas: The Big Bend of the Rio Grande*. "....Stillwell was called upon in early April of 1918 to cross into Mexico to recover a number of horses which had been stolen and driven across the river," 356.

44   Telegram, AG Harley to Captain Bates, April 3, 1918, TSA.

45   Captain Bates to AG Harley, April 6, 1918, TSA.

46   Ibid.

47   *El Paso Times,* April 4, 1918.

48   Waters, "A. G. Beard: West Texas Law Officer." The author reports that Santa Helena, Texas, no longer exists but is "very near the current Castalon in the Big Bend National Park," 26.

49   Telegram, Captain Bates to AG Harley, April 7, 1918, TSA; Harris and Sadler, *The Texas Rangers,* 358.

50   Captain Bates to AG Harley, April 6, 1918, TSA.

51   AG Harley to All Ranger Captains, May 17, 1918, TSA.

52   Captain Bates to AG Harley, April 6, 1918, TSA.

Chapter 19: Joe Robert Shaw, 1918.

1   Enlistment, Oath of Service, and Description Ranger Force, Joe R. Shaw, July 5, 1918, TRHF&M; Adjutant General James A. Harley to Captain Charles F. Stevens, July 10, 1918, TRHF&M; Harris, Harris, and Sadler, *Texas Ranger Biographies*, 346.

2   Gournay, *Texas Boundaries*, 49, 51.

3   Tise, *Texas County Sheriffs*, 43.

4   Harris and Sadler, *The Texas Rangers*, 329.

5   Ibid.

6   Captain Charles F. Stevens to Ranger John B. Sittre, January 8, 1918, TRHF&M.

7   Enlistment, Oath of Service, and Description Ranger Force, William Scott. December 13, 1917, TRHF&M.

8   Harris and Sadler, *The Texas Rangers*, 375.

9   Captain Stephens to Major Walter F. Woodul, Assistant Adjutant General, March 27, 1918: "The Army Officers have been very nice to me, and when my men are out on a scout and go into an army camp, they are always invited to eat and their horses are fed," WP-CAH. In a letter dated April 3, 1918, to Ranger Harry Wallis the sheriff of Cameron County, W.T. Vann, made his feelings known: "Now Harry, I have asked you and the rangers to return the guns that you took before but have not been able to even hear from you and I want to state here in BLACK and WHITE, that I am going to file complaint against you for robbery if you do not return the guns at once, you have no right whatever to go into those people's houses and take their guns, no more than you would have to take their money. I have talked to John Kleiber about this matter and he says it is a violation of the law for you to do this and that he will prosecute you, but I am going to give you a chance to square this matter," WP-CAH; Wesley Hall Looney, "The Texas Rangers in a Turbulent Era," MA Thesis, Texas Tech University, Lubbock, Texas, 1971, 28–33.

10   Enlistment, Oath of Service, and Description Ranger Force, William Scott, TRHF&M.

11   Captain Stevens to Assistant Adjutant General Walter F. Woodul, August, 22, 1918, TSA.

12   *Brownsville Herald*, August 22, 1918: "his [Joe Robert Shaw's] family in Harlingen."

13   Enlistment, Oath of Service, and Description Ranger Force, S. T. Chaves, December 18, 1917, TRHF&M; Harris, Harris, and Sadler, *Texas Ranger Biographies*, 59.

14   *Brownsville Herald*, August 22, 1918.

15   Sterling, *Trails and Trials of a Texas Ranger*, 423.

16   *Brownsville Herald*, August 22, 1918.

17   Captain Stevens to Assistant AG Woodul, August 22, 1918, TSA.

18   Harris and Sadler, *The Texas Rangers*. Astutely the authors mention: "Trying to enlist in the Texas Rangers as a way of dodging the draft is an aspect of the organization's history that has not been touched on," 324; Adjutant General J. A. Harley to Captain J. M. Fox, October 11, 1917, TSA; AG Harley to Captain Fox, November 24, 1917. "You are hereby instructed to inform all members of your command within the draft age and who have been enlisted as Rangers since June 5, 1917, that their service as Rangers is not intended to relieve them from the draft, and they will not claim exemption on the ground of being Rangers. If they have done so or do so, they will be discharged from the service. This department has an agreement with the War Department which exempts Rangers who were in the service before June 5, 1917, but we are not to assist in defeating the draft law by enlisting Rangers who would come under the draft," TSA.

19   Harris and Sadler, *The Texas Rangers*, 326.

20   Ibid. For thoughtful—and evenhanded—insight regarding the population shifts, both Anglos and Hispanics, moving away from the Lower Rio Grande Valley due to excessive violence from forces on each side of the border, see, Charles C. Cumberland, "Border Raids in the Lower Rio Grande Valley—1915, *Southwestern Historical Quarterly*, April 1954, 285–311. Although somewhat popular in certain writings, an excoriating indictment of the Texas Rangers resorting to indiscriminate bloodshed in the Lower Rio Grande Valley, while at the same time trying to justify other criminal acts of brutality against persons and/or property is anemic on its face: Murder is murder, criminality is criminality, whether under the color of law, or as an excuse for real or fancied social injustice. Extralegal measures may be understandable, yes; defensible, no. Likewise lame are masking thievery and robbery and stealing livestock as but a begin necessity for revolutionists reconstituting their commissary. Victimization is objectionable and unpleasant, no matter the feigned justification, no matter which side of the border.

21   Telephone interviews by author with Drs. Charles H. Harris III and Louis R. Sadler, December 16, 2011.

22   Harris and Sadler, *The Texas Rangers*, quoting Captain Stevens to Assistant AG Woodul, June 12, 1918, 380.

23   Affidavit and Personnel File [Joe R. Shaw] For Texas Peace Officers Killed in the Line of Duty, CLEAT.

24   Captain Stevens to Assistant AG Woodul, August 22, 1918, TSA.

25   Ibid.; Webb, *TheTexas Rangers*, 508.

26   Ibid.

27   Telegram, Captain Stevens to AG Harley, August 22, 1918, TSA; *Dallas Morning News*, August 23, 1918; *Austin American Statesman*, August 23, 1918.

28   Captain H. M. Harrison, USA, District Intelligence Officer to Captain Stevens, August 24, 1918, TRHF&M.

29   *Brownsville Herald*, August 22, 1918.

30   John R. Peavey, *Echoes From the Rio Grande: From the Thorny Hills of Duval to the Sleepy Rio Grande*, 178–79; Harris, Harris, and Sadler, *Texas Ranger Biographies*, 371.

Chapter 20: Lenn T. Sadler, 1918.

1   Harris, Harris, and Sadler, *Texas Ranger Biographies*, 334–35.

2   Ibid.

3   Gournay, *Texas Boundaries*, 78; Awbrey and Dooley, *Why Stop?* 379.

4   Harris, Harris, and Sadler, *Texas Ranger Biographies*, 334–35.

5   Ibid.

6   Captain Stevens to Assistant AG Woodul, March 23, 1918, TSA.

7   Captain Stevens to Assistant AG Woodul, April 25, 1918, TSA; James Randolph Ward, "The Texas Rangers, 1919-1935: A Study in Law Enforcement," Ph.D Dissertation, Texas Christian University, Fort Worth, 1972; Valley By-Liners, *Gift of the Rio: Story of Texas' Tropical Borderland*, Kitty Culwell, Cont., "The Day of the Bandit." "Many raids took place in this area of the Valley. Frank has vivid memories of his own personal encounters with some of the roving law-breakers. It was not unusual for some of the farm workers to join the night raiders," 124.

8   Ibid.; and May 23, 1918, TSA.

9   Captain Stevens to Assistant AG Woodul, May 23, 1918, TSA.

10   Captain Stevens to Assistant AG Woodul, May 25, 1918, TSA.

11   Captain Stevens to Assistant AG Woodul, June 21, 1918, TSA.

12   Enlistment, Oath of Service, and Description Ranger Force, L. T. Sadler, May 27, 1918, TRHF&M.

13   Verdon R. Adams, *Tom White: The Life of a Lawman*. 10; DeLord, *The Ultimate Sacrifice*, 82.

14   Harris and Sadler, *The Texas Rangers*, 410.

15   Special Order No. 30, Assistant AG Woodul to Captain Stevens, August 26, 1918, TRHF&M.

16   Telegram, Texas State Reprehensive J. T. Canales to AG Harley, August 31, 1918, TSA.

17   For those interested in this area's attraction for genuine and would-be train robbers the reader is referred to the comprehensive research and

adroit writing of Jeffrey Burton, particularly, *The Deadliest Outlaws: The Ketchum Gang and the Wild Bunch* (UNT Press 2009).

18   Utley, *Lone Star Lawmen*, 81.

19   Ibid.: "It leaves today's historian to conclude that these offenses may or may not have happened; we cannot know," 80.

20   Captain Stevens to AG Harley, September 14, 1918, TSA.

21   DeLord, *The Ultimate Sacrifice*, 83,

22   Harris and Sadler, *The Texas Rangers*, 418.

23   Telegram, Ranger George Sadler to AG Harley, September 15, 1918, TSA.

24   Donaly Brice, TSA, to author, December 8, 2011: "The service record for L. T. Sadler shows that he enlisted on May 27, 1918, at Mercedes, in Hidalgo County. There is also a notation that he was 'killed accidently on Devil's River Sept. 15, 1918.' I found no correspondence in the Ranger records or the Adjutant General's Records describing the situation in which he was 'accidently' shot."

25   Affidavit and Personnel Records [L.T. Sadler] For Texas Peace Officers Killed in the Line of Duty, CLEAT; Texas Certificate of Death, L. T. Sadler, September 16, 1918.

26   H. M. Johnson, Quartermaster, Ranger Force, to Southwestern Hospital, Del Rio, Texas, October 7, 1918, TSA.

Chapter 21: Delbert "Tim" Timberlake, 1918

1   There are discrepancies. Timberlake's date of birth is taken from his Death Certificate, which more or less coincides with his assertion that he was twenty-two years old when he became a Texas Ranger during 1905, though he stretched his age forward a few months as most young people are inclined to do. TSA furnished an Oath of Service for Delbert Timberlake dated January 14, 1905, and an Enlistment, Oath of Service, and Description Ranger Force, dated July 27, 1905. A 1905 Scout Report for Company A reveals Timberlake's name showing up on January 24, 1905: "scouted Webb County during month. 26 to 30 they [Privates Anglin and D. Timberlake] were at the coal mines." Clearly Delbert was a Texas Ranger as early as January 1905; Donaly Brice, TSA, to author, December 27, 2001; Spellman, *Captain J. A. Brooks, Texas Ranger*, 168; William Warren Sterling, who personally knew Timberlake avers: "Sergeant Delbert Timberlake, whom we always called Tim, was one of the best Rangers who ever died for his native state." See, Sterling, *Trails and Trials of a Texas Ranger*, 424.

2   Monthly Scout Reports [1905], Company A, Ranger Force, TSA.

3   Pay Roll, Compnay A, Ranger Force, month of August 1905, Timberlake discharged August 5th, TSA.

4   U.S. Federal Census 1910, Galveston County, Texas.

5   Harris, Harris, and Sadler, *Texas Ranger Biographies*, 379.

6   Enlistment, Oath of Service, and Description Ranger Force [without pay] for D. Timberlake, March 9, 1916, TRHF&M.

7   Tise, *Texas County Sheriffs*, 505; Harris and Sadler, *The Texas Rangers*, 315–16.

8   Harris and Sadler, *The Texas Rangers,* 419.

9   Clifford R. Caldwell, *Fort McKavett and Tales of Menard County,* 132–34; Clifford R. Caldwell and Ron DeLord, *Texas Lawmen, 1900–1940: More of the Good and the Bad.* Law enforcement agencies listed alphabetically.

10 Harris and Sadler, *The Texas Rangers,* 419.

11 *Fort Worth Record*, October 12, 1918.

12 Sterling, *Trails and Trials of a Texas Ranger*: "Vann had been advised by an informant that a bunch of smugglers would cross the river...," 423.

13 Ibid., 424.

14 Webb, *The Texas Rangers,* 529. Naturally, H. Gordon Frost and John H. Jenkins in *"I'm Frank Hamer" The Life of a Texas Peace Officer* offer their own version of similar dialogue, 82.

15 Ibid., 528.

16 Sterling, *Trails and Trials of a Texas Ranger:* "The *hombre* who served as *guia* literally had to walk into the mouth of the gun, and his courage was bolstered by mescal or marihuana," 423.

17 Harris and Sadler, *The Texas Rangers,* 420–21; W. M. Hanson, Ranger Inspector to Adjutant General James A. Harley, October 13, 1918: "On account of the scarcity of liquor in Texas, the Mescal business from Mexico is flurishing [sic]. It is very cheap on the other side, worth probably, two or three dollars a gallon, and on this side it is worth up to ten dollars a quart," WP-CAH.

18 *San Antonio Daily Light*, October 18, 1918; Sterling, *Trails and Trials of a Texas Ranger*, 424. The official report of the incident—though a touch confusing—seems to award the death shots to Sheriff Vann: "When Vann and Hamer saw the blaze from Delgado's pistol they returned the fire, Vann wounding him in the right hand and side with his automatic rifle [shotgun in other accounts], hitting him three times, twice in the body, both of which were death shots, and the other shot in the leg. Delgado ran about thirty or forty feet and fell dead." See report of "Murder of Ranger Delbert Timberlake," W. M. Hanson, Ranger Inspector to AG Harley, WP-CAH.

19 Death Certificate, Delbert Timberlake, October 11, 1918; Affidavit and Personnel File [Delbert Timberlake] For Texas Peace Officers Killed in the Line of Duty, CLEAT; *Temple Daily Telegram*, October 12, 1918.

20 *San Antonio Daily Light*, October 18, 1918.

21 Affidavit and Personnel File [Delbert Timberlake] For Texas Peace Officers Killed in the Line of Duty, CLEAT; Texas State Death Certificate.

22 Resolution, Brownsville Board of City Development, October 15, 1918, Signed, S. C. Tucker, President, TRHF&M.

23 Captain J. M. Fox to Assistant AG Woodul, January 22, 1918: "and am leaving him [Pennington] there [Alpine] until I hear from you as the boys are all afraid to work with him," TSA; Captain W. W. Davis to AG Harley, March 18, 1918: "Ranger Pennington who was transferred to me from Captain Fox's Company will not stay sober. I have talked to him but it does no good. I had him here, but to get him away I sent him to Fabens, and Perkins who is in charge of the Fabens Camp thinks he is buying whiskey for the soldiers as he drinks with them.... and if you could transfer him to some Company in a dry territory where he could not get boose he would make a good ranger, but if he can get anything to drink he gets down and out," TSA; Captain Davis to AG Harley, March 23, 1918, after a fight with Mexican revolutionists: "Ranger Pennington showed good nerve & judgment and as he promised never to take another drink would you please give him another showing," TSA; Assistant AG Woodul to Captain Davis, March 26, 1918: "As to Pennington, if he ever so much as touches another drop you will immediately dismiss him from service...," TSA; Affidavit and Personnel File [Ben L. Pennington] For Texas Peace Officers Killed in the Line of Duty, CLEAT; *El Paso Times*, October 13, 1918. For a brief sketch of Ben Pennington see Mike Cox's *Texas Ranger Tales II*, 162–74.

24 DeLord, *The Ultimate Sacrifice*, 83.

25 Captain Davis to AG Harley, April 27, 1918: "One of my men, Hyde, is very sick with dysentery and has been in bed two weeks and the Doctors think he has small chance to get well," TSA; Captain Davis to Assistant AG Woodul, April 30, 1918: "P.S. Since writing the above Ranger Hyde has died," TSA; Captain Davis to P. A. Cardwell, May 9, 1918: "and all of us badly scared and it is a wonder I could make out any Kind of report. Ranger Hyde and his little girl died with emebic [*sic*] dysentery, two [of] the other boys and his wife had it and the rest of us had diarrhea and it looked like a general die up might occur but we are all well now," TSA; Harris, Harris, and Sadler, *Texas Ranger Biographies*, 196.

Chapter 22: T. E. Paul Perkins, 1918.

1   Enlistment, Oath of Service, and Description Ranger Force, T.E.P. Perkins, September 1, 1918, TSA.
2   *Cameron Herald*, November 14, 1918.
3   Awbrey and Dooley, *Why Stop?* 78.
4   Captain W. W. Davis to Adjutant General James A. Harley, March 14, 1918, TSA.
5   Captain Davis to AG Harley, April 4, 1918, TSA.
6   Captain Davis to AG Harley, March 7, 1918, TSA.
7   Captain Davis to AG Harley, March 23, 1918, TSA.
8   Ibid.; Report of Incident, Captain Davis to AG Harley, TSA; Telegram, Captain Davis to AG Harley, March 3, 1918. The date on the telegram is incorrect and should read March 23, rather than March 3, an apparent typographical error, TSA.
9   Ibid.; Harris and Sadler, *The Texas Rangers,* 346.
10 Captain Davis to AG Harley, March 27, 1918, TSA; Though not specific to this instance of combat the role women played during the Mexican Revolution is a fascinating side story. In fact, Elena Poniatowska in her delightful and insightful and photo-packed *Las Soldaderas: Women of the Mexican Revolution* is not hesitant: "Without the soldaeras, there is no Mexican Revolution—they kept it alive and fertile, like the earth," 16.
11 Captain Davis to AG Harley, April 4, 1918, TSA.
12 Harris, Harris, and Sadler, *Texas Ranger Biographies*, 122–23.
13 Captain Davis to AG Harley, March 31, 1918, TSA.
14 Ibid.
15 Captain Davis to AG Harley, March 27, 1918, TSA.
16 Captain Davis to Assistant AG Walter F. Woodul, April 30, 1918, TSA.
17 Captain Davis to AG Harley, March 18, 1918, TSA.
18 Enlistment, Oath of Service, and Description Ranger Force, T. E. P. Perkins, September 1, 1918, TRHF&M; State of Texas Commission as Private in "the Texas Ranger Force," Dated September 10, 1918, Signed by Adjutant General James A. Harley, TRHF&M.
19 One of the best, with a single chapter even titled "Gunrunning," is the recent award-winning treatment by Charles H. Harris III and Louis R. Sadler, *The Secret War in El Paso: Mexican Revolutionary Intrigue, 1906–1920.* Also refer to *War Along the Border: The Mexican Revolution and Tejano Communities*, Arnoldo De León, ed. Specifically the subject is addressed in separate chapters: "Smugglers in Dangerous Times: Revolution and Communities in the Tejano Borderlands," by George T. Díaz and "'The Population is Overwhelmingly Mexican: Most of It Is in

Sympathy With the Revolution': Mexico's Revolution of 1910 and the Tejano Community in the Bid Bend" by John Euebio Kingemann.

[20]   Harris, Harris, and Sadler, *Texas Ranger Biographies*, 307.

[21]   DeLord, *The Ultimate Sacrifice*, 84.

[22]   Captain Davis to AG Harley, December 23, 1918, TSA.

[23]   A snippet in the *Beaumont Journal*, November 8, 1918, places the episode as occurring "on the island, thirty-two miles southeast of El Paso. The international boundary passes through the island." Likewise, commentary in the *Fort Worth Record*, November 9, 1898, is near verbatim. The *Austin American*, November 9, 1918, positions the fight as taking place "on the island three miles southeast of El Paso where the international boundary passes through the island."

[24]   Affidavit and Personnel File [T. E. P. Perkins] For Texas Peace Officers Killed in the Line of Duty, CLEAT; Death Certificate, Ellezy Prkins, "Gun shot wound parties unknown."

[25]   Telegram, Captain Davis to AG Harley, November 8, 1918, TSA.

[26]   Sam D. W. Low, Acting Adjutant General to Captain Davis, November 8, 1918, TSA.

[27]   *El Paso Times*, November 9, 1918.

[28]   *Cameron Herald*, November 14, 1918.

Chapter 23: William M. Alsobrook, 1919.

[1]   Death Certificate, William Alsobrook; Harris, Harris, and Sadler, *Texas Ranger Biographies*, 7.

[2]   Ibid.; Enlistment, Oath of Service, and Description Ranger Force, William M. Alsobrook, June 16, 1919, TRHF&M. There are discrepancies associated with these two documents. The first states Will Alsobrook's POB was Manchester (Red River County), Texas, and the second, data furnished by Will, indicates he was born in neighboring Lamar County (Paris), Texas. Likewise, in the first instance a birth year of 1881 is recorded, whereas the latter document indicates a birth year of 1884; Lawrence and Sue Dale, eds., *Burial, Cemetery and Death Records for Red River County, Texas, thru 31 December 2004*, Volume 1, 28.

[3]   Letterhead Stationery: "Will Alsobrook, Constable. Precinct No. One. Clarksville, Texas," TRHF&M.

[4]   M. R. Butts, *Lawmakers and Lawbreakers of Red River County*, vol. 1, 38.

[5]   Blackburn, *Wanted: Historic County Jails of Texas*, 278.

[6]   Harris and Sadler, *The Texas Rangers*, 396–97.

[7]   Enlistment, Oath of Service and Description Ranger Force, Will Alsobrook, June 1, 1918. "Without Pay," "Loyalty Ranger," Station: "Clarksville," TRHF&M.

8   Ibid.
9   Harris and Sadler, *The Texas Rangers*. Quoting Captain Hanson's instructions to Loyalty Rangers, 397.
10   Harris, Harris, and Sadler, *Texas Ranger Biographies*, 7.
11   Harris and Sadler, *The Texas Rangers*, 453.
12   Ward, "The Texas Rangers, 1919–1935: A Study in Law Enforcement," 19.
13   Harris, Harris, and Sadler, *Texas Ranger Biographies*, 79, 204, 249, 388.
14   DeLord, *The Ultimate Sacrifice*, 84.
15   Harris and Sadler, *The Texas Rangers*, 453.
16   Will Alsobrook to AG James A. Harley, February 25, 1919, TRHF&M.
17   Enlistment, Oath of Service, and Description Ranger Force, William M. Alsobrook, June 16, 1919, TRHF&M; Private Will Alsobrook to Captain R. W. Aldrich, Austin, July 29, 1919, TRHF&M; Captain Aldrich to Will Alsobrook, August 14, 1919, TRHF&M.
18   Ibid.
19   Captain Aldrich to Private Alsobrook, September 8, 1919, TSA.
20   Captain Aldrich to Ranger Ben Tumlinson, Jr., December 1919, TSA.
21   On letterhead of Edds & Acklen Lumber Company, Hebbronville, Texas, Private Will Alsobrook to Captain Aldrich, July 29, 1919, TRHF&M.
22   Gournay, *Texas Boundaries*, 119.
23   Tise, *Texas County Sheriffs*, 288; Gilliland, *Wilson County Texas Rangers*, 48–49.
24   Jack Shipman, ed., "Mexican Payrolls and American Bandits," *Voice of the Mexican Border*, El Paso Issue, December 1933, 146.
25   Harris and Sadler, *The Texas Rangers*, 478–80.
26   Shipman, "Mexican Payrolls and American Bandits," 146.
27   Captain W. M. Hanson to C. E. Breniman, Bureau of Investigation, San Antonio, August 18, 1919. "This will introduce to you Captain Jerry Gray of Marfa, Texas, who has been making a very careful and extensive investigation with reference to the matter...," Webb Papers, Center for American History; hereafter WP-CA, Austin, Texas.
28   Jefferson Eagle Vaughn to Adjutant General W. D. Cope, February 17, 1920, WP-CA.
29   Harris and Sadler, *The Texas Rangers*, 478–80; Tise, *Texas County Sheriffs*, 410.
30   Waters, "A. G. Beard: West Texas Law Officer," quoting Bureau of Investigation report from Gus Jones, August 21, 1919, 54.
31   Captain Aldrich to Private Alsobrook, September 8, 1919, two separate letters, TSA.
32   Private Alsobrook to Captain Aldrich, September 13, 1919, TSA.
33   Ranger Tumlinson to Captain Aldrich, December 12, 1919, TSA.

34   Captain Aldrich to Ranger Tumlinson, December 18, 1919, TSA.
35   *Laredo Times*, December 14, 1919.
36   *Austin American Statesman*, December 11, 1919: "inflicted from a .45 caliber Colts...."
37   Donaly Brice, to author January 17, 2012, TSA. A diligent search at the Texas State Library and Archives has thus far failed to produce primary source documents adequately detailing Ranger Will Alsobrook's death.
38   Affidavit and Personnel File [William Alsobrook] For Texas Peace Officers Killed in the Line of Duty, CLEAT; Death Certificate, William Alsobrook: "Gunshot wound abdomen"; pinpointing where an incident actually occurred on a moving train is near impossible. The fact he died at Mercy Hospital, Laredo, Texas, and was a Texas Ranger when he passed, seems justification enough for his inclusion in *Riding Lucifer's Line*.
39   *Dallas Morning News*, December 10, 1919.
40   Affidavit and Personnel File, William Alsobrook, CLEAT; *Clarksville Times*, December 12, 1919.
41   Typescript: Family History of the Geer Family, 19, courtesy Lisa Cornelius, Director, Red River County Public Library, Clarksville, Texas.
42   *Dallas Morning News*, December 10, 1919; *Deport Times*, December 26, 1919.
43   Oath of Members of Ranger Force, Will M. Alsobrook, June 16, 1919, TRHF&M.
44   Ranger Tumlinson to Captain Aldrich, December 15, 1919, TRHF&M.
45   Waters, "A. G. Beard: West Texas Law Officer," 55; Harris and Sadler, *The Texas Rangers*, 480.
46   Tise, *Texas County Sheriffs*. 288; Gilliland, *Horsebackers of the Brush Country*, 134.

Chapter 24: Joe Ben Buchanan, 1921.

1   Enlistment, Oath of Service, and Description Ranger Force, J. B. Buchanan, March 1, 1921, TRHF&M.
2   Interview by author with Sarah Bellian, Curator, Scurry County Museum, Snyder, Texas, January 18, 2012; Doris Lavinia Buchanan Driscoll and Constance Ruth Buchanan McJimsey, co-contributors, *Footprints Across Scurry County, 1884–1984*, 163–64.
3   Hooper Shelton, *History of Scurry County, Texas: From Buffalo ... to Oil*, 18. A statue of the white buffalo is situated on the Scurry County courthouse grounds in Snyder, Texas. Also, Charles G. Anderson, *In Search of the Buffalo: The Story of J. Wright Mooar*, 82–87.

4   J. Wright Mooar, "The Frontier Experiences of J. Wright Mooar," *West Texas Historical Association Yearbook*, 1928, 89–92.

5   Gournay, *Texas Boundaries*, 95, 105; Awbrey and Dooley, *Why Stop?* 470–71.

6   Tise, *Texas County Sheriffs*, 460.

7   William Curry Holden, *The Espuela Land and Cattle Company: A Study of a Foreign-Owned Ranch in Texas*, 228.

8   Kathryn Cotten, *Saga of Scurry*, 80.

9   Driscoll and McJimsey, *Footprints Across Scurry County*, 164.

10   Aline Parks and Jeff Corkran, eds., *The Coming West: True Stories of Trails Grown Dim*, 201.

11   Harris, Harris, and Sadler, *Texas Ranger Biographies*, 46.

12   Enlistment, Oath of Service, and Description Ranger Force, J. B. Buchanan, December 7, 1917, TRHF&M.

13   Warrant of Authority and Descriptive List, J. B. Buchanan, December 7, 1918, TRHF&M.

14   Enlistment, Oath of Service, and Description Ranger Force, J. B. Buchanan, March 1, 1921, TRHF&M.

15   Captain Aldrich to Sergeant Trimble, November 3, 1921, TSA.

16   Sheriff Everett Ewing "E. E." Townsend, Brewster County, to Adjutant General Barton, November 29, 1921, TSA.

17   *Waco Times Herald*, December 27, 1921; *Austin American Statesman*, December 27 and 31, 1921.

18   Affidavit and Personnel File [J. B. Buchanan] For Peace Officers Killed in the Line of Duty, CLEAT.

19   Captain Gray's report to the adjutant general was printed in the December 31, 1921, edition of the *Austin American Statesman*.

20   Captain Aldrich to Sheriff J. E. Vaughan, Marfa, Texas, December 29, 1921, TSA.

21   DeLord, *The Ultimate Sacrifice*, 87.

22   Captain Gray to Captain Aldrich, January 12, 1922, TRHF&M.

23   Death Certificate, Joseph Benjamin Buchanan, December 26, 1921, "Examined after death. Gun Shot."

Afterword

1   Interview by author with Brenda Tisdale, Museum Administrator, Border Patrol Museum and Memorial Library Foundation, El Paso, Texas, January 19, 2012. One book-length U.S. Border Patrol history is John Myers Myers' treatment *The Border Wardens*. Also, for a contemporary look at Border Patrolmen working out of a Texas Post of Duty, see, Robert Lee Marill, *Patrolling Chaos: The U.S. Border Patrol In Deep South Texas*.

2   Just for Texas the reader is referred to *The Thirteenth Biennial Texas Peace Officers' Memorial Services Program* for 2011. Line of Duty Deaths for U.S Border Patrolmen, pages 69-70; Line of Duty Deaths for U.S. Customs Inspectors, page 71.

3   Tisdale to author, January 24, 2012. Interestingly, in April 2012 the U.S. Border Patrol graduated class number 1000 at their National Training Academy in Artesia, New Mexico. Also, Peter Andreas, *Border Games: Policing the U.S.-Mexico Divide*, 156.

4   *Thirteenth Biennial Texas Peace Officers. Memorial Services Program* for 2011. The Line of Duty Deaths for Texas Rangers after creation of the Frontier Battalion and Special Force in 1874 may be found on pages 63–64 and 66–67.

5   Numerous interviews by author with Kirby Dendy, the Chief of the Texas Rangers.

Bibliography

Non-published sources—manuscripts, typescripts, theses, dissertations, tape recordings, official documents, courthouse records, tax rolls, petitions, correspondence, prison records, census records, licensing records, interviews, etc.—are cited with specificity in chapter endnotes.

The three principal sources for recovering primary documents were the Texas State Library and Archives Commission, Austin, Texas; The Texas Ranger Hall of Fame and Ranger Museum, Research Center, Waco, Texas; and the Affidavits and Personnel Files for Texas Peace Officers Killed in the Line of Duty, Peace Officers Memorial Foundation, Inc., Austin, Texas.

Books:

Adams, Ramon F. *Western Words: A Dictionary of the Old West*. New York: Hippocrene Books, 1998.

Adams, Verdon R. *Tom White: The Life of a Lawman*. El Paso: Texas Western Press, 1972.

Aguirre, Jr., Adalberto, and Jonathan H. Turner. *American Ethnicity: The Dynamics and Consequences of Discrimination*. Boston: McGraw-Hill, 1998.

Alexander, Bob. *Rawhide Ranger, Ira Aten: Enforcing Law on the Texas Frontier*. Denton: University of North Texas Press, 2011.

———. *Winchester Warriors: Texas Rangers of Company D, 1874–1901*. Denton: University of North Texas Press, 2009.

———. *Lawmen, Outlaws, and S.O.Bs*. Silver City, NM: High-Lonesome Books, 2004.

———. *Lawmen, Outlaws, and S.O.Bs*. Vol. 2. Silver City, NM: High-Lonesome Books, 2007.

———. *Fearless Dave Allison: Border Lawman*. Silver City, NM: High-Lonesome Books, 2003.

———. *Desert Desperadoes: The Banditti of Southwestern New Mexico*. Silver City, NM: Gila Books, 2006.

———. *John H. Behan: Sacrificed Sheriff*. Silver City, NM: High-Lonesome Books, 2002.

———. *Dangerous Dan Tucker: New Mexico's Deadly Lawman*. Silver City, NM: High-Lonesome Books, 2001.

Amberson, Mary Margaret McAllen, James A. McAllen and Margaret H. McAllen. *I Would Rather Sleep in Texas: A History of the Lower Rio Grande Valley and the People of the Santa Anita Land Grant*. Austin: Texas State Historical Association, 2003.

Anderson, Charles G. *In Search of the Buffalo*. Union City, TN: Pioneer Press, 1996.

Andreas, Peter. *Border Games: Policing the U.S.-Mexico Divide*. Ithaca, NY: Cornell University Press, 2009.

Aros, Joyce. *The Cochise County Cowboys: Who Were These Men?* Tombstone, AZ: Goose Flats Publishing, 2011.

Austerman, Wayne R. *Sharps Rifles and Spanish Mules: The San Antonio–El Paso Mail, 1851–1881*. College Station: Texas A&M University Press, 1985.

Awbrey, Betty Dooley, and Claude Dooley. *Why Stop? A Guide to Texas Historical Roadside Markers*. Houston: Lone Star Books, 1978.

Baker, T. Lindsey. *Ghost Towns of Texas*. Norman: University of Oklahoma Press, 1986.

Ball, Larry D. *Desert Lawmen: The High Sheriffs of New Mexico and Arizona Territories, 1846–1912*. Albuquerque: University of New Mexico Press, 1992.

———. *The United States Marshals of New Mexico and Arizona Territories, 1846–1912*. Albuquerque: University of New Mexico Press, 1978.

Banta, Cindy, Chairman. *Footprints Across Scurry County, 1884–1984*. Snyder, TX: Scurry County Book Committee, 1984.

Barkley, Roy R., and Mark F. Odintz, eds. *The Portable Handbook of Texas*. Austin: Texas State Historical Association, 2000.

Bartholomew, Ed. *Jesse Evans: A Texas Hide-Burner*. Houston: Frontier Press of Texas, 1955.

———. *The Biographical Album of Western Gunfighters*. Houston: Frontier Press of Texas, 1958.

Baylor County Historical Society. *From Salt Pork to Sirloin: A History of Baylor County, Texas—1879 to 1930*. Quanah, TX: Nortex Publishing, 1972.

Baylor, George Wythe. *Into the Far, Wild Country: True Tales of the Old Southwest*. Edited by Jerry Thompson. El Paso: Texas Western Press, 1996.

Beith, Malcolm. *The Last Narco: Inside the Hunt for El Chapo, The World's Most Wanted Drug Lord*. New York: Grove Press, 2010.

Biggers, Don H. *Shackelford County Sketches*. Edited by Joan Farmer. Albany, TX: Clear Fork Press, 1974.

Blackburn, Ed. *Wanted: Historic County Jails of Texas*. College Station: Texas A&M University Press, 2006.

Blumenson, Martin. *The Patton Papers, 1885–1940*. New York: Da Capo Press, 1998.

Boardman, Mark, ed. *Revenge! And Other True Tales of the Old West*. Lafayette, IN: Scarlet Mask Enterprises. 2004.

Bohm, Robert M., and Keith N. Haley. *Introduction to Criminal Justice*. New York: McGraw-Hill, 2002.

Bowden, Charles. *Murder City: Ciudad Juárez and the Global Economy's New Killing Field*. New York: Nation Books, 2011.

———. *Juárez: The Laboratory of Our Future*. New York: Aperture Foundation, 1998.

Brice, Donaly E. *The Great Comanche Raid: Boldest Indian Attack of the Texas Republic*. Austin: Eakin Press, 1987.

———, and Barry A. Crouch. *The Governor's Hounds: The Texas State Police, 1870–1873*. Austin: University of Texas Press, 2011.

Broaddus, J. Morgan. *The Legal Heritage of El Paso*. El Paso: Texas Western College Press, 1963.

Browning, James A. *Violence Was No Stranger: A Guide to the Grave Sites of Famous Westerners*. Stillwater, OK: Barbed-Wire Press, 1993.

Burton, Jeffrey. *The Deadliest Outlaws: The Ketchum Gang and the Wild Bunch*. Denton: University of North Texas Press, 2009.

Butts, M. R. *Lawmakers and Lawbreakers of Red River County*. 2 vols. Clarksville, TX: Self-published, 2006.

Caldwell, Clifford R. *Dead Right: The Lincoln County War*. Mountain Home, TX: Self-published, 2008.

———. *Fort McKavett and Tales of Menard County*. Mountain Home, TX: Self-published, 2012.

———, and Ron DeLord. *Texas Lawmen, 1835–1899: The Good and the Bad*. Charleston, SC: The History Press, 2011.

———, and Ron DeLord. *Texas Lawmen, 1900–1940: More of the Good and the Bad*. Charleston, SC: The History Press, 2012.

Campbell, Howard. *Drug War Zone: Frontline Dispatches from the Streets of El Paso and Juárez*. Austin: University of Texas Press, 2011.

Cano, Tony, and Anne Sochat. *BANDIDO: The True Story of Chico Canto, The Last Western Bandit*. Canutillo, TX: Reata Publishing Co., 1997.

Cartwright, Gary. *Dirty Dealing: Drug Smuggling on the Mexican Border and the Assassination of a Federal Judge*. El Paso: Cinco Puntos Press, 1998.

Casey, Robert. *The Texas Border and Some Borderliners*. New York: Bobbs-Merrill Co., 1950.

Casey, Clifford B. *Mirages, Mysteries and Reality: Brewster County, Texas, the Big Bend and the Rio Grande*. Hereford, TX: Pioneer Books Publishers, 1973.

Clayton, Lawrence, and Joan Halford Farmer, eds. *Tracks Along the Clear Fork: Stories From Shackelford and Throckmorton Counties*. Abilene, TX: McWhiney Foundation Press, 2000.

Collinson, Frank. *Life in the Saddle*. Edited by Mary Whatley Clarke. Norman: University of Oklahoma Press, 1963.

Cool, Paul. *Salt Warriors: Insurgency on the Rio Grande*. College Station: Texas A&M University Press, 2008.

Coolidge, Dane. *Fighting Men of the West*. New York: E. P. Dutton and Company, 1932.

Cotten, Kathryn. *Saga of Scurry*. San Antonio: The Naylor Company, 1957.

Cox, Mike. *The Texas Rangers: Wearing the Cinco Peso, 1821–1900*. New York: Forge Books, 2008.

———. *Time of the Rangers: Texas Rangers From 1900 to the Present*. New York: Forge Books, 2009.

———. *Texas Ranger Tales: Stories That Need Telling*. Plano, TX: Republic of Texas Press, 1997.

———. *Texas Ranger Tales II*. Plano, TX: Republic of Texas Press, 1999.

Davis, John L. *The Texas Rangers: The First 150 Years*. San Antonio: University of Texas at San Antonio, Institute of Texas Cultures, 1975.

Daywood, Victoria Dunnahoo, and Peggy White Engledow. *The Bad Boys of Caldwell County, Texas: Book One, Murders in the 1800s*. Lockhart, TX: Ericson Books, 2011.

DeArment, Robert K. *Deadly Dozen: Twelve Forgotten Gunfighters of the Old West*. Norman: University of Oklahoma Press, 2003.

———. *George Scarborough: The Life and Death of a Lawman on the Closing Frontier*. Norman: University of Oklahoma Press, 1992.

———. *Bravo of the Brazos: John Larn of Fort Griffin*. Norman: University of Oklahoma Press, 2002.

DeLeón, Arnoldo. *They Called Them Greasers: Anglo Attitudes Toward Mexicans in Texas, 1821–1900*. Austin: University of Texas Press, 1983.

———. *The Tejano Community, 1836–1900*. Albuquerque: University of New Mexico Press, 1982.

———, ed. *War Along the Border: The Mexican Revolution and Tejano Communities*. College Station: Texas A&M University Press, 2012.

DeLord, Ronald G. *The Ultimate Sacrifice: Trials and Triumphs of the Texas Peace Officer, 1823–2000*. Austin: Police Officers Memorial Fund, 2000.

Devereaux, Jan. *Pistols, Petticoats, and Poker: The Real Lottie Deno, No Lies or Alibis*. Silver City, NM: High-Lonesome Books, 2008.

Dobie, J. Frank. *Vaquero of the Brush Country*. Boston: Little, Brown and Company, 1929.

Douglas, C. L. *The Gentlemen in the White Hats: Dramatic Episodes in the History of the Texas Rangers*. Dallas: South-West Press, 1934.

DuCoin, Candice. *Lawmen on the Texas Frontier: Rangers and Sheriffs*. Round Rock, TX: Riata Books, 2007.

Dukes, Doug. *Ben Thompson: Iron Marshal of Austin*. Austin: Self-published, 2011.

Dunn, J. B. (Red) John. *Perilous Trails of Texas*. Dallas: Southwest Press, 1932.

Durham, George. *Taming the Nueces Strip: The Story of McNelly's Rangers*. Austin: University of Texas Press, 1962.

Ernst, Robert. *Deadly Affrays: The Violent Deaths of the US Marshals*. Lafayette, IN: Scarlet Mask, 2006.

Fehrenbach, T. R. *Lone Star: A History of Texas and the Texans*. New York: Macmillan Publishing, 1968.

Ferguson, Harvey. *Rio Grande*. New York: Alfred A. Knopf, 1936.

Frost, H. Gordon. *The Gentlemen's Club: The Story of Prostitution In El Paso*. El Paso. Mangan Books. 1983.

———, and John H. Jenkins. *"I'm Frank Hamer": The Life of a Texas Peace Officer*. Austin: The Pemberton Press, 1968.

Galbreath, Lester W. *Fort Griffin and the Clear Fork Country: 100 Years of History, 1850–1950, on 25 Miles of the Clear Fork of the Brazos River*. Albany, TX: Self-published, 1997.

Gammel, Hans Peter. *The Laws of Texas, 1822–1897*. 10 Volumes. Austin: Gammel Books, 1898.

Garner, Diane. *Letters From the Big Bend: Legacy of a Pioneer*. Bloomington, IN: iUniverse Books Inc., 2011.

Gatto, Steve. *The Real Wyatt Earp: A Documentary Biography*. Edited by Neil B. Carmony. Silver City, NM: High-Lonesome Books, 2000.

———. *Johnny Ringo*. Lansing, MI: Protar House, 2002.

Gillett, James B. *Six Years with the Texas Rangers*. New Haven: Yale University Press, 1925.

Gilliland, Maude T. *Wilson County Texas Rangers, 1837–1977*. Pleasanton, TX: Self-published, 1977.

———. *Horsebackers of the Brush Country: A Study of Texas Rangers and Mexican Liquor Smugglers*. Pleasanton, TX: Self-published, 1968.

Gournay, Luke. *Texas Boundaries: Evolution of the State's Counties*. College Station: Texas A&M University Press, 1995.

Graham, Don. *Kings of Texas: The 150-Year Saga of an American Ranching Empire*. Hoboken, NJ: John Wiley & Sons, 2003.

Graybill, Andrew R. *Policing the Great Plains: Rangers, Mounties, and the North American Frontier, 1875–1910*. Lincoln: University of Nebraska Press, 2007.

Grayson, George W. *Mexico: Narco-Violence and a Failed State?* New Brunswick, NJ: Transaction Publishers, 2011.

Grillo, Ioan. *El Narco: Inside Mexico's Criminal Insurgency*. New York: Bloomsbury Press, 2011.

Habermeyer, Christopher Lance. *Gringo's Curve: Pancho Villa's Massacre of American Miners in Mexico, 1916*. El Paso: Book Publishers of El Paso, 2004.

Haley, J. Evetts. *Jeff Milton: A Good Man with a Gun*. Norman: University of Oklahoma Press, 1948.

Harris, Charles H. III, and Louis R. Sadler, *The Texas Rangers and the Mexican Revolution: The Bloodiest Decade, 1910–1920*. Albuquerque: University of New Mexico Press, 2004.

———. *The Secret War in El Paso: Mexican Revolutionary Intrigues, 1906–1920*. Albuquerque: University of New Mexico Press, 2009.

———. *The Border and the Revolution: Clandestine Activities of the Mexican Revolution, 1910–1920*. Silver City, NM: High-Lonesome Books, 1988.

———. *Plan de San Diego: Tejano Rebellion, Mexican Intrigue*. Lincoln: University of Nebraska, 2013.

———. and Frances E. Harris. *Texas Ranger Biographies: Those Who Served, 1910–1921*. Albuquerque: University of New Mexico Press, 2009.

Hendricks, Rick, and W. H. Timmons. *San Elizario: Spanish Presidio to Texas County Seat*. El Paso: Texas Western Press, University of Texas at El Paso, 1998.

Holden, William Curry. *The Espuela Land and Cattle Company: A Study of a Foreign-Owned Ranch in Texas*. Austin: Texas State Historical Association, 1970.

Horgan, Paul. *Great River: The Rio Grande in North American History*. 2 vols. New York: Rinehart & Company, 1954.

Howell, Kenneth W., ed. *Still the Arena of Civil War: Violence and Turmoil in Reconstruction Texas*. Denton: University of North Texas Press, 2012.

Hunter, J. Marvin, ed. *The Trail Drivers of Texas*. Austin: University of Texas Press, 1985.

Ivey, Darren L. *The Texas Rangers: A Registry and History*. Jefferson, NC: McFarland & Co., 2010.

Jacobson, Lucy Miller, and Nored, Mildred. *Jeff Davis County, Texas*. Fort Davis, TX: Fort Davis County Historical Society, 1993.

Jennings, N. A. *A Texas Ranger*. Dallas: Turner Company, 1930.

Johnson, David. *John Ringo, King of the Cowboys: His Life and Times from the Hoo Doo War to Tombstone*. Denton: University of North Texas Press, 2008.

———. *The Mason County "Hoo Doo" War, 1874–1902*. Denton: University of North Texas Press, 2006.

Jones, Harriot Howze, ed. *El Paso: A Centennial Portrait*. El Paso: El Paso County Historical Society, 1972.

Justice, Glenn. *Little Known History of the Texas Big Bend: Documented Chronicles From Cabeza DeVaca to the Era of Pancho Villa*. Odessa, TX: Rimrock Press, 2001.

———. *Revolution on the Rio Grande: Mexican Raids and Army Pursuits, 1916–1919*. El Paso: Texas Western Press, University of Texas at El Paso, 1992.

Keil, Robert. *Bosque Bonito: Violent Times Along the Borderland During the Mexican Revolution*. Edited by Elizabeth McBride. Alpine, TX: Center for Big Bend Studies, Sul Ross University, 2002.

Kearney, Milo, and Anthony Knopp. *Boom and Bust: The Historical Cycles of Matamoros and Brownsville*. Austin: Eakin Press, 1991.

Kilgore, D. E. *A Ranger Legacy: 150 Years of Service to Texas*. Austin: Madrona Press, 1973.

McAlavy, Don, and Harold Kilmer, eds. *High Plains History: 100 Years of History of East Central New Mexico*. Portales, NM: High Plains Historical Press, 1980.

McCampbell, Coleman. *Texas Seaport: The Story of the Growth of Corpus Christi and the Coastal Bend Area*. New York: Exposition Press, 1952.

McCaslin, Richard B. *Fighting Stock: John S. "Rip" Ford of Texas*. Fort Worth: Texas Christian University Press, 2011.

McCright, Grady E., and James H. Powell. *Jessie Evans: Lincoln County Badman*. College Station: Creative Publishing, 1983.

McLane, Curren Rogers, ed. *The Rogers Family Genealogy. The Texas Rangers*. Self-published, 1995.

MacCallum, Esther Darbyshire. *The History of St. Clement's Church*. El Paso. The McMath Co. 1925.

Madison, Virginia. *The Big Bend Country of Texas*. New York: October House, 1968.

Marill, Robert Lee. *Patrolling Chaos: The U.S. Border Patrol in Deep South Texas*. Lubbock: Texas Tech University Press, 2004.

Marks, Paula Mitchell. *In a Barren Land: American Indian Dispossession and Survival*. New York: William Morrow and Company, 1998.

Marohn, Richard C. *The Last Gunfighter: John Wesley Hardin*. College Station: Creative Publishing, 1995.

Mason, Herbert Molloy, Jr. *The Texas Rangers*. New York: Meredith Press, 1967.

Matthews, Sallie Reynolds. *Interwoven: A Pioneer Chronicle*. College Station: Texas A&M University Press, 1997.

Means, Joyce E. *Pancho Villa Days at Pilares*. Tucson: Self-published, 1994.

Meed, Douglas V. *Bloody Border: Riots, Battles and Adventures Along the Turbulent U.S Mexico Borderlands*. Tucson: Westernlore, 1992.

Meketa, Jacqueline. *From Martyrs to Murderers: The Old Southwest's Saints, Sinners and Scalawags*. Las Cruces: Yucca Tree Press, 1993.

Metz, Leon Claire. *The Shooters*. El Paso: Mangan Books, 1976.

———. *Border: The U.S.-Mexican Line*. El Paso: Mangan Books, 1990.

———. *John Wesley Hardin: Dark Angel of Texas*. El Paso: Mangan Books, 1996.

———. *John Selman: Texas Gunfighter*. New York: Hastings House, 1966.

———. *The Encyclopedia of Lawmen, Outlaws, and Gunfighters*. New York: Checkmark Books, 2003.

Michno, Gregory. *The Settlers' War: The Struggle for the Texas Frontier in the 1860s*. Caldwell, ID: Caxton Press, 2011.

Miles, Elton. *Stray Tales of the Big Bend*. College Station: Texas A&M University Press, 1993.

Miller, Rick. *Bloody Bill Longley: The Mythology of a Gunfighter*. Denton: University of North Texas Press, 2011.

———. *Texas Ranger John B. Jones and the Frontier Battalion, 1874–1881*. Denton: University of North Texas Press, 2012.

———. *Sam Bass and Gang*. Austin: State House Press, 1999.

Mills, W. W. *Forty Years at El Paso, 1858–1898*. El Paso: Carl Hertzog, 1962.

Monday, Jane Clements, and Frances B. Vick. *Petra's Legacy: The South Texas Ranching Empire of Petra Vela and Mifflin Kenedy*. College Station: Texas A&M University Press, 2007.

———. *Letters to Alice: Birth of the Kleberg-King Ranch Dynasty*. College Station: Texas A&M University Press, 2012.

Moneyhon, Carl H. *Edmund J. Davis: Civil War General, Republican Leader, Reconstruction Governor*. Fort Worth: Texas Christian University Press, 2010.

Mooar, J. Wright. *Buffalo Days: Stories from J. Wright Mooar as Told to James Winford Hunt*. Edited by Robert F. Pace. Abilene, TX: State House Press-McMurry University, 2005.

Moore, Stephen L. *Savage Frontier: Rangers, Riflemen, and Indian Wars in Texas*. 4 Vols. Denton: University of North Texas Press, 2002–2010.

Morgenthaler, Jefferson. *The River Has Never Divided Us: A Border History of La Junta de los Rios*. Austin: University of Texas Press, 2004.

Myers, John Myers. *The Border Wardens*. Englewod Cliffs, NJ: Prentice-Hall, 1971.

Oden, Alonzo V. *Texas Ranger's Diary and Scrapbook*. Edited by Ann Jensen. Dallas: Kaleidograph Press, 1936.

Oppenheimer, Andres. *Bordering on Chaos: Mexico's Roller-Coaster Journey Toward Prosperity*. New York: Little, Brown and Company/A Back Bay Book, 1998.

O'Rear, Mary Jo. *Storm Over the Bay: The People of Corpus Christi and Their Port*. College Station: Texas A&M University Press, 2009.

Paredes, Américo. *With His Pistol in His Hand: A Border Ballad and Its Hero*. Austin: University of Texas Press, 1958.

Parks, Aline, and Jeff Corkran, eds. *The Coming West: True Stories of Trails Grown Dim*. Snyder, TX: iMAJiKA Productions, 1995.

Parsons, Chuck. *Captain John R. Hughes: Lone Star Ranger*. Denton: University of North Texas Press, 2011.

———. *The Sutton-Taylor Feud: The Deadliest Blood Feud in Texas*. Denton: University of North Texas Press, 2009.

———. *John B. Armstrong: Texas Ranger and Pioneer Ranchman*. College Station: Texas A&M University Press, 2007.

———. *James Madison Brown: Texas Sheriff, Texas Turfman*. Wolfe City, TX: Hennington Publishing, 1993.

———. *"Pidge": A Texas Ranger from Virginia*. Luling, TX: Self-published, 1985.

———, and Marianne E. Hall. *Captain L. H. McNelly, Texas Ranger: The Life and Times of a Fighting Man*. Austin: State House Press, 2001.

Peavey, John R. *Echoes of the Rio Grande: From the Thorny Hills of Duval to the Sleepy Rio Grande*. Brownsville, TX: Springman-King Company, 1963.

Perkins, Clifford Alan. *Border Patrol: With the U.S. Immigration Service on the Mexican Boundary, 1910–1954*. El Paso: Texas Western Press, 1978.

Poniatowska, Elena. *Las Soldaderas: Women of the Mexican Revolution*. El Paso: Cinco Puntos Press, 2006.

Poppa, Terrence E. *Drug Lord: The Life and Death of a Mexican Kingpin*. El Paso: Cinco Puntos Press, 2010.

Prassel, Frank Richard. *The Western Peace Officer: A Legacy of Law and Order*. Norman: University of Oklahoma Press, 1972.

Proctor, Ben. *Just One Riot: Episodes of Texas Rangers in the 20ᵗʰ Century*. Austin: Eakin Press, 1991.

Pylant, James. *Sins of the Pioneers: Crimes and Scandals in a Small Town*. Stephenville, TX: Jacobus Books, 2009.

Ragsdale, Kenneth B. *Big Bend Country: Land of the Unexpected*. College Station: Texas A&M University Press, 1998.

Raht, Carlysle G. *The Romance of Davis Mountains and Big Bend Country*. Odessa, TX: Rahtbooks, 1963.

Rasch, Philip J. *Desperadoes of Arizona Territory*. Edited by Robert K. DeArment. Stillwater, OK: Western Publications, 1999.

———. *Warriors of Lincoln County*. Edited by Robert K. DeArment. Stillwater, OK: NOLA, 1998.

Rayburn, John C., and Virginia Kemp Rayburn, eds. *Century of Conflict, 1821–1913: Incidents in the Lives of William Neale and William A. Neale, Early Settlers in South Texas*. Waco: Texian Press, 1966.

Roberts, Dan W. *Rangers and Sovereignty*. Austin: State House Press, 1987.

Robinson, Charles M. III. *The Men Who Wear the Star: The Story of the Texas Rangers*. New York: Random House, 2000.

————. *Frontier Forts of Texas*. Houston: Lone Star Books, 1986.

Romo, David Dorado. *Ringside Seat to a Revolution: An Underground Cultural History of El Paso and Juárez, 1893-1923*. El Paso: Cinco Puntos Press, 2005.

Rose, Peter R. *The Reckoning: The Triumph of Order on the Texas Outlaw Frontier*. Lubbock: Texas Tech University Press, 2012.

Samaha, Joel. *Criminal Law*. Belmont, CA: Wadsworth Group/Thomson Learning, Inc. 2002.

Samora, Julian, Joe Bernal, and Albert Peña. *Gunpowder Justice: A Reassessment of the Texas Rangers*. Notre Dame, IN: Notre Dame University Press, 1979.

Scott, Bob. *Leander McNelly, Texas Ranger: He Just Kept On Keepin' On*. Austin: Eakin Press, 1998.

Selcer, Richard F. and Kevin S. Foster. *Written in Blood: The History of Fort Worth's Fallen Lawmen, Volume I, 1861–1909*. Denton: University of North Texas Press, 2010.

————. *Written in Blood: The History of Fort Worth's Fallen Lawmen, Volume II, 1910–1928*. Denton: University of North Texas Press, 2011.

Shannon, Elaine. *Desperados: Latin Drug Lords, U.S. Lawmen, and the War America Can't Win*. New York: Viking Penguin, 1988.

Shelton, Hooper. *History of Scurry County, Texas: From Buffalo... to Oil*. Snyder, TX: Scurry County Historical Survey Committee, 1973.

Smith, Cornelius C., Jr. *Emilio Kosterlitzky: Eagle of Sonora and the Southwest Border*. Glendale, CA: Arthur H. Clark Company, 1970.

Smithers, W. D. *Chronicles of the Big Bend: A Photographic Memoir of Life on the Border*. Austin. Texas State Historical Association, 1999.

————. *Pancho Villa's Last Hangout—On Both Sides of the Rio Grande in the Big Bend Country*. Privately Published, No date.

Sonnichsen, C. L. *Pass of the North: Four Centuries on the Rio Grande*. El Paso: Texas Western University, 1968.

————. *Ten Texas Feuds*. Albuquerque: University of New Mexico Press, 1971.

————. *Tularosa: Last of the Frontier West*. Albuquerque: University of New Mexico Press, 1960.

————. *The El Paso Salt War*. El Paso: Texas Western Press, 1963.

Spellman, Paul N. *Captain J. A. Brooks: Texas Ranger*. Denton: University of North Texas Press, 2007.

————. *Captain John H. Rogers, Texas Ranger*. Denton: University of North Texas Press, 2003.

Stephens, Robert W. *Texas Ranger Sketches*. Dallas: Self-published, 1972.

————. *Texas Ranger Captain Dan Roberts: The Untold Story*. Dallas: Self-published, 2009.

————. *Bullets and Buckshot in Texas*. Dallas: Self-published, 2002.

—————. *Walter Durbin: Texas Ranger and Sheriff*. Clarendon, TX: Clarendon Press, 1970.

Sterling, William Warren. *Trails and Trials of a Texas Ranger*. Norman: University of Oklahoma Press, 1959.

Stillwell, Hallie Crawford. *I'll Gather My Geese*. College Station: Texas A&M University Press, 1991.

Tanner, Karen Holliday, and John D. Tanner, Jr. *Directory of Inmates: New Mexico Territorial Penitentiary, 1884–1912*. Fall Brook, CA: Runnin' Iron Books, 2006.

Tefertiller, Casey. *Wyatt Earp: The Life Behind the Legend*. New York: John Wiley & Sons, 1997.

Thompson, Jerry D. *Cortina: Defending the Mexican Name in Texas*. College Station: Texas A&M University Press, 2007.

—————. *A Wild and Vivid Land: An Illustrated History of the South Texas Border*. Austin: Texas State Historical Association, 1997.

Thrapp, Dan L. *Encyclopedia of Frontier Biography*. 3 Vols. Lincoln: University of Nebraska Press, 1998.

Tise, Sammy. *Texas County Sheriffs*. Hallettsville, TX: Tise Genealogical Research. 1989.

Tyler, Ronnie C. *The Big Bend: A History of the Last Texas Frontier*. Washington, D.C.: National Park Service, 1975.

Uglow, Loyd M. *Standing in the Gap: Army Outposts, Picket Stations, and the Pacification of the Texas Frontier, 1866–1886*. Fort Worth: Texas Christian University Press, 2001.

Underwood, Martha Deen, and Hamilton Underwood. *Concordia Cemetery, El Paso: A Walking Tour*. El Paso: Self-Published, 2009.

Utley, Robert M. *Lone Star Justice: The First Century of the Texas Rangers*. New York: Oxford University Press, 2002.

—————. *Lone Star Lawmen: The Second Century of the Texas Rangers*. New York: Oxford University Press, 2007.

Valley By-Liners. *Gift of the Rio: Story of Texas' Tropical Borderland*. Mission, TX: Border Kingdom Press, 1975.

Vulliamy Ed. *AMEXIA: War Along the Borderline*. New York: Farrar, Straus and Giroux, 2010.

Watts, Peter. *A Dictionary of the Old West*. New York: Promontory Press, 1977.

Webb, Walter Prescott. *The Texas Rangers: A Century of Frontier Defense*. Austin: University of Texas Press, 1965.

—————. *The Story of the Texas Rangers*. Austin: Encino Press, 1957.

Weiss, Harold J., Jr. *Yours to Command: The Life and Legend of Texas Ranger Captain Bill McDonald*. Denton: University of North Texas Press, 2009.

White, Owen P. *Lead and Likker*. New York: Minton, Balch & Company, 1932.

————. *Out of the Desert: The Historical Romance of El Paso*. New York: The McMath Company, 1924.

Wilkins, Frederick. *The Law Comes to Texas: The Texas Rangers, 1870–1901*. Austin: State House Press, 1999.

Williams, Clayton W. *Texas' Last Frontier: Fort Stockton and the Trans-Pecos, 1861–1895*. College Station: Texas A&M University Press, 1982.

Wooten, Dudley G., ed. *A Comprehensive History of Texas, 1685–1897*. 2 vols. Dallas: William Scharff, 1898.

Young, Elliott. *Catarino Garza's Revolution on the Texas-Mexico Border*. Durham, NC: Duke University Press, 2004.

Periodicals:

Alexander, Bob. "Square Deals and Real McCoys." *Wild West History Association Journal*. (WWHA) June 2011.

————. "Tucker x Texas = Trouble." WWHA *Journal*. June 2008.

————. "Hell Paso" *National Outlaw/Lawman History Association Quarterly* (NOLA). April–June 2002.

Baenziger, Ann Patton. "The Texas State Police During Reconstruction: A Reexamination." *Southwestern Historical Quarterly*. April 1969.

Bailey, Tom and Ralph J. Weaver. "The Nine Lives of Captain Frank Jones." *Frontier Times*. Spring 1960.

Brand, Peter. "Sherman W. McMaster(s): The El Paso Salt War, Texas Rangers and Tombstone." *Western Outlaw and Lawman History Association Journal* (WOLA). Winter. 1999.

Barton, Henry W. "The Untied States Cavalry and the Texas Rangers." *Southwestern Historical Quarterly*. April 1960.

Bowser, David. "Reconstruction State Police Not Entirely Evil, Says Archivist." *Livestock Weekly*. May 24, 2012.

Caldwell, Cliff. "Davey Thomas 'Tom' Carson, Texas Ranger." *WWHA Journal*. June 2009.

Cool, Paul. "J. A. Tays: The Frontier Battalion's Forgotten Officer." *Texas Ranger Dispatch*. Summer. 2004.

————. "Salt War Sheriff: El Paso's Charles Kerber." *NOLA Quarterly*. January–March 2003.

Cox, Mike. "The Ranger from Washington County." *Round Top Register*, Fall 2011.

Crnal, Ed. "Reminiscences of a Texas Ranger." *Frontier Times*. December 1923.

Croce, Antonio. "In the Line of Duty." *The Texas Gun Collector*. Fall 1996.

Cumberland, Charles C. "Border Raids in the Lower Rio Grande Valley— 1915." *Southwestern Historical Quarterly*. January 1954.

Cunningham, Eugene. "Bass Outlaw." *Frontier Times*. January 1928.

Draper, Robert. "The Twilight of the Texas Rangers." *Texas Monthly*. February. 1994.

Dodson, Ruth. "The Noakes Raid." *Frontier Times*. July 1945.

Doughtery, Frank W. "Las Vegas de los Ladrones and the Flynt Gang." *Journal of Big Bend Studies*. 1991.

Dukes, Doug. "Frank McMahan: In Custody." *WWHA Journal*. August 2009.

Hager, William M. "The Nuecestown Raid of 1875: A Border Incident." *Arizona and the West*. Autumn 1959.

Fox, Dorothea Magdalene. "Marked for Death." *Frontier Times*. March 1965.

Harris, Charles H. III, and Louis R. Sadler. "The 1911 Reyes Conspiracy: The Texas Side." *Southwestern Historical Quarterly*. April 1980.

Hunter, J. Marvin, ed. "Texas Rangers on the Border." *Frontier Times*. April 1924.

———. "Texas Rangers Battle With Outlaws in 1880." *Frontier Times*. August 1927.

Jones, Julia. "Brief History of Lee County." *Frontier Times*. January 1942.

Kelton, Elmer. "Generational Chauvinism." *West Texas Historical Association Yearbook*. 1991.

Kieffe, Glenna D. "Finis: The Final Entry." *Customs Today*. Fall 1990.

McCampbell, Coleman. "Romance Had Role in Founding of Corpus Christi." *Frontier Times*. June 1939.

Mayfield, Mrs. G. C. "Interesting Narrative of Capt. W. L. Rudd, Ex-Ranger." *Frontier Times*. December 1932.

Meed, Douglas V. "Daggers on the Gallows: The Revenge of Texas Ranger Captain 'Boss' Hughes." *True West*, May 1999.

Metz, Leon. "Gunfighters of the Old West—Texas Posse Stuns New Mexican Wagon Train in Opening Round of the Magoffin's Salt War." (A series) *El Paso Times*. February 17, 1974.

Michaels, Kevin. "Tracker." *Great West*. September 1974.

Mooar, J. Wright. "The Frontier Experiences of J. Wright Mooar." *West Texas Historical Association Yearbook*. 1928.

Morris, Lepold. "The Mexican Raid of 1875 on Corpus Christi." *Texas Historical Association Quarterly*. July 1900.

Nelson, Scott L. "Trailing Jerry Barton." *NOLA Quarterly*. January–March 2002.

Parrish, Joe. "Ranger Killed in Gun Battle Gave Fusselman Canyon Name." *Sundial Magazine*. September 26, 1965.

Parsons, Chuck. "The Jesse Evans Gang and the Death of Texas Ranger George Bingham." *Journal of Big Bend Studies*, 2008.

———. "An Incident in West Texas: The Jesse Evans Gang and the Death of Texas Ranger George Bingham." *WOLA Journal*. Winter 2006.

———. "Charles H. Fusselman." *Texas Ranger Dispatch*. Summer 2004.

Richardson, T. C. "Corpus Christi: The Naples of the Gulf." *Frontier Times*. June 1939.

Ritter, Al. "Death on the Rio Grande." *DPSOA Magazine*. (Department of Public Safety Officers Association). March/April 1996.

———. "Captain Fox's Colt." *Handguns*. February 1997.

———, and Chick Davis. "Captain Monroe Fox and the Incident at Porvenir." *Oklahoma State Trooper*. Winter 1995.

Saenz, Luz Maria Hernandez. "Smuggling for the Revolution: Illegal Traffic of Arms on the Arizona-Sonora Border, 1912–1914." *Arizona and the West*. Winter 1986.

Shipman, Jack. "The Killing of Ranger Hulin." *Voice of the Mexican Border*. Centennial Edition. 1936.

———, ed. "Villa Takes Ojinaga." *Voice of the Mexican Border*. Centennial Edition. 1936.

———, ed. "Mexican Payrolls and American Bandits." *Voice of the Mexican Border*. El Paso issue. December 1933.

———. "The Salt War of San Elizario." *Voice of the Mexican Border*. January 1934.

Sparks, John E. "Tom Goff, Texas Ranger. *True West*. December 1987.

Spellman, Paul N. "Dark Days of the Texas Rangers, 1915–1918." *Journal of South Texas Studies*. Spring 2001.

Stivison, Roy Edward. "Night of Terror." *Old West*. Summer 1974.

Trimble. Lee. "The Oral Memoirs of Lee Trimble." *The Texas Ranger Annual*. 1982.

Tyler, Ronnie C. "Notes and Documents: The Little Punitive Expedition in the Big Bend." *Southwestern Historical Quarterly*. January 1975.

Walker, Wayne T. "Joe Sitters, The Best Damn Tracker in Texas." *Oldtimers Wild West*. December 1978.

Webb, Walter Prescott. "Rangers Reorganized." *The State Trooper*. July 1927.

———. "Texas Rangers in Eclipse." *The State Trooper*. January 1926.

Webster, Michael G. "Intrigue on the Rio Grande: The Rio Bravo Affair, 1875." *Southwestern Historical Quarterly*. October 1972.

Weiss Jr., Harold J. "Western Lawmen: Image and Reality." *Journal of the West*. January 1985.

———. "Organized Constabularies: The Texas Rangers and the Early State Police Movement in the American Southwest." *Journal of the West*. January 1995.

———. "The Texas Rangers Revisited: Old Themes and New Viewpoints." *Southwestern Historical Quarterly*. April 1994.

Wright, Charles L. "A Western Tragedy." *Customs Today*. Fall 1992.

Newspapers:

Alice Echo
Alpine Avalanche
Alpine Times
Arizona Daily Star
Austin Daily Democrat
Austin Daily Statesman
Beaumont Enterprise
Beaumont Journal
Brooklyn Daily Eagle
Brownsville Daily Herald
Cameron Herald
Clarksville Times
Corpus Christi Caller
Daily State Journal
Dallas Daily Herald
Dallas Morning News
Dallas Times Herald
Deport Times
El Paso Daily Times
Floresville Chronicle

Galveston Daily News
Grant County Herald
Houston Chronicle
Jeff Davis Mt. Dispatch
Knoxville Journal
Laredo Times
Los Angles Times
Luling Signal
Mercedes Enterprise
Omaha World Herald
Round Top Register
San Antonio Daily Express
San Antonio Daily Light
San Antonio Daily News
San Antonio Daily Times
Stephenville-Empire
Temple Daily Telegram
Waco Daily Examiner
Waco-Times Herald

Index